STAR TREK®

ALIEN SPOTLIGHT

Volume 1

IDW Publishing • San Diego, CA

SPECIAL THANKS

Special thanks to Paula Block of CBS Consumer Products for her invaluable assistance.

www.idwpublishing.com

SBN: 978-1-60010-179-3

11 10 09 08   1 2 3 4 5

IDW Publishing
Operations
Ted Adams, Presiden
Clifford Meth, EVP of Strategie
Matthew Ruzicka, CPA, Controlle
Alan Payne, VP of Sales
Lorelei Bunjes, Dir. of Digital Services
Marci Kahn, Executive Assistant
Alonzo Simon, Shipping Manager

Editorial
Chris Ryall, Publisher/Editor-in-Chie
Justin Eisinger, Edito
Andrew Steven Harris, Edito
Kris Oprisko, Editor/Foreign Lic
Denton J. Tipton, Edito
Tom Waltz, Edito

Design
Robbie Robbins, EVP/Sr. Graphic Artis
Neil Uyetake, Art Directo
Chris Mowry, Graphic Artis
Amauri Osorio, Graphic Artis

GORN
page 4
Written by
Scott & David Tipton
Art by **David Messina**
Art Assist by **Sara Pichelli**
Colors by **Paolo Maddaleni**
Letters by **Chris Mowry**
Alien Tech Designs by
Paolo Maddaleni
Edits by **Dan Taylor**

VULCANS
page 28
Written by **James Patrick**
Art by
Josep Maria Beroy
Colors by **Mario Boon**
Color Assist by
Andrew Elder
Letters by **Chris Mowry**
Edits by
Andrew Steven Harris

ANDORIANS
page 52
Written by
Paul D. Storrie
Art by **Leonard O'Grady**
Colors by
Leonard O'Grady
Letters by **Chris Mowry**
Edits by
Andrew Steven Harris

ORIONS
page 76
Written by
Scott & David Tipton
Art by **Elena Casagrande**
Colors by
Mirco Pierfederici
Letters by **Chris Mowry**
Edits by
Andrew Steven Harris

BORG
page 100
Written by
Andrew Steven Harris
Art by **Sean Murphy**
Colors by
Leonard O'Grady
Letters by **Chris Mowry**
Edits by **Chris Ryall**

ROMULANS
page 124
Written by **John Byrne**
Art by **John Byrne**
Colors by
Leonard O'Grady
Letters by **Neil Uyetake**
Edits by **Chris Ryall**

ART GALLERY
page 147

Collection Edits by
Justin Eisinger

Collection Design by
Tom B. Long

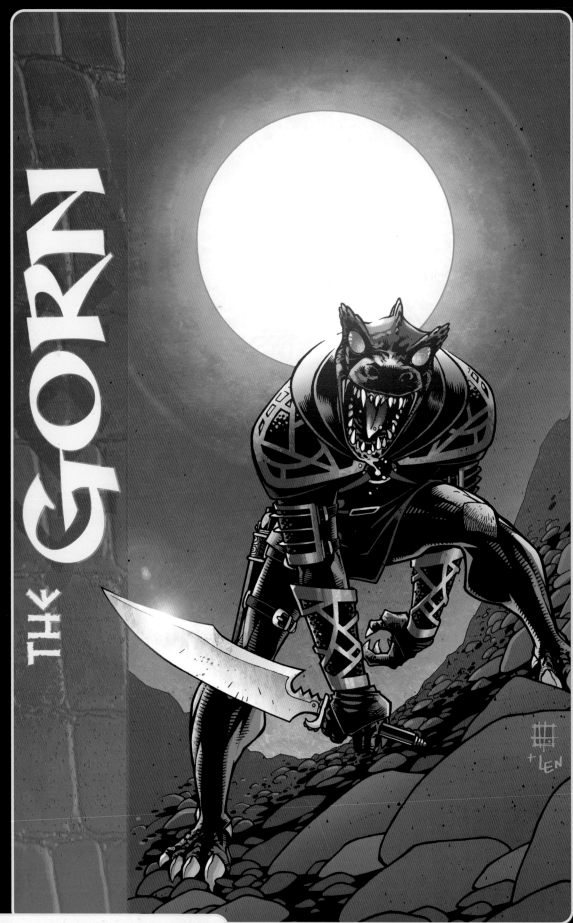

THE GORN

art by Zach Howard
colors and logo by Len O'Grady

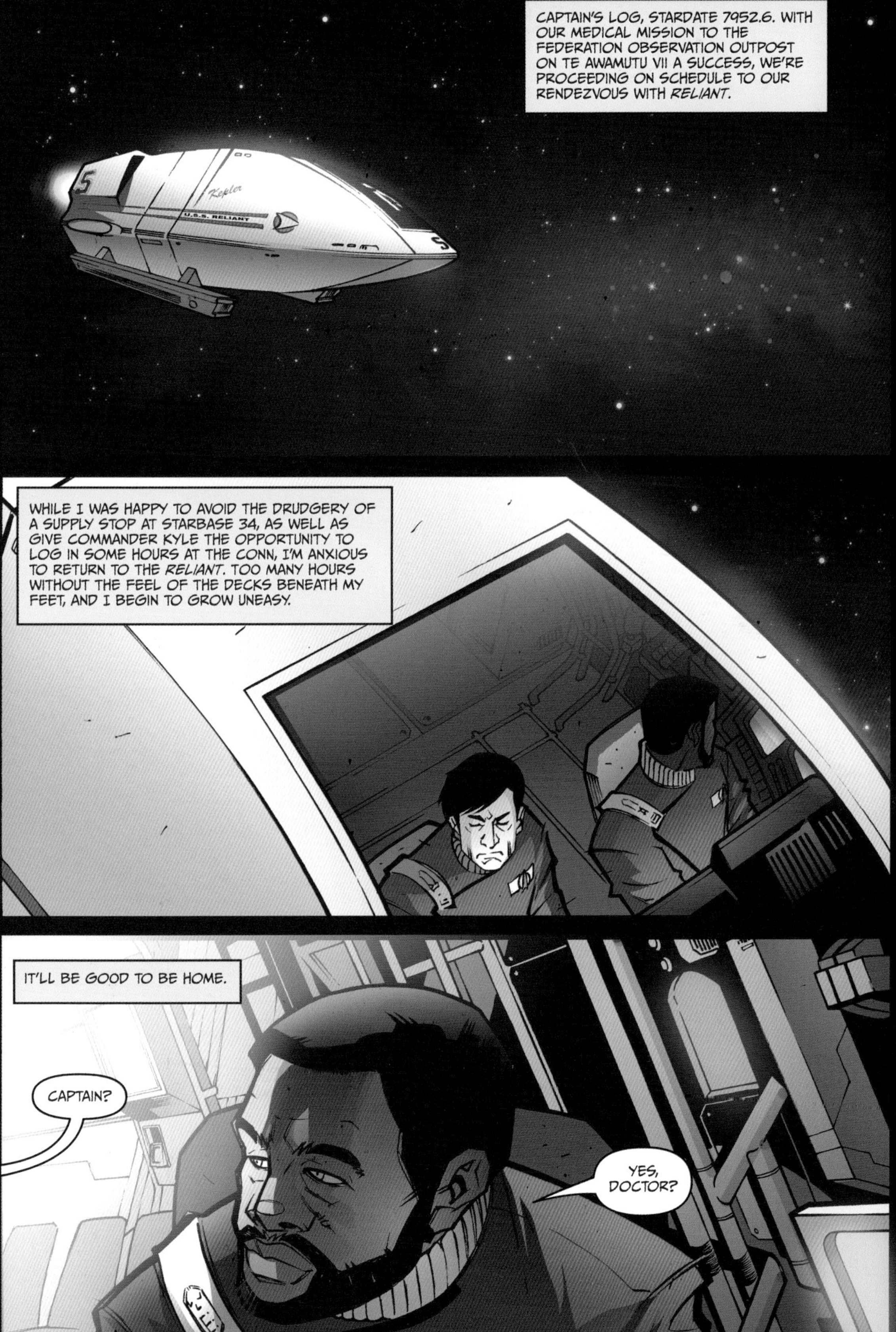
CAPTAIN'S LOG, STARDATE 7952.6. WITH OUR MEDICAL MISSION TO THE FEDERATION OBSERVATION OUTPOST ON TE AWAMUTU VII A SUCCESS, WE'RE PROCEEDING ON SCHEDULE TO OUR RENDEZVOUS WITH *RELIANT*.
Kepler
U.S.S. RELIANT
WHILE I WAS HAPPY TO AVOID THE DRUDGERY OF A SUPPLY STOP AT STARBASE 34, AS WELL AS GIVE COMMANDER KYLE THE OPPORTUNITY TO LOG IN SOME HOURS AT THE CONN, I'M ANXIOUS TO RETURN TO THE *RELIANT*. TOO MANY HOURS WITHOUT THE FEEL OF THE DECKS BENEATH MY FEET, AND I BEGIN TO GROW UNEASY.
IT'LL BE GOOD TO BE HOME.
CAPTAIN?
YES, DOCTOR?

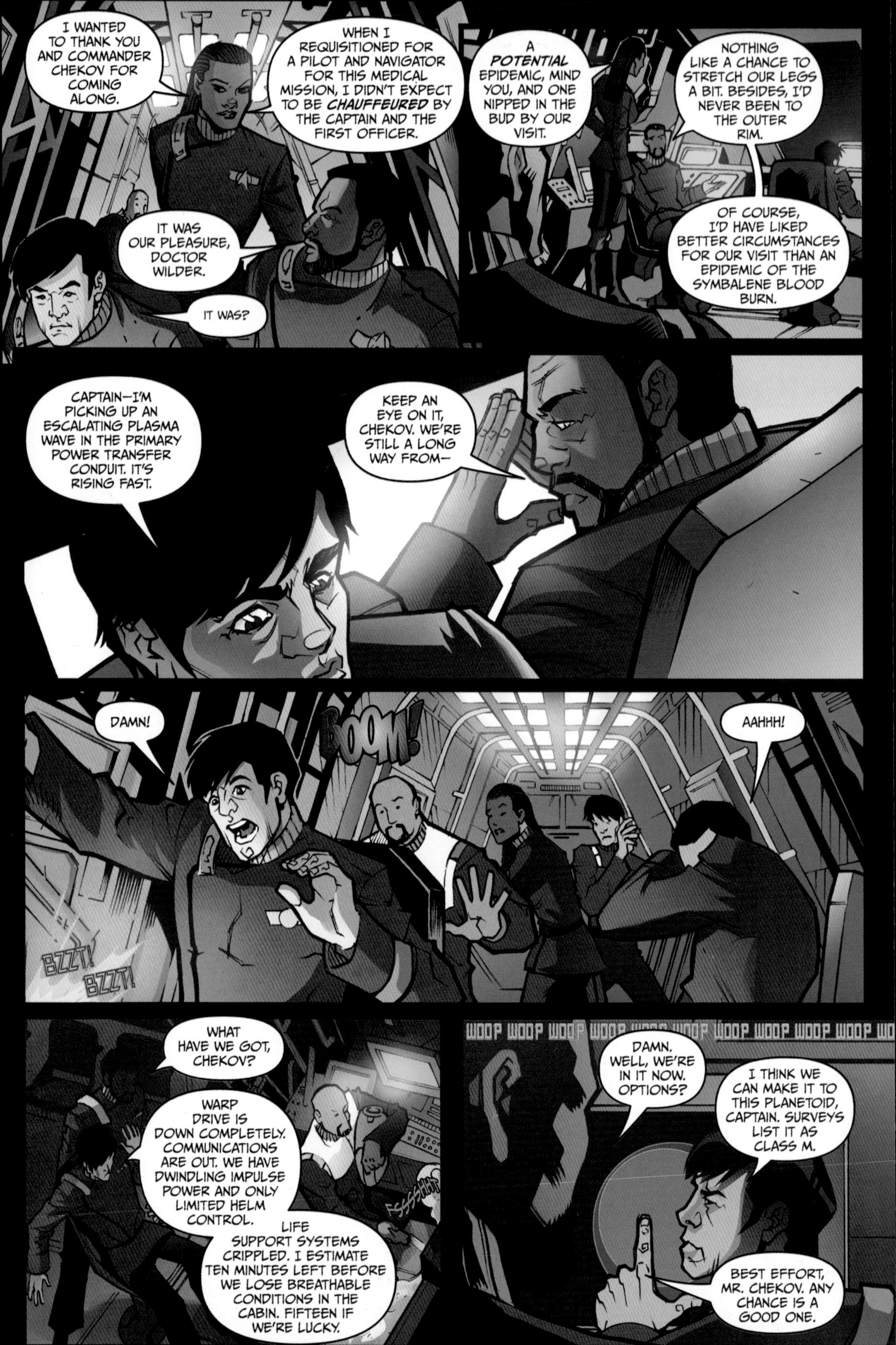
I WANTED TO THANK YOU AND COMMANDER CHEKOV FOR COMING ALONG.
WHEN I REQUISITIONED FOR A PILOT AND NAVIGATOR FOR THIS MEDICAL MISSION, I DIDN'T EXPECT TO BE *CHAUFFEURED* BY THE CAPTAIN AND THE FIRST OFFICER.
IT WAS OUR PLEASURE, DOCTOR WILDER.
IT WAS?
A *POTENTIAL* EPIDEMIC, MIND YOU, AND ONE NIPPED IN THE BUD BY OUR VISIT.
NOTHING LIKE A CHANCE TO STRETCH OUR LEGS A BIT. BESIDES, I'D NEVER BEEN TO THE OUTER RIM.
OF COURSE, I'D HAVE LIKED BETTER CIRCUMSTANCES FOR OUR VISIT THAN AN EPIDEMIC OF THE SYMBALENE BLOOD BURN.
CAPTAIN—I'M PICKING UP AN ESCALATING PLASMA WAVE IN THE PRIMARY POWER TRANSFER CONDUIT. IT'S RISING FAST.
KEEP AN EYE ON IT, CHEKOV. WE'RE STILL A LONG WAY FROM—
DAMN!
BOOM!
AAHHH!
BZZZT! BZZZT!
WHAT HAVE WE GOT, CHEKOV?
WARP DRIVE IS DOWN COMPLETELY. COMMUNICATIONS ARE OUT. WE HAVE DWINDLING IMPULSE POWER AND ONLY LIMITED HELM CONTROL.
LIFE SUPPORT SYSTEMS CRIPPLED. I ESTIMATE TEN MINUTES LEFT BEFORE WE LOSE BREATHABLE CONDITIONS IN THE CABIN. FIFTEEN IF WE'RE LUCKY.
FSSSSHHT
WOOP WOOP WOOP WOOP WOOP WOOP WOOP WOOP WOOP
DAMN. WELL, WE'RE IN IT NOW. OPTIONS?
I THINK WE CAN MAKE IT TO THIS PLANETOID, CAPTAIN. SURVEYS LIST IT AS CLASS M.
BEST EFFORT, MR. CHEKOV. ANY CHANCE IS A GOOD ONE.

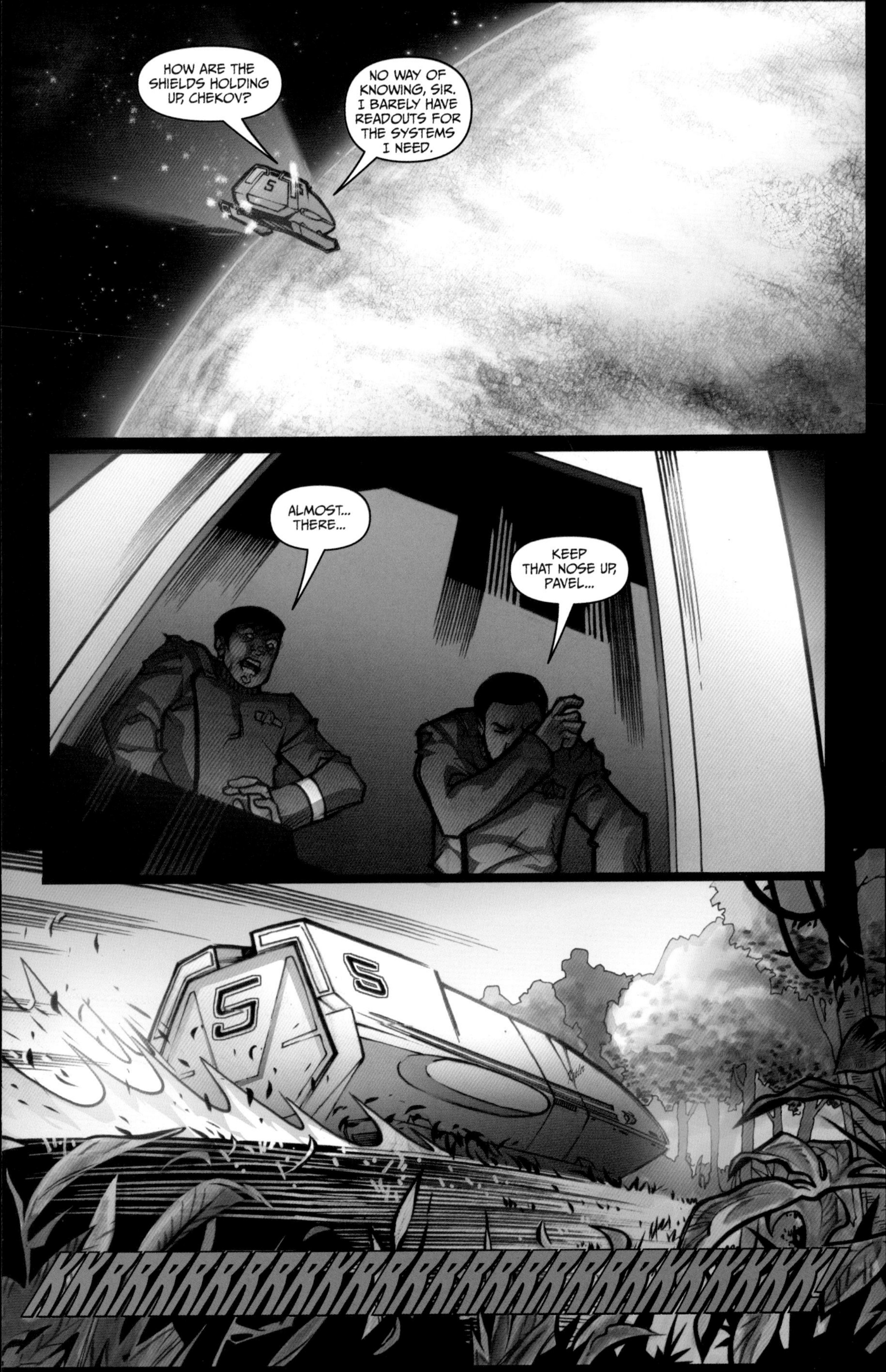
HOW ARE THE SHIELDS HOLDING UP, CHEKOV?
NO WAY OF KNOWING, SIR. I BARELY HAVE READOUTS FOR THE SYSTEMS I NEED.
ALMOST... THERE...
KEEP THAT NOSE UP, PAVEL...
KKRRRRRRRRKRRRRRRRRRRRRRKKKKKK!!

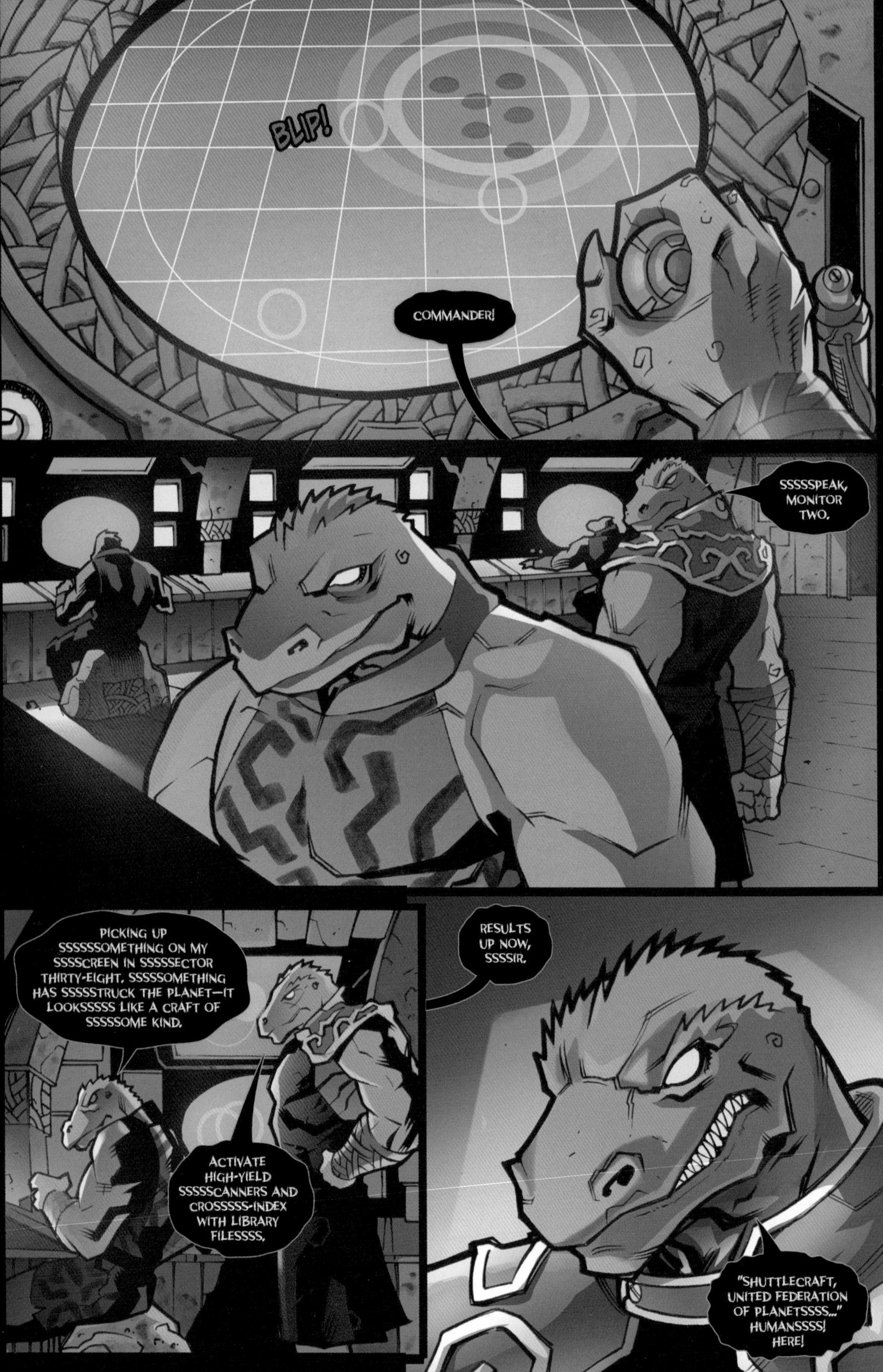
BLIP!
COMMANDER!
SSSSSPEAK, MONITOR TWO.
PICKING UP SSSSSSOMETHING ON MY SSSSCREEN IN SSSSSECTOR THIRTY-EIGHT. SSSSSOMETHING HAS SSSSSTRUCK THE PLANET—IT LOOKSSSSS LIKE A CRAFT OF SSSSSOME KIND.
ACTIVATE HIGH-YIELD SSSSSCANNERS AND CROSSSSS-INDEX WITH LIBRARY FILESSSS.
RESULTS UP NOW, SSSSSIR.
"SHUTTLECRAFT, UNITED FEDERATION OF PLANETSSSS..." HUMANSSSS! HERE!

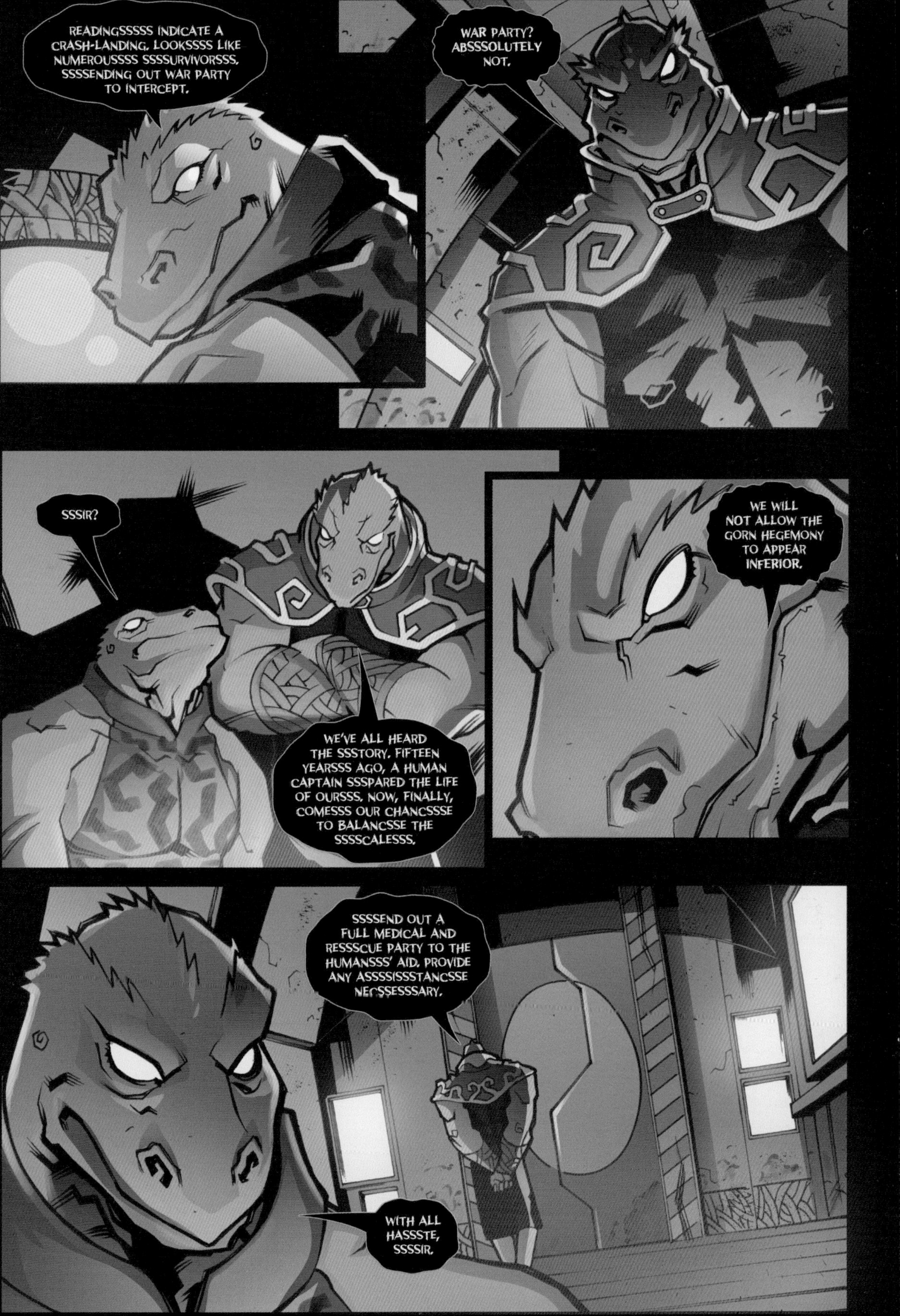
READINGSSSSS INDICATE A CRASH-LANDING. LOOKSSSS LIKE NUMEROUSSSS SSSSURVIVORSSS. SSSSENDING OUT WAR PARTY TO INTERCEPT.
WAR PARTY? ABSSSOLUTELY NOT.
SSSIR?
WE'VE ALL HEARD THE SSSTORY. FIFTEEN YEARSSS AGO, A HUMAN CAPTAIN SSSPARED THE LIFE OF OURSSS. NOW, FINALLY, COMESSS OUR CHANCSSSE TO BALANCSSE THE SSSSCALESSS.
WE WILL NOT ALLOW THE GORN HEGEMONY TO APPEAR INFERIOR.
SSSSEND OUT A FULL MEDICAL AND RESSSCUE PARTY TO THE HUMANSSS' AID. PROVIDE ANY ASSSSISSSTANCSSE NECSSESSSARY.
WITH ALL HASSSTE, SSSSIR.

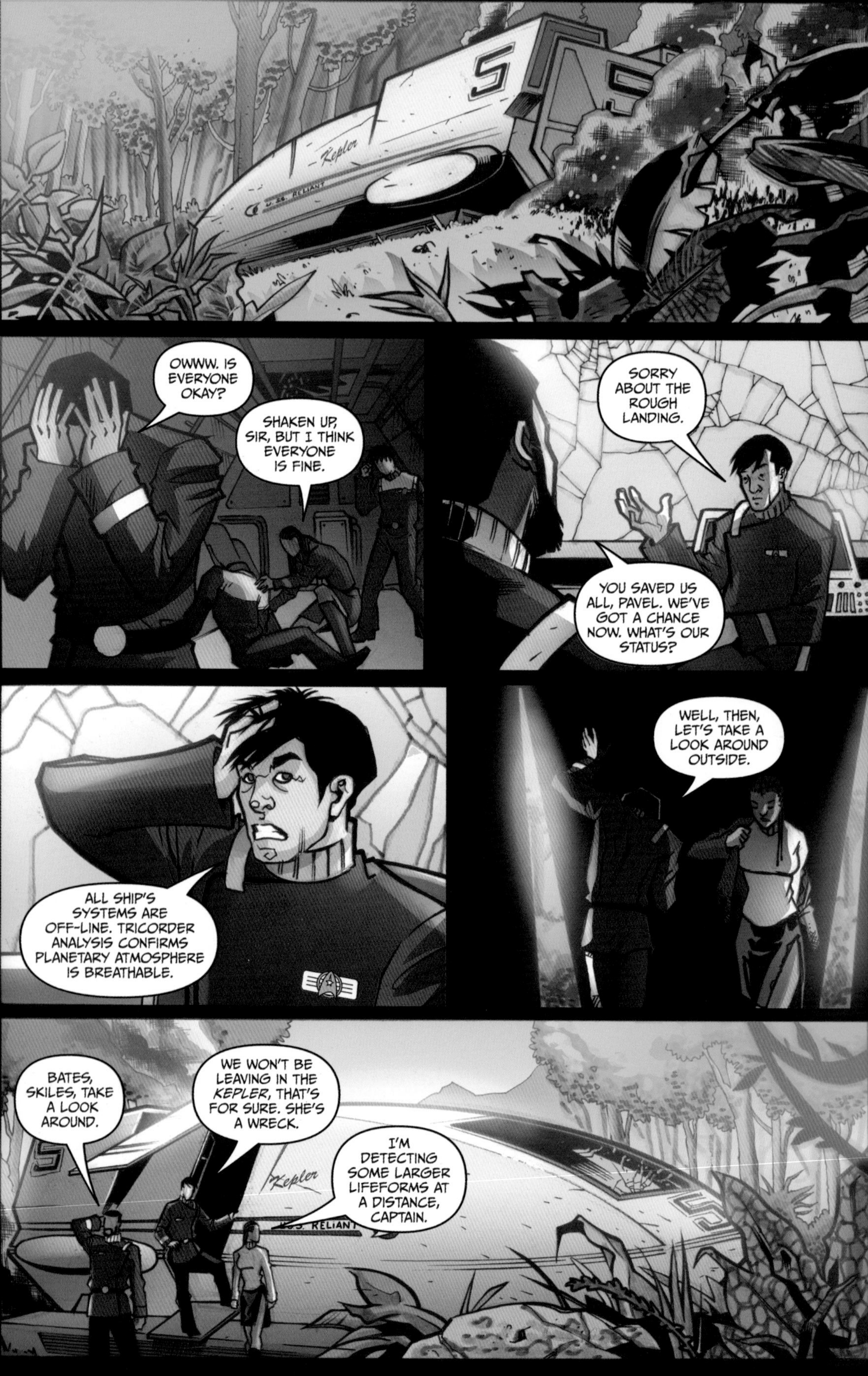
Kepler
OWWW. IS EVERYONE OKAY?
SHAKEN UP, SIR, BUT I THINK EVERYONE IS FINE.
SORRY ABOUT THE ROUGH LANDING.
YOU SAVED US ALL, PAVEL. WE'VE GOT A CHANCE NOW. WHAT'S OUR STATUS?
ALL SHIP'S SYSTEMS ARE OFF-LINE. TRICORDER ANALYSIS CONFIRMS PLANETARY ATMOSPHERE IS BREATHABLE.
WELL, THEN, LET'S TAKE A LOOK AROUND OUTSIDE.
BATES, SKILES, TAKE A LOOK AROUND.
WE WON'T BE LEAVING IN THE *KEPLER*, THAT'S FOR SURE. SHE'S A WRECK.
I'M DETECTING SOME LARGER LIFEFORMS AT A DISTANCE, CAPTAIN.

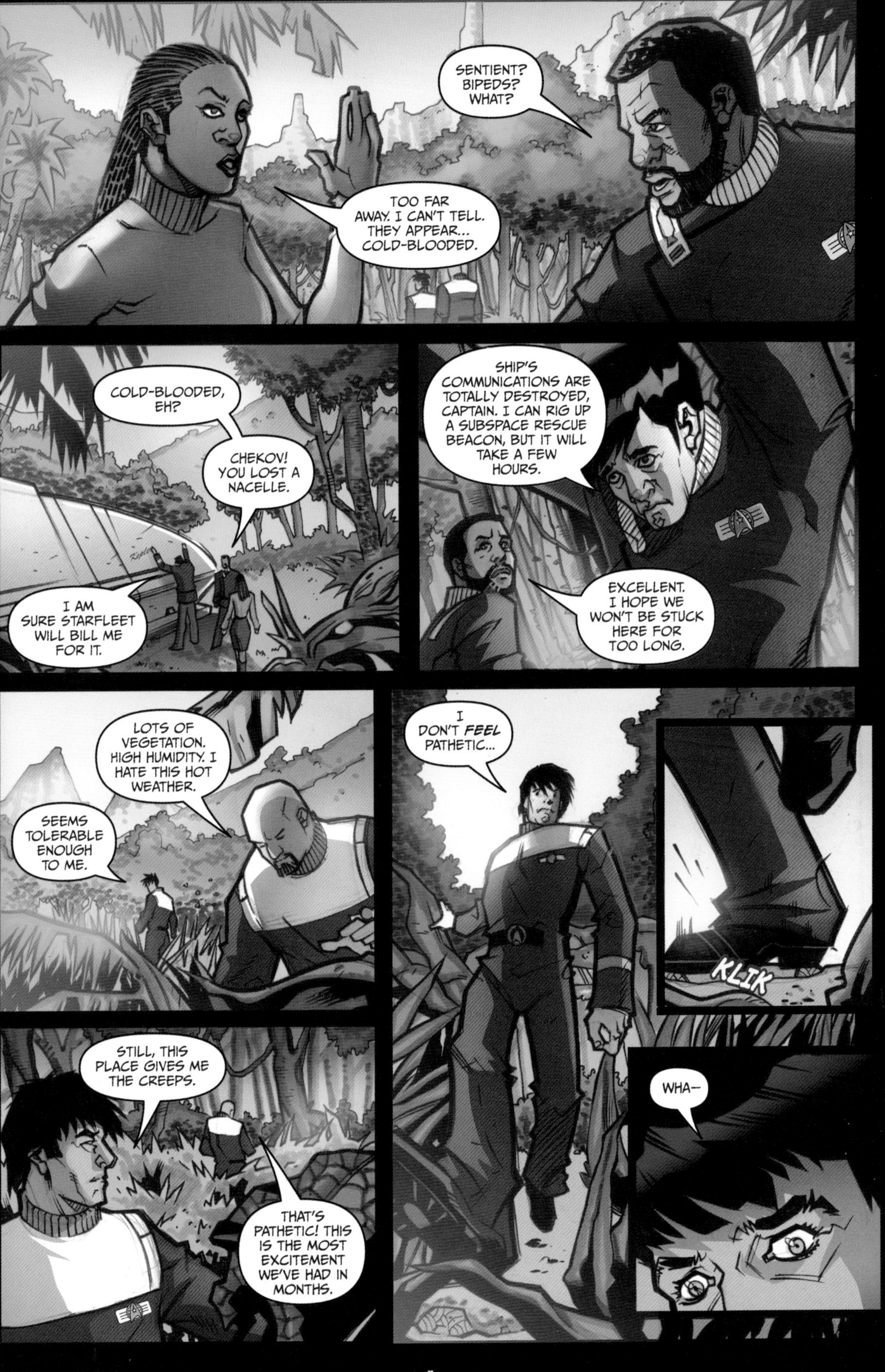
SENTIENT? BIPEDS? WHAT?
TOO FAR AWAY. I CAN'T TELL. THEY APPEAR... COLD-BLOODED.
COLD-BLOODED, EH?
CHEKOV! YOU LOST A NACELLE.
I AM SURE STARFLEET WILL BILL ME FOR IT.
SHIP'S COMMUNICATIONS ARE TOTALLY DESTROYED, CAPTAIN. I CAN RIG UP A SUBSPACE RESCUE BEACON, BUT IT WILL TAKE A FEW HOURS.
EXCELLENT. I HOPE WE WON'T BE STUCK HERE FOR TOO LONG.
LOTS OF VEGETATION. HIGH HUMIDITY. I HATE THIS HOT WEATHER.
SEEMS TOLERABLE ENOUGH TO ME.
STILL, THIS PLACE GIVES ME THE CREEPS.
THAT'S PATHETIC! THIS IS THE MOST EXCITEMENT WE'VE HAD IN MONTHS.
I DON'T FEEL PATHETIC...
KLIK
WHA–

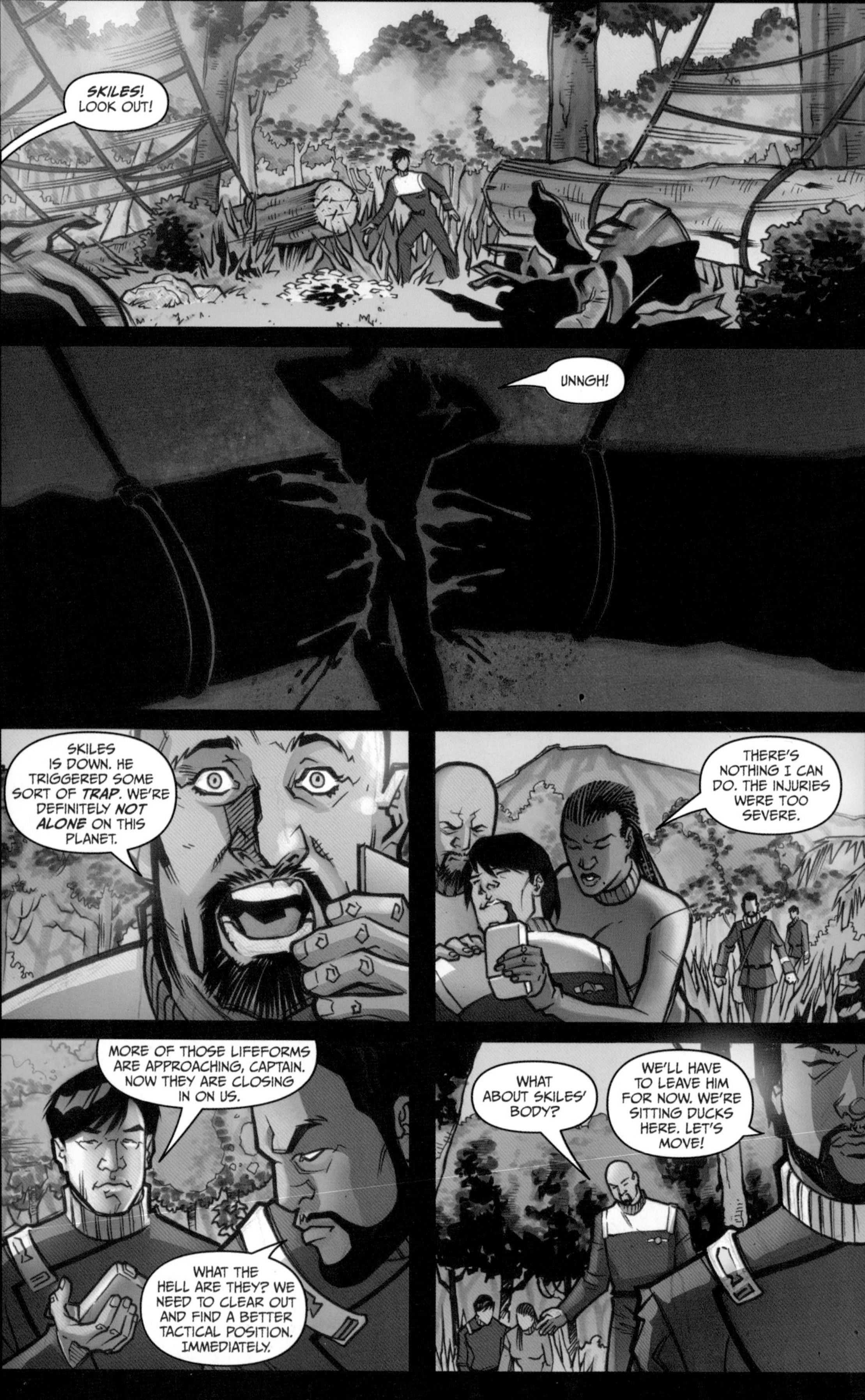
SKILES! LOOK OUT!
UNNGH!
SKILES IS DOWN. HE TRIGGERED SOME SORT OF TRAP. WE'RE DEFINITELY NOT ALONE ON THIS PLANET.
THERE'S NOTHING I CAN DO. THE INJURIES WERE TOO SEVERE.
MORE OF THOSE LIFEFORMS ARE APPROACHING, CAPTAIN. NOW THEY ARE CLOSING IN ON US.
WHAT THE HELL ARE THEY? WE NEED TO CLEAR OUT AND FIND A BETTER TACTICAL POSITION. IMMEDIATELY.
WHAT ABOUT SKILES' BODY?
WE'LL HAVE TO LEAVE HIM FOR NOW. WE'RE SITTING DUCKS HERE. LET'S MOVE!

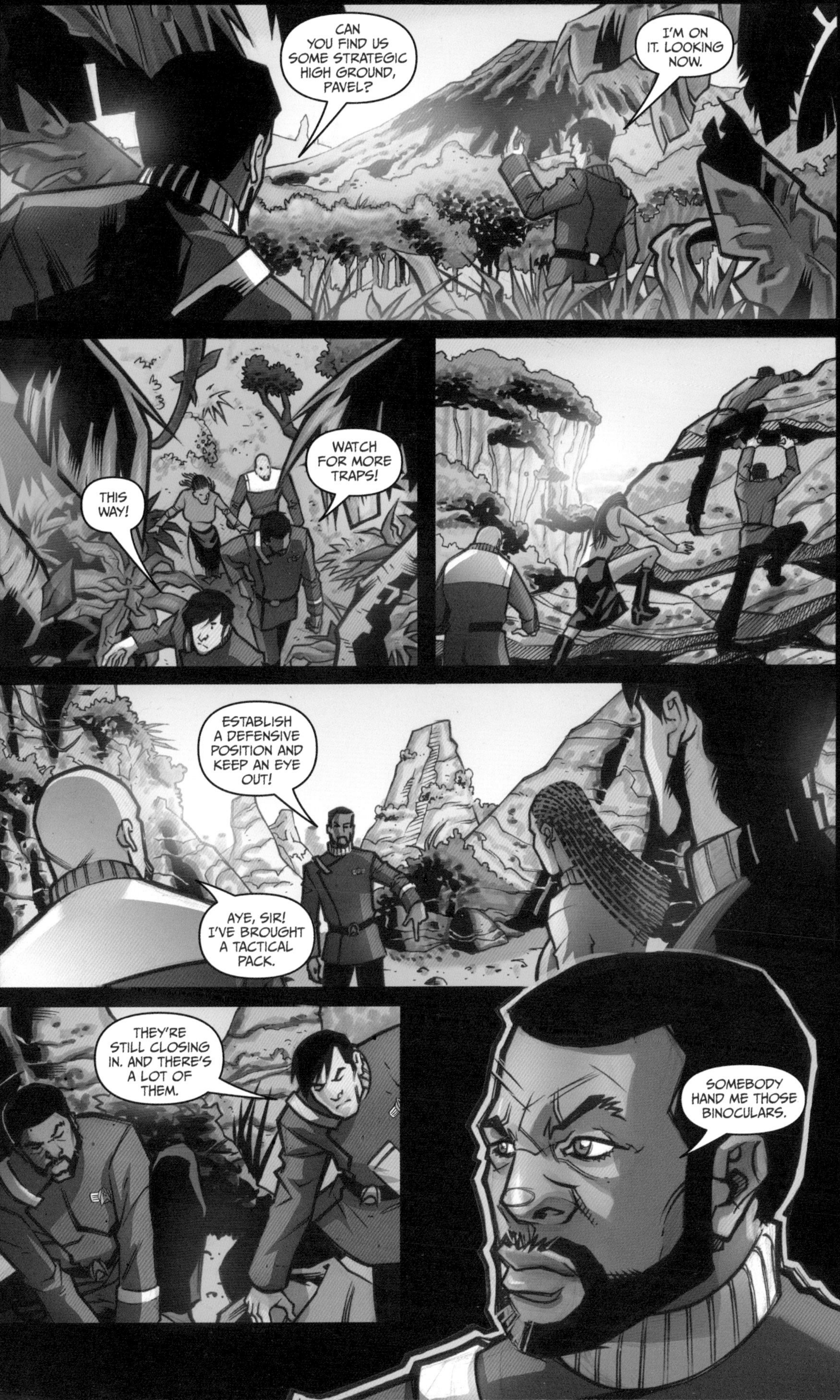
CAN YOU FIND US SOME STRATEGIC HIGH GROUND, PAVEL?
I'M ON IT. LOOKING NOW.
THIS WAY!
WATCH FOR MORE TRAPS!
ESTABLISH A DEFENSIVE POSITION AND KEEP AN EYE OUT!
AYE, SIR! I'VE BROUGHT A TACTICAL PACK.
THEY'RE STILL CLOSING IN. AND THERE'S A LOT OF THEM.
SOMEBODY HAND ME THOSE BINOCULARS.

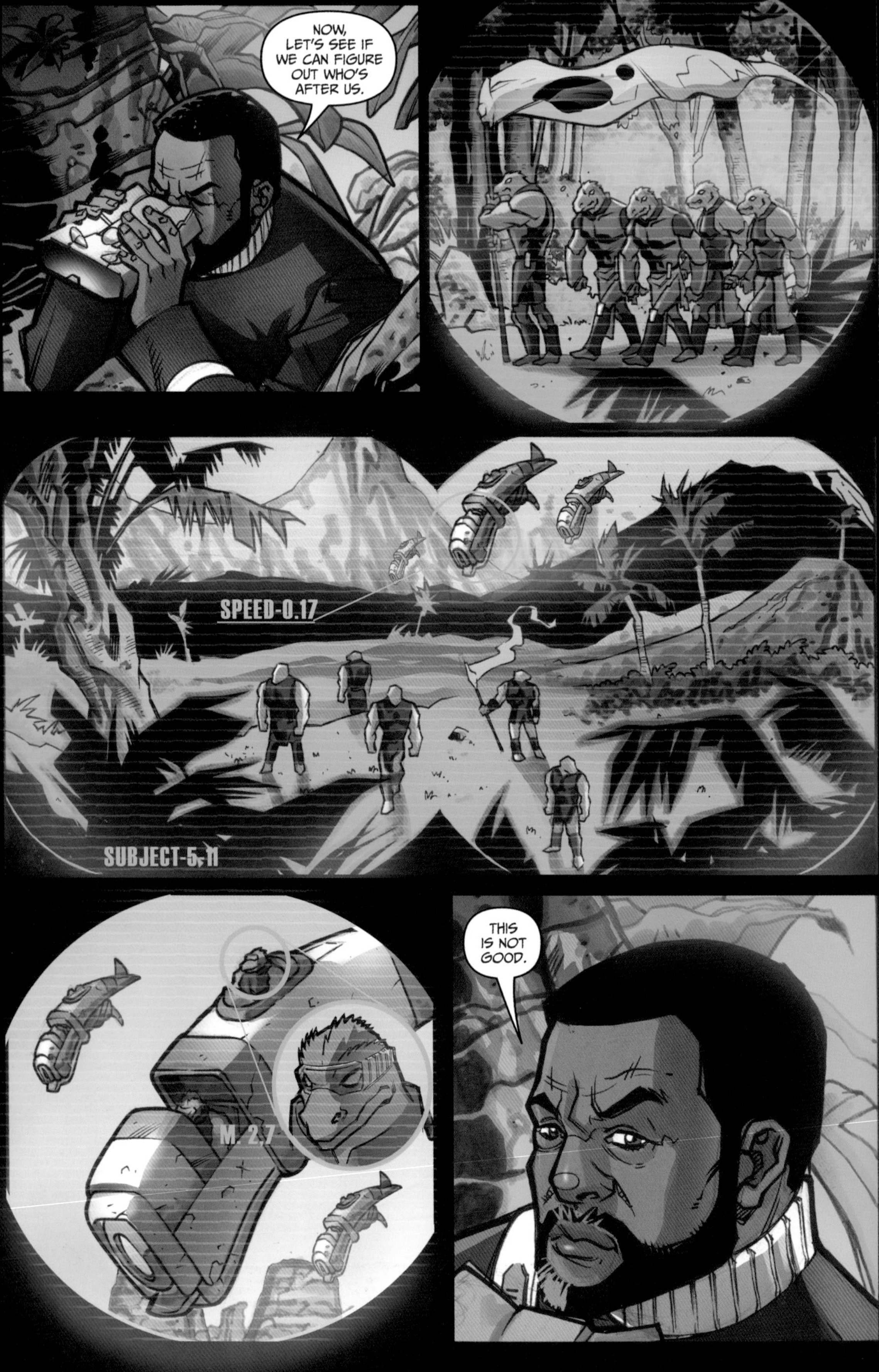
NOW, LET'S SEE IF WE CAN FIGURE OUT WHO'S AFTER US.
SPEED-0.17
SUBJECT-5.11
M. 2.7
THIS IS NOT GOOD.

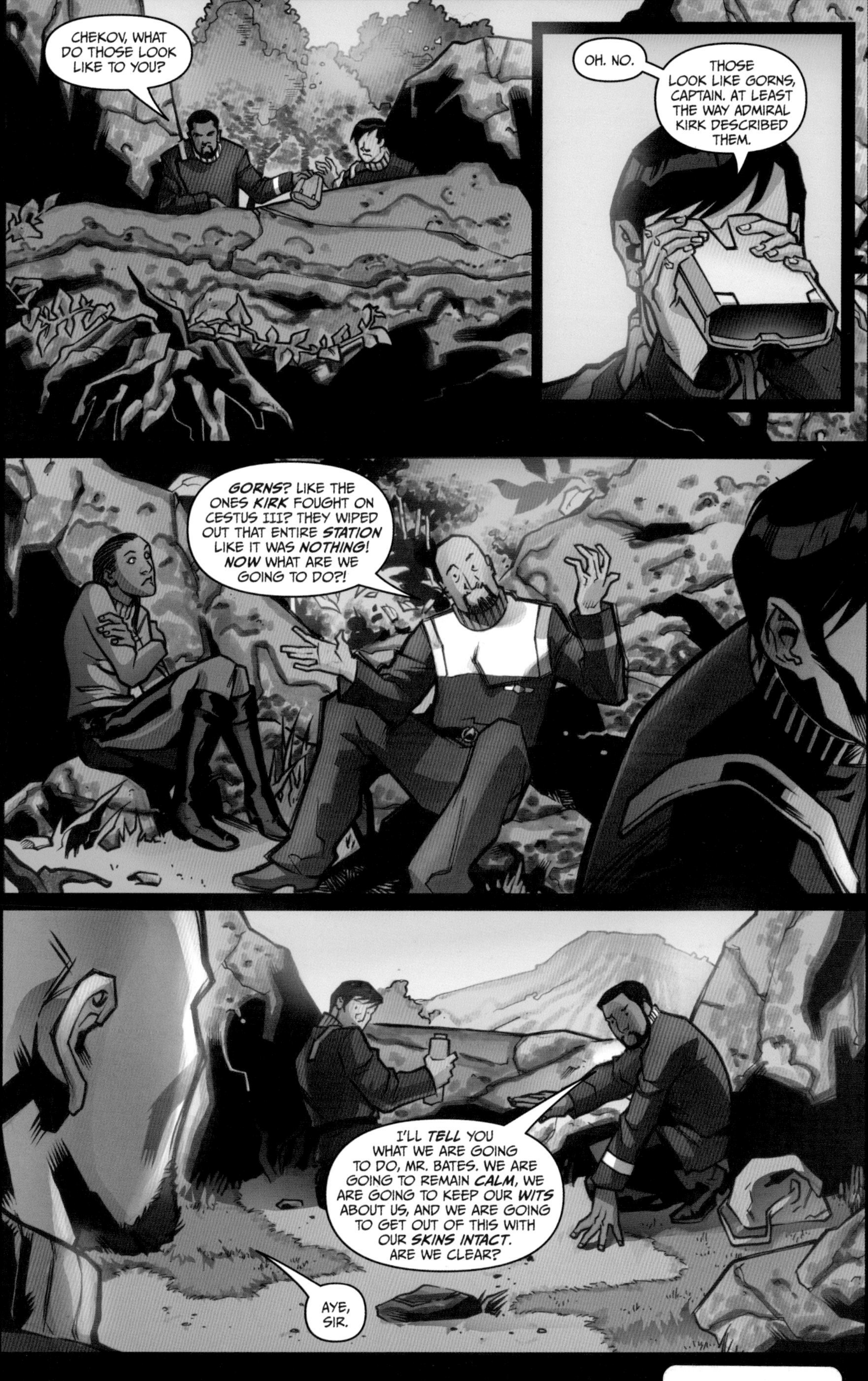
CHEKOV, WHAT DO THOSE LOOK LIKE TO YOU?
OH. NO.
THOSE LOOK LIKE GORNS, CAPTAIN. AT LEAST THE WAY ADMIRAL KIRK DESCRIBED THEM.
GORNS? LIKE THE ONES KIRK FOUGHT ON CESTUS III? THEY WIPED OUT THAT ENTIRE STATION LIKE IT WAS NOTHING! NOW WHAT ARE WE GOING TO DO?!
I'LL TELL YOU WHAT WE ARE GOING TO DO, MR. BATES. WE ARE GOING TO REMAIN CALM, WE ARE GOING TO KEEP OUR WITS ABOUT US, AND WE ARE GOING TO GET OUT OF THIS WITH OUR SKINS INTACT. ARE WE CLEAR?
AYE, SIR.

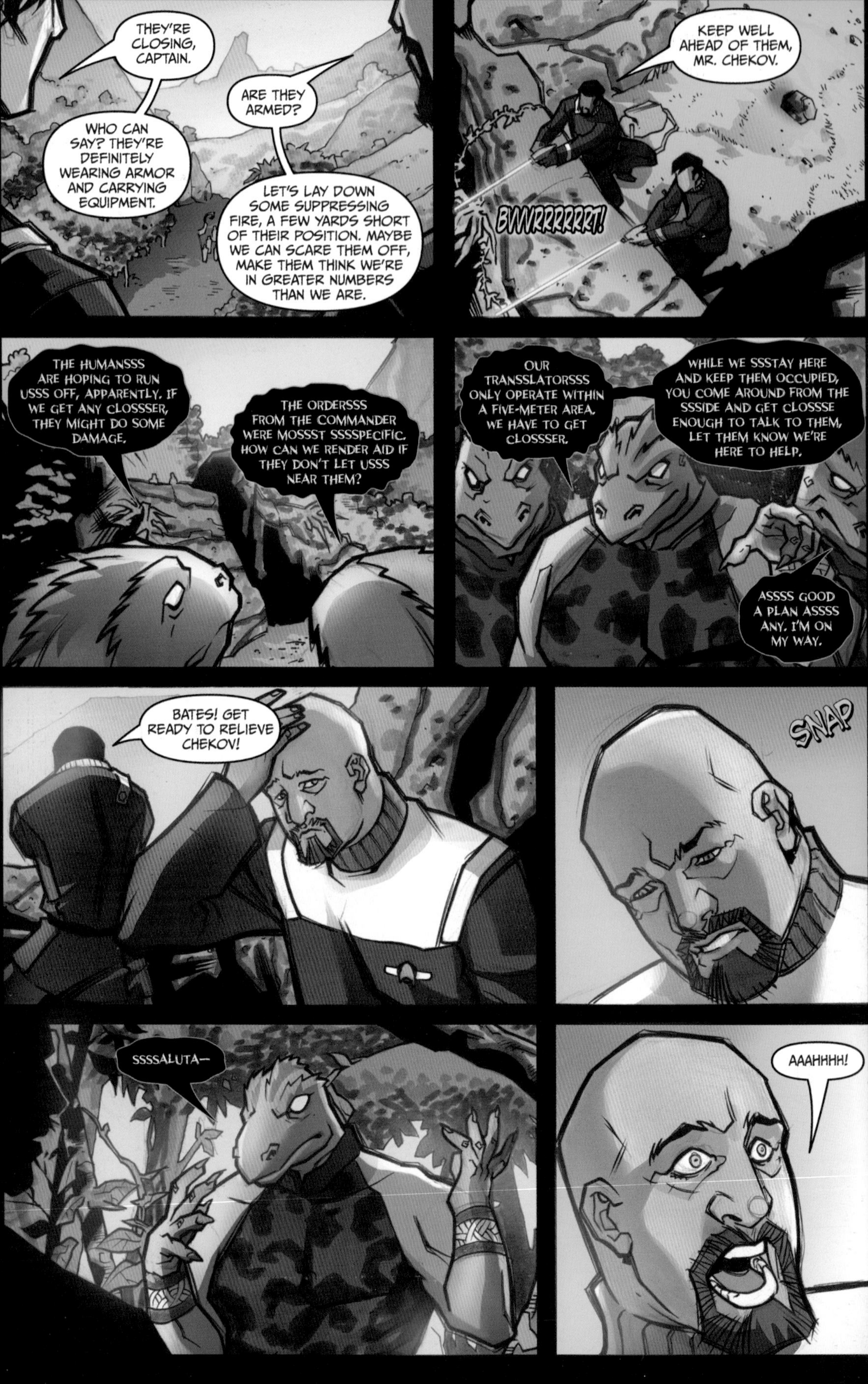

THEY'RE CLOSING, CAPTAIN.
ARE THEY ARMED?
WHO CAN SAY? THEY'RE DEFINITELY WEARING ARMOR AND CARRYING EQUIPMENT.
LET'S LAY DOWN SOME SUPPRESSING FIRE, A FEW YARDS SHORT OF THEIR POSITION. MAYBE WE CAN SCARE THEM OFF, MAKE THEM THINK WE'RE IN GREATER NUMBERS THAN WE ARE.
KEEP WELL AHEAD OF THEM, MR. CHEKOV.
BVVVRRRRRRT!
THE HUMANSSS ARE HOPING TO RUN USSS OFF, APPARENTLY. IF WE GET ANY CLOSSSER, THEY MIGHT DO SOME DAMAGE.
THE ORDERSSS FROM THE COMMANDER WERE MOSSST SSSSPECIFIC. HOW CAN WE RENDER AID IF THEY DON'T LET USSS NEAR THEM?
OUR TRANSSLATORSSS ONLY OPERATE WITHIN A FIVE-METER AREA. WE HAVE TO GET CLOSSSER.
WHILE WE SSSTAY HERE AND KEEP THEM OCCUPIED, YOU COME AROUND FROM THE SSSIDE AND GET CLOSSSE ENOUGH TO TALK TO THEM, LET THEM KNOW WE'RE HERE TO HELP.
ASSSS GOOD A PLAN ASSSS ANY. I'M ON MY WAY.
BATES! GET READY TO RELIEVE CHEKOV!
SNAP
SSSSALUTA—
AAAHHHH!

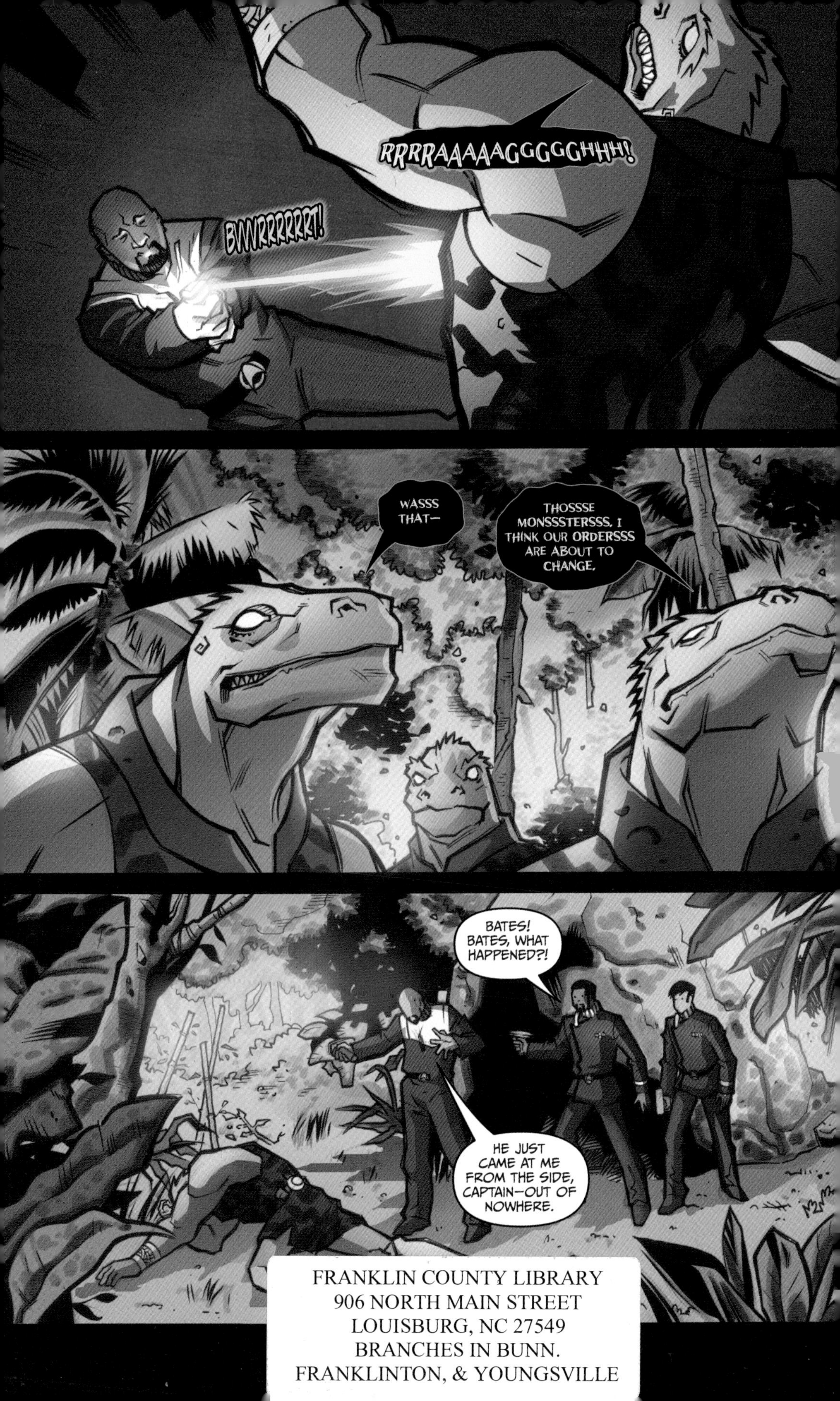
RRRRAAAAAGGGGGHHH!
BWRRRRRRT!
WASSS THAT—
THOSSSE MONSSSTERSSS. I THINK OUR ORDERSSS ARE ABOUT TO CHANGE.
BATES! BATES, WHAT HAPPENED?!
HE JUST CAME AT ME FROM THE SIDE, CAPTAIN—OUT OF NOWHERE.

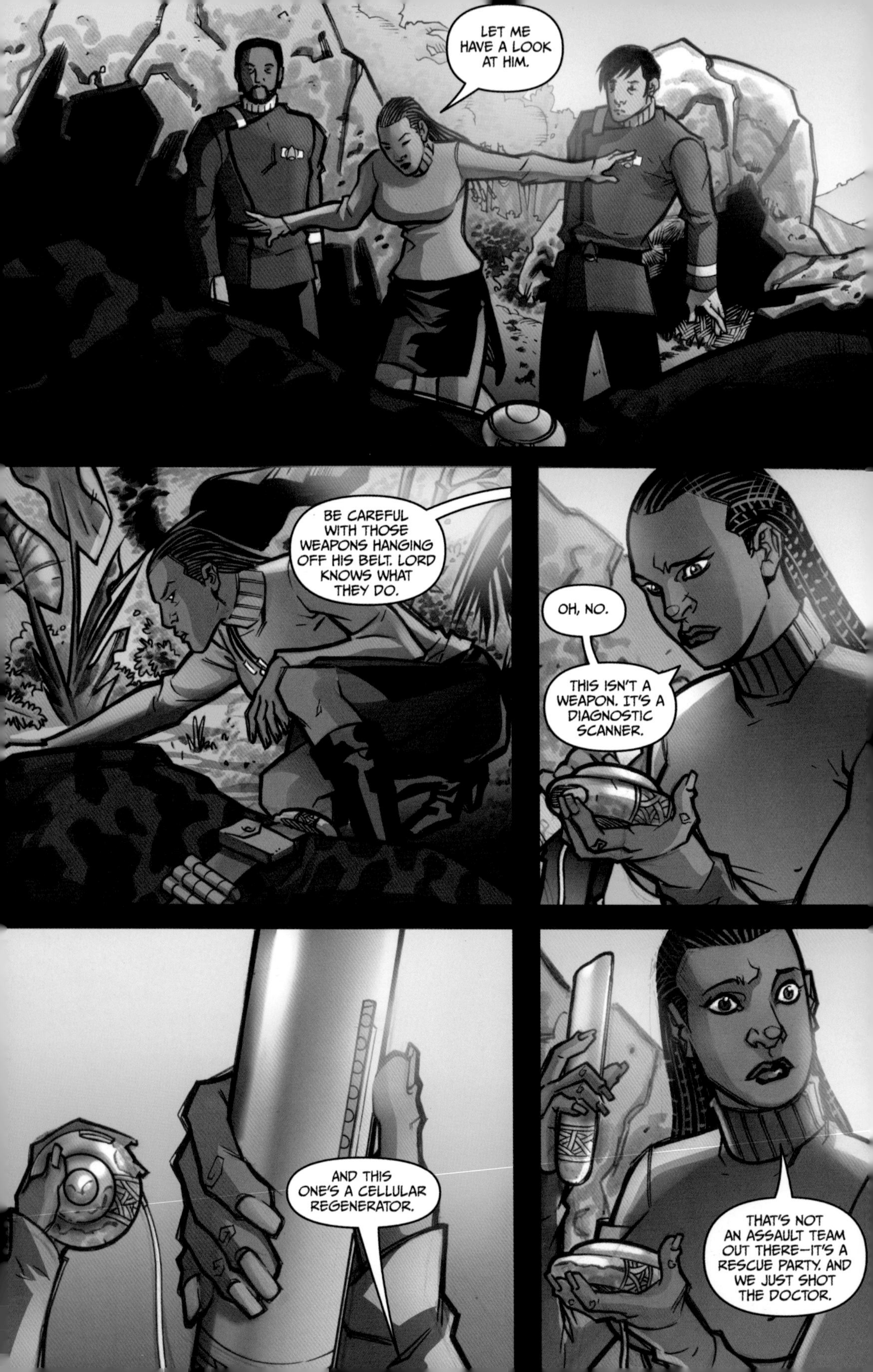
LET ME HAVE A LOOK AT HIM.
BE CAREFUL WITH THOSE WEAPONS HANGING OFF HIS BELT. LORD KNOWS WHAT THEY DO.
OH, NO.
THIS ISN'T A WEAPON. IT'S A DIAGNOSTIC SCANNER.
AND THIS ONE'S A CELLULAR REGENERATOR.
THAT'S NOT AN ASSAULT TEAM OUT THERE—IT'S A RESCUE PARTY. AND WE JUST SHOT THE DOCTOR.

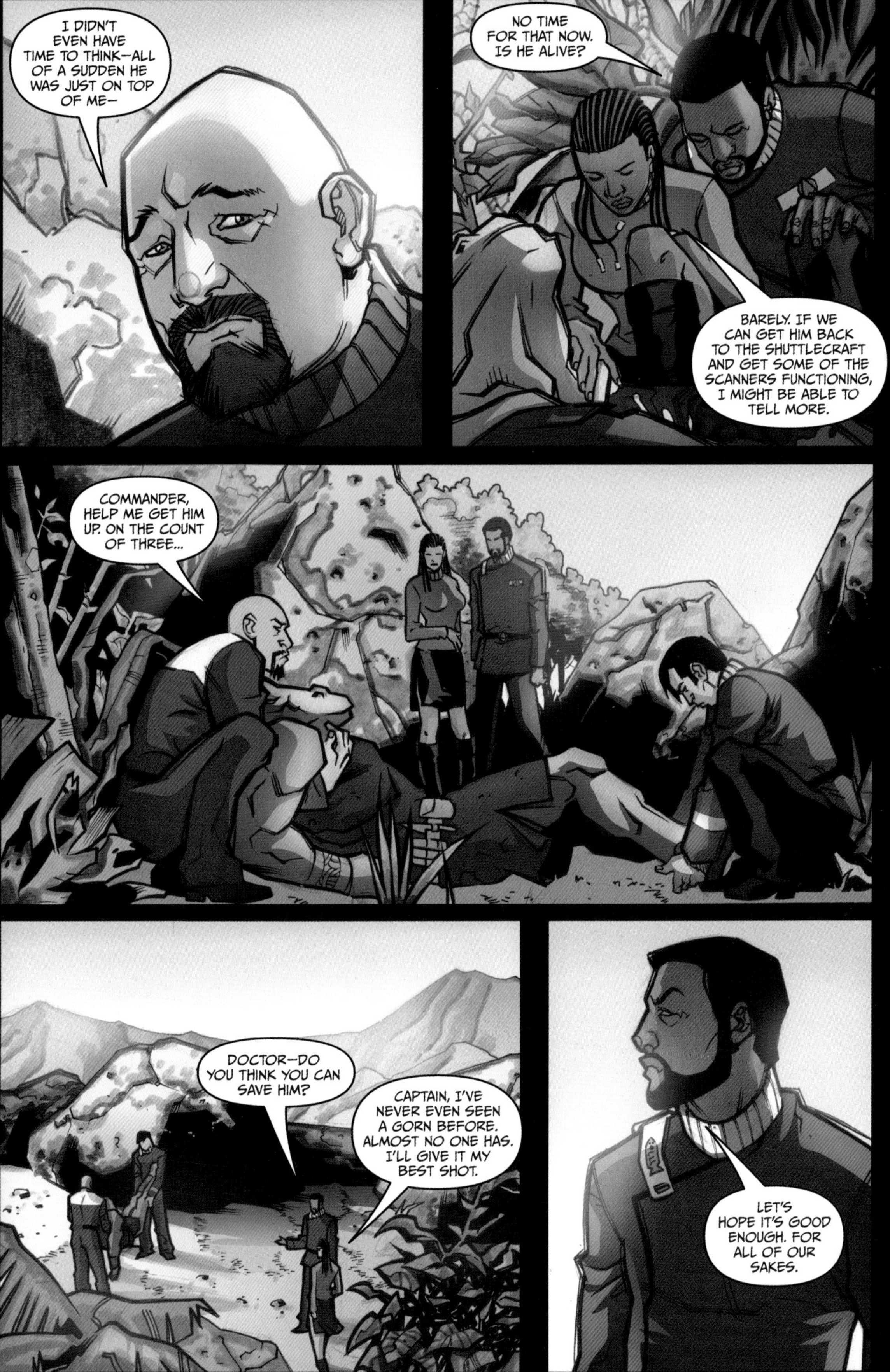
I DIDN'T EVEN HAVE TIME TO THINK--ALL OF A SUDDEN HE WAS JUST ON TOP OF ME--
NO TIME FOR THAT NOW. IS HE ALIVE?
BARELY. IF WE CAN GET HIM BACK TO THE SHUTTLECRAFT AND GET SOME OF THE SCANNERS FUNCTIONING, I MIGHT BE ABLE TO TELL MORE.
COMMANDER, HELP ME GET HIM UP. ON THE COUNT OF THREE...
DOCTOR--DO YOU THINK YOU CAN SAVE HIM?
CAPTAIN, I'VE NEVER EVEN SEEN A GORN BEFORE. ALMOST NO ONE HAS. I'LL GIVE IT MY BEST SHOT.
LET'S HOPE IT'S GOOD ENOUGH. FOR ALL OF OUR SAKES.

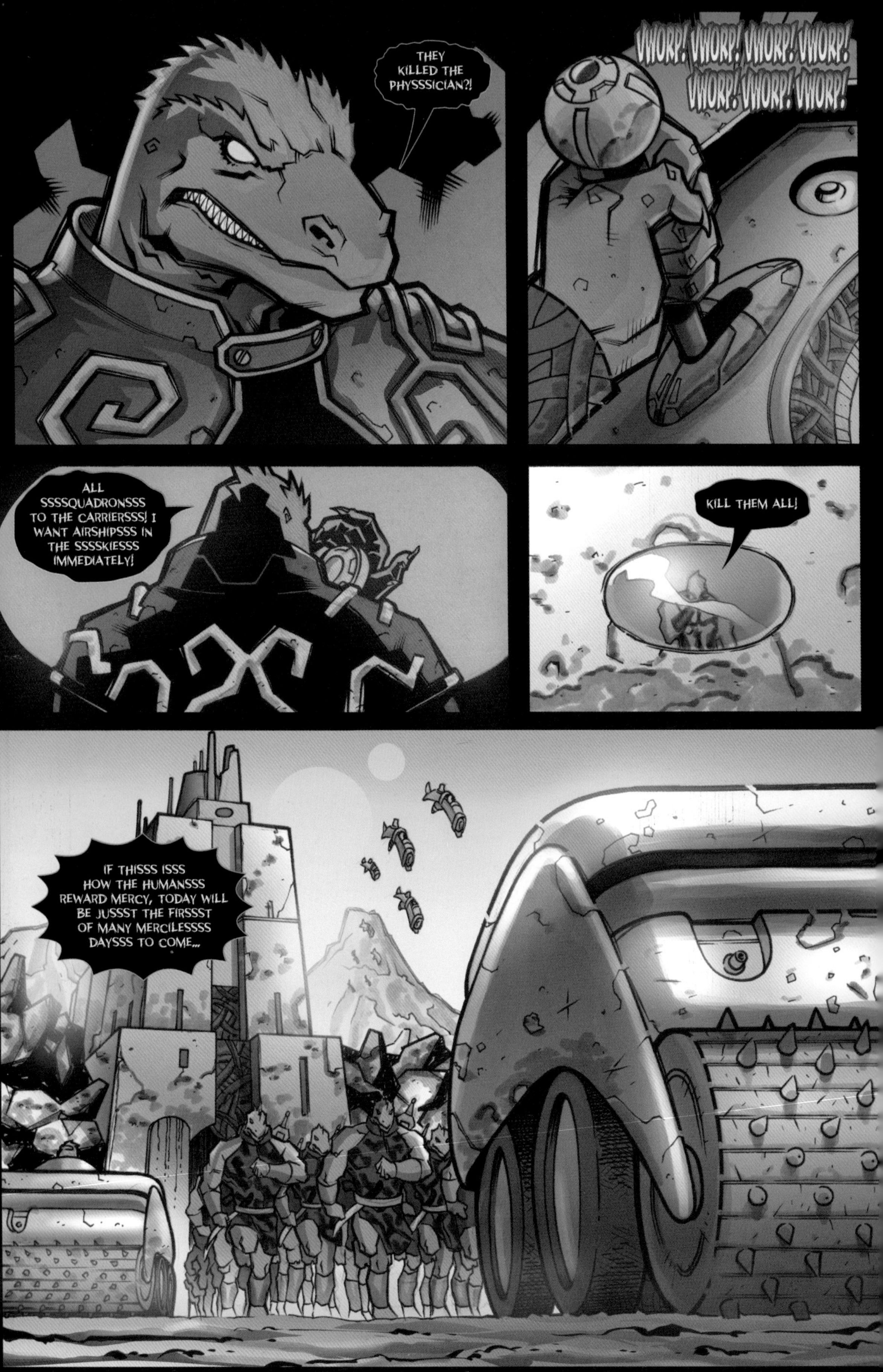
THEY KILLED THE PHYSSSICIAN?!
VWORP! VWORP! VWORP! VWORP! VWORP! VWORP! VWORP!
ALL SSSSQUADRONSSS TO THE CARRIERSSS! I WANT AIRSHIPSSS IN THE SSSSKIESSS IMMEDIATELY!
KILL THEM ALL!
IF THISSS ISSS HOW THE HUMANSSS REWARD MERCY, TODAY WILL BE JUSSST THE FIRSSST OF MANY MERCILESSSS DAYSSS TO COME...

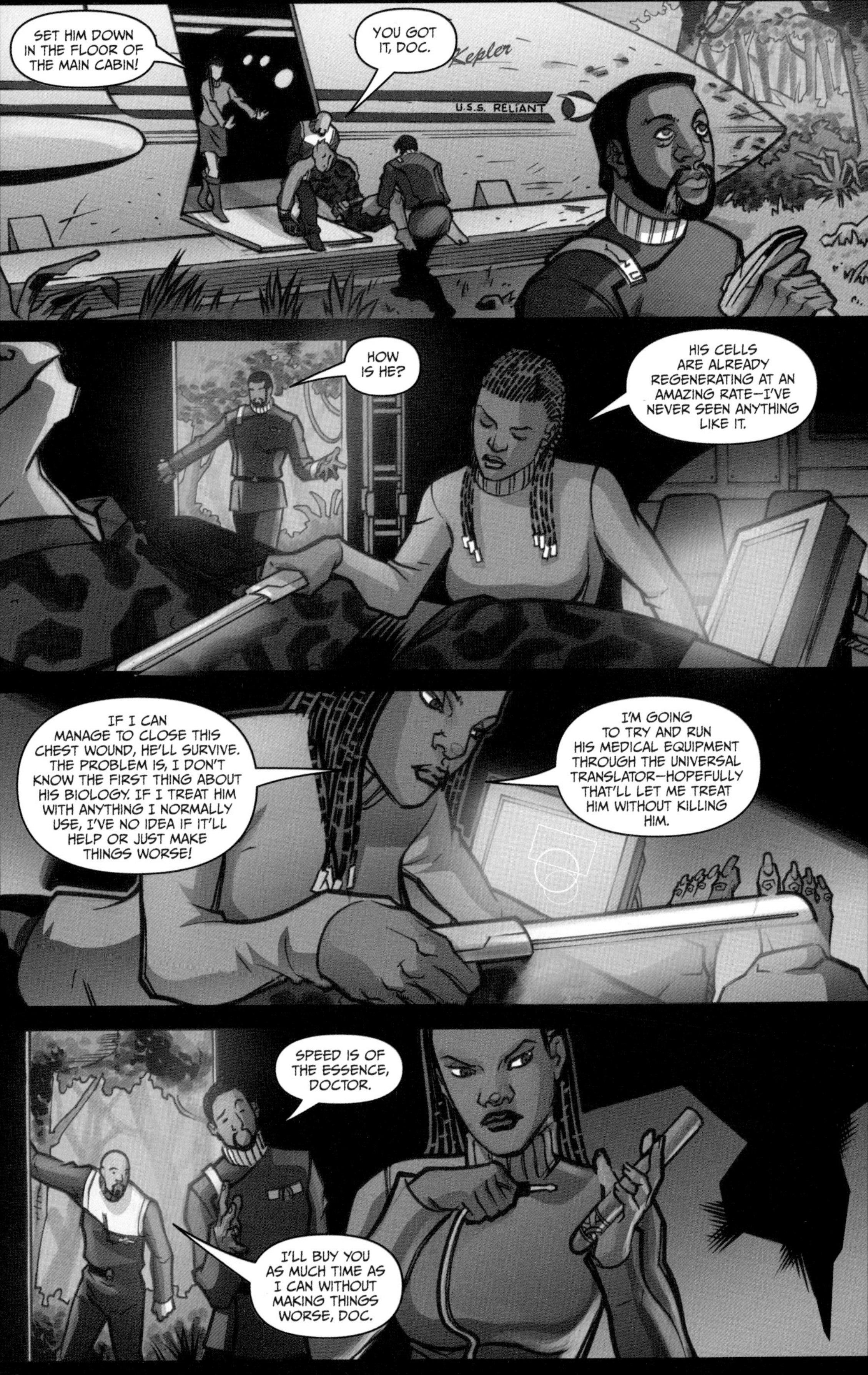
SET HIM DOWN IN THE FLOOR OF THE MAIN CABIN!
YOU GOT IT, DOC.
Kepler
U.S.S. RELIANT
HOW IS HE?
HIS CELLS ARE ALREADY REGENERATING AT AN AMAZING RATE--I'VE NEVER SEEN ANYTHING LIKE IT.
IF I CAN MANAGE TO CLOSE THIS CHEST WOUND, HE'LL SURVIVE. THE PROBLEM IS, I DON'T KNOW THE FIRST THING ABOUT HIS BIOLOGY. IF I TREAT HIM WITH ANYTHING I NORMALLY USE, I'VE NO IDEA IF IT'LL HELP OR JUST MAKE THINGS WORSE!
I'M GOING TO TRY AND RUN HIS MEDICAL EQUIPMENT THROUGH THE UNIVERSAL TRANSLATOR--HOPEFULLY THAT'LL LET ME TREAT HIM WITHOUT KILLING HIM.
SPEED IS OF THE ESSENCE, DOCTOR.
I'LL BUY YOU AS MUCH TIME AS I CAN WITHOUT MAKING THINGS WORSE, DOC.

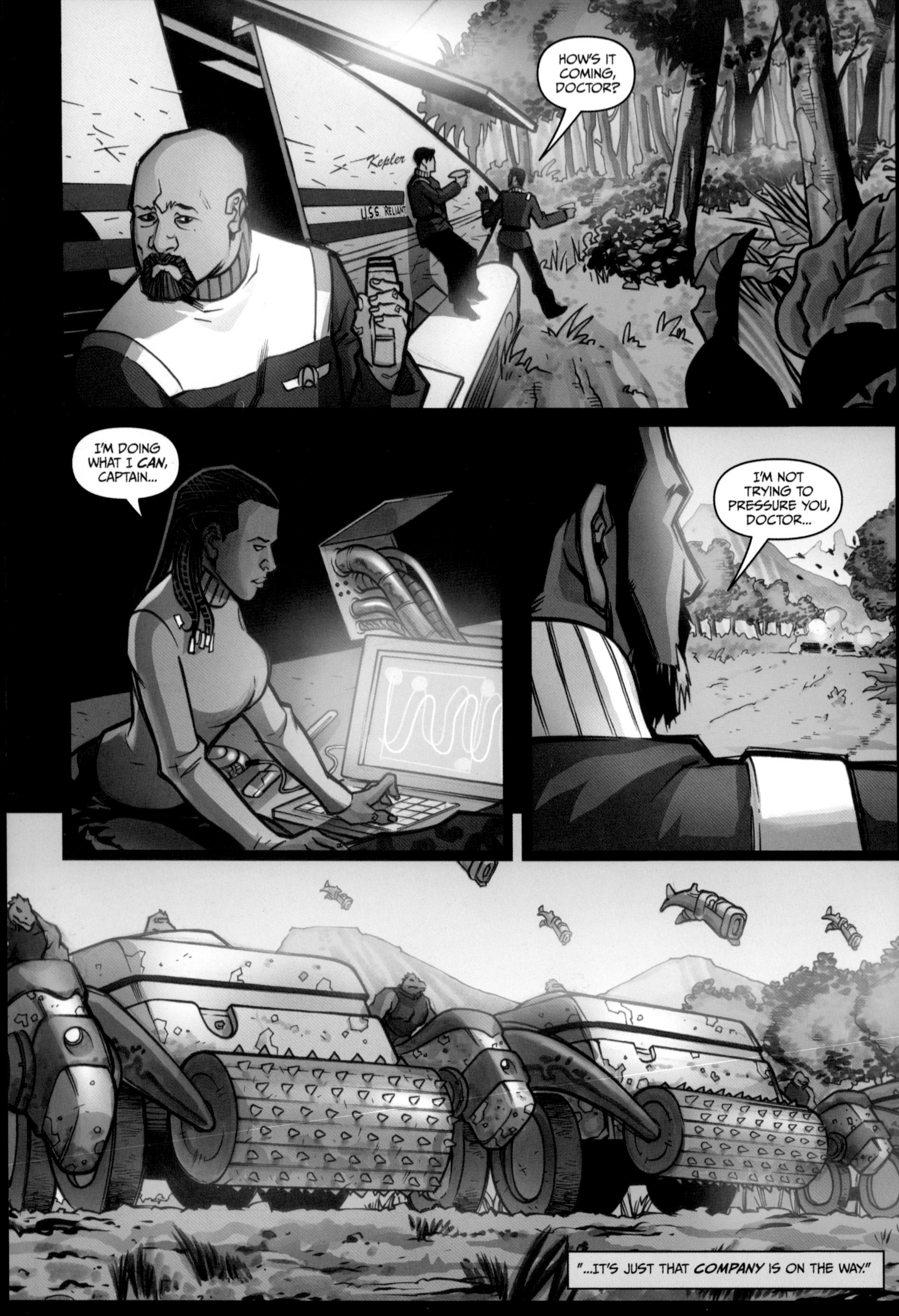
Kepler
U.S.S. RELIANT
HOW'S IT COMING, DOCTOR?
I'M DOING WHAT I *CAN*, CAPTAIN...
I'M NOT TRYING TO PRESSURE YOU, DOCTOR...
"...IT'S JUST THAT *COMPANY* IS ON THE WAY."

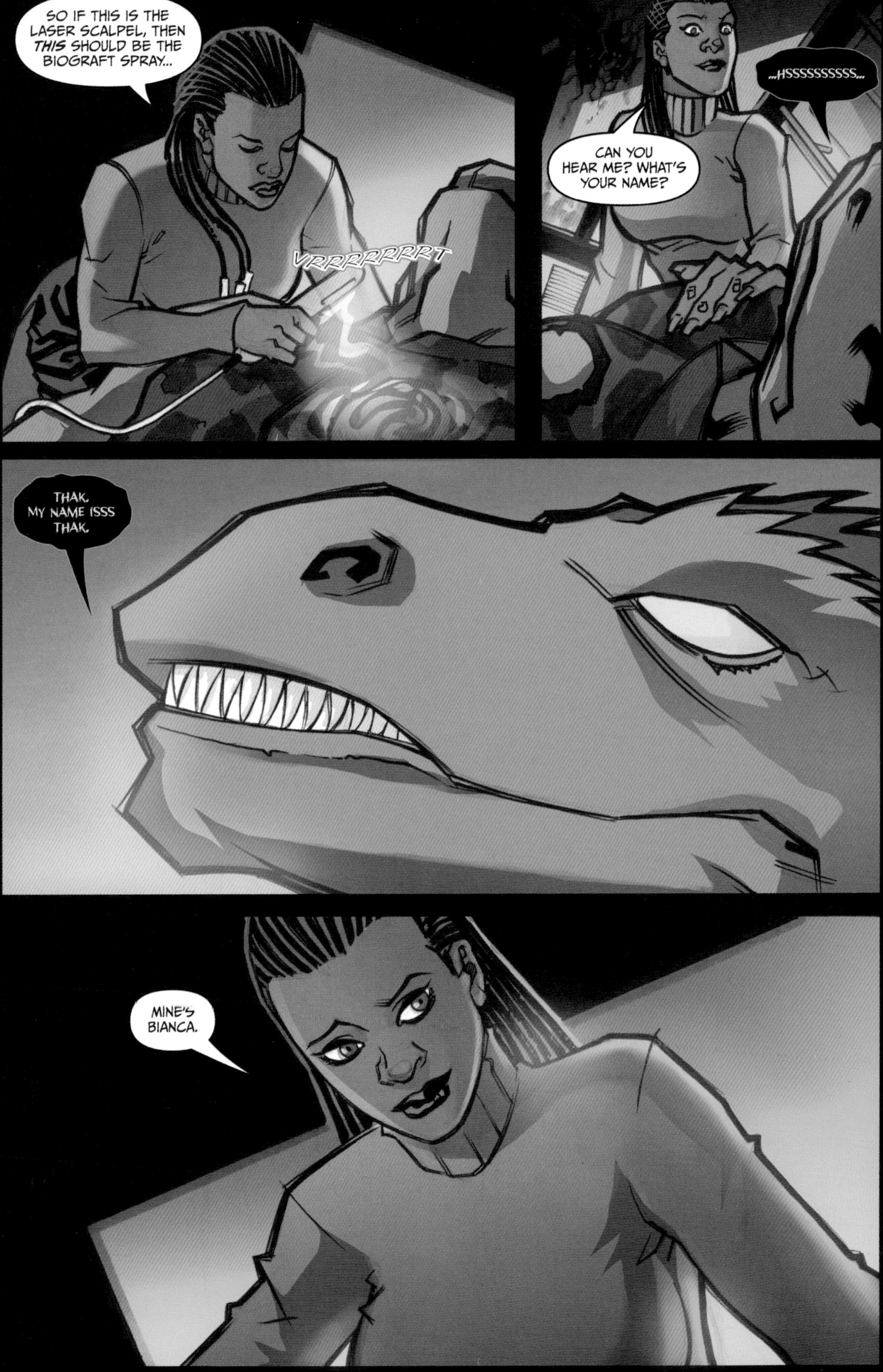
SO IF THIS IS THE LASER SCALPEL, THEN *THIS* SHOULD BE THE BIOGRAFT SPRAY...
VRRRRRRRRT
CAN YOU HEAR ME? WHAT'S YOUR NAME?
...HSSSSSSSSSS...
THAK. MY NAME ISSS THAK.
MINE'S BIANCA.

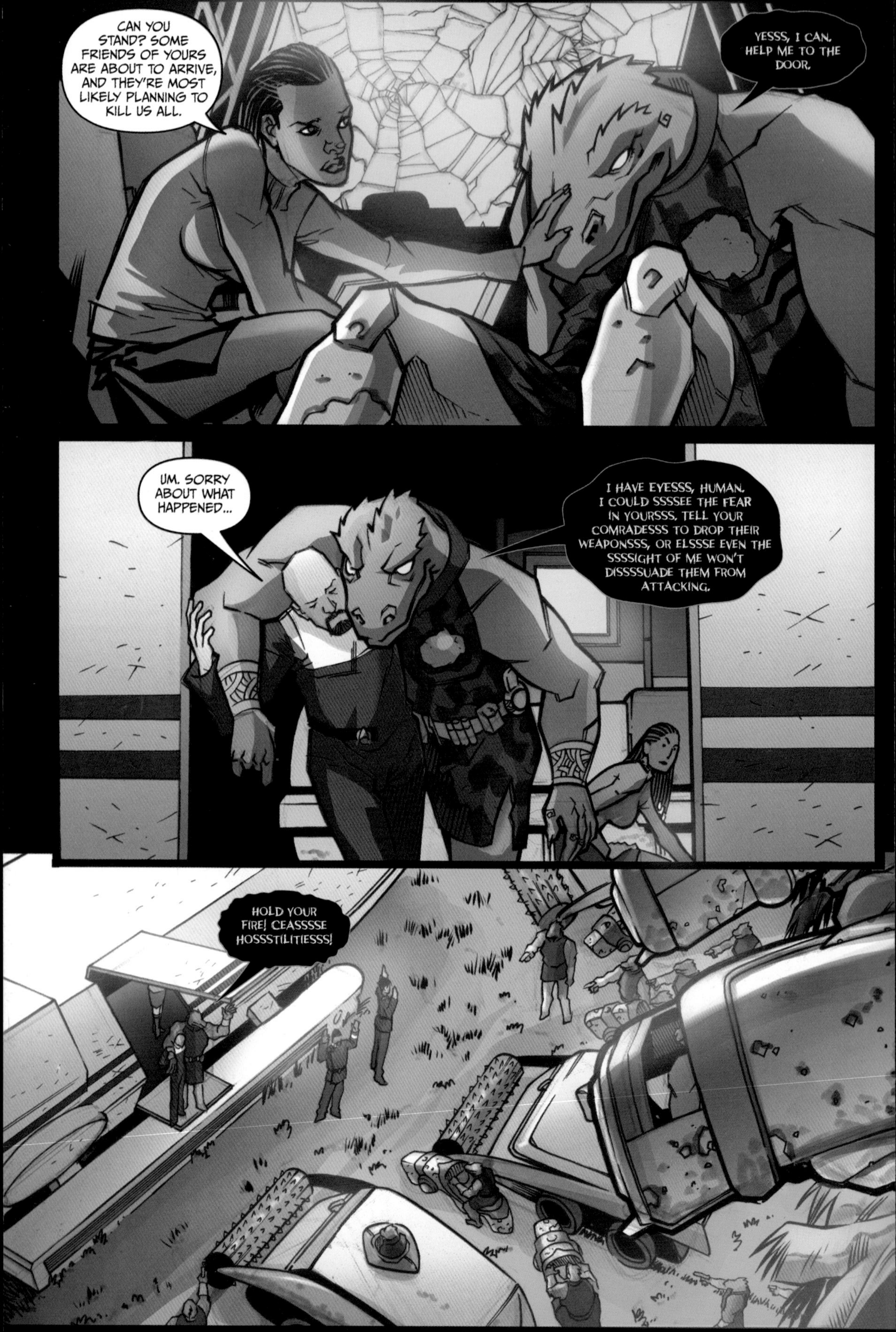
CAN YOU STAND? SOME FRIENDS OF YOURS ARE ABOUT TO ARRIVE, AND THEY'RE MOST LIKELY PLANNING TO KILL US ALL.
YESSS, I CAN. HELP ME TO THE DOOR.
UM. SORRY ABOUT WHAT HAPPENED...
I HAVE EYESSS, HUMAN. I COULD SSSSEE THE FEAR IN YOURSSS. TELL YOUR COMRADESSS TO DROP THEIR WEAPONSSS, OR ELSSSE EVEN THE SSSSIGHT OF ME WON'T DISSSSUADE THEM FROM ATTACKING.
HOLD YOUR FIRE! CEASSSSE HOSSSTILITIESSS!

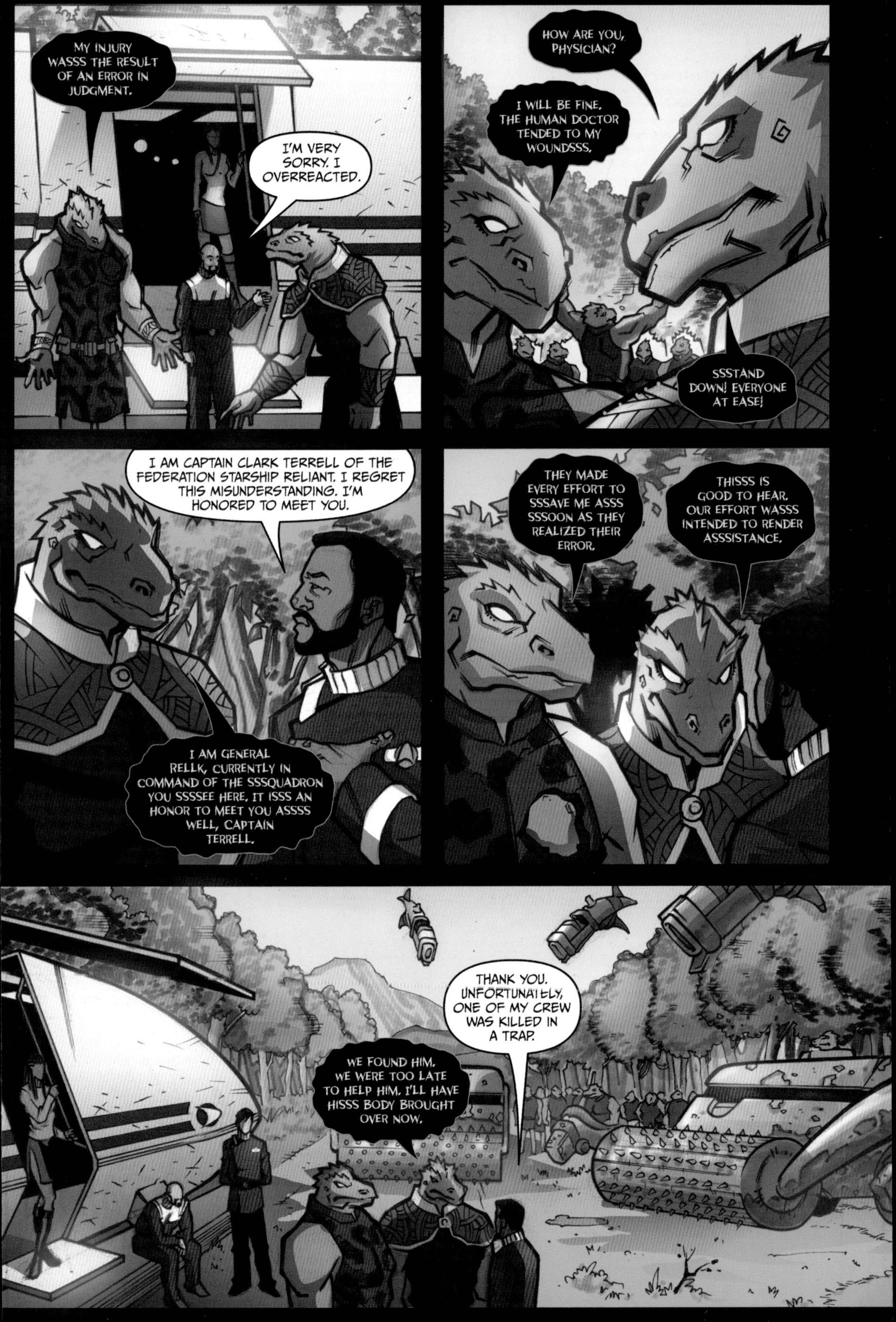
MY INJURY WASSS THE RESULT OF AN ERROR IN JUDGMENT.
I'M VERY SORRY. I OVERREACTED.
HOW ARE YOU, PHYSICIAN?
I WILL BE FINE. THE HUMAN DOCTOR TENDED TO MY WOUNDSSS.
SSSTAND DOWN! EVERYONE AT EASE!
I AM CAPTAIN CLARK TERRELL OF THE FEDERATION STARSHIP RELIANT. I REGRET THIS MISUNDERSTANDING. I'M HONORED TO MEET YOU.
I AM GENERAL RELLK, CURRENTLY IN COMMAND OF THE SSSQUADRON YOU SSSSEE HERE. IT ISSS AN HONOR TO MEET YOU ASSSS WELL, CAPTAIN TERRELL.
THEY MADE EVERY EFFORT TO SSSAVE ME ASSS SSSOON AS THEY REALIZED THEIR ERROR.
THISSS IS GOOD TO HEAR. OUR EFFORT WASSS INTENDED TO RENDER ASSSISTANCE.
THANK YOU. UNFORTUNATELY, ONE OF MY CREW WAS KILLED IN A TRAP.
WE FOUND HIM. WE WERE TOO LATE TO HELP HIM. I'LL HAVE HISSS BODY BROUGHT OVER NOW.

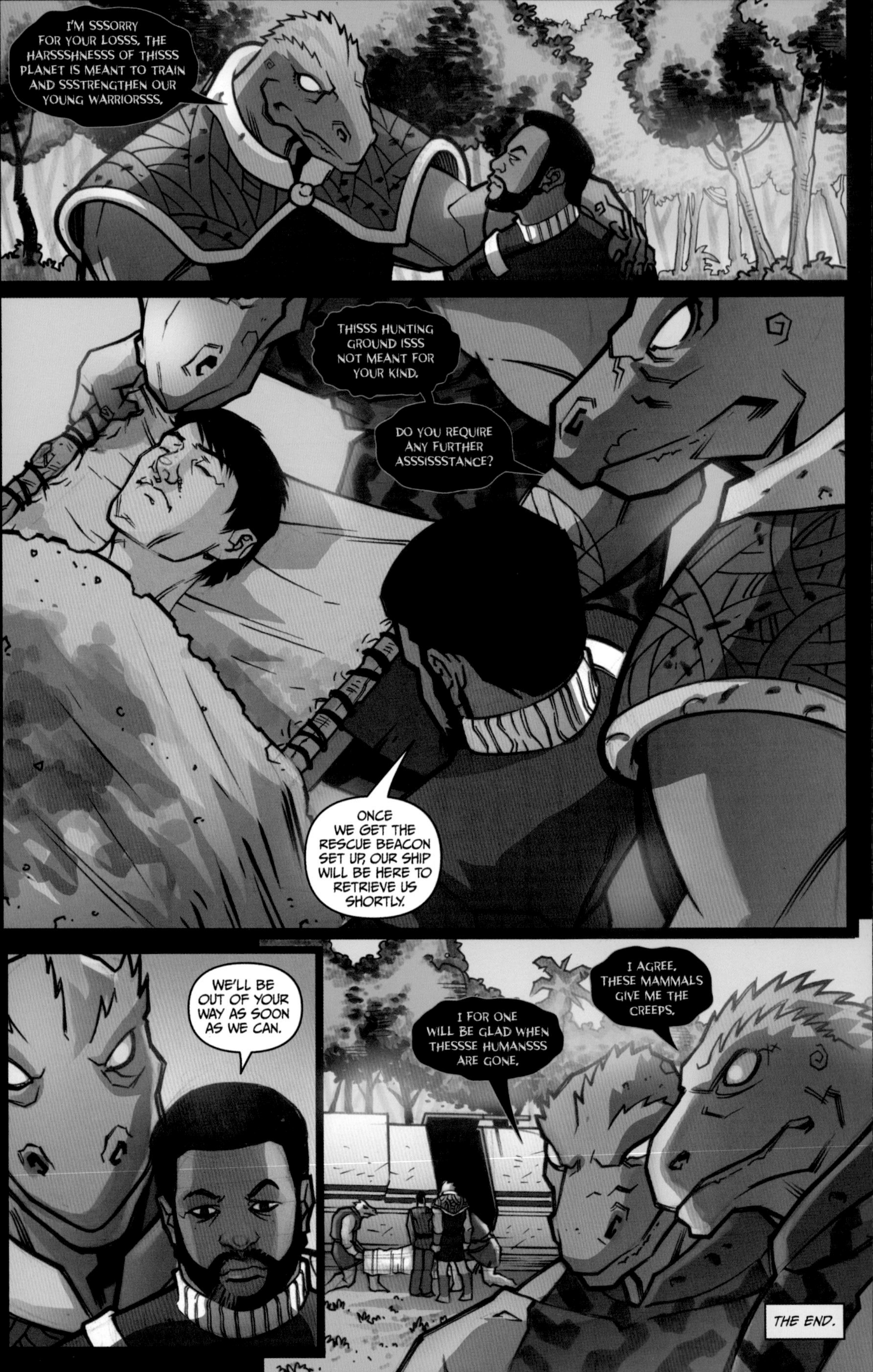
I'M SSSORRY FOR YOUR LOSSS. THE HARSSSHNESSS OF THISSS PLANET IS MEANT TO TRAIN AND SSSTRENGTHEN OUR YOUNG WARRIORSSS.
THISSS HUNTING GROUND ISSS NOT MEANT FOR YOUR KIND.
DO YOU REQUIRE ANY FURTHER ASSSISSSTANCE?
ONCE WE GET THE RESCUE BEACON SET UP, OUR SHIP WILL BE HERE TO RETRIEVE US SHORTLY.
WE'LL BE OUT OF YOUR WAY AS SOON AS WE CAN.
I FOR ONE WILL BE GLAD WHEN THESSSE HUMANSSS ARE GONE.
I AGREE. THESE MAMMALS GIVE ME THE CREEPS.
THE END.

art and color by David Messina

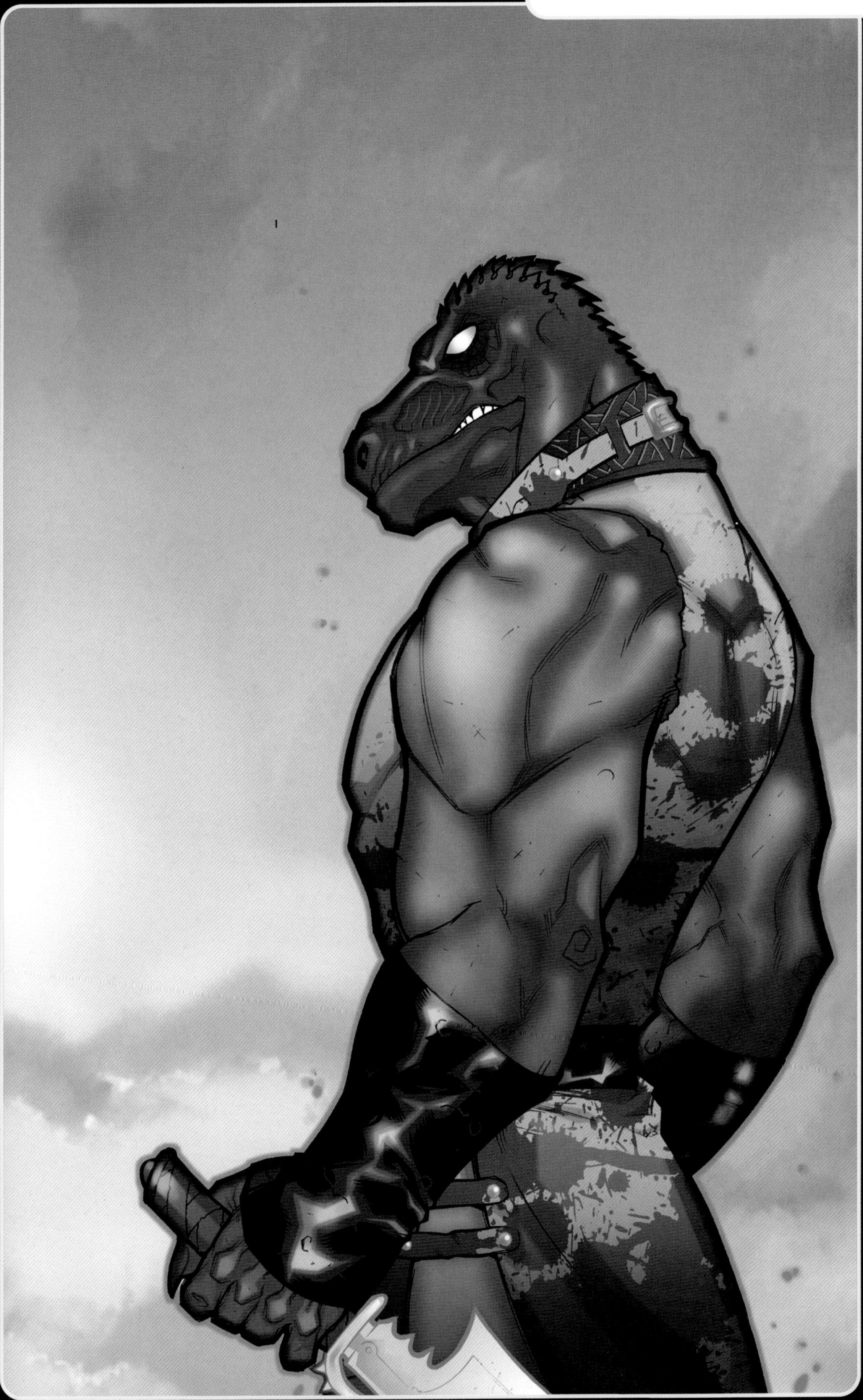

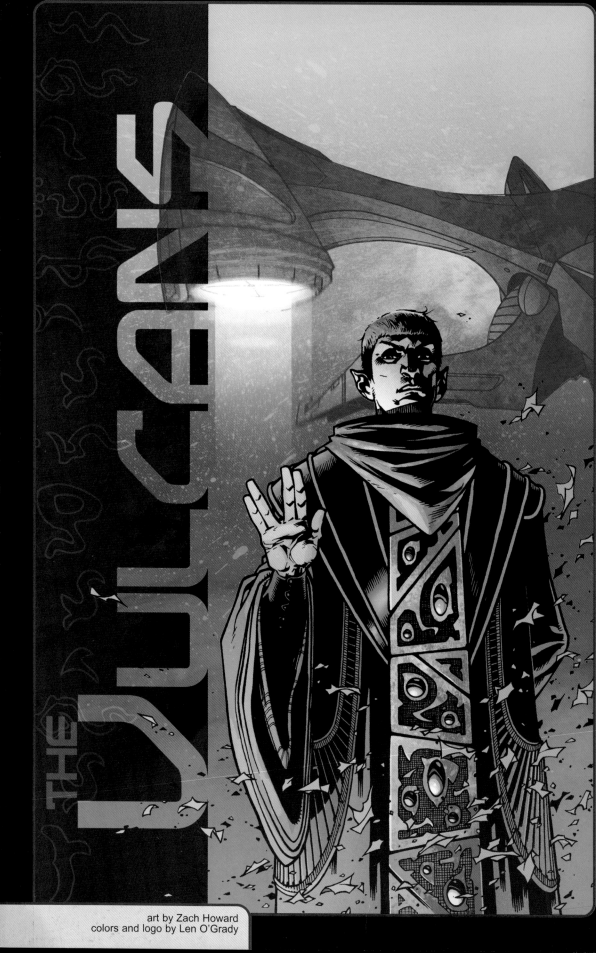

THE VULCANS

art by Zach Howard
colors and logo by Len O'Grady

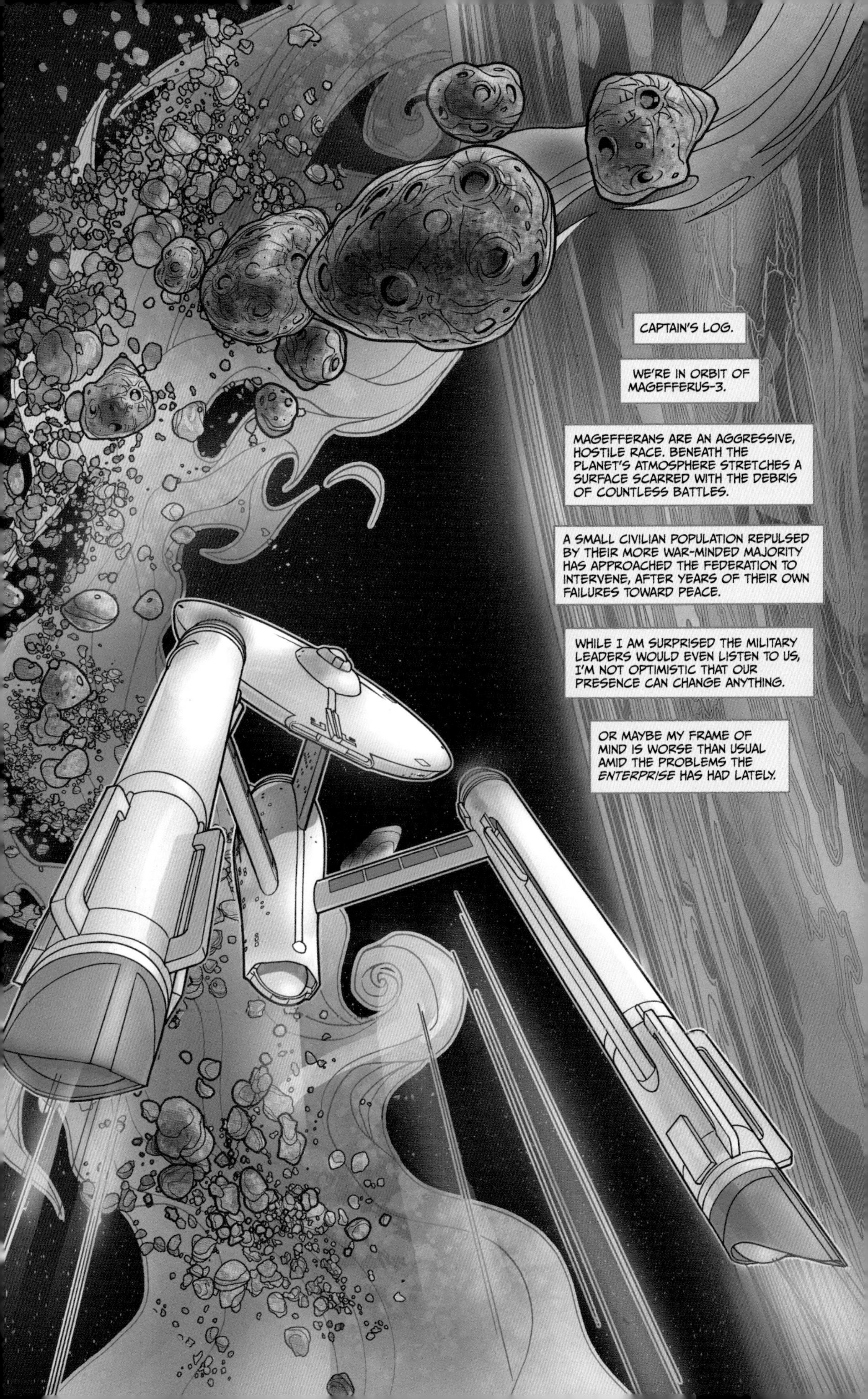
CAPTAIN'S LOG.
WE'RE IN ORBIT OF MAGEFFERUS-3.
MAGEFFERANS ARE AN AGGRESSIVE, HOSTILE RACE. BENEATH THE PLANET'S ATMOSPHERE STRETCHES A SURFACE SCARRED WITH THE DEBRIS OF COUNTLESS BATTLES.
A SMALL CIVILIAN POPULATION REPULSED BY THEIR MORE WAR-MINDED MAJORITY HAS APPROACHED THE FEDERATION TO INTERVENE, AFTER YEARS OF THEIR OWN FAILURES TOWARD PEACE.
WHILE I AM SURPRISED THE MILITARY LEADERS WOULD EVEN LISTEN TO US, I'M NOT OPTIMISTIC THAT OUR PRESENCE CAN CHANGE ANYTHING.
OR MAYBE MY FRAME OF MIND IS WORSE THAN USUAL AMID THE PROBLEMS THE *ENTERPRISE* HAS HAD LATELY.

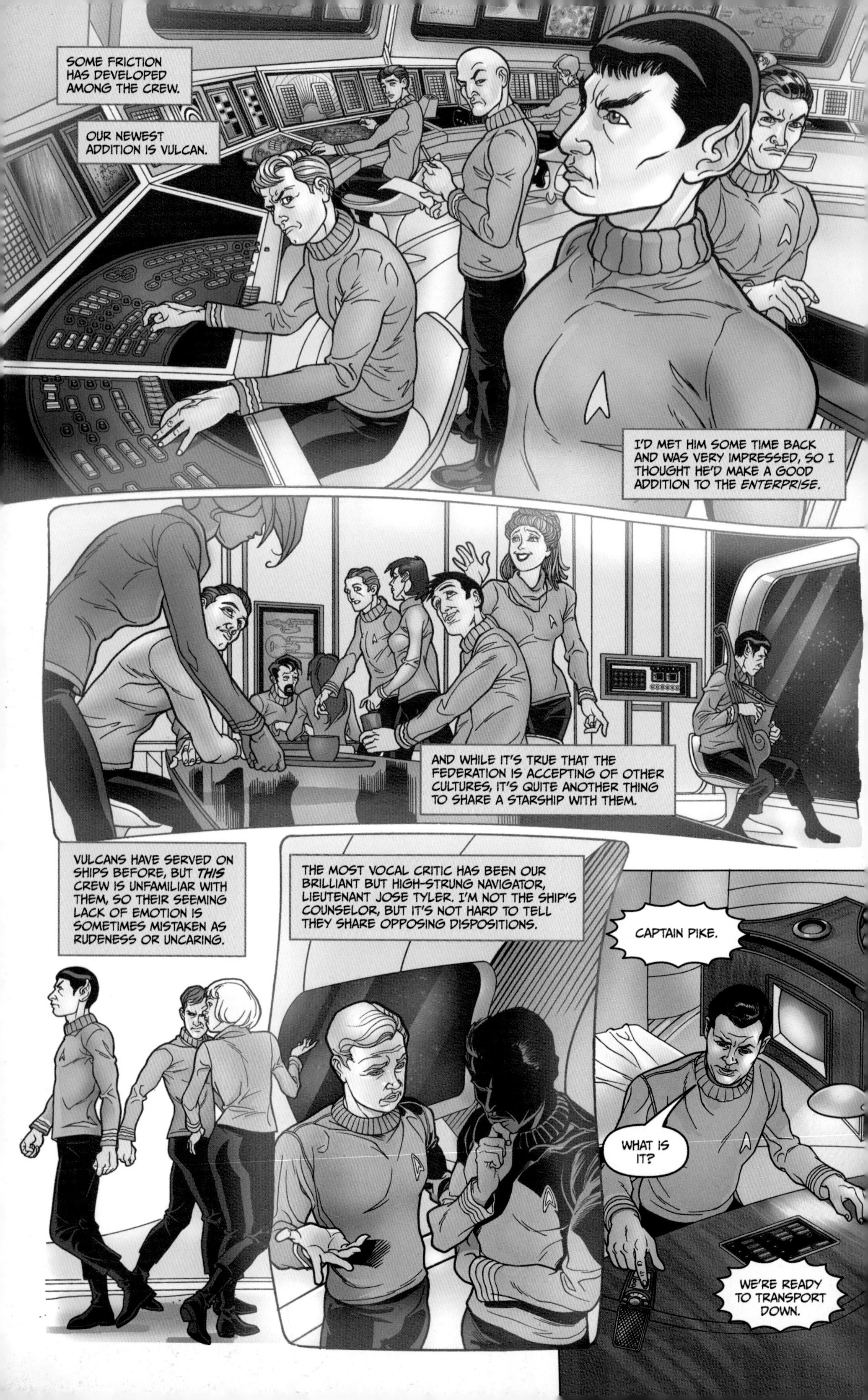
SOME FRICTION HAS DEVELOPED AMONG THE CREW.
OUR NEWEST ADDITION IS VULCAN.
I'D MET HIM SOME TIME BACK AND WAS VERY IMPRESSED, SO I THOUGHT HE'D MAKE A GOOD ADDITION TO THE *ENTERPRISE*.
AND WHILE IT'S TRUE THAT THE FEDERATION IS ACCEPTING OF OTHER CULTURES, IT'S QUITE ANOTHER THING TO SHARE A STARSHIP WITH THEM.
VULCANS HAVE SERVED ON SHIPS BEFORE, BUT *THIS* CREW IS UNFAMILIAR WITH THEM, SO THEIR SEEMING LACK OF EMOTION IS SOMETIMES MISTAKEN AS RUDENESS OR UNCARING.
THE MOST VOCAL CRITIC HAS BEEN OUR BRILLIANT BUT HIGH-STRUNG NAVIGATOR, LIEUTENANT JOSE TYLER. I'M NOT THE SHIP'S COUNSELOR, BUT IT'S NOT HARD TO TELL THEY SHARE OPPOSING DISPOSITIONS.
CAPTAIN PIKE.
WHAT IS IT?
WE'RE READY TO TRANSPORT DOWN.

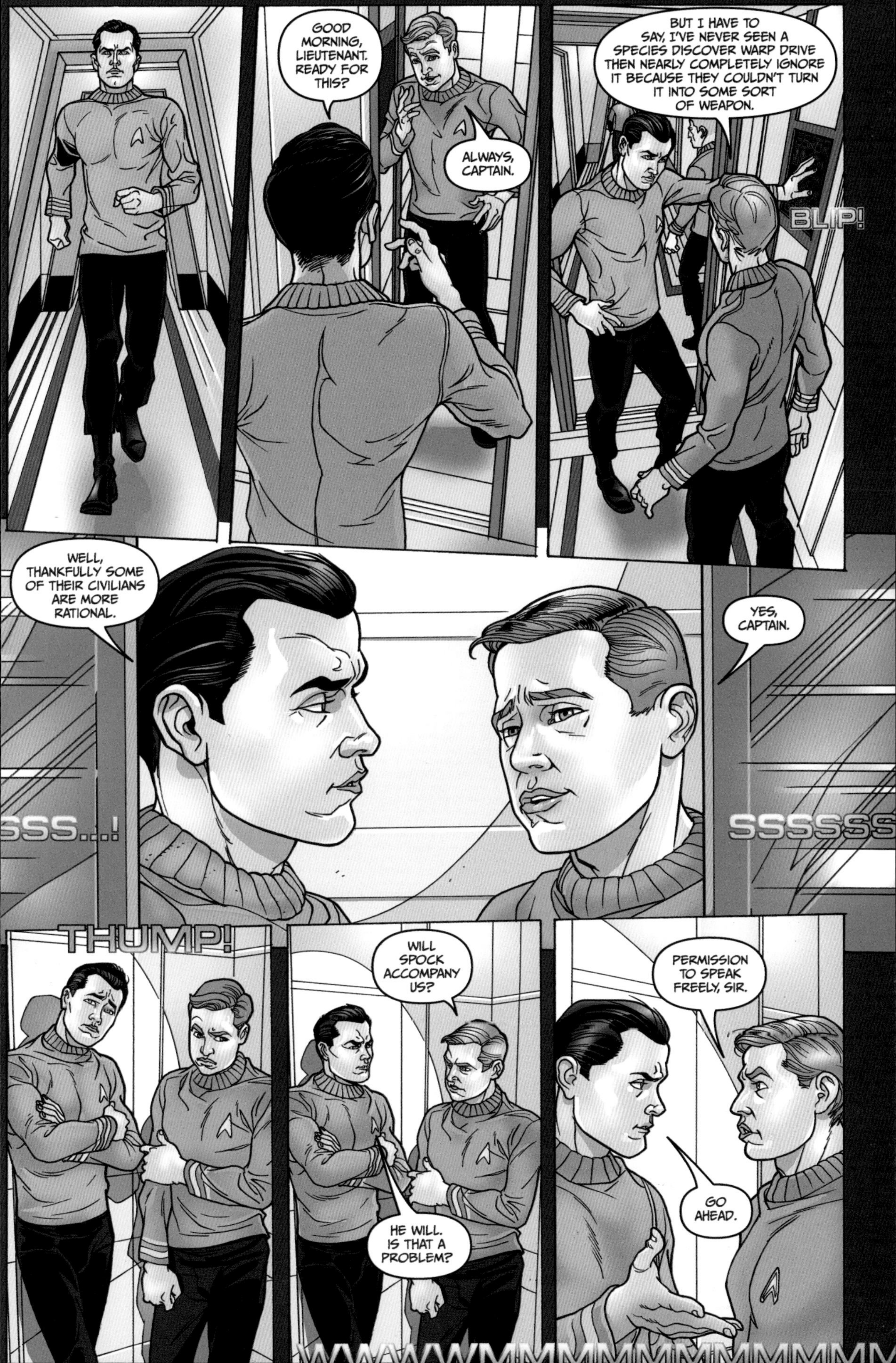

GOOD MORNING, LIEUTENANT. READY FOR THIS?
ALWAYS, CAPTAIN.
BUT I HAVE TO SAY, I'VE NEVER SEEN A SPECIES DISCOVER WARP DRIVE THEN NEARLY COMPLETELY IGNORE IT BECAUSE THEY COULDN'T TURN IT INTO SOME SORT OF WEAPON.
BLIP!
WELL, THANKFULLY SOME OF THEIR CIVILIANS ARE MORE RATIONAL.
YES, CAPTAIN.
SSS...!
SSSSSS
THUMP!
WILL SPOCK ACCOMPANY US?
HE WILL. IS THAT A PROBLEM?
PERMISSION TO SPEAK FREELY, SIR.
GO AHEAD.
WWWWWMMMMMMMMMMMM

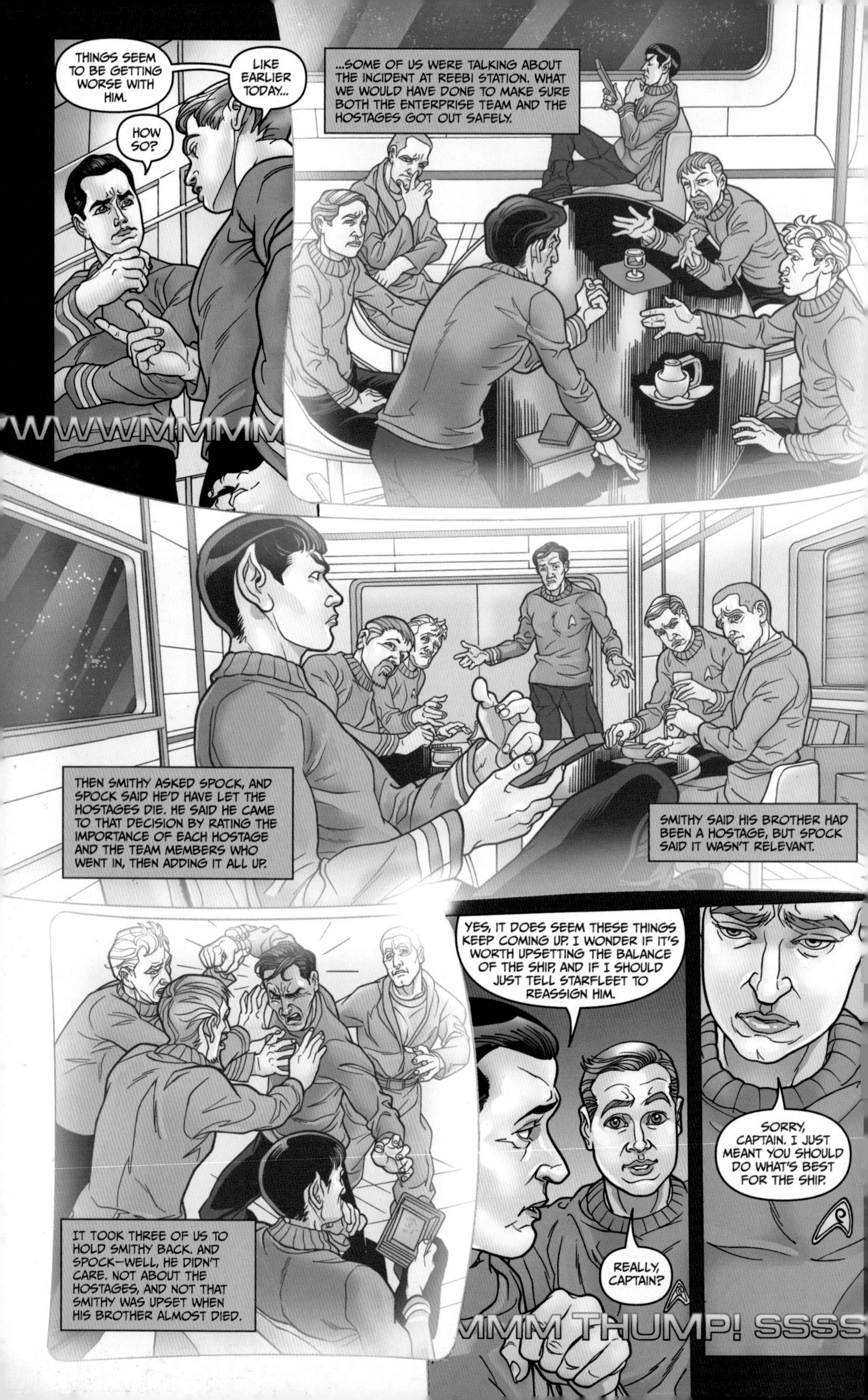

THINGS SEEM TO BE GETTING WORSE WITH HIM.
HOW SO?
LIKE EARLIER TODAY...
...SOME OF US WERE TALKING ABOUT THE INCIDENT AT REEBI STATION. WHAT WE WOULD HAVE DONE TO MAKE SURE BOTH THE ENTERPRISE TEAM AND THE HOSTAGES GOT OUT SAFELY.
WWWWMMMM
THEN SMITHY ASKED SPOCK, AND SPOCK SAID HE'D HAVE LET THE HOSTAGES DIE. HE SAID HE CAME TO THAT DECISION BY RATING THE IMPORTANCE OF EACH HOSTAGE AND THE TEAM MEMBERS WHO WENT IN, THEN ADDING IT ALL UP.
SMITHY SAID HIS BROTHER HAD BEEN A HOSTAGE, BUT SPOCK SAID IT WASN'T RELEVANT.
IT TOOK THREE OF US TO HOLD SMITHY BACK. AND SPOCK—WELL, HE DIDN'T CARE. NOT ABOUT THE HOSTAGES, AND NOT THAT SMITHY WAS UPSET WHEN HIS BROTHER ALMOST DIED.
YES, IT DOES SEEM THESE THINGS KEEP COMING UP. I WONDER IF IT'S WORTH UPSETTING THE BALANCE OF THE SHIP, AND IF I SHOULD JUST TELL STARFLEET TO REASSIGN HIM.
REALLY, CAPTAIN?
MMM THUMP! SSSS
SORRY, CAPTAIN. I JUST MEANT YOU SHOULD DO WHAT'S BEST FOR THE SHIP.

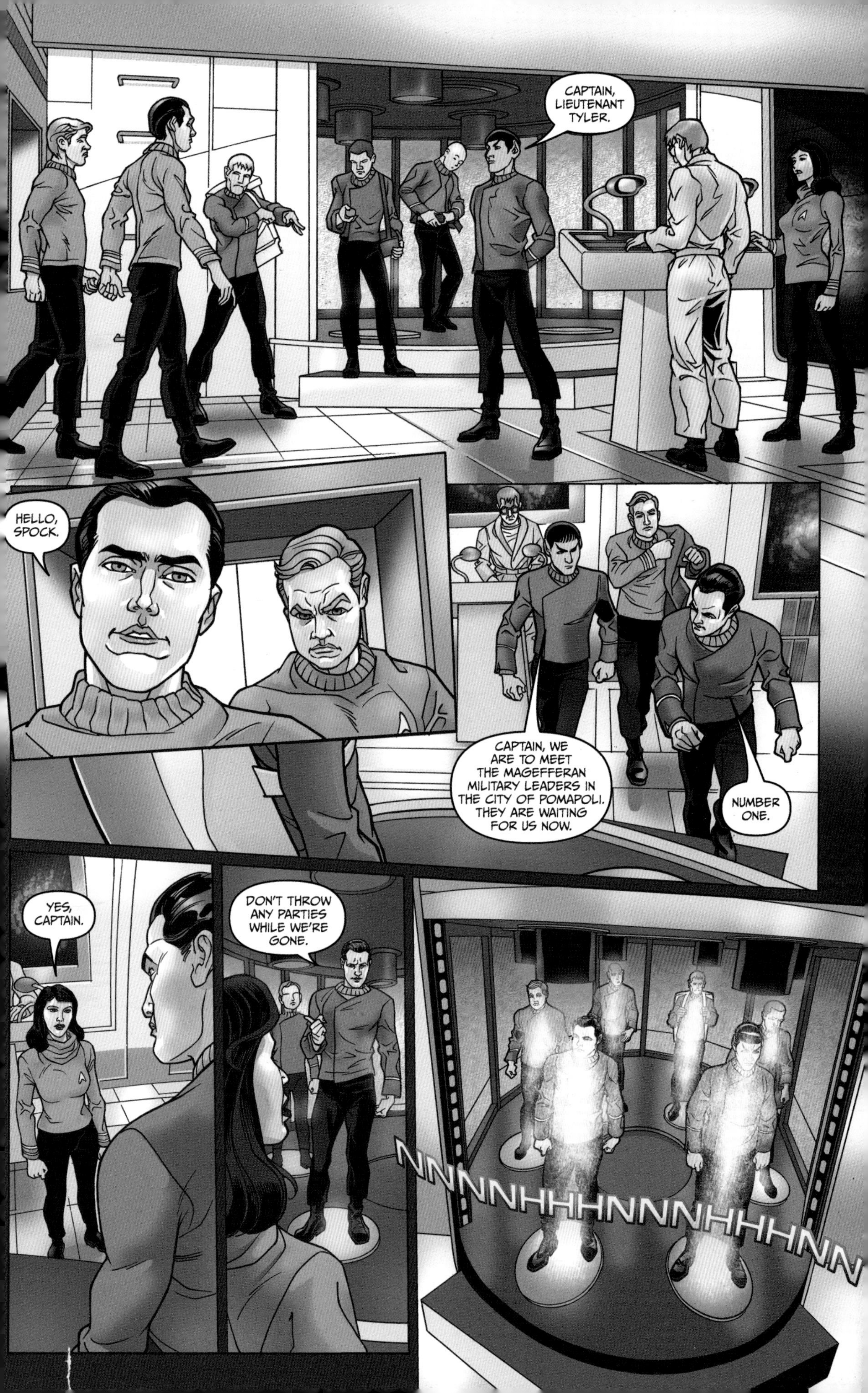
CAPTAIN, LIEUTENANT TYLER.
HELLO, SPOCK.
CAPTAIN, WE ARE TO MEET THE MAGEFFERAN MILITARY LEADERS IN THE CITY OF POMAPOLI. THEY ARE WAITING FOR US NOW.
NUMBER ONE.
YES, CAPTAIN.
DON'T THROW ANY PARTIES WHILE WE'RE GONE.
NNNNHHHNNNNHHHHNN

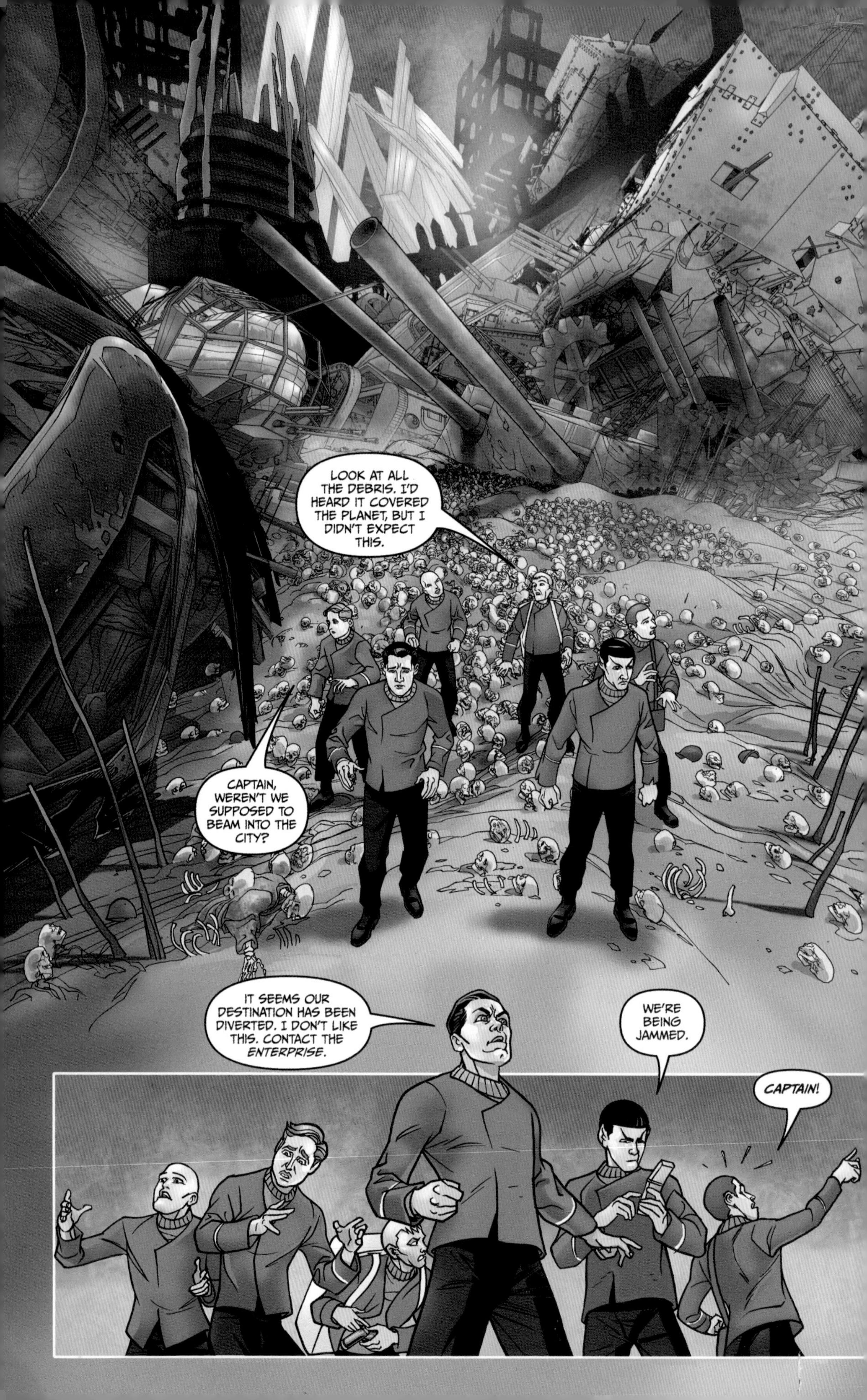
LOOK AT ALL THE DEBRIS. I'D HEARD IT COVERED THE PLANET, BUT I DIDN'T EXPECT THIS.
CAPTAIN, WEREN'T WE SUPPOSED TO BEAM INTO THE CITY?
IT SEEMS OUR DESTINATION HAS BEEN DIVERTED. I DON'T LIKE THIS. CONTACT THE *ENTERPRISE*.
WE'RE BEING JAMMED.
CAPTAIN!

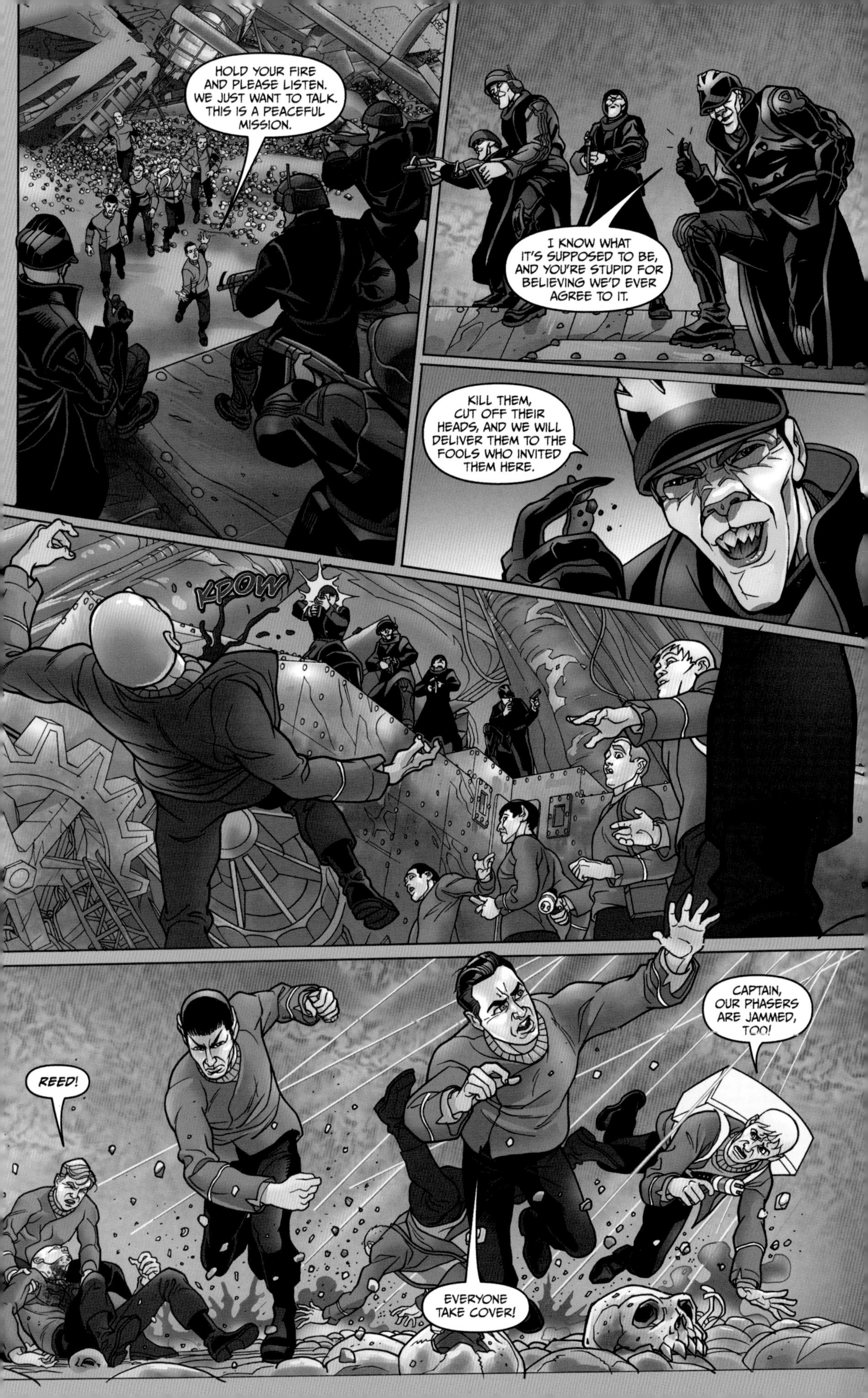
HOLD YOUR FIRE AND PLEASE LISTEN. WE JUST WANT TO TALK. THIS IS A PEACEFUL MISSION.
I KNOW WHAT IT'S SUPPOSED TO BE, AND YOU'RE STUPID FOR BELIEVING WE'D EVER AGREE TO IT.
KILL THEM, CUT OFF THEIR HEADS, AND WE WILL DELIVER THEM TO THE FOOLS WHO INVITED THEM HERE.
KPOW
REED!
CAPTAIN, OUR PHASERS ARE JAMMED, TOO!
EVERYONE TAKE COVER!

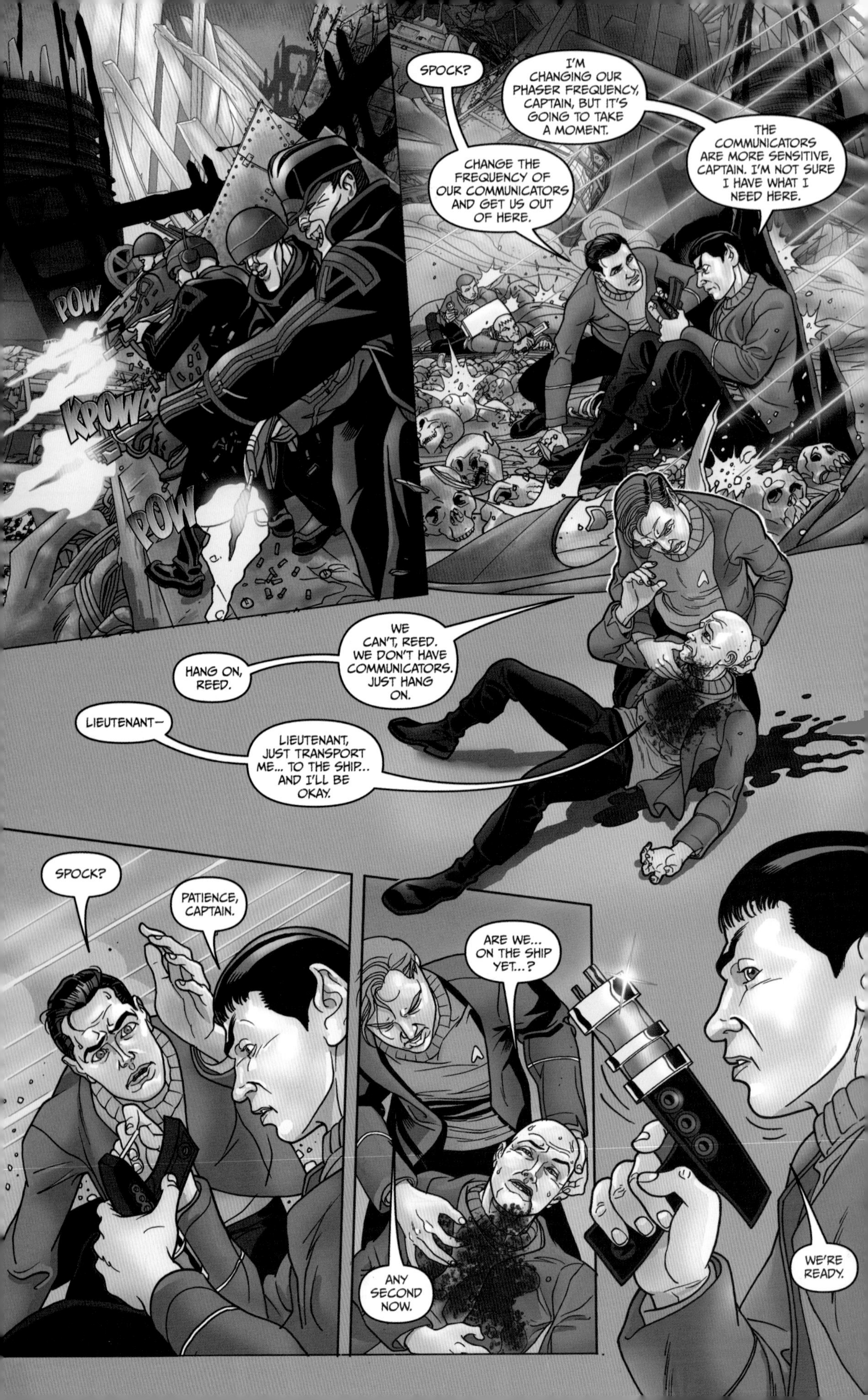
POW
KPOW
POW
SPOCK?
CHANGE THE FREQUENCY OF OUR COMMUNICATORS AND GET US OUT OF HERE.
I'M CHANGING OUR PHASER FREQUENCY, CAPTAIN, BUT IT'S GOING TO TAKE A MOMENT.
THE COMMUNICATORS ARE MORE SENSITIVE, CAPTAIN. I'M NOT SURE I HAVE WHAT I NEED HERE.
LIEUTENANT—
LIEUTENANT, JUST TRANSPORT ME... TO THE SHIP... AND I'LL BE OKAY.
HANG ON, REED.
WE CAN'T, REED. WE DON'T HAVE COMMUNICATORS. JUST HANG ON.
SPOCK?
PATIENCE, CAPTAIN.
ARE WE... ON THE SHIP YET...?
ANY SECOND NOW.
WE'RE READY.

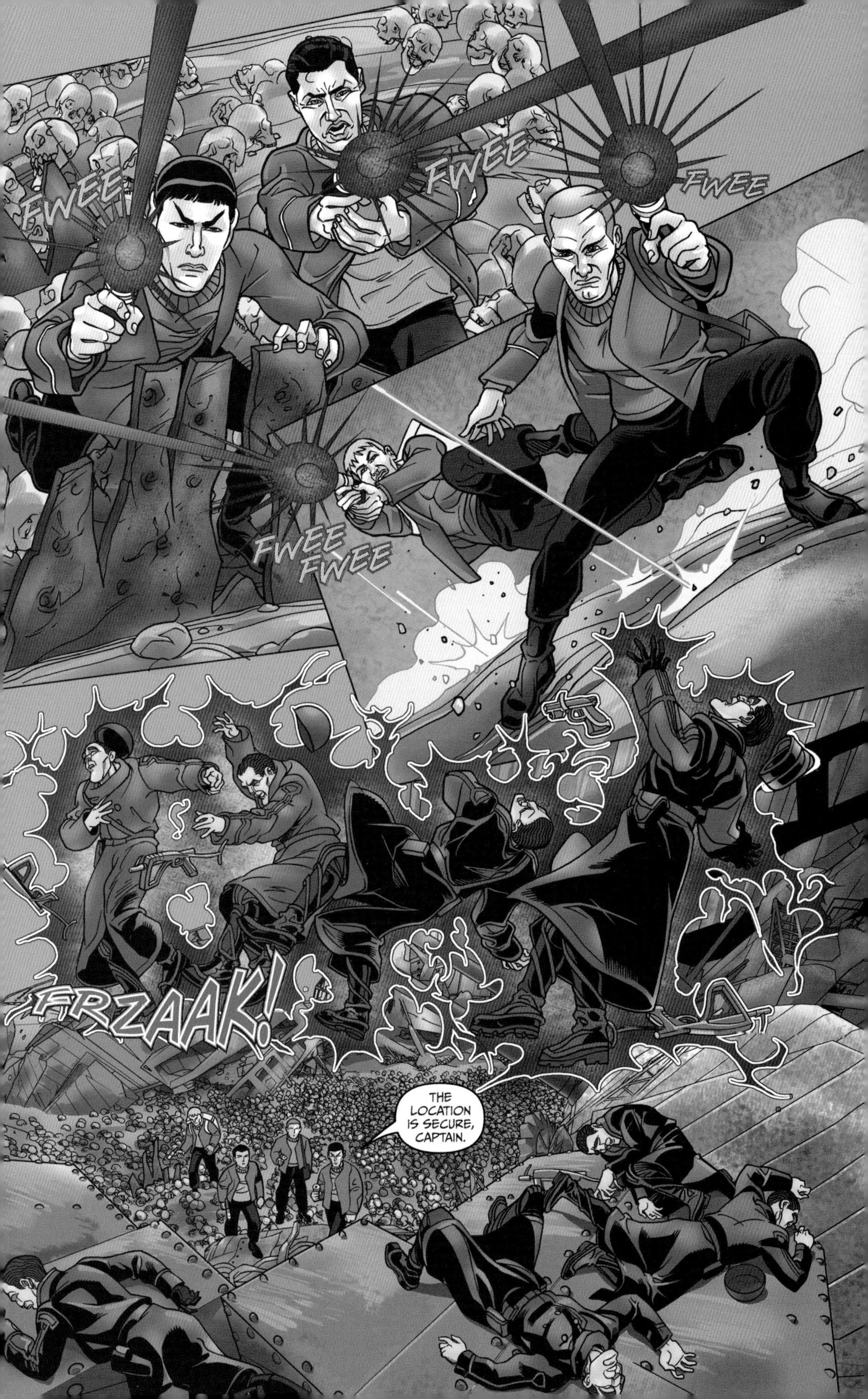
FWEE
FWEE
FWEE
FWEE
FWEE
FWEE
FRZAAK!
THE LOCATION IS SECURE, CAPTAIN.

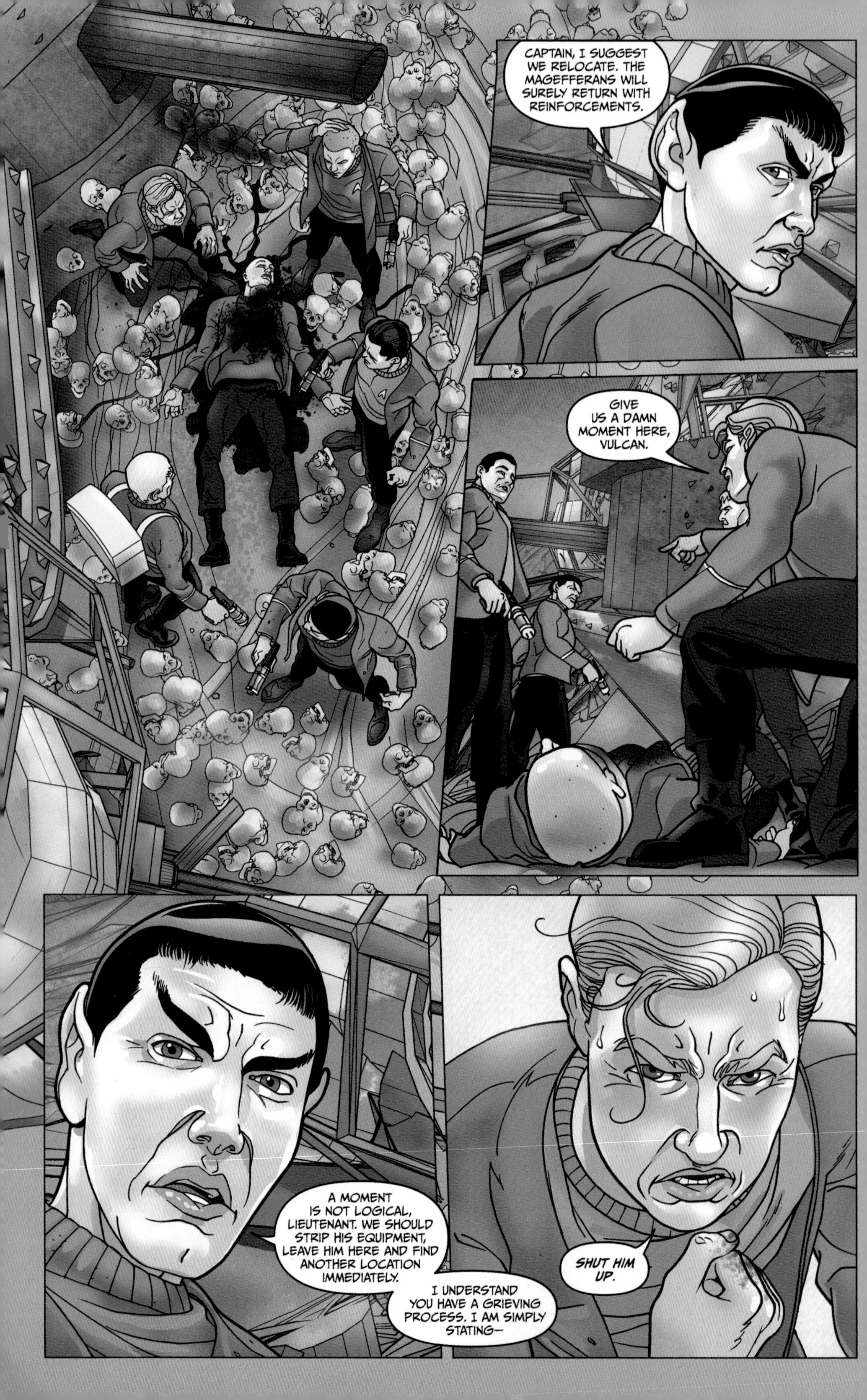

CAPTAIN, I SUGGEST WE RELOCATE. THE MAGEFFERANS WILL SURELY RETURN WITH REINFORCEMENTS.
GIVE US A DAMN MOMENT HERE, VULCAN.
A MOMENT IS NOT LOGICAL, LIEUTENANT. WE SHOULD STRIP HIS EQUIPMENT, LEAVE HIM HERE AND FIND ANOTHER LOCATION IMMEDIATELY.
I UNDERSTAND YOU HAVE A GRIEVING PROCESS. I AM SIMPLY STATING—
SHUT HIM UP.

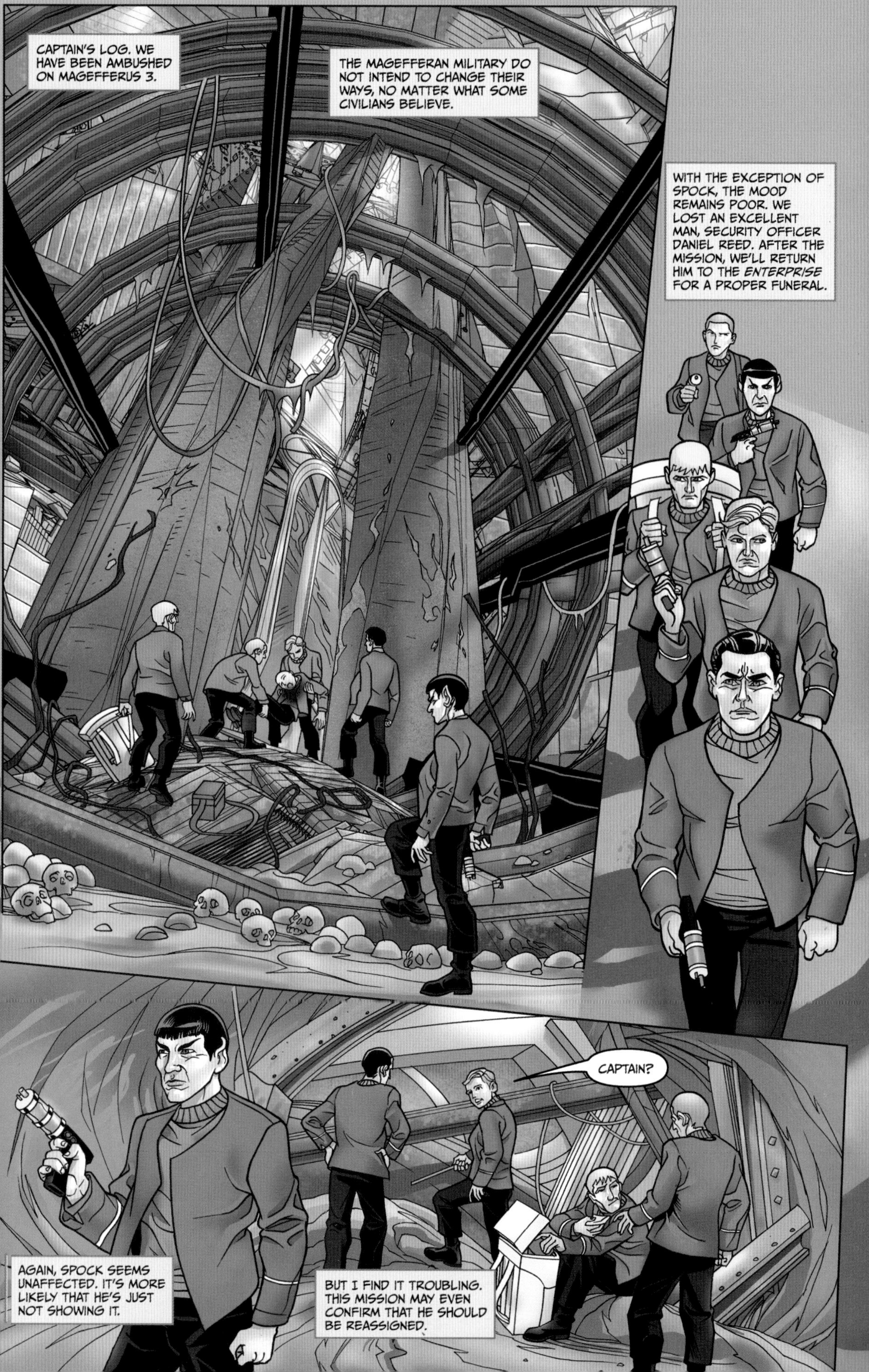
CAPTAIN'S LOG. WE HAVE BEEN AMBUSHED ON MAGEFFERUS 3.
THE MAGEFFERAN MILITARY DO NOT INTEND TO CHANGE THEIR WAYS, NO MATTER WHAT SOME CIVILIANS BELIEVE.
WITH THE EXCEPTION OF SPOCK, THE MOOD REMAINS POOR. WE LOST AN EXCELLENT MAN, SECURITY OFFICER DANIEL REED. AFTER THE MISSION, WE'LL RETURN HIM TO THE *ENTERPRISE* FOR A PROPER FUNERAL.
CAPTAIN?
AGAIN, SPOCK SEEMS UNAFFECTED. IT'S MORE LIKELY THAT HE'S JUST NOT SHOWING IT.
BUT I FIND IT TROUBLING. THIS MISSION MAY EVEN CONFIRM THAT HE SHOULD BE REASSIGNED.

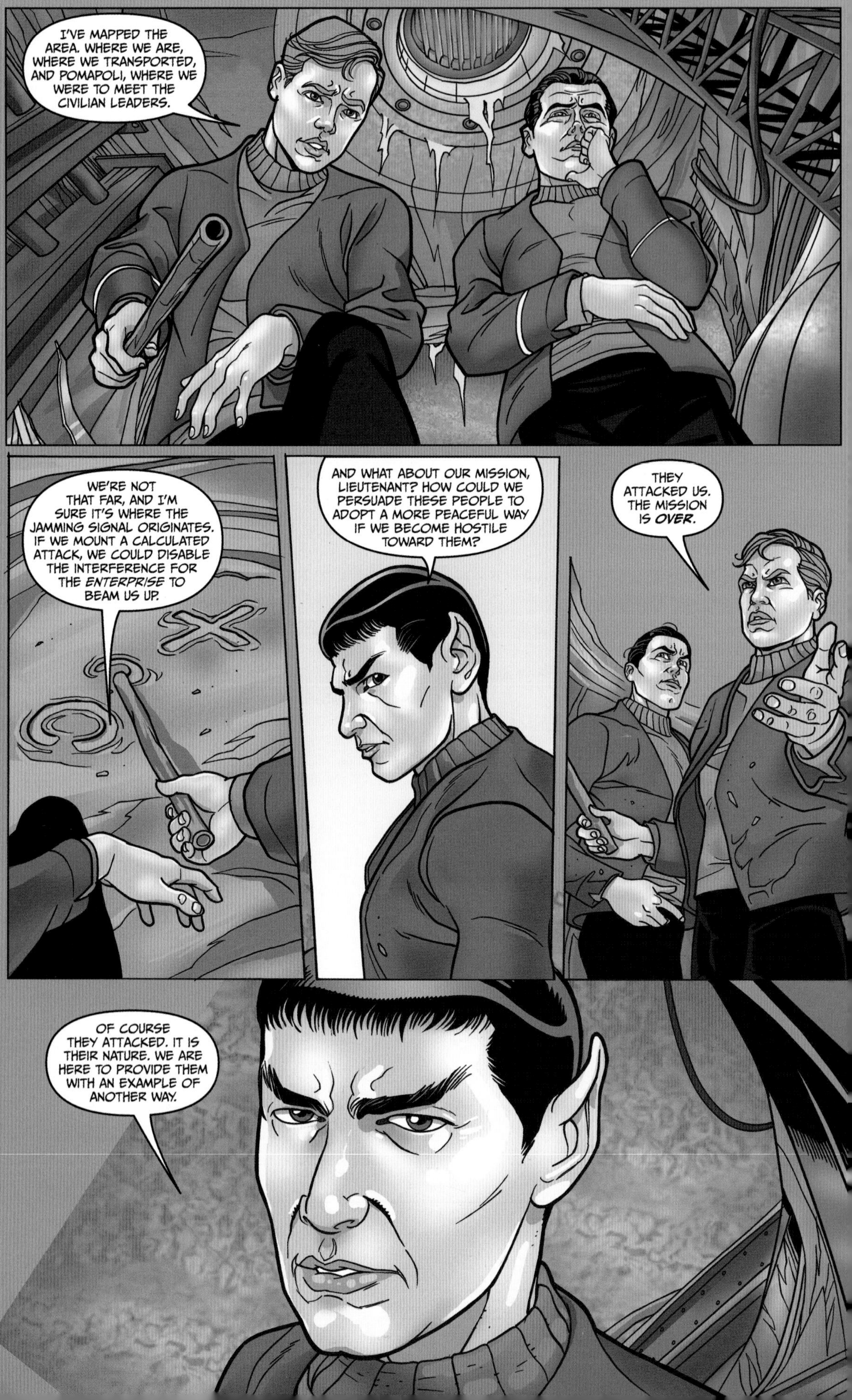
I'VE MAPPED THE AREA. WHERE WE ARE, WHERE WE TRANSPORTED, AND POMAPOLI, WHERE WE WERE TO MEET THE CIVILIAN LEADERS.
WE'RE NOT THAT FAR, AND I'M SURE IT'S WHERE THE JAMMING SIGNAL ORIGINATES. IF WE MOUNT A CALCULATED ATTACK, WE COULD DISABLE THE INTERFERENCE FOR THE *ENTERPRISE* TO BEAM US UP.
AND WHAT ABOUT OUR MISSION, LIEUTENANT? HOW COULD WE PERSUADE THESE PEOPLE TO ADOPT A MORE PEACEFUL WAY IF WE BECOME HOSTILE TOWARD THEM?
THEY ATTACKED US. THE MISSION IS ***OVER***.
OF COURSE THEY ATTACKED. IT IS THEIR NATURE. WE ARE HERE TO PROVIDE THEM WITH AN EXAMPLE OF ANOTHER WAY.

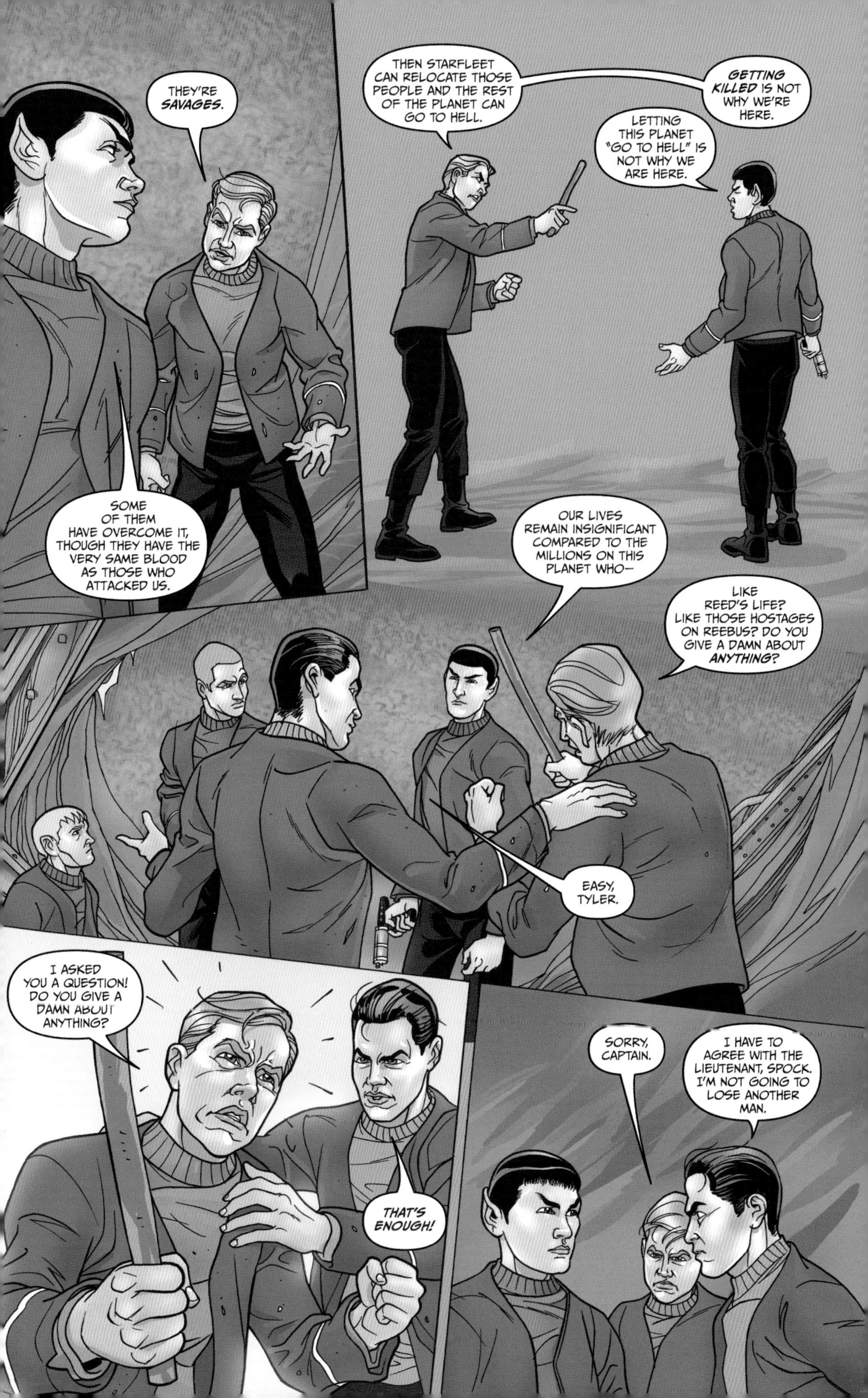
THEY'RE SAVAGES.
SOME OF THEM HAVE OVERCOME IT, THOUGH THEY HAVE THE VERY SAME BLOOD AS THOSE WHO ATTACKED US.
THEN STARFLEET CAN RELOCATE THOSE PEOPLE AND THE REST OF THE PLANET CAN GO TO HELL.
GETTING KILLED IS NOT WHY WE'RE HERE.
LETTING THIS PLANET "GO TO HELL" IS NOT WHY WE ARE HERE.
OUR LIVES REMAIN INSIGNIFICANT COMPARED TO THE MILLIONS ON THIS PLANET WHO—
LIKE REED'S LIFE? LIKE THOSE HOSTAGES ON REEBUS? DO YOU GIVE A DAMN ABOUT ANYTHING?
EASY, TYLER.
I ASKED YOU A QUESTION! DO YOU GIVE A DAMN ABOUT ANYTHING?
THAT'S ENOUGH!
SORRY, CAPTAIN.
I HAVE TO AGREE WITH THE LIEUTENANT, SPOCK. I'M NOT GOING TO LOSE ANOTHER MAN.

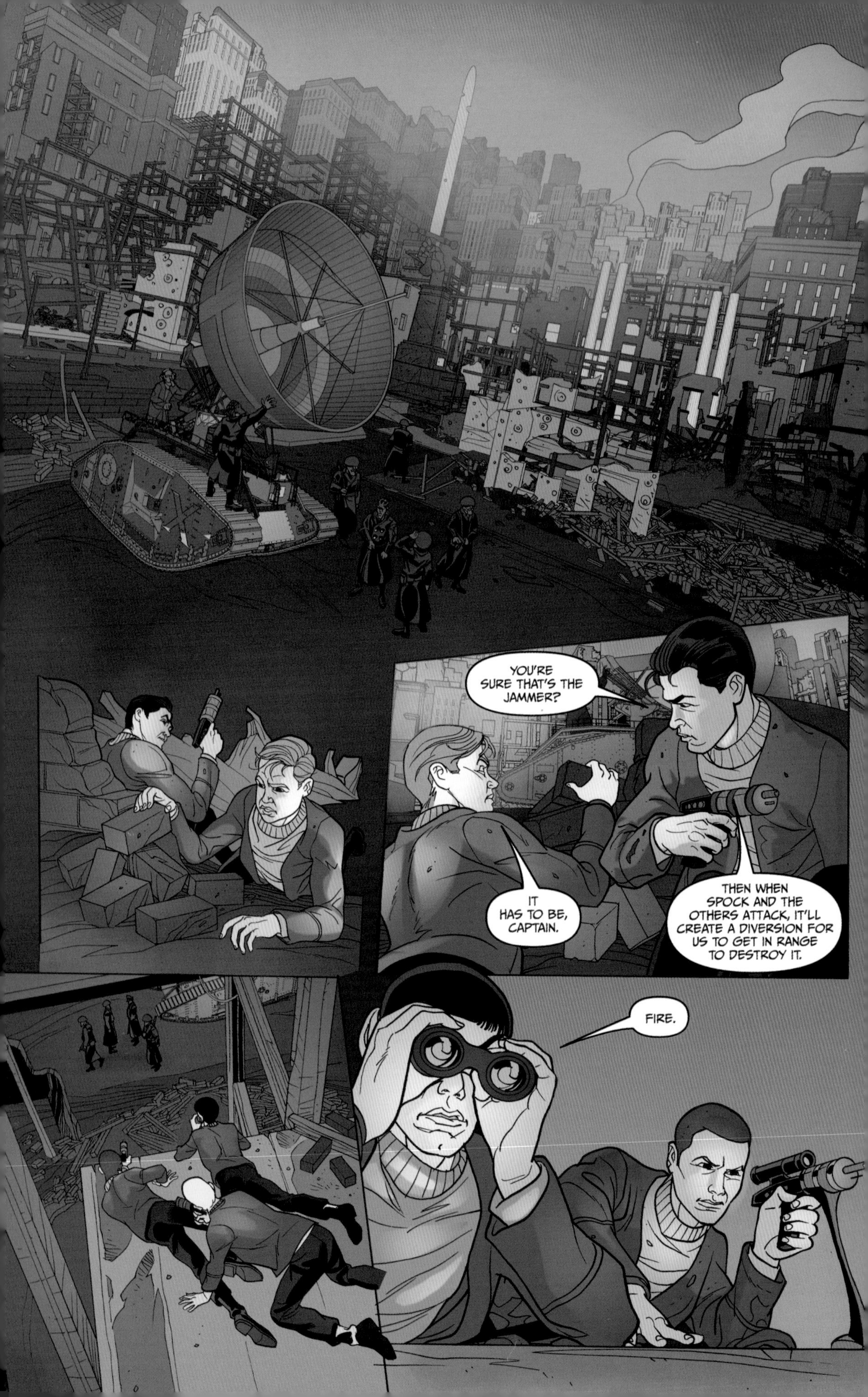

YOU'RE SURE THAT'S THE JAMMER?
IT HAS TO BE, CAPTAIN.
THEN WHEN SPOCK AND THE OTHERS ATTACK, IT'LL CREATE A DIVERSION FOR US TO GET IN RANGE TO DESTROY IT.
FIRE.

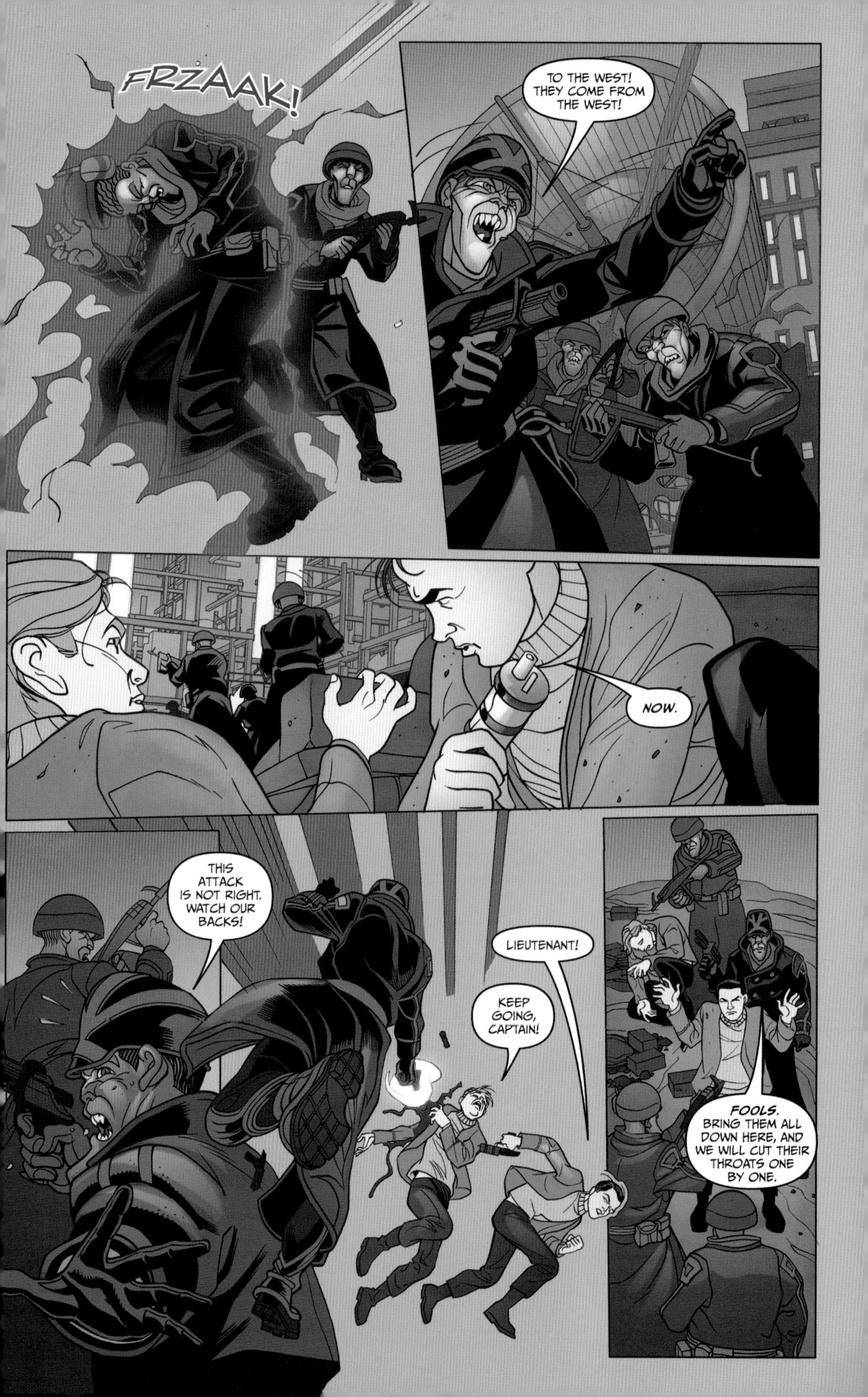
FRZAAK!
TO THE WEST! THEY COME FROM THE WEST!
NOW.
THIS ATTACK IS NOT RIGHT. WATCH OUR BACKS!
LIEUTENANT!
KEEP GOING, CAPTAIN!
FOOLS. BRING THEM ALL DOWN HERE, AND WE WILL CUT THEIR THROATS ONE BY ONE.

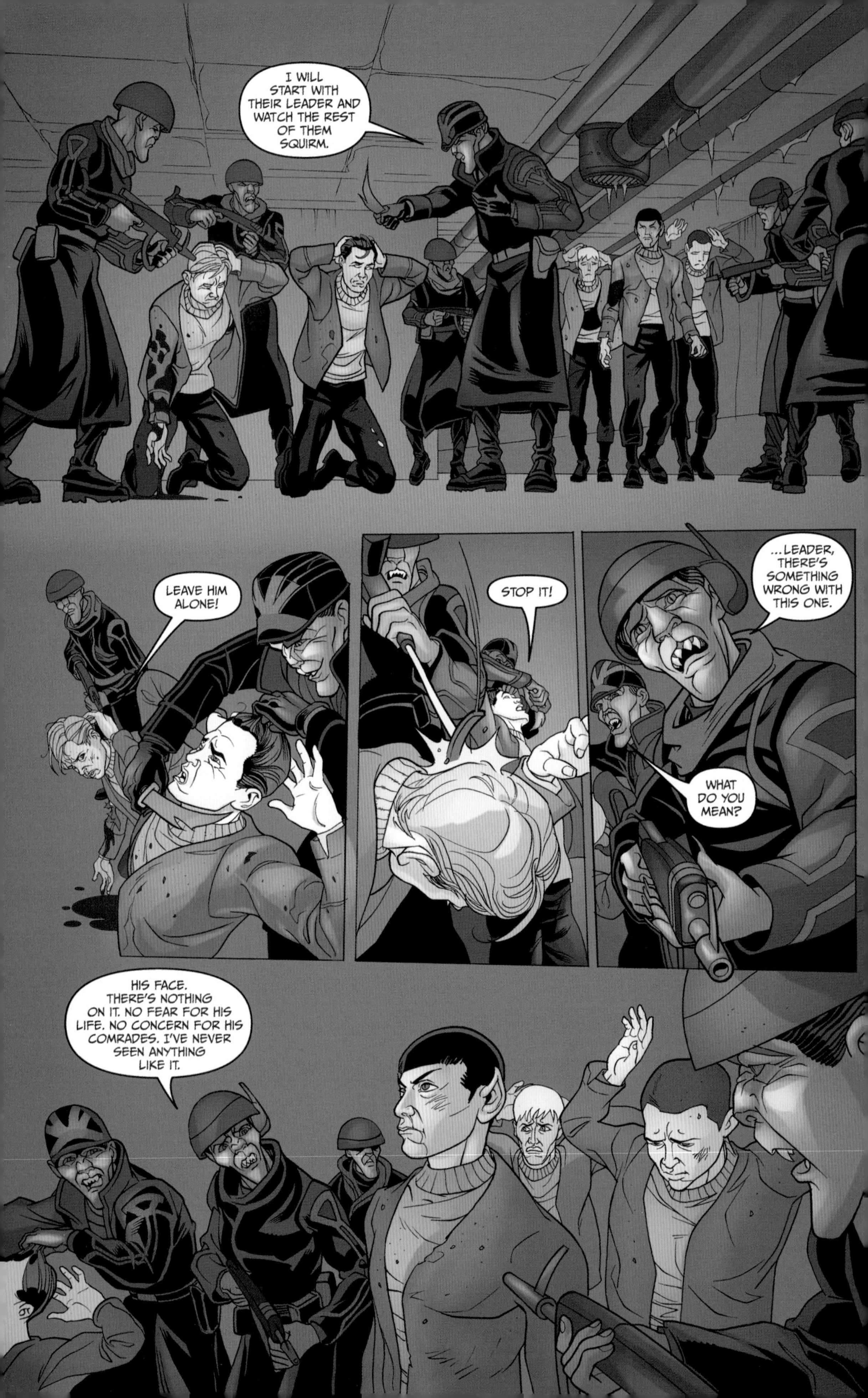
I WILL START WITH THEIR LEADER AND WATCH THE REST OF THEM SQUIRM.
LEAVE HIM ALONE!
STOP IT!
...LEADER, THERE'S SOMETHING WRONG WITH THIS ONE.
WHAT DO YOU MEAN?
HIS FACE. THERE'S NOTHING ON IT. NO FEAR FOR HIS LIFE. NO CONCERN FOR HIS COMRADES. I'VE NEVER SEEN ANYTHING LIKE IT.

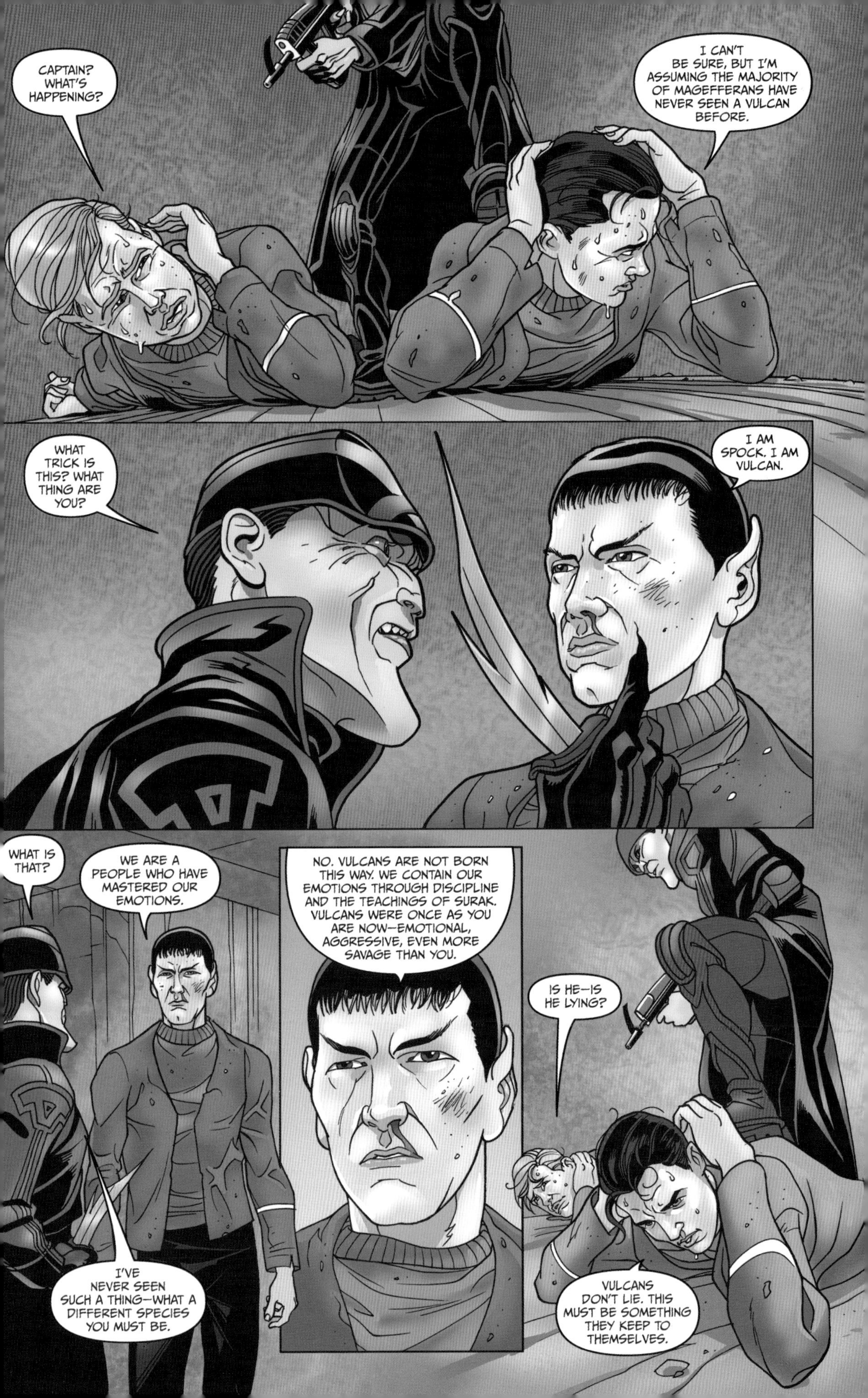
CAPTAIN? WHAT'S HAPPENING?
I CAN'T BE SURE, BUT I'M ASSUMING THE MAJORITY OF MAGEFFERANS HAVE NEVER SEEN A VULCAN BEFORE.
WHAT TRICK IS THIS? WHAT THING ARE YOU?
I AM SPOCK. I AM VULCAN.
WHAT IS THAT?
WE ARE A PEOPLE WHO HAVE MASTERED OUR EMOTIONS.
I'VE NEVER SEEN SUCH A THING—WHAT A DIFFERENT SPECIES YOU MUST BE.
NO. VULCANS ARE NOT BORN THIS WAY. WE CONTAIN OUR EMOTIONS THROUGH DISCIPLINE AND THE TEACHINGS OF SURAK. VULCANS WERE ONCE AS YOU ARE NOW—EMOTIONAL, AGGRESSIVE, EVEN MORE SAVAGE THAN YOU.
IS HE—IS HE LYING?
VULCANS DON'T LIE. THIS MUST BE SOMETHING THEY KEEP TO THEMSELVES.

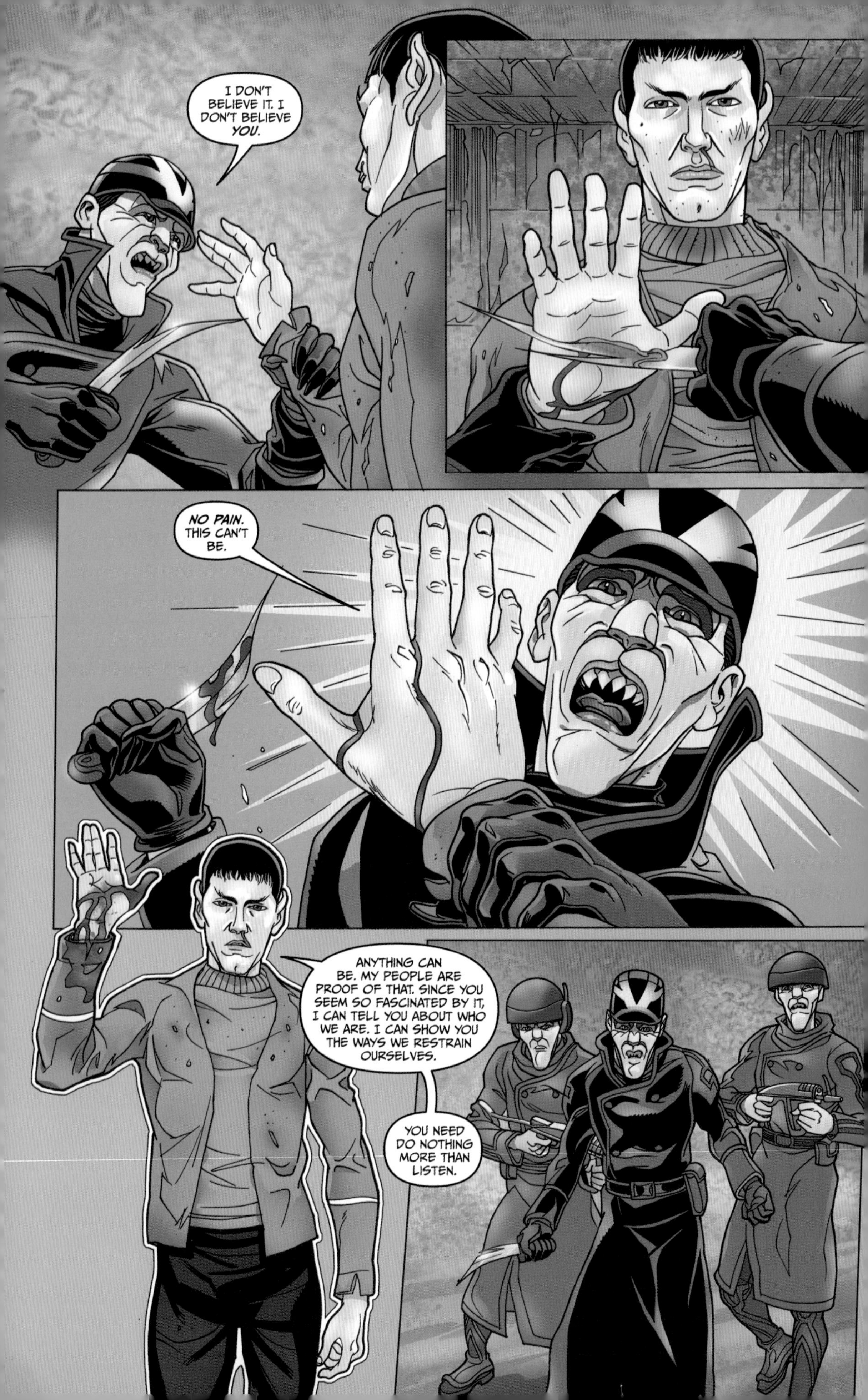
I DON'T BELIEVE IT. I DON'T BELIEVE *YOU*.
NO PAIN. THIS CAN'T BE.
ANYTHING CAN BE. MY PEOPLE ARE PROOF OF THAT. SINCE YOU SEEM SO FASCINATED BY IT, I CAN TELL YOU ABOUT WHO WE ARE. I CAN SHOW YOU THE WAYS WE RESTRAIN OURSELVES.
YOU NEED DO NOTHING MORE THAN LISTEN.

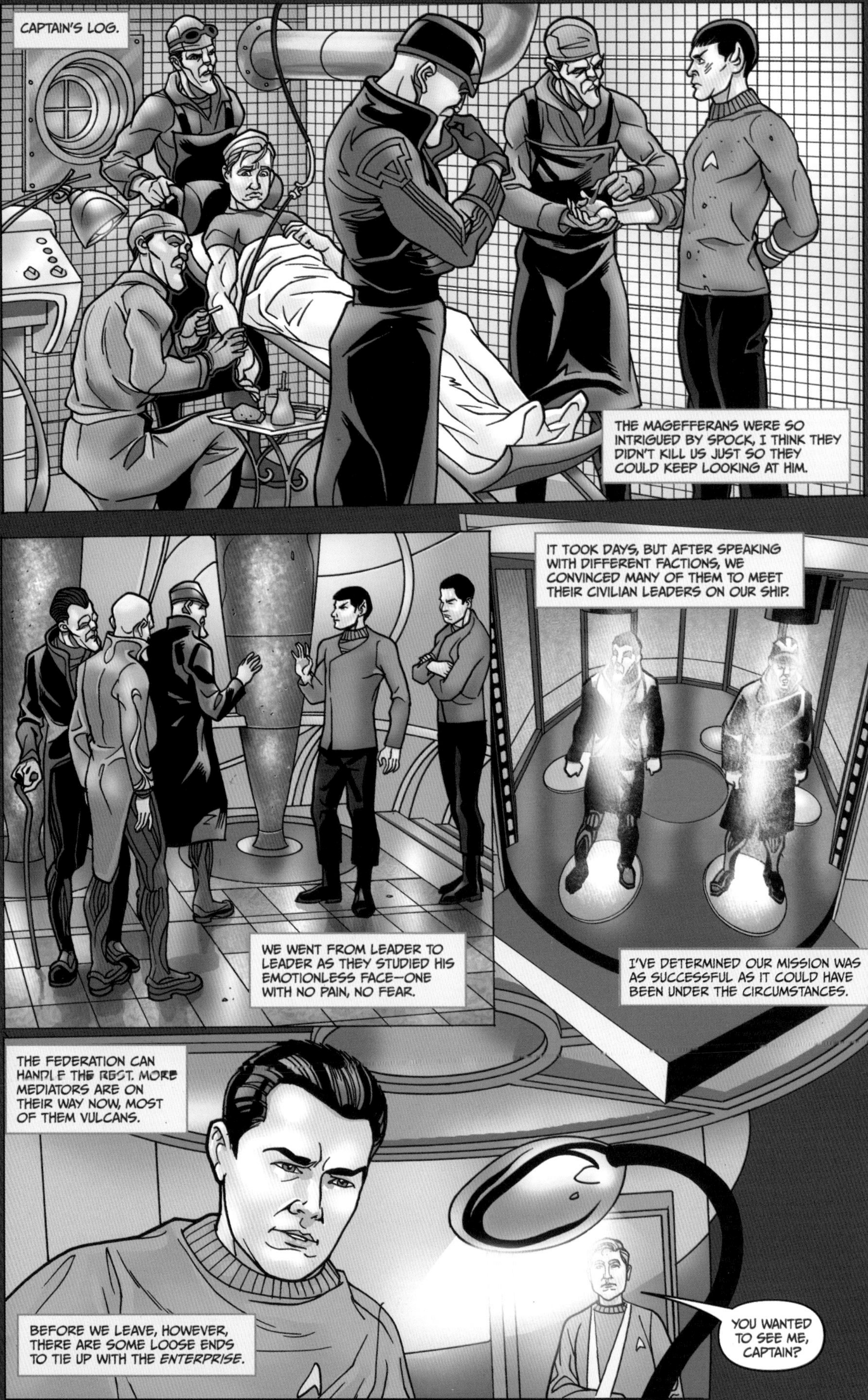
CAPTAIN'S LOG.
THE MAGEFFERANS WERE SO INTRIGUED BY SPOCK, I THINK THEY DIDN'T KILL US JUST SO THEY COULD KEEP LOOKING AT HIM.
WE WENT FROM LEADER TO LEADER AS THEY STUDIED HIS EMOTIONLESS FACE—ONE WITH NO PAIN, NO FEAR.
IT TOOK DAYS, BUT AFTER SPEAKING WITH DIFFERENT FACTIONS, WE CONVINCED MANY OF THEM TO MEET THEIR CIVILIAN LEADERS ON OUR SHIP.
I'VE DETERMINED OUR MISSION WAS AS SUCCESSFUL AS IT COULD HAVE BEEN UNDER THE CIRCUMSTANCES.
THE FEDERATION CAN HANDLE THE REST. MORE MEDIATORS ARE ON THEIR WAY NOW, MOST OF THEM VULCANS.
BEFORE WE LEAVE, HOWEVER, THERE ARE SOME LOOSE ENDS TO TIE UP WITH THE *ENTERPRISE*.
YOU WANTED TO SEE ME, CAPTAIN?

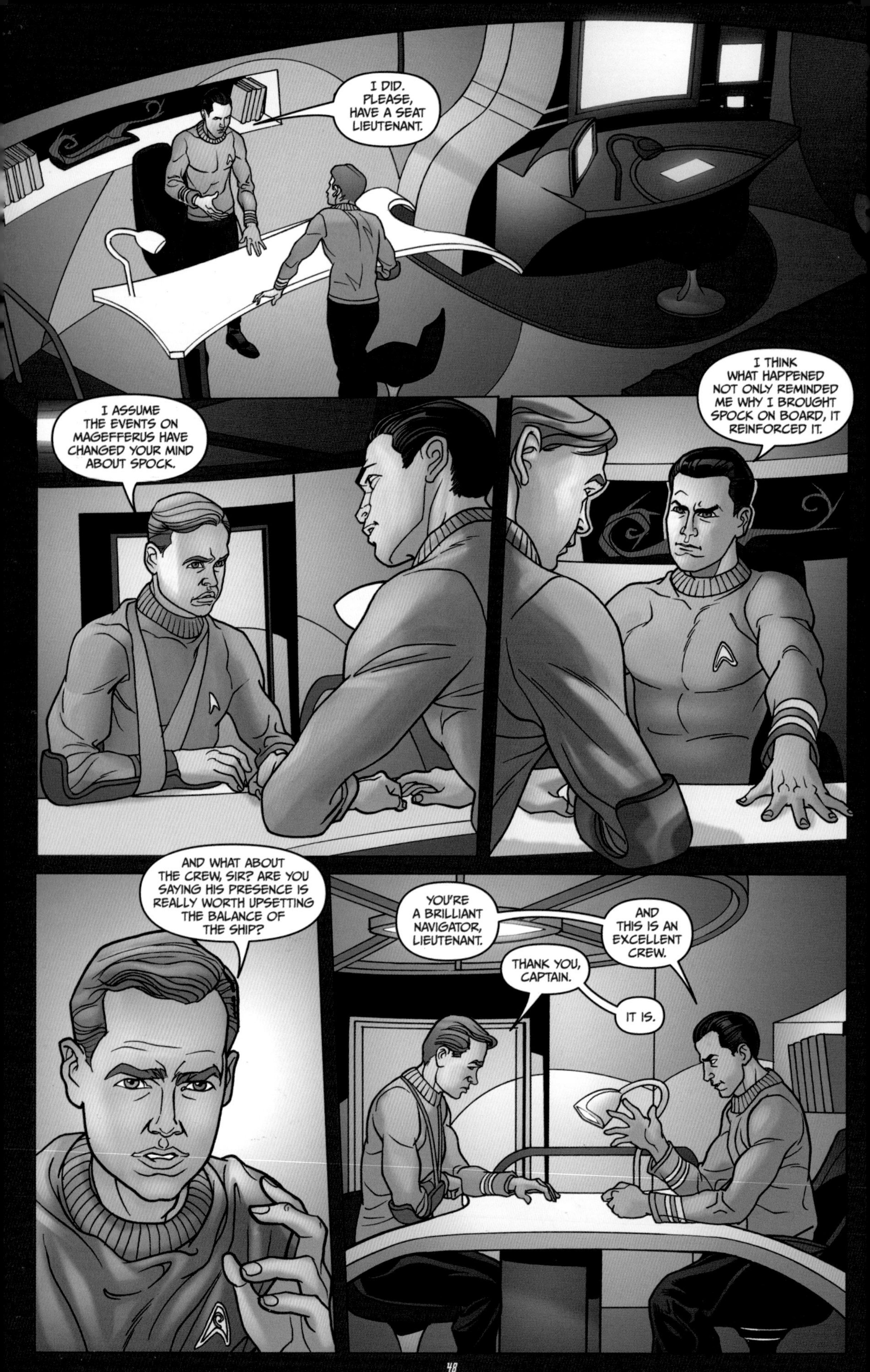
I DID. PLEASE, HAVE A SEAT LIEUTENANT.
I ASSUME THE EVENTS ON MAGEFFERUS HAVE CHANGED YOUR MIND ABOUT SPOCK.
I THINK WHAT HAPPENED NOT ONLY REMINDED ME WHY I BROUGHT SPOCK ON BOARD, IT REINFORCED IT.
AND WHAT ABOUT THE CREW, SIR? ARE YOU SAYING HIS PRESENCE IS REALLY WORTH UPSETTING THE BALANCE OF THE SHIP?
YOU'RE A BRILLIANT NAVIGATOR, LIEUTENANT.
AND THIS IS AN EXCELLENT CREW.
THANK YOU, CAPTAIN.
IT IS.

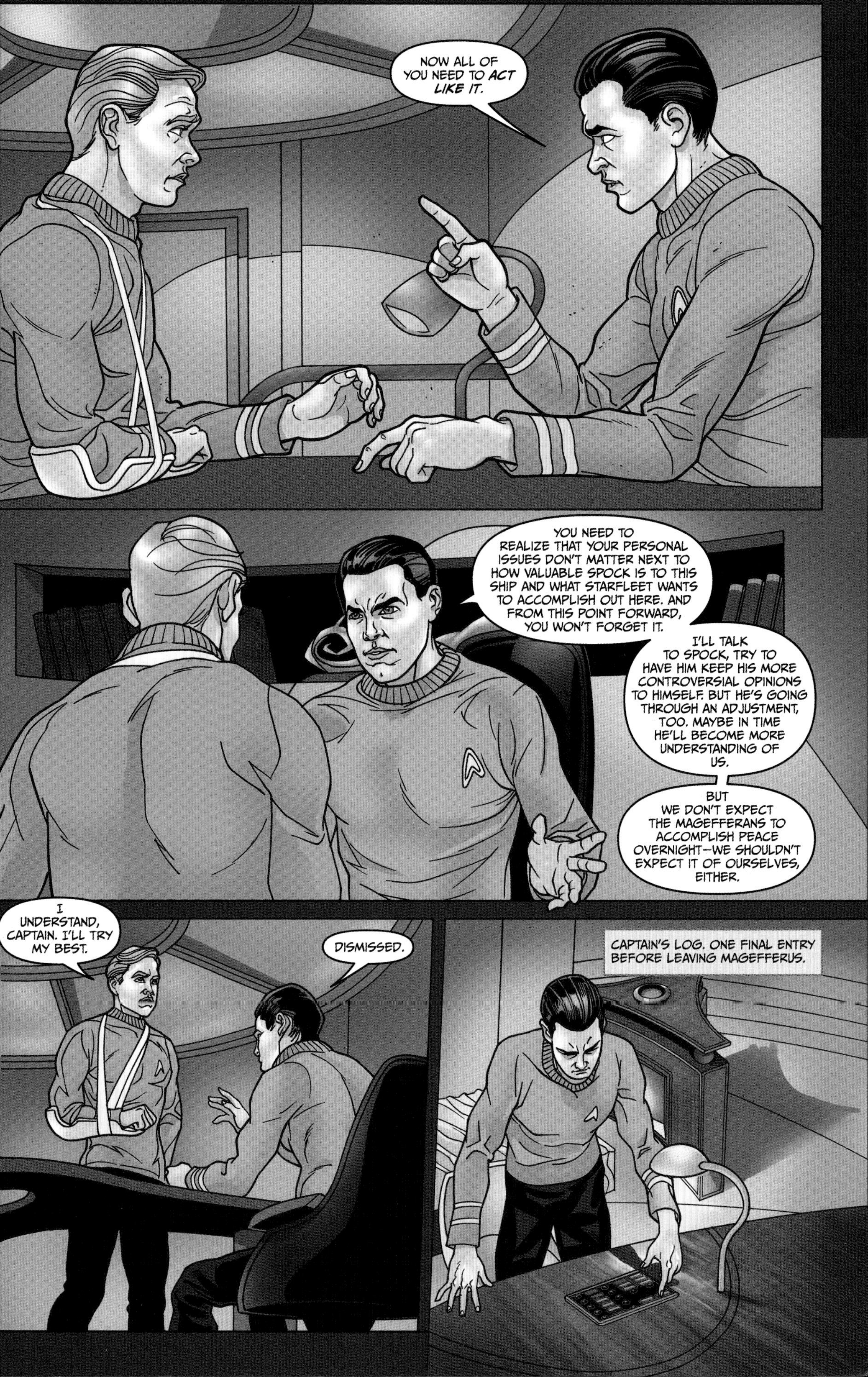
NOW ALL OF YOU NEED TO *ACT LIKE IT*.
YOU NEED TO REALIZE THAT YOUR PERSONAL ISSUES DON'T MATTER NEXT TO HOW VALUABLE SPOCK IS TO THIS SHIP AND WHAT STARFLEET WANTS TO ACCOMPLISH OUT HERE. AND FROM THIS POINT FORWARD, YOU WON'T FORGET IT.
I'LL TALK TO SPOCK, TRY TO HAVE HIM KEEP HIS MORE CONTROVERSIAL OPINIONS TO HIMSELF. BUT HE'S GOING THROUGH AN ADJUSTMENT, TOO. MAYBE IN TIME HE'LL BECOME MORE UNDERSTANDING OF US.
BUT WE DON'T EXPECT THE MAGEFFERANS TO ACCOMPLISH PEACE OVERNIGHT—WE SHOULDN'T EXPECT IT OF OURSELVES, EITHER.
I UNDERSTAND, CAPTAIN. I'LL TRY MY BEST.
DISMISSED.
CAPTAIN'S LOG. ONE FINAL ENTRY BEFORE LEAVING MAGEFFERUS.

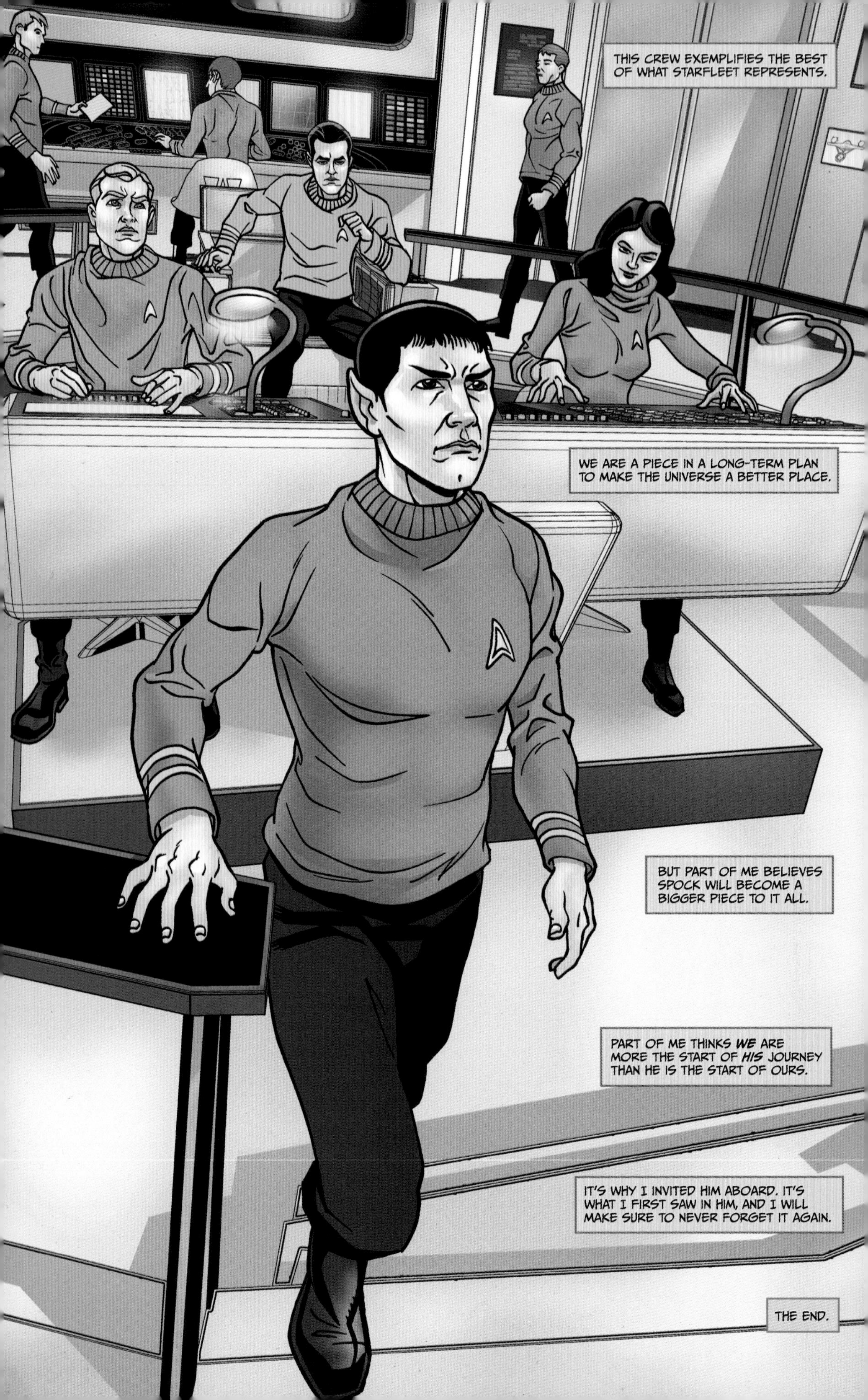
THIS CREW EXEMPLIFIES THE BEST OF WHAT STARFLEET REPRESENTS.
WE ARE A PIECE IN A LONG-TERM PLAN TO MAKE THE UNIVERSE A BETTER PLACE.
BUT PART OF ME BELIEVES SPOCK WILL BECOME A BIGGER PIECE TO IT ALL.
PART OF ME THINKS *WE* ARE MORE THE START OF *HIS* JOURNEY THAN HE IS THE START OF OURS.
IT'S WHY I INVITED HIM ABOARD. IT'S WHAT I FIRST SAW IN HIM, AND I WILL MAKE SURE TO NEVER FORGET IT AGAIN.
THE END.

art and color by Josep Maria Beroy

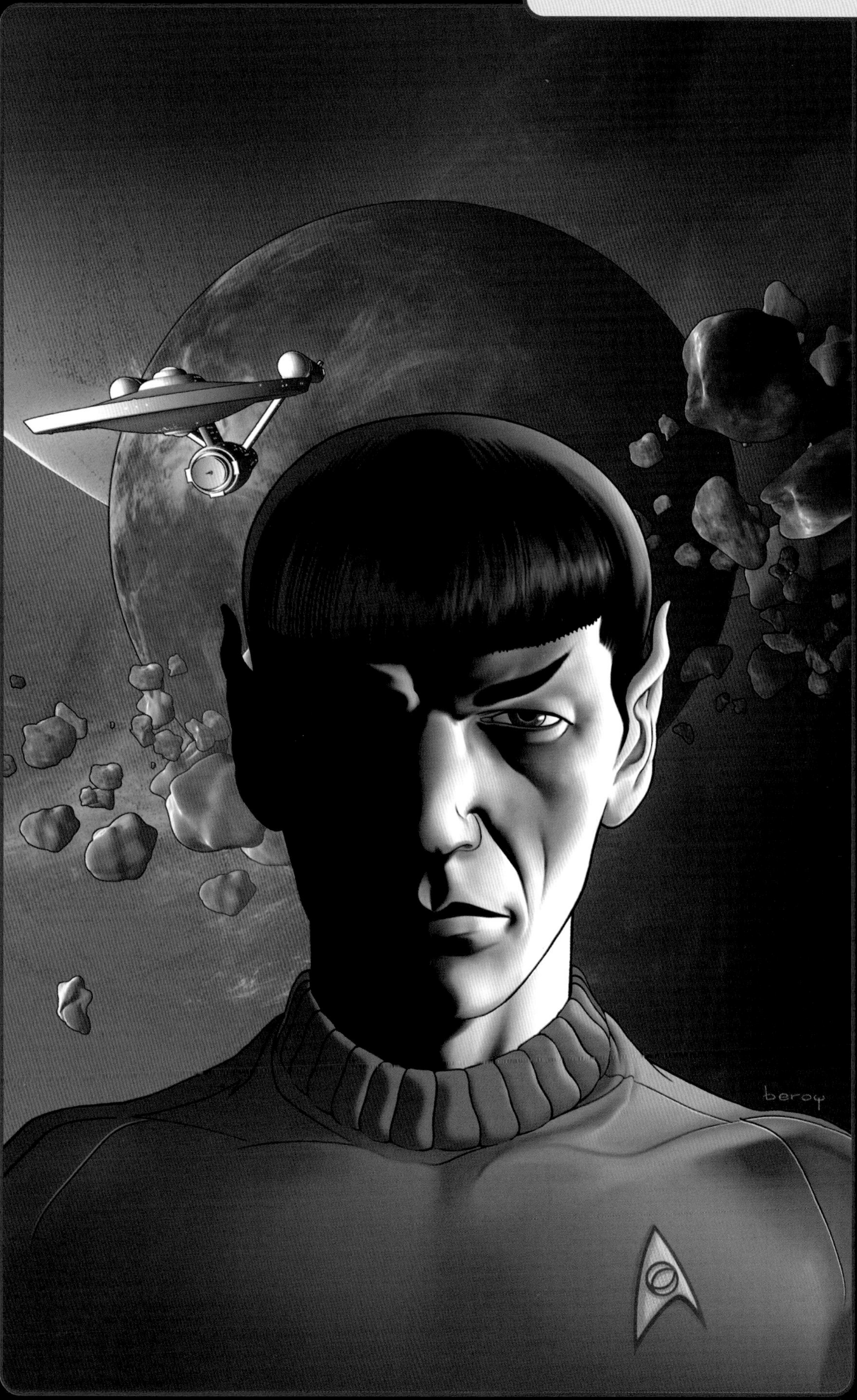
beroy

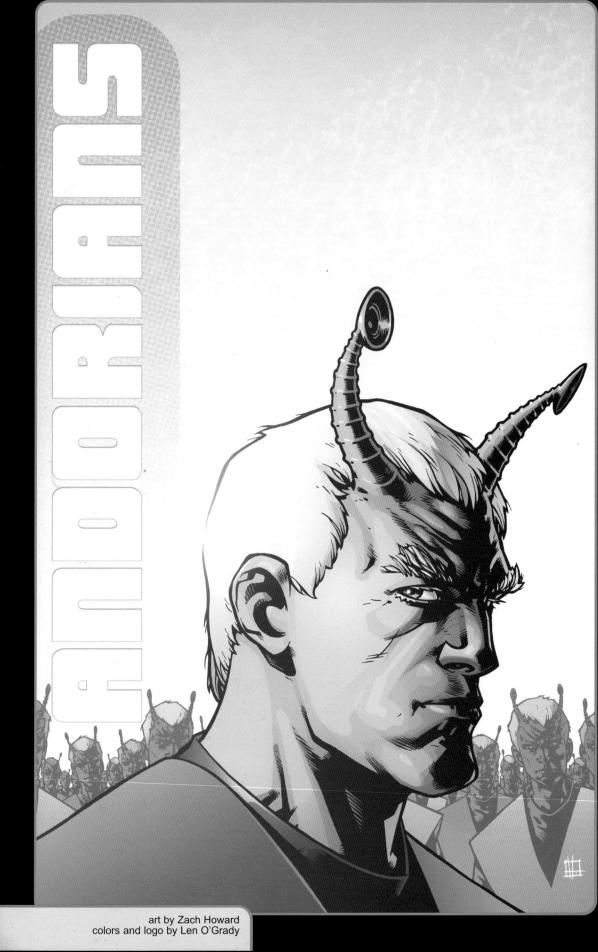

ANDORIANS

art by Zach Howard
colors and logo by Len O'Grady

STAR TREK: ALIEN SPOTLIGHT: ANDORIANS

THE OLD WAYS

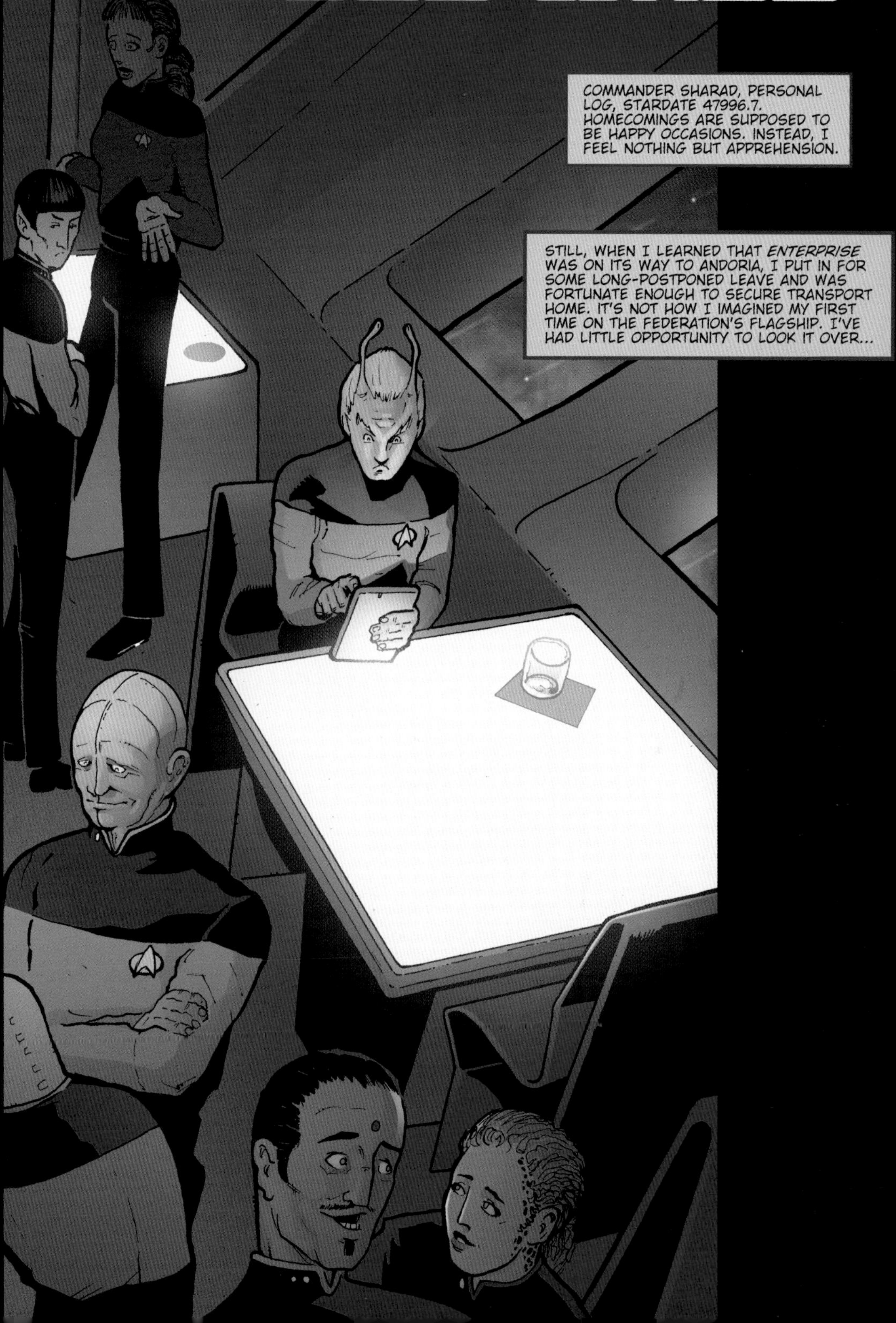
COMMANDER SHARAD, PERSONAL LOG, STARDATE 47996.7. HOMECOMINGS ARE SUPPOSED TO BE HAPPY OCCASIONS. INSTEAD, I FEEL NOTHING BUT APPREHENSION.
STILL, WHEN I LEARNED THAT *ENTERPRISE* WAS ON ITS WAY TO ANDORIA, I PUT IN FOR SOME LONG-POSTPONED LEAVE AND WAS FORTUNATE ENOUGH TO SECURE TRANSPORT HOME. IT'S NOT HOW I IMAGINED MY FIRST TIME ON THE FEDERATION'S FLAGSHIP. I'VE HAD LITTLE OPPORTUNITY TO LOOK IT OVER...

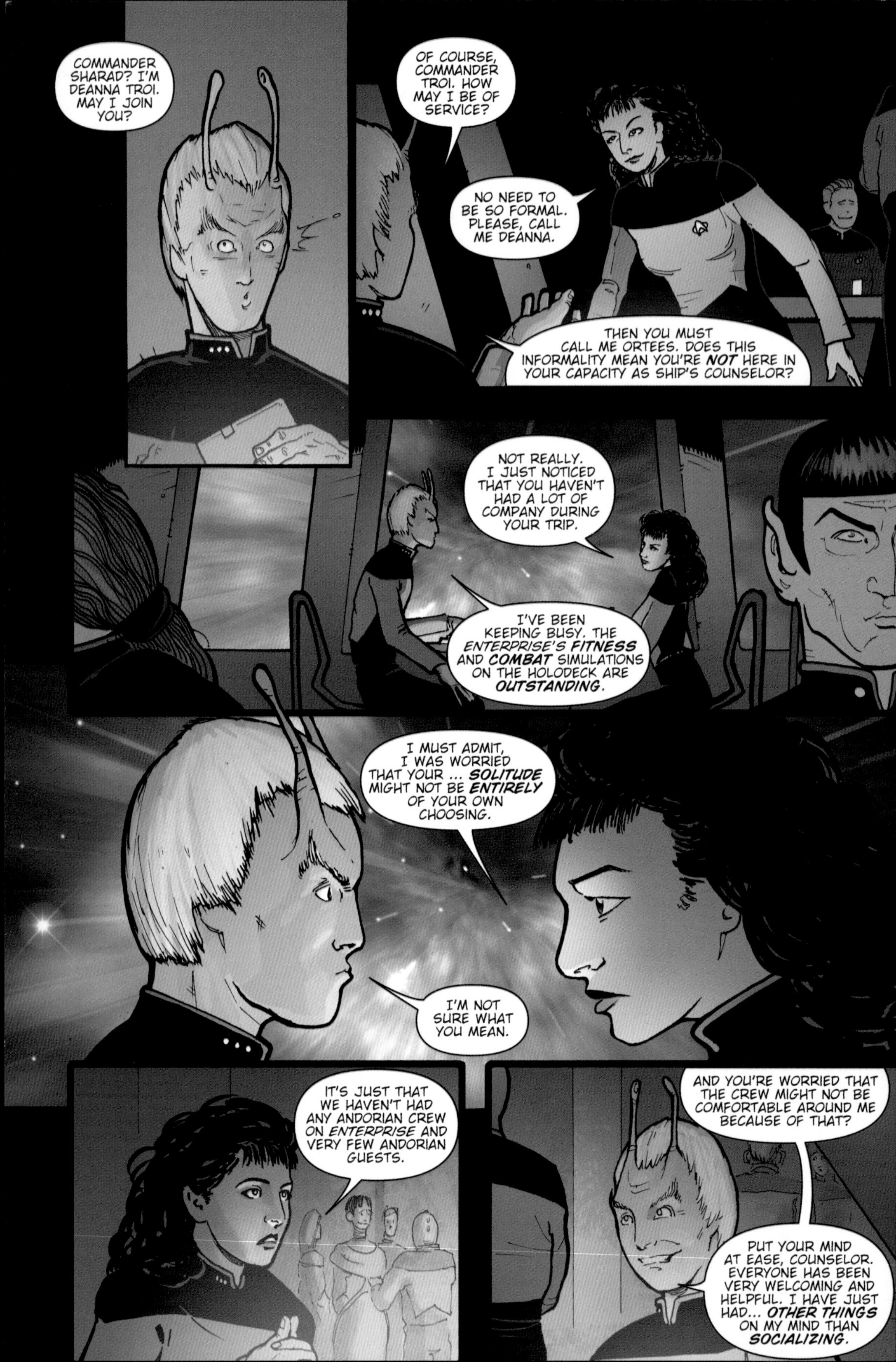
COMMANDER SHARAD? I'M DEANNA TROI. MAY I JOIN YOU?
OF COURSE, COMMANDER TROI. HOW MAY I BE OF SERVICE?
NO NEED TO BE SO FORMAL. PLEASE, CALL ME DEANNA.
THEN YOU MUST CALL ME ORTEES. DOES THIS INFORMALITY MEAN YOU'RE NOT HERE IN YOUR CAPACITY AS SHIP'S COUNSELOR?
NOT REALLY. I JUST NOTICED THAT YOU HAVEN'T HAD A LOT OF COMPANY DURING YOUR TRIP.
I'VE BEEN KEEPING BUSY. THE ENTERPRISE'S FITNESS AND COMBAT SIMULATIONS ON THE HOLODECK ARE OUTSTANDING.
I MUST ADMIT, I WAS WORRIED THAT YOUR ... SOLITUDE MIGHT NOT BE ENTIRELY OF YOUR OWN CHOOSING.
I'M NOT SURE WHAT YOU MEAN.
IT'S JUST THAT WE HAVEN'T HAD ANY ANDORIAN CREW ON ENTERPRISE AND VERY FEW ANDORIAN GUESTS.
AND YOU'RE WORRIED THAT THE CREW MIGHT NOT BE COMFORTABLE AROUND ME BECAUSE OF THAT?
PUT YOUR MIND AT EASE, COUNSELOR. EVERYONE HAS BEEN VERY WELCOMING AND HELPFUL. I HAVE JUST HAD... OTHER THINGS ON MY MIND THAN SOCIALIZING.

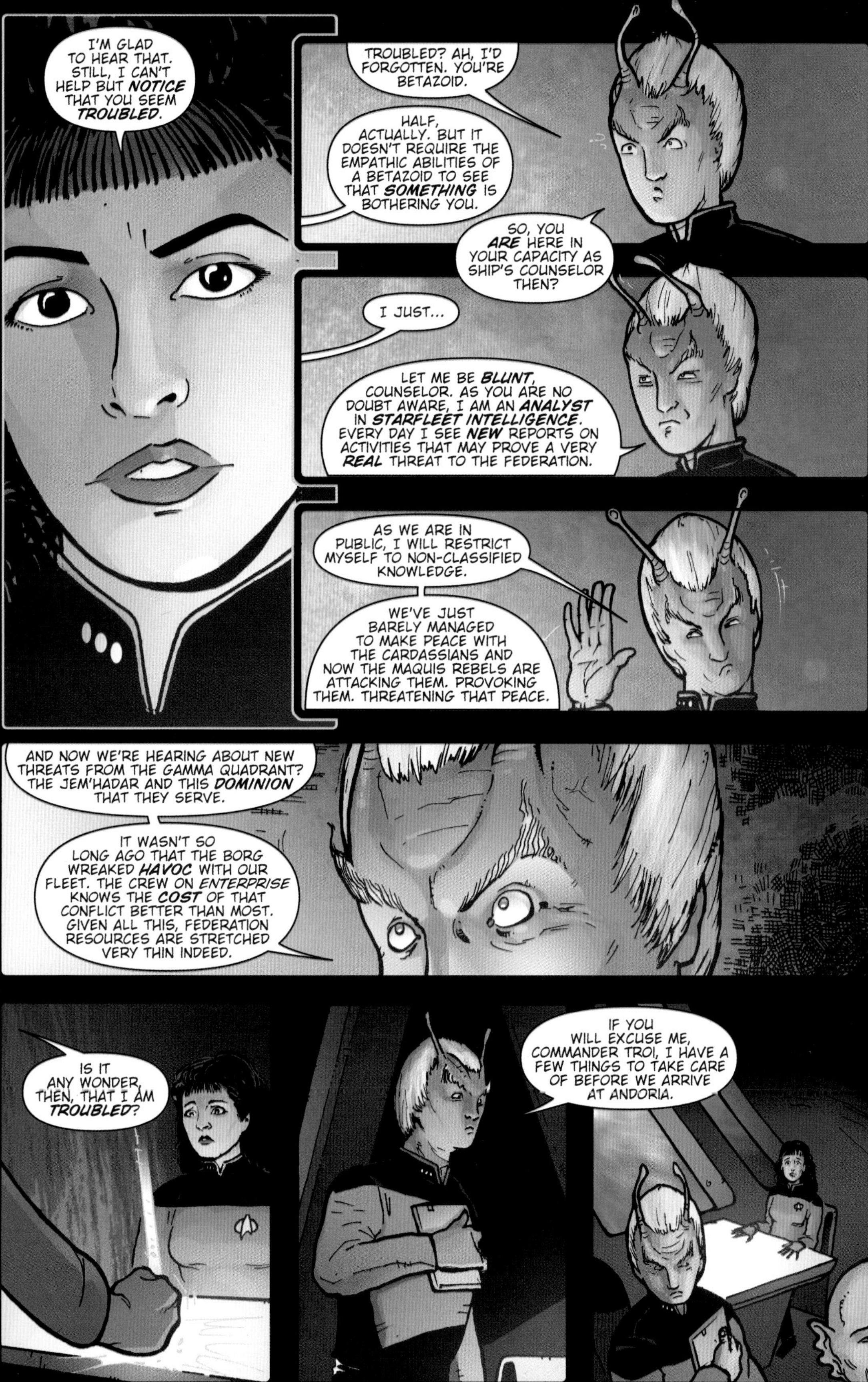
I'M GLAD TO HEAR THAT. STILL, I CAN'T HELP BUT NOTICE THAT YOU SEEM TROUBLED.
TROUBLED? AH, I'D FORGOTTEN. YOU'RE BETAZOID.
HALF, ACTUALLY. BUT IT DOESN'T REQUIRE THE EMPATHIC ABILITIES OF A BETAZOID TO SEE THAT SOMETHING IS BOTHERING YOU.
SO, YOU ARE HERE IN YOUR CAPACITY AS SHIP'S COUNSELOR THEN?
I JUST...
LET ME BE BLUNT, COUNSELOR. AS YOU ARE NO DOUBT AWARE, I AM AN ANALYST IN STARFLEET INTELLIGENCE. EVERY DAY I SEE NEW REPORTS ON ACTIVITIES THAT MAY PROVE A VERY REAL THREAT TO THE FEDERATION.
AS WE ARE IN PUBLIC, I WILL RESTRICT MYSELF TO NON-CLASSIFIED KNOWLEDGE.
WE'VE JUST BARELY MANAGED TO MAKE PEACE WITH THE CARDASSIANS AND NOW THE MAQUIS REBELS ARE ATTACKING THEM. PROVOKING THEM. THREATENING THAT PEACE.
AND NOW WE'RE HEARING ABOUT NEW THREATS FROM THE GAMMA QUADRANT? THE JEM'HADAR AND THIS DOMINION THAT THEY SERVE.
IT WASN'T SO LONG AGO THAT THE BORG WREAKED HAVOC WITH OUR FLEET. THE CREW ON ENTERPRISE KNOWS THE COST OF THAT CONFLICT BETTER THAN MOST. GIVEN ALL THIS, FEDERATION RESOURCES ARE STRETCHED VERY THIN INDEED.
IS IT ANY WONDER, THEN, THAT I AM TROUBLED?
IF YOU WILL EXCUSE ME, COMMANDER TROI, I HAVE A FEW THINGS TO TAKE CARE OF BEFORE WE ARRIVE AT ANDORIA.

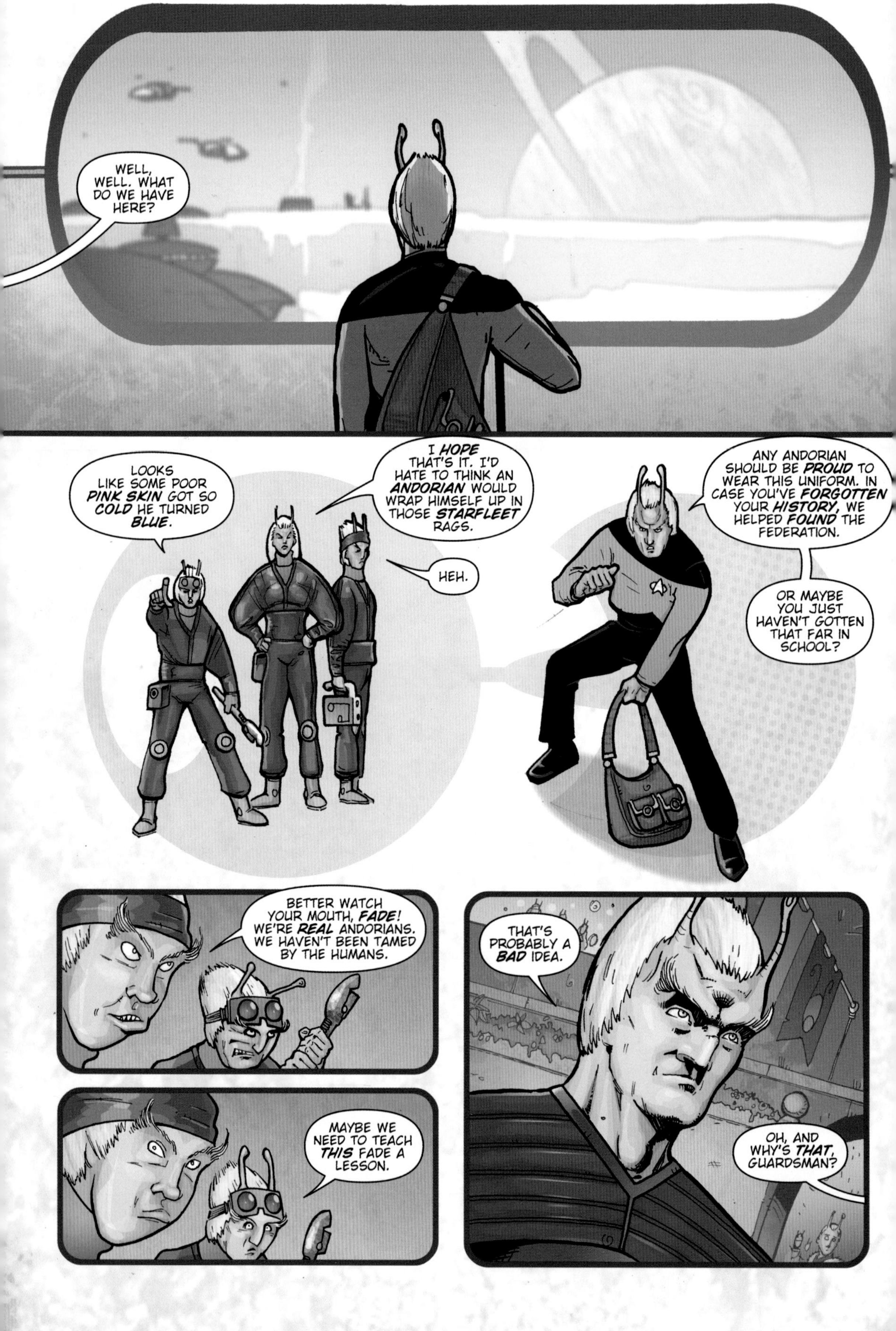
WELL, WELL. WHAT DO WE HAVE HERE?
LOOKS LIKE SOME POOR PINK SKIN GOT SO COLD HE TURNED BLUE.
I HOPE THAT'S IT. I'D HATE TO THINK AN ANDORIAN WOULD WRAP HIMSELF UP IN THOSE STARFLEET RAGS.
HEH.
ANY ANDORIAN SHOULD BE PROUD TO WEAR THIS UNIFORM. IN CASE YOU'VE FORGOTTEN YOUR HISTORY, WE HELPED FOUND THE FEDERATION.
OR MAYBE YOU JUST HAVEN'T GOTTEN THAT FAR IN SCHOOL?
BETTER WATCH YOUR MOUTH, FADE! WE'RE REAL ANDORIANS. WE HAVEN'T BEEN TAMED BY THE HUMANS.
MAYBE WE NEED TO TEACH THIS FADE A LESSON.
THAT'S PROBABLY A BAD IDEA.
OH, AND WHY'S THAT, GUARDSMAN?

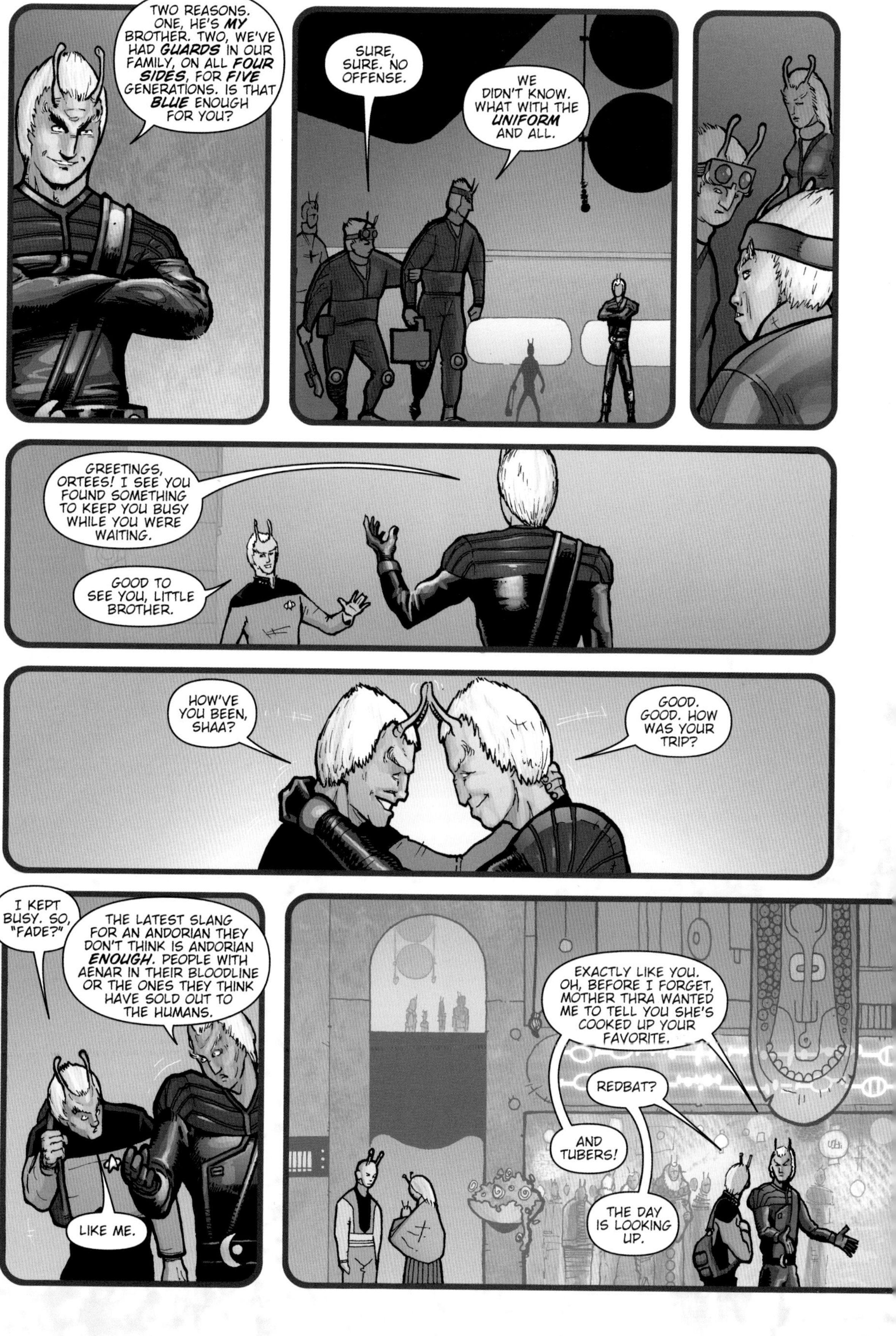
TWO REASONS. ONE, HE'S MY BROTHER. TWO, WE'VE HAD GUARDS IN OUR FAMILY, ON ALL FOUR SIDES, FOR FIVE GENERATIONS. IS THAT BLUE ENOUGH FOR YOU?
SURE, SURE. NO OFFENSE.
WE DIDN'T KNOW. WHAT WITH THE UNIFORM AND ALL.
GREETINGS, ORTEES! I SEE YOU FOUND SOMETHING TO KEEP YOU BUSY WHILE YOU WERE WAITING.
GOOD TO SEE YOU, LITTLE BROTHER.
HOW'VE YOU BEEN, SHAA?
GOOD. GOOD. HOW WAS YOUR TRIP?
I KEPT BUSY. SO, "FADE?"
THE LATEST SLANG FOR AN ANDORIAN THEY DON'T THINK IS ANDORIAN ENOUGH. PEOPLE WITH AENAR IN THEIR BLOODLINE OR THE ONES THEY THINK HAVE SOLD OUT TO THE HUMANS.
LIKE ME.
EXACTLY LIKE YOU. OH, BEFORE I FORGET, MOTHER THRA WANTED ME TO TELL YOU SHE'S COOKED UP YOUR FAVORITE.
REDBAT?
AND TUBERS!
THE DAY IS LOOKING UP.

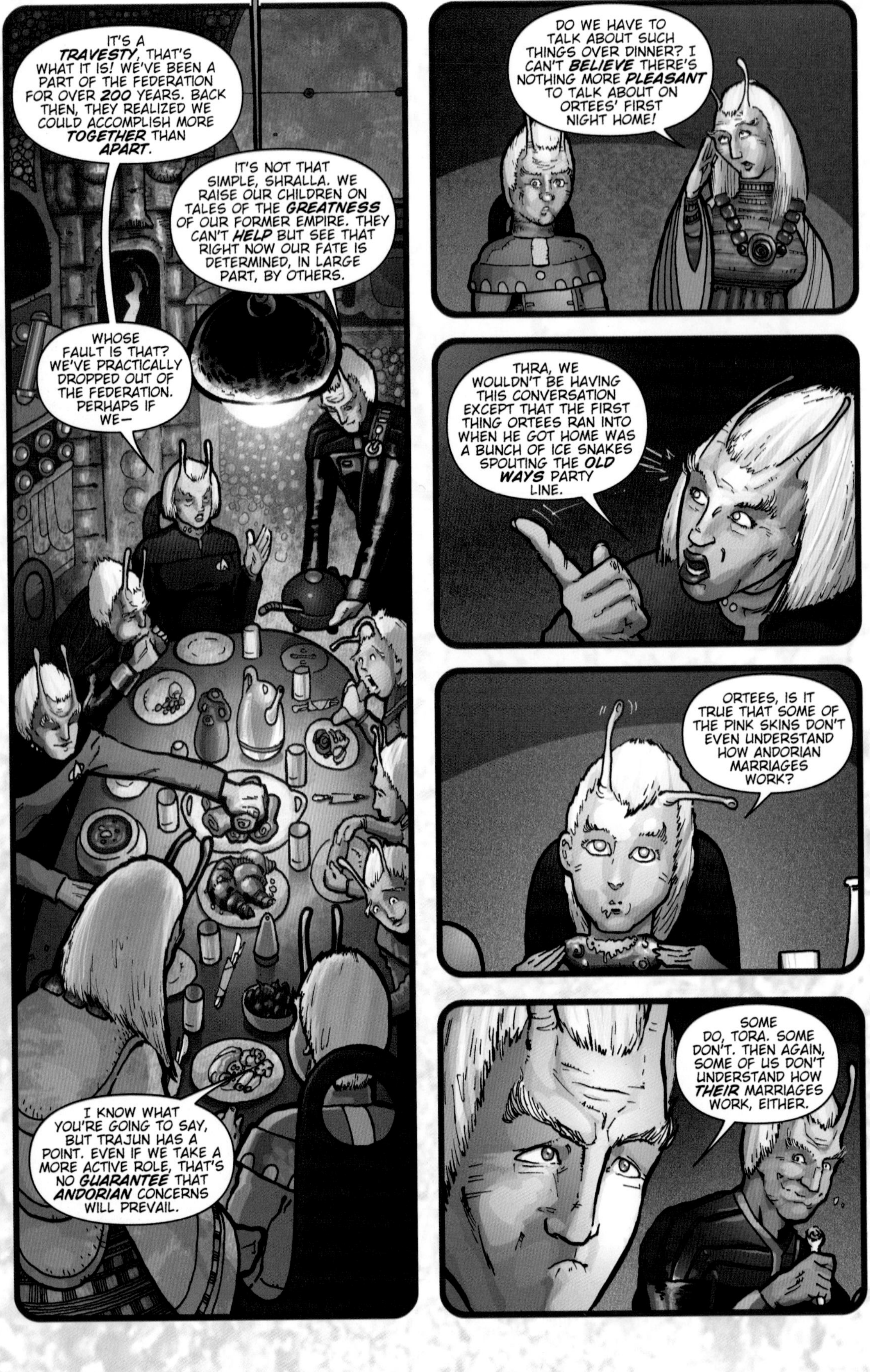
IT'S A TRAVESTY, THAT'S WHAT IT IS! WE'VE BEEN A PART OF THE FEDERATION FOR OVER 200 YEARS. BACK THEN, THEY REALIZED WE COULD ACCOMPLISH MORE TOGETHER THAN APART.
IT'S NOT THAT SIMPLE, SHRALLA. WE RAISE OUR CHILDREN ON TALES OF THE GREATNESS OF OUR FORMER EMPIRE. THEY CAN'T HELP BUT SEE THAT RIGHT NOW OUR FATE IS DETERMINED, IN LARGE PART, BY OTHERS.
WHOSE FAULT IS THAT? WE'VE PRACTICALLY DROPPED OUT OF THE FEDERATION. PERHAPS IF WE—
I KNOW WHAT YOU'RE GOING TO SAY, BUT TRAJUN HAS A POINT. EVEN IF WE TAKE A MORE ACTIVE ROLE, THAT'S NO GUARANTEE THAT ANDORIAN CONCERNS WILL PREVAIL.
DO WE HAVE TO TALK ABOUT SUCH THINGS OVER DINNER? I CAN'T BELIEVE THERE'S NOTHING MORE PLEASANT TO TALK ABOUT ON ORTEES' FIRST NIGHT HOME!
THRA, WE WOULDN'T BE HAVING THIS CONVERSATION EXCEPT THAT THE FIRST THING ORTEES RAN INTO WHEN HE GOT HOME WAS A BUNCH OF ICE SNAKES SPOUTING THE OLD WAYS PARTY LINE.
ORTEES, IS IT TRUE THAT SOME OF THE PINK SKINS DON'T EVEN UNDERSTAND HOW ANDORIAN MARRIAGES WORK?
SOME DO, TORA. SOME DON'T. THEN AGAIN, SOME OF US DON'T UNDERSTAND HOW THEIR MARRIAGES WORK, EITHER.

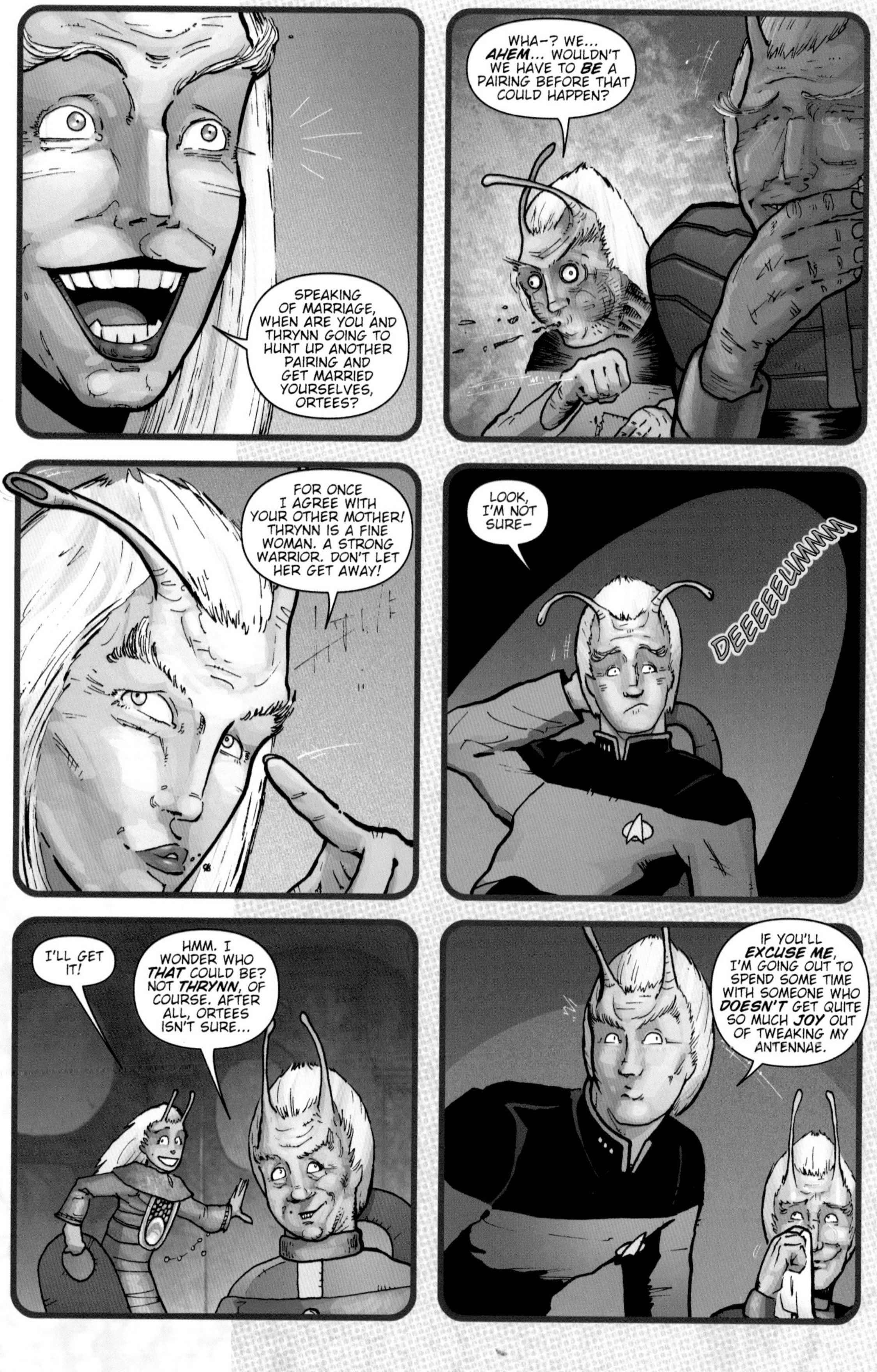
SPEAKING OF MARRIAGE, WHEN ARE YOU AND THRYNN GOING TO HUNT UP ANOTHER PAIRING AND GET MARRIED YOURSELVES, ORTEES?
WHA-? WE... AHEM... WOULDN'T WE HAVE TO BE A PAIRING BEFORE THAT COULD HAPPEN?
FOR ONCE I AGREE WITH YOUR OTHER MOTHER! THRYNN IS A FINE WOMAN. A STRONG WARRIOR. DON'T LET HER GET AWAY!
LOOK, I'M NOT SURE-
DEEEEEUMMM
I'LL GET IT!
HMM. I WONDER WHO THAT COULD BE? NOT THRYNN, OF COURSE. AFTER ALL, ORTEES ISN'T SURE...
IF YOU'LL EXCUSE ME, I'M GOING OUT TO SPEND SOME TIME WITH SOMEONE WHO DOESN'T GET QUITE SO MUCH JOY OUT OF TWEAKING MY ANTENNAE.

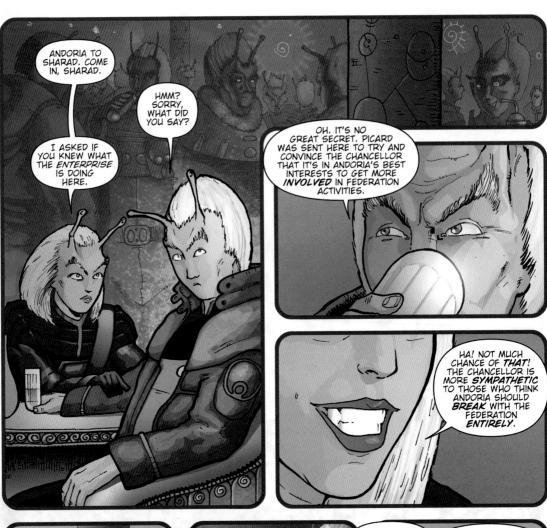

ANDORIA TO SHARAD. COME IN, SHARAD.

HMM? SORRY, WHAT DID YOU SAY?

I ASKED IF YOU KNEW WHAT THE *ENTERPRISE* IS DOING HERE.

OH. IT'S NO GREAT SECRET. PICARD WAS SENT HERE TO TRY AND CONVINCE THE CHANCELLOR THAT IT'S IN ANDORIA'S BEST INTERESTS TO GET MORE *INVOLVED* IN FEDERATION ACTIVITIES.

HA! NOT MUCH CHANCE OF *THAT!* THE CHANCELLOR IS MORE *SYMPATHETIC* TO THOSE WHO THINK ANDORIA SHOULD *BREAK* WITH THE FEDERATION *ENTIRELY.*

HE'S A *FOOL!* ALONE, ANDORIA IS *VULNERABLE.*

YOU *MIGHT* WANT TO KEEP IT *DOWN.*

ANYWAY, WHAT WOULD YOU *EXPECT?* THE *OLD WAYERS* GOT HIM ELECTED AND A LOT OF THEM ARE TIRED OF THE HUMANS AND THE *VULCANS* AND THE REST TELLING US WHAT WE SHOULD AND SHOULDN'T DO.

WHEN DID IT GET THIS BAD, THRYNN? THERE WAS A TIME WHEN HALF THE CUSTOMERS IN THIS PLACE WERE STARFLEET. NO ONE GAVE THE UNIFORM A SECOND GLANCE. NOW...

TIMES CHANGE, SHARAD. I *TOLD* YOU TO WEAR SOMETHING ELSE. *SOME* OF THE PEOPLE HERE SEE STARFLEET AS THE *THREAT* THAT THE FEDERATION USES TO KEEP US IN LINE.

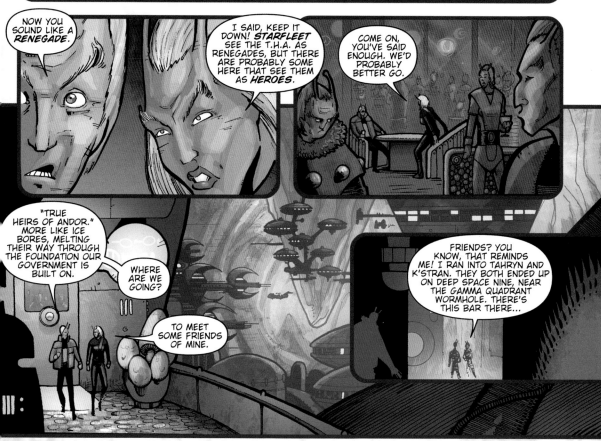

NOW YOU SOUND LIKE A *RENEGADE.*

I SAID, KEEP IT DOWN! *STARFLEET* SEE THE T.H.A. AS RENEGADES, BUT THERE ARE PROBABLY SOME HERE THAT SEE THEM AS *HEROES.*

COME ON, YOU'VE SAID ENOUGH. WE'D PROBABLY BETTER GO.

"TRUE HEIRS OF ANDOR." MORE LIKE ICE BORES, MELTING THEIR WAY THROUGH THE FOUNDATION OUR GOVERNMENT IS BUILT ON.

WHERE ARE WE GOING?

TO MEET SOME FRIENDS OF MINE.

FRIENDS? YOU KNOW, THAT REMINDS ME! I RAN INTO TAHRYN AND K'STRAN. THEY BOTH ENDED UP ON DEEP SPACE NINE, NEAR THE GAMMA QUADRANT WORMHOLE. THERE'S THIS BAR THERE...

GREETINGS, COMMANDER! WE'VE BEEN WAITING FOR YOU.

THIS IS BAD! CHECK BEHIND US. MORE OF THEM MAY TRY TO CUT OFF OUR RETREAT!

WHUD!

GUH!

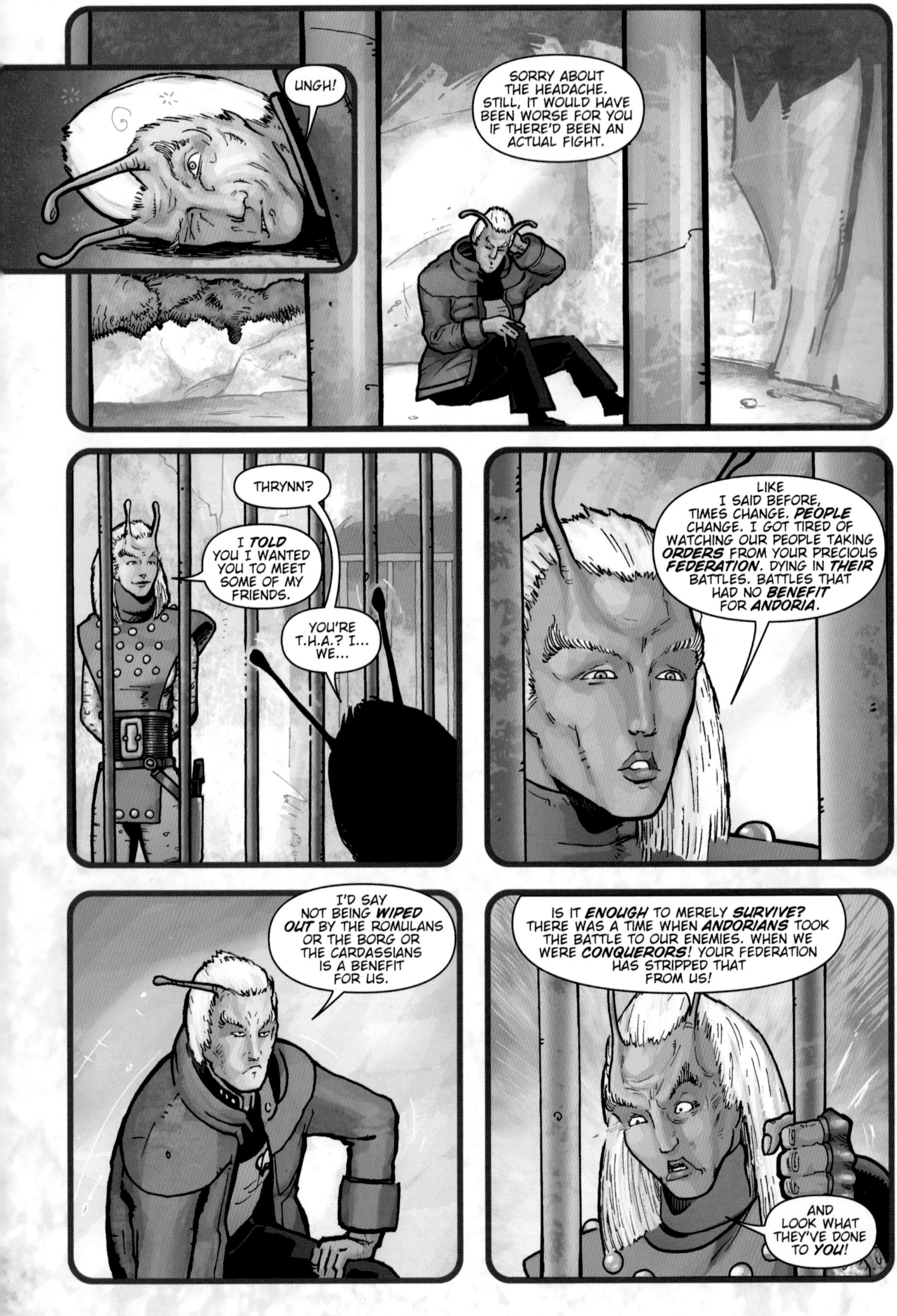
UNGH!
SORRY ABOUT THE HEADACHE. STILL, IT WOULD HAVE BEEN WORSE FOR YOU IF THERE'D BEEN AN ACTUAL FIGHT.
THRYNN?
I TOLD YOU I WANTED YOU TO MEET SOME OF MY FRIENDS.
YOU'RE T.H.A.? I... WE...
LIKE I SAID BEFORE, TIMES CHANGE. PEOPLE CHANGE. I GOT TIRED OF WATCHING OUR PEOPLE TAKING ORDERS FROM YOUR PRECIOUS FEDERATION. DYING IN THEIR BATTLES. BATTLES THAT HAD NO BENEFIT FOR ANDORIA.
I'D SAY NOT BEING WIPED OUT BY THE ROMULANS OR THE BORG OR THE CARDASSIANS IS A BENEFIT FOR US.
IS IT ENOUGH TO MERELY SURVIVE? THERE WAS A TIME WHEN ANDORIANS TOOK THE BATTLE TO OUR ENEMIES. WHEN WE WERE CONQUERORS! YOUR FEDERATION HAS STRIPPED THAT FROM US!
AND LOOK WHAT THEY'VE DONE TO YOU!

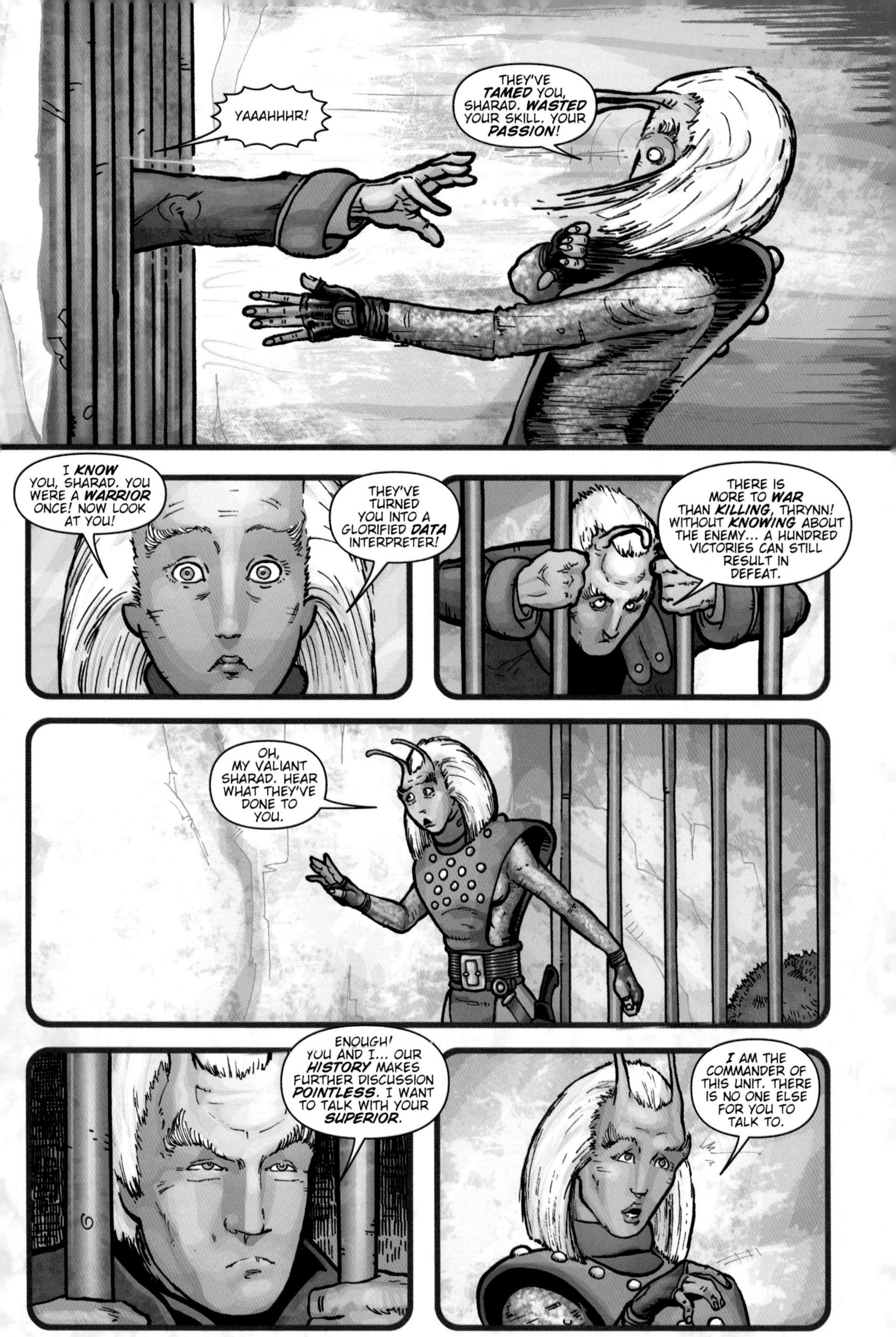
YAAAHHHR!
THEY'VE TAMED YOU, SHARAD. WASTED YOUR SKILL. YOUR PASSION!
I KNOW YOU, SHARAD. YOU WERE A WARRIOR ONCE! NOW LOOK AT YOU!
THEY'VE TURNED YOU INTO A GLORIFIED DATA INTERPRETER!
THERE IS MORE TO WAR THAN KILLING, THRYNN! WITHOUT KNOWING ABOUT THE ENEMY... A HUNDRED VICTORIES CAN STILL RESULT IN DEFEAT.
OH, MY VALIANT SHARAD. HEAR WHAT THEY'VE DONE TO YOU.
ENOUGH! YOU AND I... OUR HISTORY MAKES FURTHER DISCUSSION POINTLESS. I WANT TO TALK WITH YOUR SUPERIOR.
I AM THE COMMANDER OF THIS UNIT. THERE IS NO ONE ELSE FOR YOU TO TALK TO.

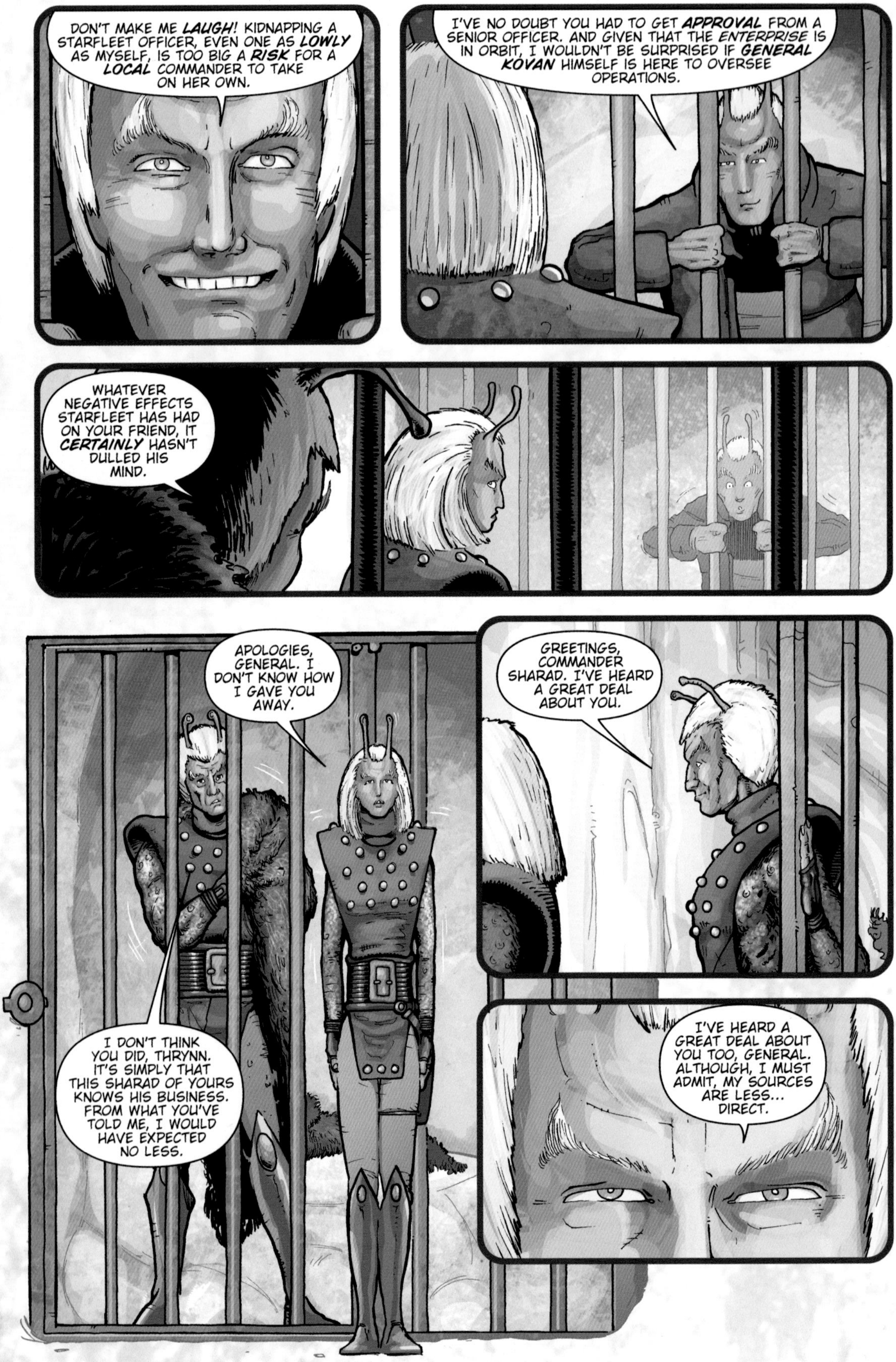

DON'T MAKE ME LAUGH! KIDNAPPING A STARFLEET OFFICER, EVEN ONE AS LOWLY AS MYSELF, IS TOO BIG A RISK FOR A LOCAL COMMANDER TO TAKE ON HER OWN.
I'VE NO DOUBT YOU HAD TO GET APPROVAL FROM A SENIOR OFFICER. AND GIVEN THAT THE ENTERPRISE IS IN ORBIT, I WOULDN'T BE SURPRISED IF GENERAL KOVAN HIMSELF IS HERE TO OVERSEE OPERATIONS.
WHATEVER NEGATIVE EFFECTS STARFLEET HAS HAD ON YOUR FRIEND, IT CERTAINLY HASN'T DULLED HIS MIND.
APOLOGIES, GENERAL. I DON'T KNOW HOW I GAVE YOU AWAY.
I DON'T THINK YOU DID, THRYNN. IT'S SIMPLY THAT THIS SHARAD OF YOURS KNOWS HIS BUSINESS. FROM WHAT YOU'VE TOLD ME, I WOULD HAVE EXPECTED NO LESS.
GREETINGS, COMMANDER SHARAD. I'VE HEARD A GREAT DEAL ABOUT YOU.
I'VE HEARD A GREAT DEAL ABOUT YOU TOO, GENERAL. ALTHOUGH, I MUST ADMIT, MY SOURCES ARE LESS... DIRECT.

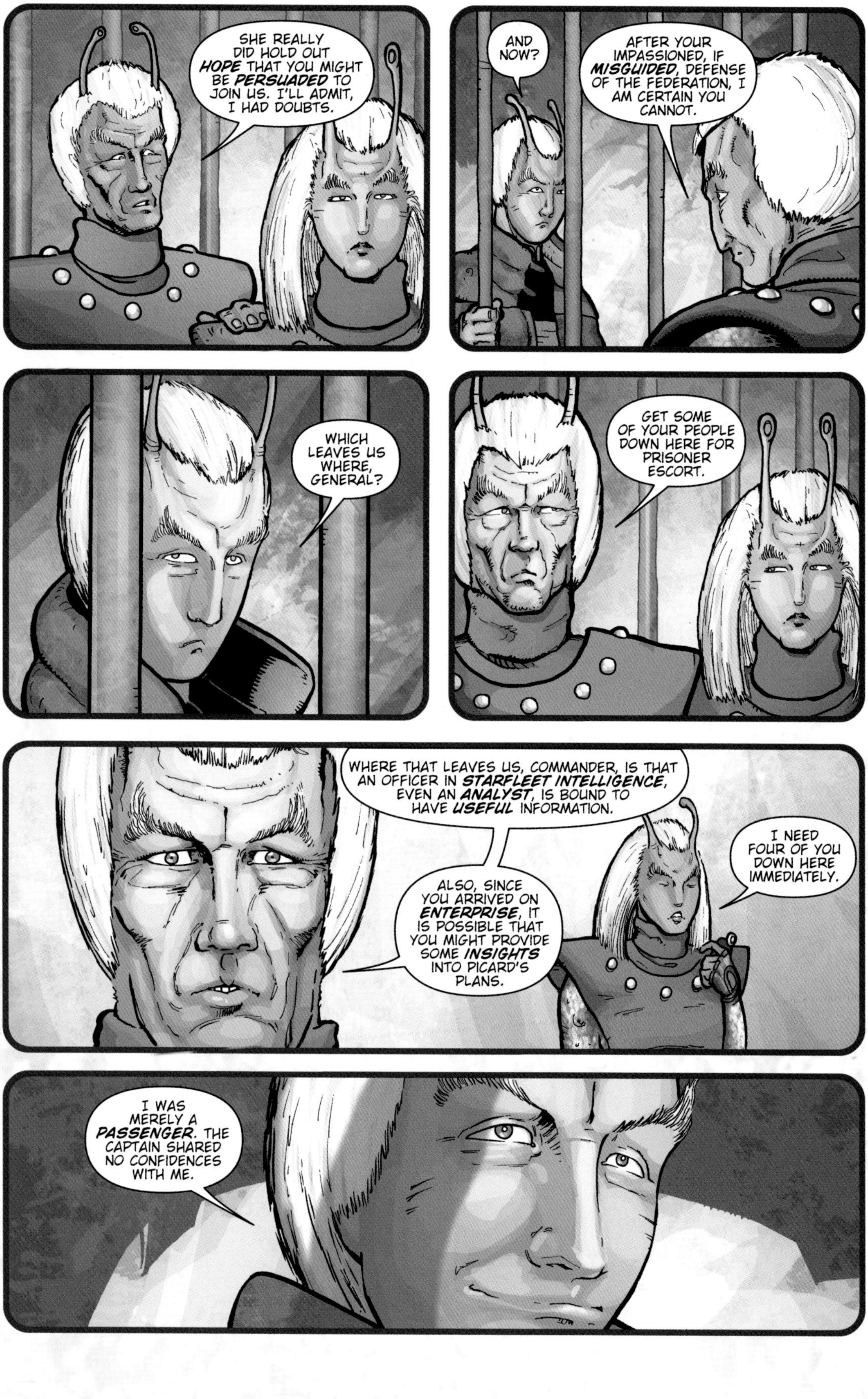
SHE REALLY DID HOLD OUT HOPE THAT YOU MIGHT BE PERSUADED TO JOIN US. I'LL ADMIT, I HAD DOUBTS.
AND NOW?
AFTER YOUR IMPASSIONED, IF MISGUIDED, DEFENSE OF THE FEDERATION, I AM CERTAIN YOU CANNOT.
WHICH LEAVES US WHERE, GENERAL?
GET SOME OF YOUR PEOPLE DOWN HERE FOR PRISONER ESCORT.
WHERE THAT LEAVES US, COMMANDER, IS THAT AN OFFICER IN STARFLEET INTELLIGENCE, EVEN AN ANALYST, IS BOUND TO HAVE USEFUL INFORMATION.
ALSO, SINCE YOU ARRIVED ON ENTERPRISE, IT IS POSSIBLE THAT YOU MIGHT PROVIDE SOME INSIGHTS INTO PICARD'S PLANS.
I NEED FOUR OF YOU DOWN HERE IMMEDIATELY.
I WAS MERELY A PASSENGER. THE CAPTAIN SHARED NO CONFIDENCES WITH ME.

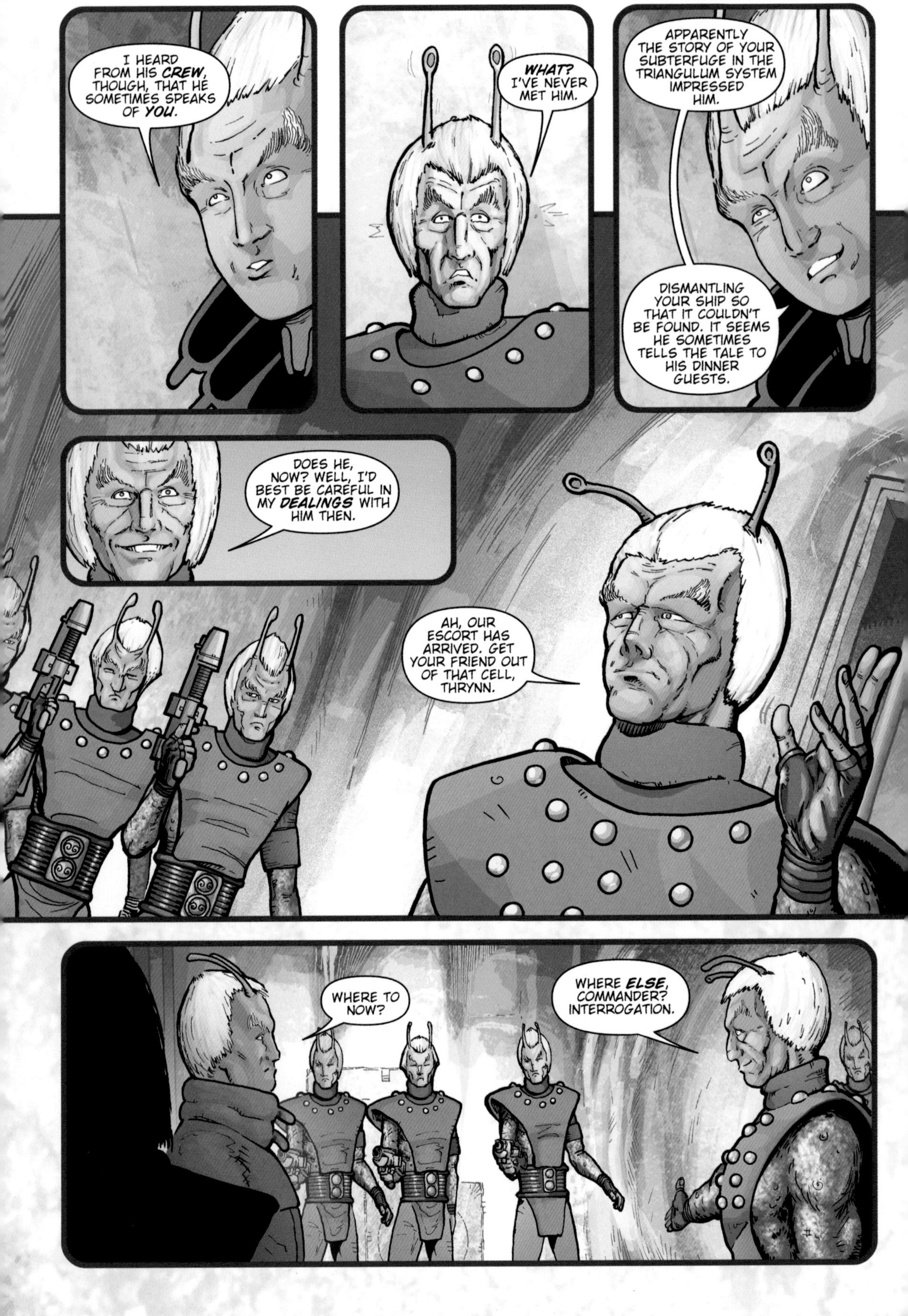
I HEARD FROM HIS **CREW**, THOUGH, THAT HE SOMETIMES SPEAKS OF **YOU**.
WHAT? I'VE NEVER MET HIM.
APPARENTLY THE STORY OF YOUR SUBTERFUGE IN THE TRIANGULUM SYSTEM IMPRESSED HIM.
DISMANTLING YOUR SHIP SO THAT IT COULDN'T BE FOUND. IT SEEMS HE SOMETIMES TELLS THE TALE TO HIS DINNER GUESTS.
DOES HE, NOW? WELL, I'D BEST BE CAREFUL IN MY **DEALINGS** WITH HIM THEN.
AH, OUR ESCORT HAS ARRIVED. GET YOUR FRIEND OUT OF THAT CELL, THRYNN.
WHERE TO NOW?
WHERE **ELSE**, COMMANDER? INTERROGATION.

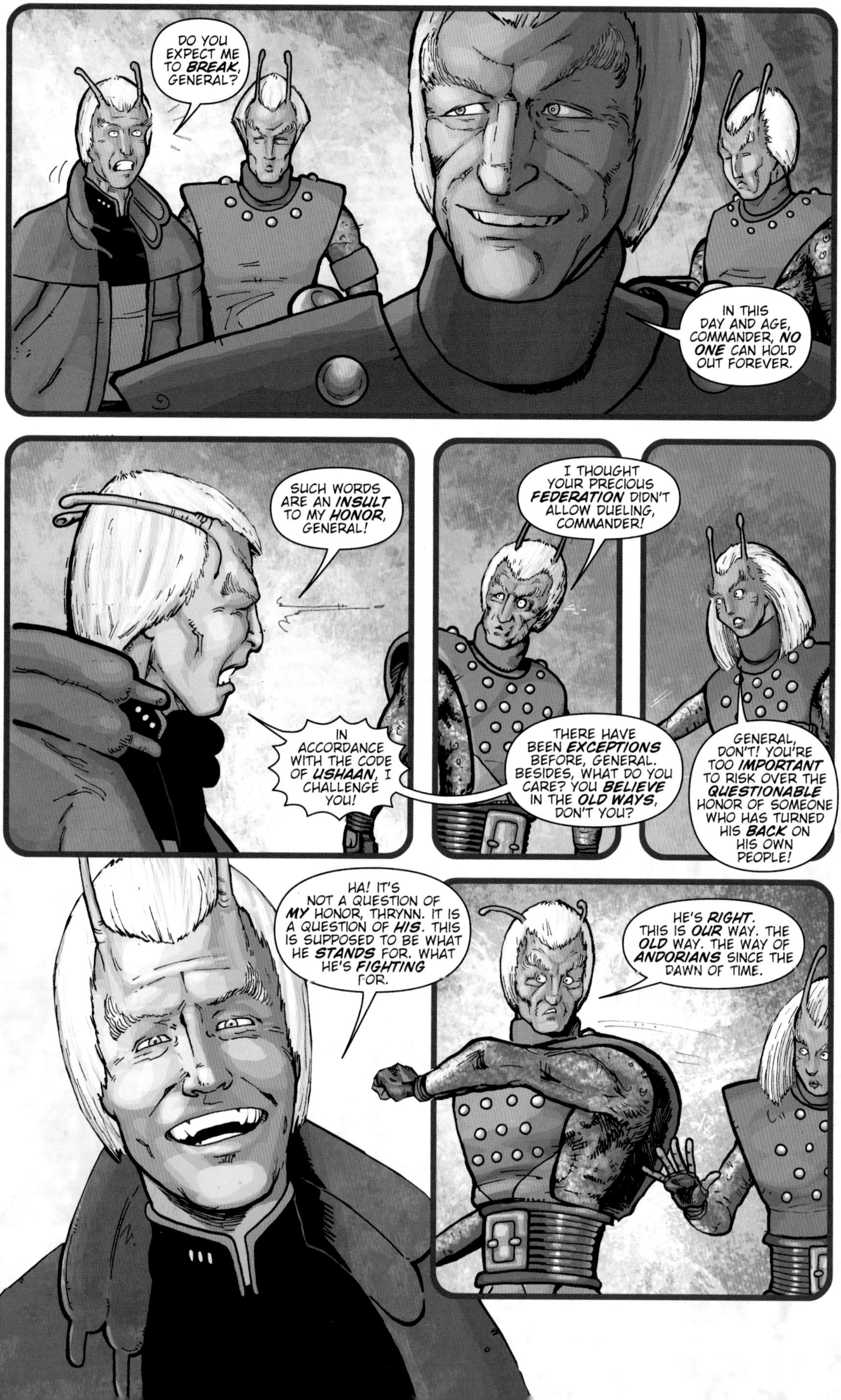
DO YOU EXPECT ME TO BREAK, GENERAL?
IN THIS DAY AND AGE, COMMANDER, NO ONE CAN HOLD OUT FOREVER.
SUCH WORDS ARE AN INSULT TO MY HONOR, GENERAL!
IN ACCORDANCE WITH THE CODE OF USHAAN, I CHALLENGE YOU!
I THOUGHT YOUR PRECIOUS FEDERATION DIDN'T ALLOW DUELING, COMMANDER!
THERE HAVE BEEN EXCEPTIONS BEFORE, GENERAL. BESIDES, WHAT DO YOU CARE? YOU BELIEVE IN THE OLD WAYS, DON'T YOU?
GENERAL, DON'T! YOU'RE TOO IMPORTANT TO RISK OVER THE QUESTIONABLE HONOR OF SOMEONE WHO HAS TURNED HIS BACK ON HIS OWN PEOPLE!
HA! IT'S NOT A QUESTION OF MY HONOR, THRYNN. IT IS A QUESTION OF HIS. THIS IS SUPPOSED TO BE WHAT HE STANDS FOR. WHAT HE'S FIGHTING FOR.
HE'S RIGHT. THIS IS OUR WAY. THE OLD WAY. THE WAY OF ANDORIANS SINCE THE DAWN OF TIME.

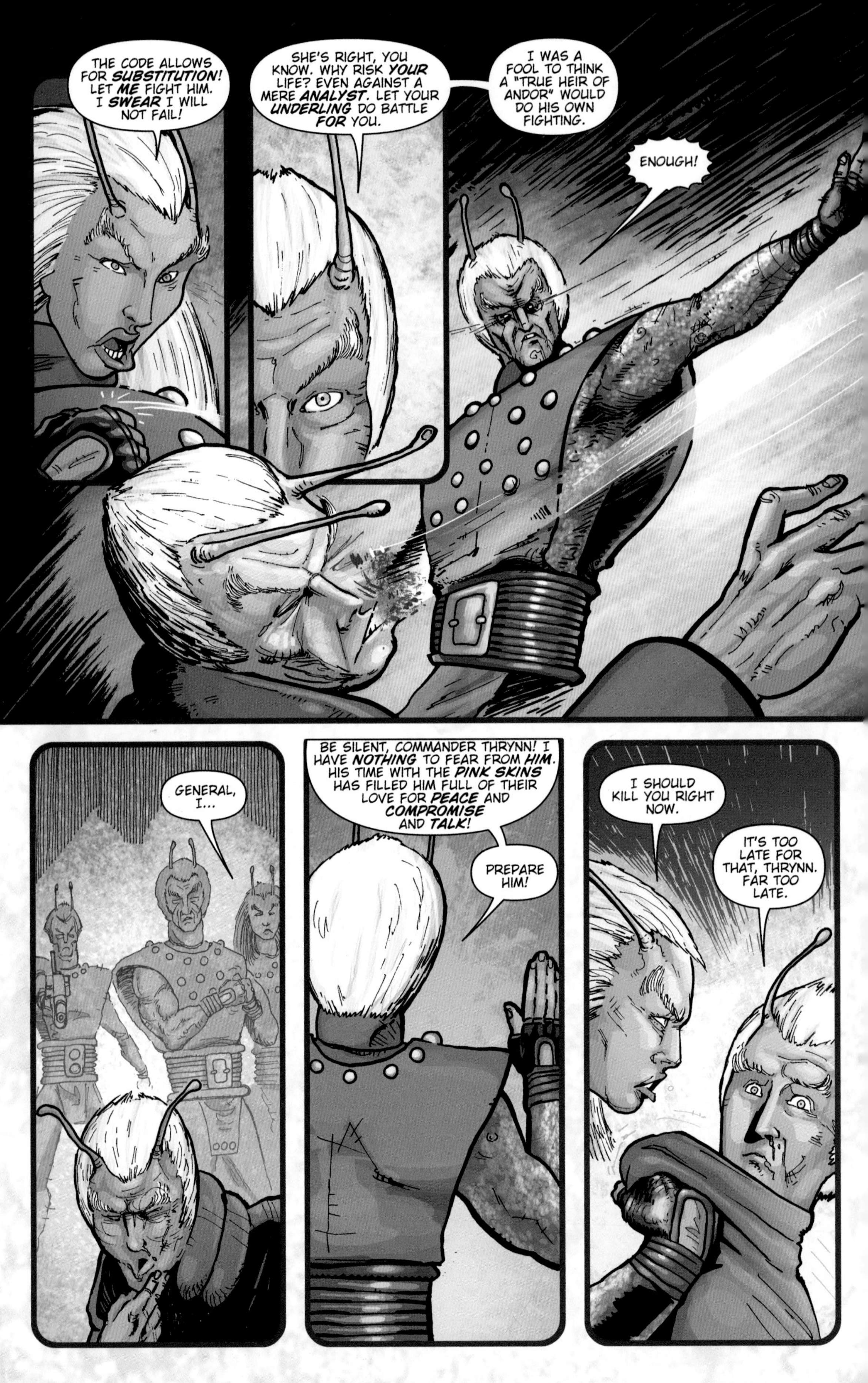
THE CODE ALLOWS FOR SUBSTITUTION! LET ME FIGHT HIM. I SWEAR I WILL NOT FAIL!
SHE'S RIGHT, YOU KNOW. WHY RISK YOUR LIFE? EVEN AGAINST A MERE ANALYST. LET YOUR UNDERLING DO BATTLE FOR YOU.
I WAS A FOOL TO THINK A "TRUE HEIR OF ANDOR" WOULD DO HIS OWN FIGHTING.
ENOUGH!
GENERAL, I...
BE SILENT, COMMANDER THRYNN! I HAVE NOTHING TO FEAR FROM HIM. HIS TIME WITH THE PINK SKINS HAS FILLED HIM FULL OF THEIR LOVE FOR PEACE AND COMPROMISE AND TALK!
PREPARE HIM!
I SHOULD KILL YOU RIGHT NOW.
IT'S TOO LATE FOR THAT, THRYNN. FAR TOO LATE.

KOVAN! KOVAN! KOVAN! KOVAN! KOVAN! KOVAN!

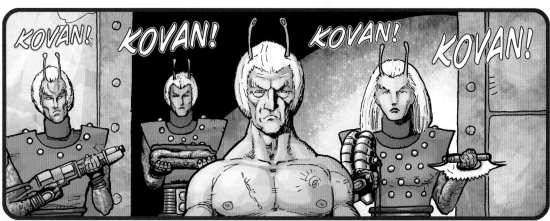

KOVAN! KOVAN! KOVAN! KOVAN!

WELL PLAYED, COMMANDER. AFTER I'D HAD A CHANCE TO REFLECT, I REALIZED EXACTLY WHY YOU GOADED ME INTO THIS FIGHT.

AND WHY IS THAT, GENERAL?

EVEN IF I WIN, I LOSE. USHAAN IS TO THE DEATH. DEAD, YOUR INFORMATION IS BEYOND MY REACH.

THEN YOU'LL JUST HAVE TO HOPE I WIN.

APOLOGIES, COMMANDER, BUT MY PEOPLE NEED *ME* MORE THAN WE NEED YOUR *INFORMATION*.

I DON'T SUPPOSE THERE IS ANY CHANCE THAT I CAN CONVINCE YOU TO *DROP* YOUR CHALLENGE? ANDORIA COULD USE A MAN LIKE YOU IN HER SERVICE.

ALL THAT I DO, I DO FOR *ANDORIA*!

THE REASONS WE JOINED THE *FEDERATION* ARE STILL SOUND AND IT IS *WITH* THE FEDERATION THAT HER *BEST* AND *BRIGHTEST* FUTURE LIES.

HER HOPE LIES IN THE OLD WAYS, SHARAD!

YOU CANNOT WIN THE *FUTURE* BY HIDING IN THE *PAST*, THRYNN.

ENOUGH WORDS! LET US BEGIN.

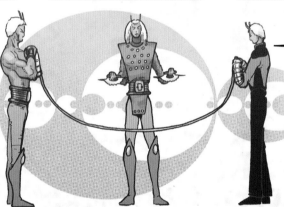

AS YOU DO NOT HAVE YOUR *OWN* USHAAN-TOR TO FIGHT WITH, COMMANDER, CHOICE OF WEAPONS IS YOURS.

IT MAKES NO DIFFERENCE, GENERAL. SO LONG AS IT'S *SHARP*.

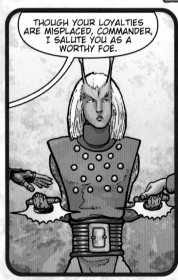

THOUGH YOUR LOYALTIES ARE MISPLACED, COMMANDER, I SALUTE YOU AS A WORTHY FOE.

I WISH I COULD DO THE SAME, GENERAL, BUT YOU ARE A DANGEROUS *LUNATIC* WHOSE MADNESS WOULD DRAG ANDORIA INTO *DESTRUCTION*.

W-WHAT?!

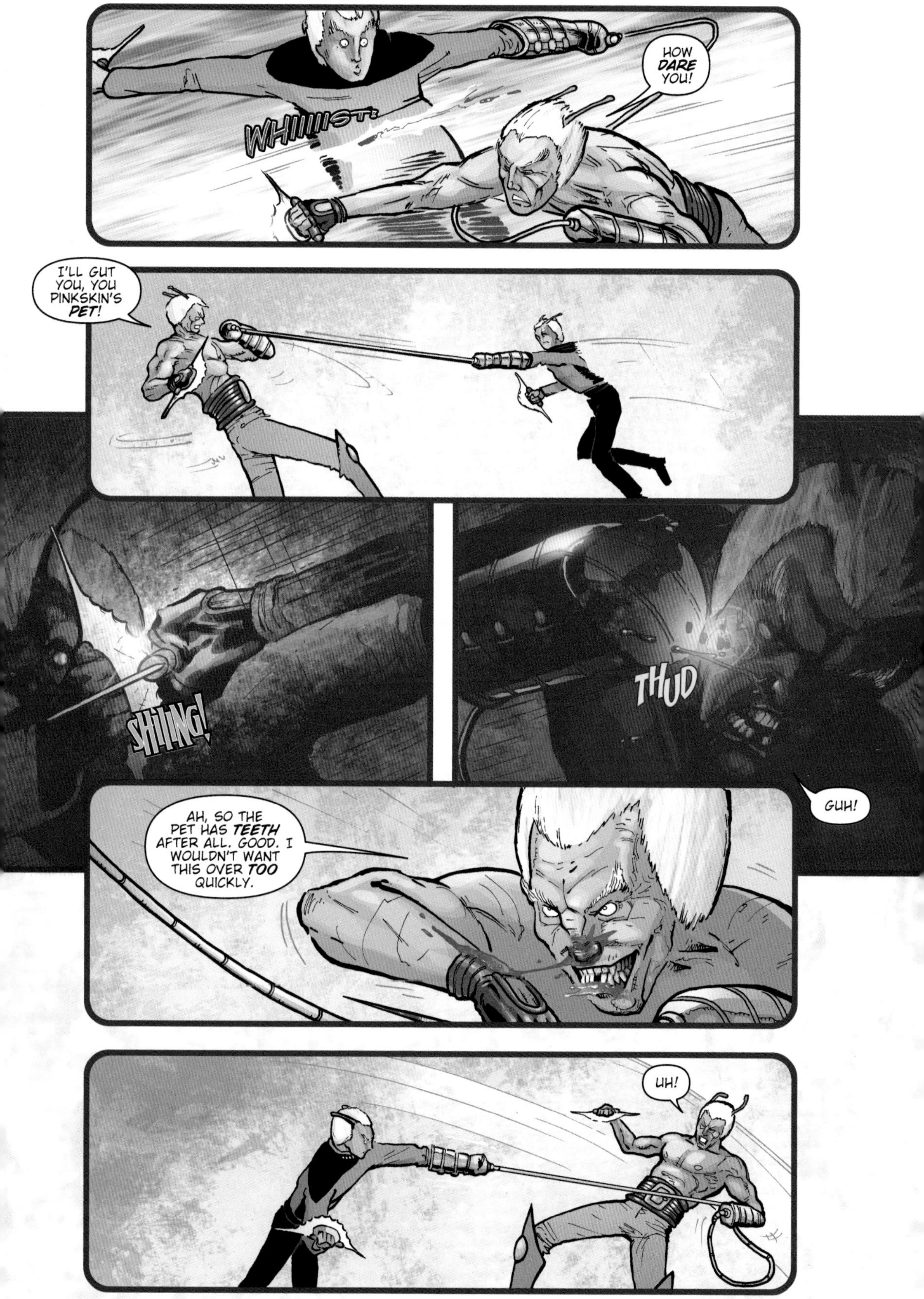
HOW DARE YOU!
WHIIIIIST!
I'LL GUT YOU, YOU PINKSKIN'S PET!
SHILLNG!
THUD
GUH!
AH, SO THE PET HAS TEETH AFTER ALL. GOOD. I WOULDN'T WANT THIS OVER TOO QUICKLY.
UH!

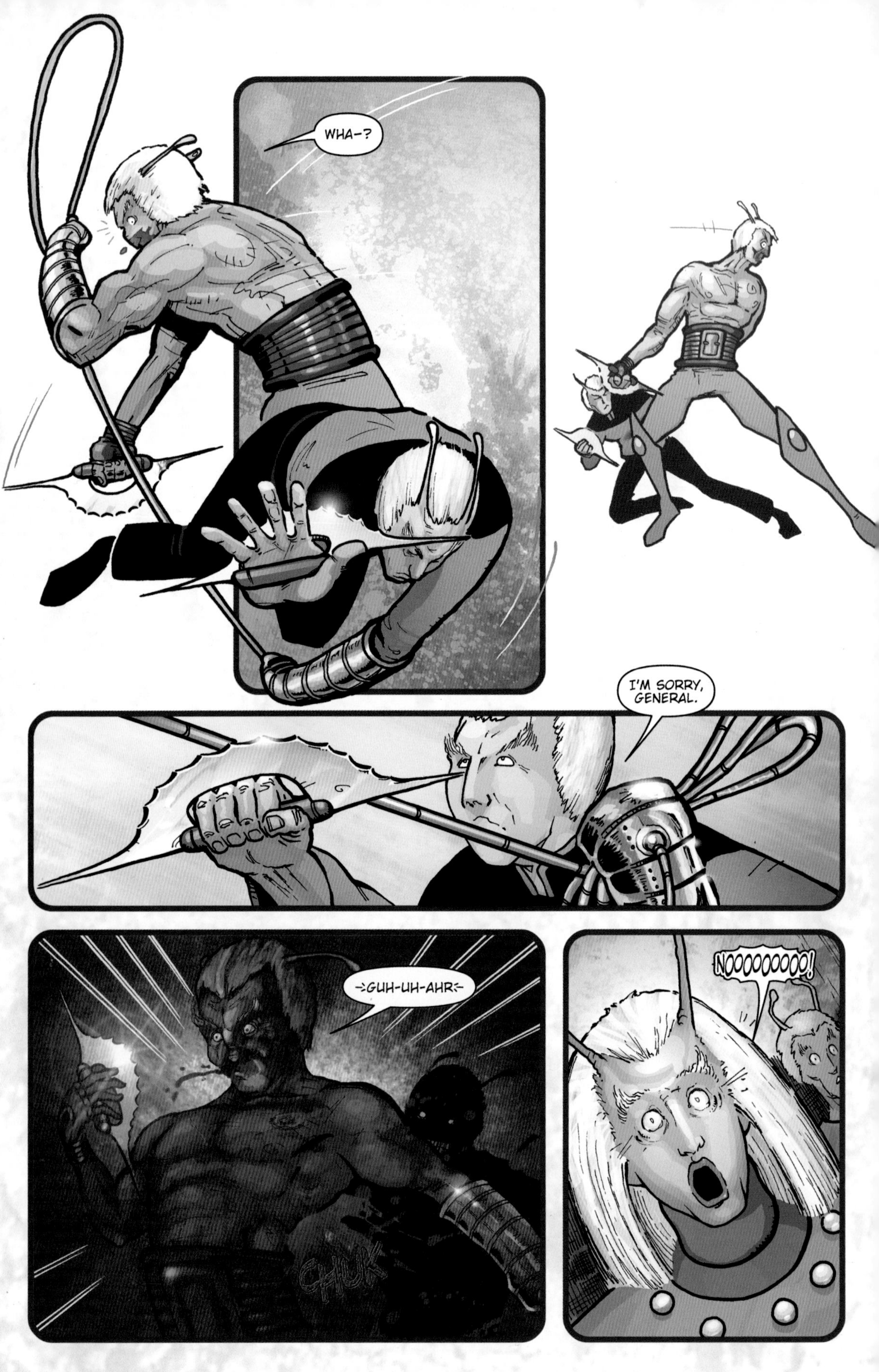
WHA-?
I'M SORRY, GENERAL.
-GUH-UH-AHR-
CHUK
NOOOOOOOOO!

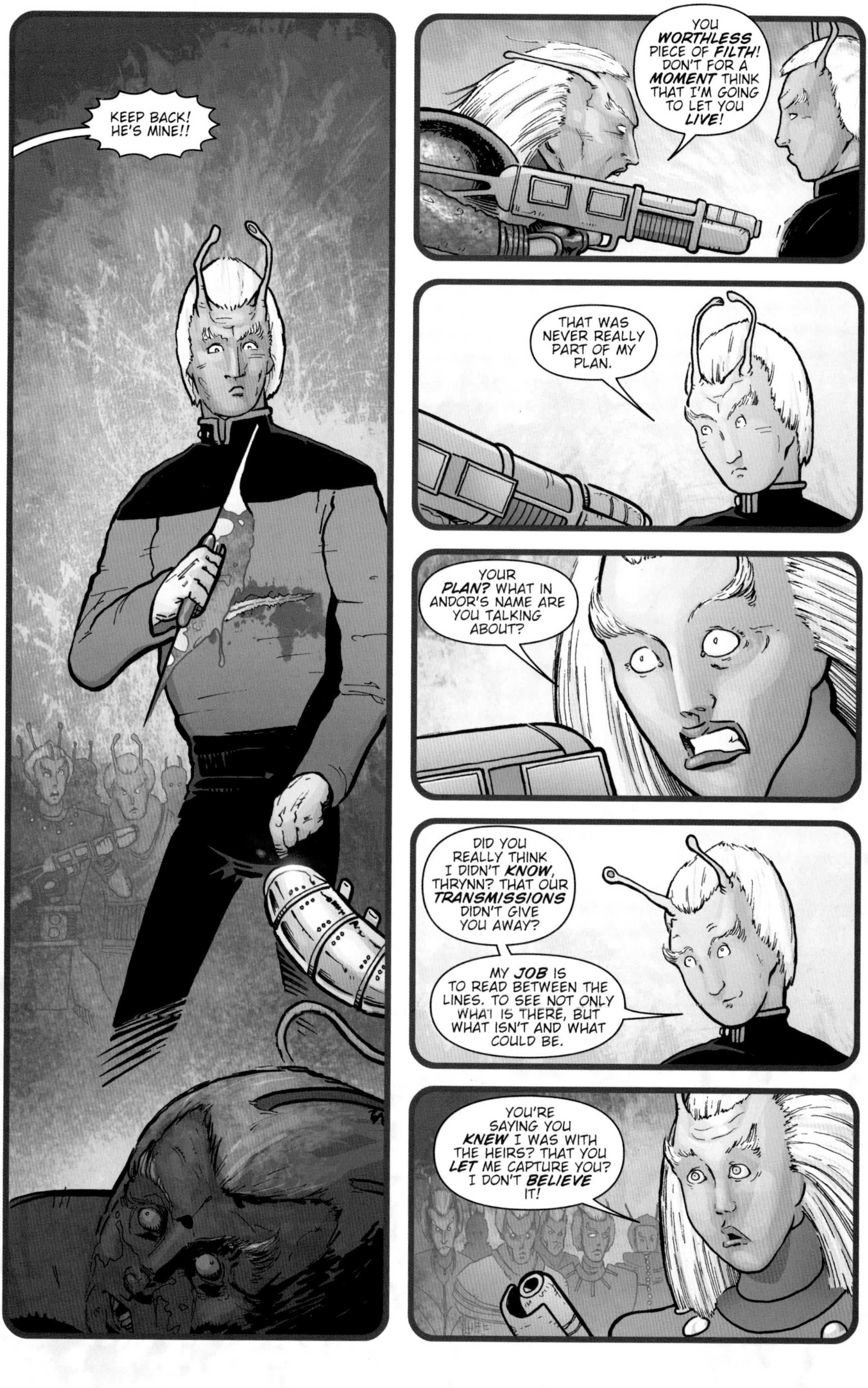
KEEP BACK! HE'S MINE!!
YOU WORTHLESS PIECE OF FILTH! DON'T FOR A MOMENT THINK THAT I'M GOING TO LET YOU LIVE!
THAT WAS NEVER REALLY PART OF MY PLAN.
YOUR PLAN? WHAT IN ANDOR'S NAME ARE YOU TALKING ABOUT?
DID YOU REALLY THINK I DIDN'T KNOW, THRYNN? THAT OUR TRANSMISSIONS DIDN'T GIVE YOU AWAY?
MY JOB IS TO READ BETWEEN THE LINES. TO SEE NOT ONLY WHAT IS THERE, BUT WHAT ISN'T AND WHAT COULD BE.
YOU'RE SAYING YOU KNEW I WAS WITH THE HEIRS? THAT YOU LET ME CAPTURE YOU? I DON'T BELIEVE IT!

I *KNEW* YOU WERE WORKING WITH KOVAN. I *KNEW* THAT IF I COULD *GET* HIM FACE TO FACE, I COULD FORCE HIM INTO A DUEL.

YOU... YOU'RE NOT *REALLY* AN ANALYST AT ALL! YOU'RE A *SPY!* AN *ASSASSIN!*

KOVAN SAID IT HIMSELF—*HE* WAS MORE IMPORTANT THAN ANYTHING YOU COULD GET OUT OF ME. HE WAS YOUR BEST STRATEGIST. YOUR STRONGEST LEADER.

DON'T BE A *FOOL! STARFLEET* WOULD NEVER RISK AN AGENT ON SUCH A DESPERATE GAMBLE.

SO YOU'RE SAYING YOU DID ALL *THIS* ON YOUR OWN? *WHY?* EVEN IF YOU ESCAPED, YOU'D BE *THROWN OUT* OF YOUR PRECIOUS *STARFLEET.*

THAT DOESN'T MATTER.

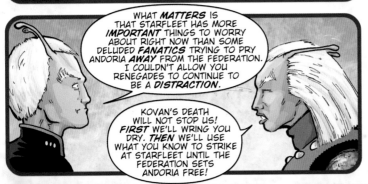

WHAT *MATTERS* IS THAT STARFLEET HAS MORE *IMPORTANT* THINGS TO WORRY ABOUT RIGHT NOW THAN SOME DELUDED *FANATICS* TRYING TO PRY ANDORIA *AWAY* FROM THE FEDERATION. I COULDN'T ALLOW YOU RENEGADES TO CONTINUE TO BE A *DISTRACTION.*

KOVAN'S DEATH WILL NOT STOP US! *FIRST* WE'LL WRING YOU DRY. *THEN* WE'LL USE WHAT YOU KNOW TO STRIKE AT STARFLEET UNTIL THE FEDERATION SETS ANDORIA FREE!

AS FOR WRINGING ME DRY, YOU *TRADITIONALISTS* HAVE NO *STUN* SETTINGS ON YOUR WEAPONS AND *I'M* NOT GOING LET YOU TAKE ME ALIVE.

I HAVE DONE WHAT I SET OUT TO DO BY CUNNING AND SKILL, PASSION AND HONOR! I AM A *TRUE* ANDORIAN AND I AM *PREPARED* TO DIE!

ARE *YOU?*

END.

art and color by Len O'Grady

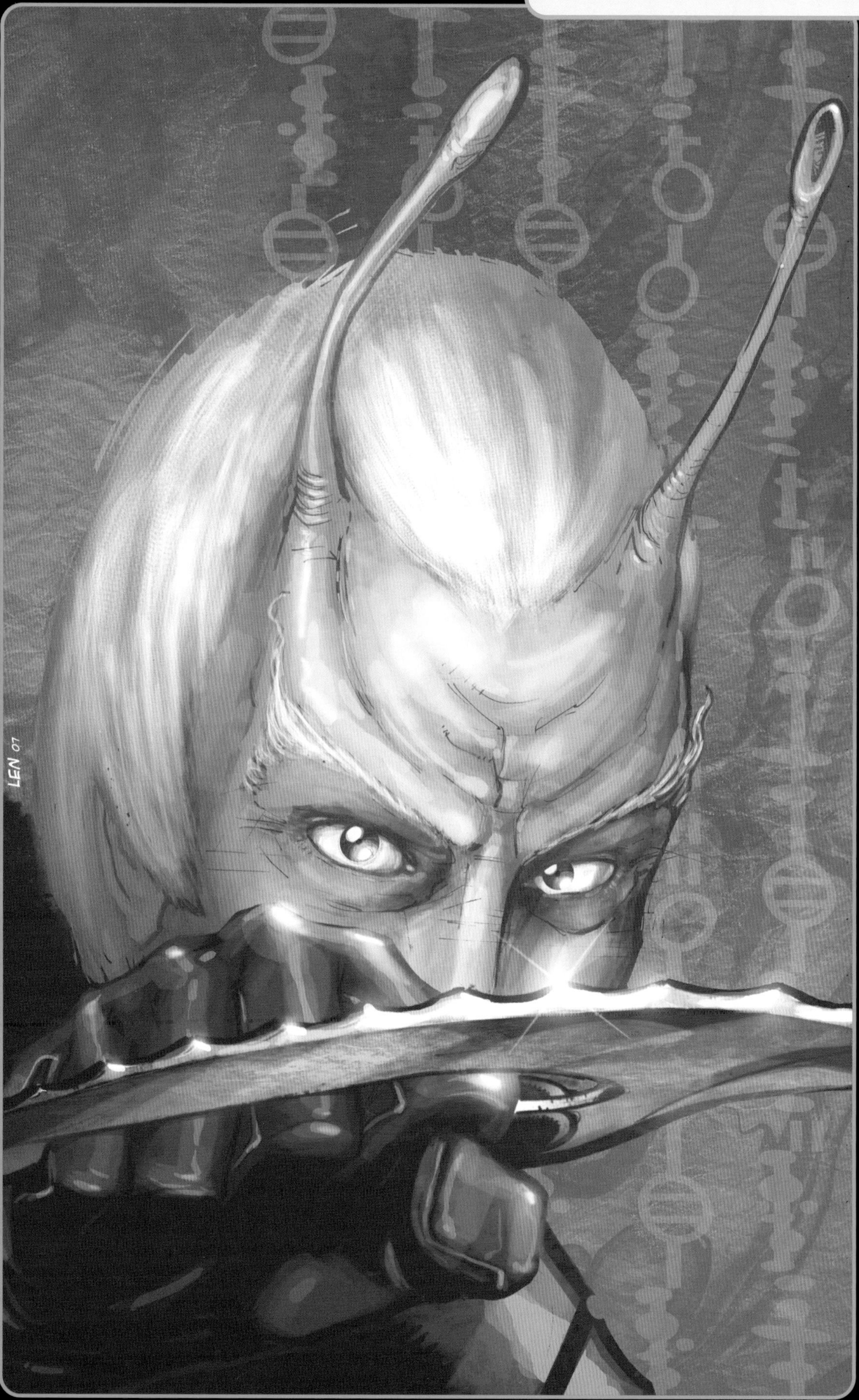
LEN 07

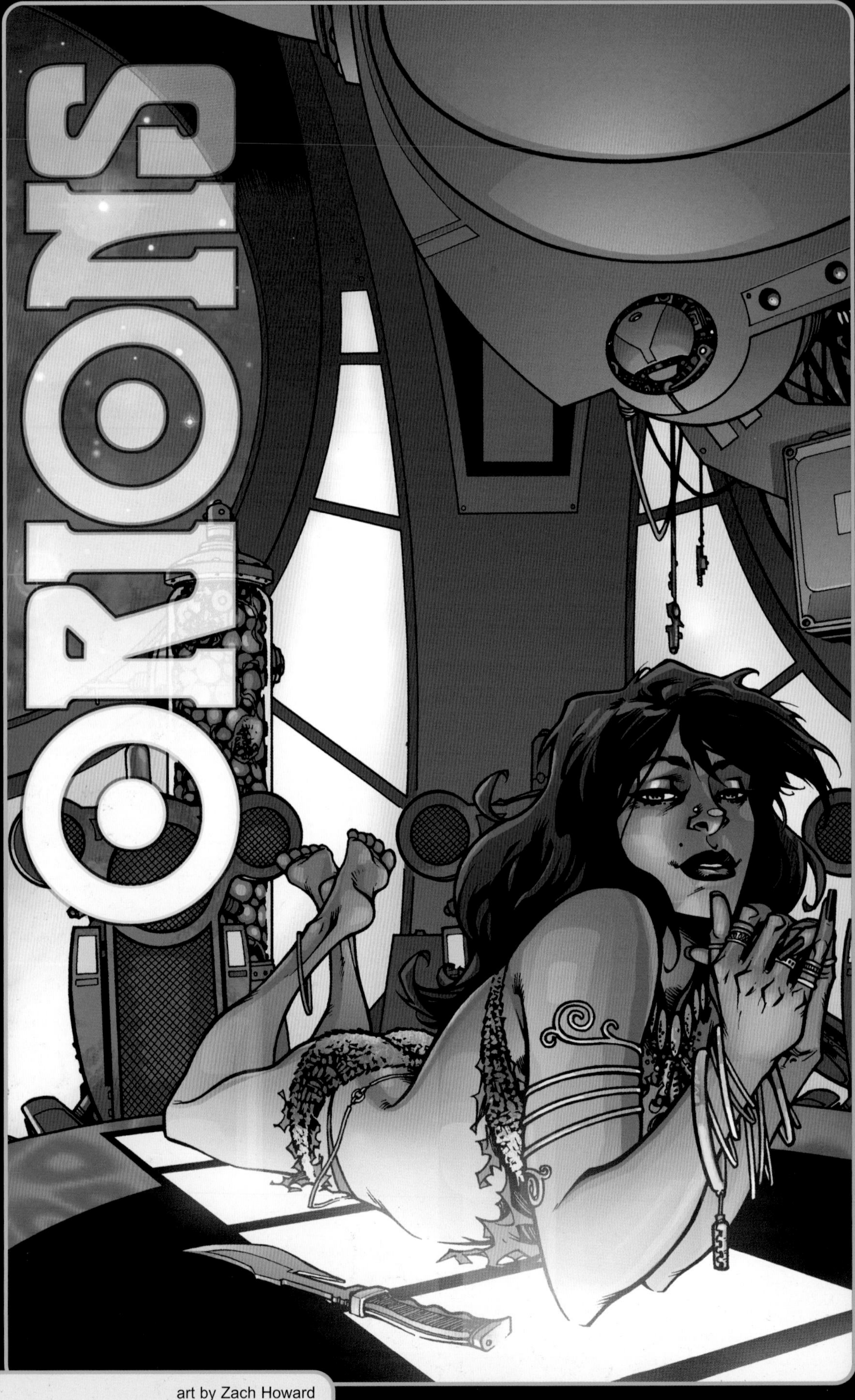
ORIONS

art by Zach Howard
colors and logo by Len O'Grady

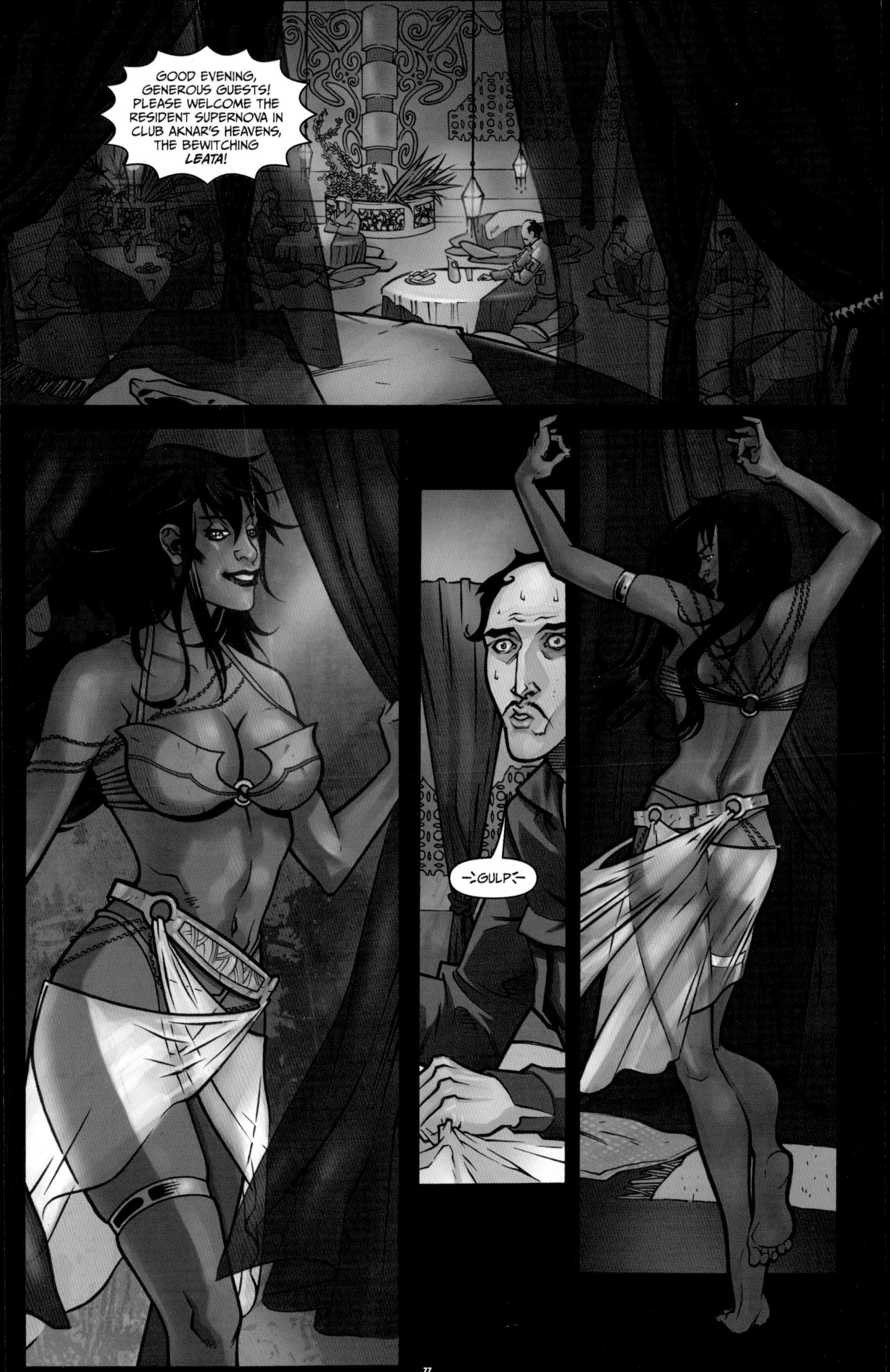
GOOD EVENING, GENEROUS GUESTS! PLEASE WELCOME THE RESIDENT SUPERNOVA IN CLUB AKNAR'S HEAVENS, THE BEWITCHING *LEATA!*
GULP

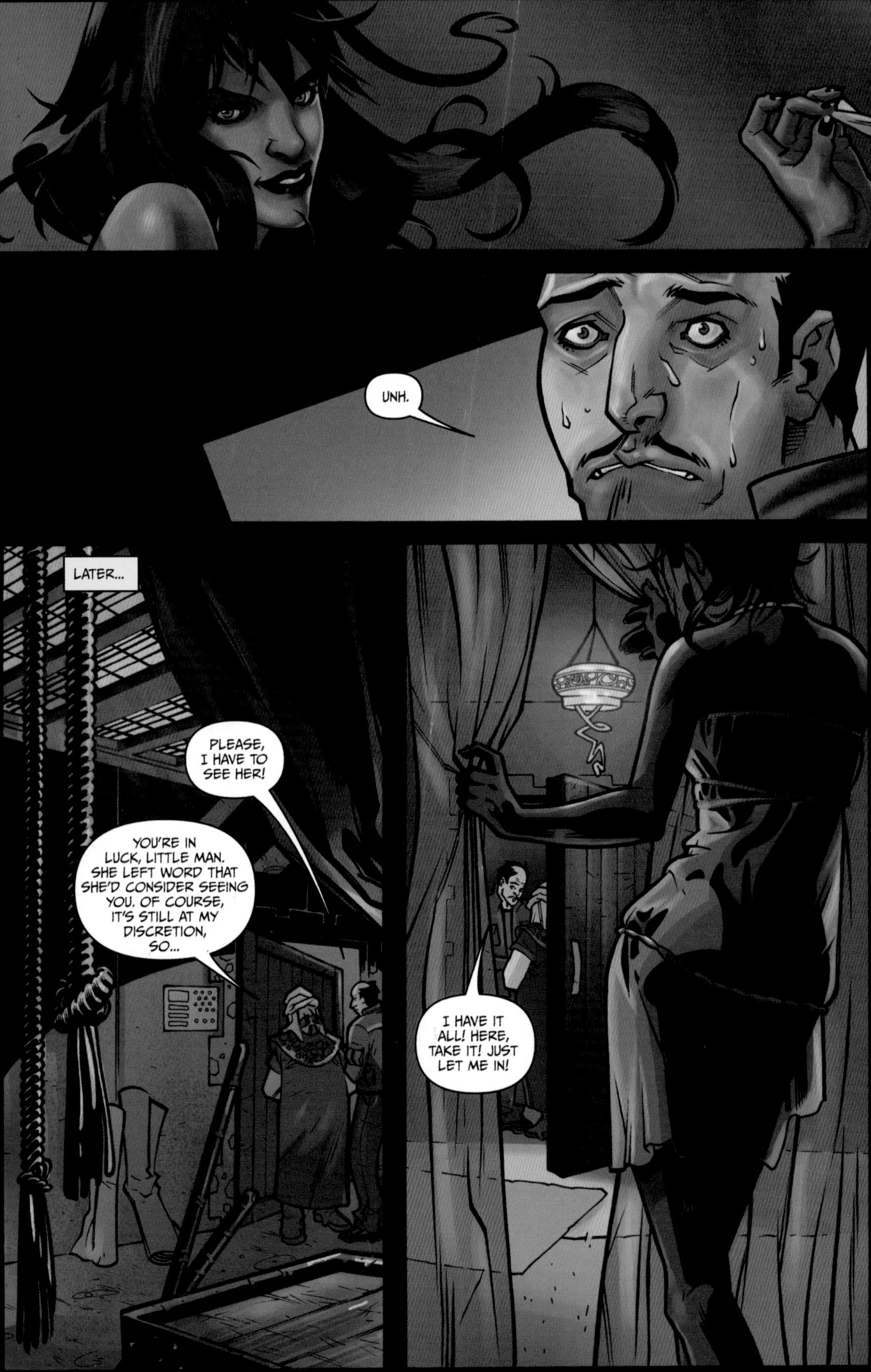
UNH.
LATER...
PLEASE, I HAVE TO SEE HER!
YOU'RE IN LUCK, LITTLE MAN. SHE LEFT WORD THAT SHE'D CONSIDER SEEING YOU. OF COURSE, IT'S STILL AT MY DISCRETION, SO...
I HAVE IT ALL! HERE, TAKE IT! JUST LET ME IN!

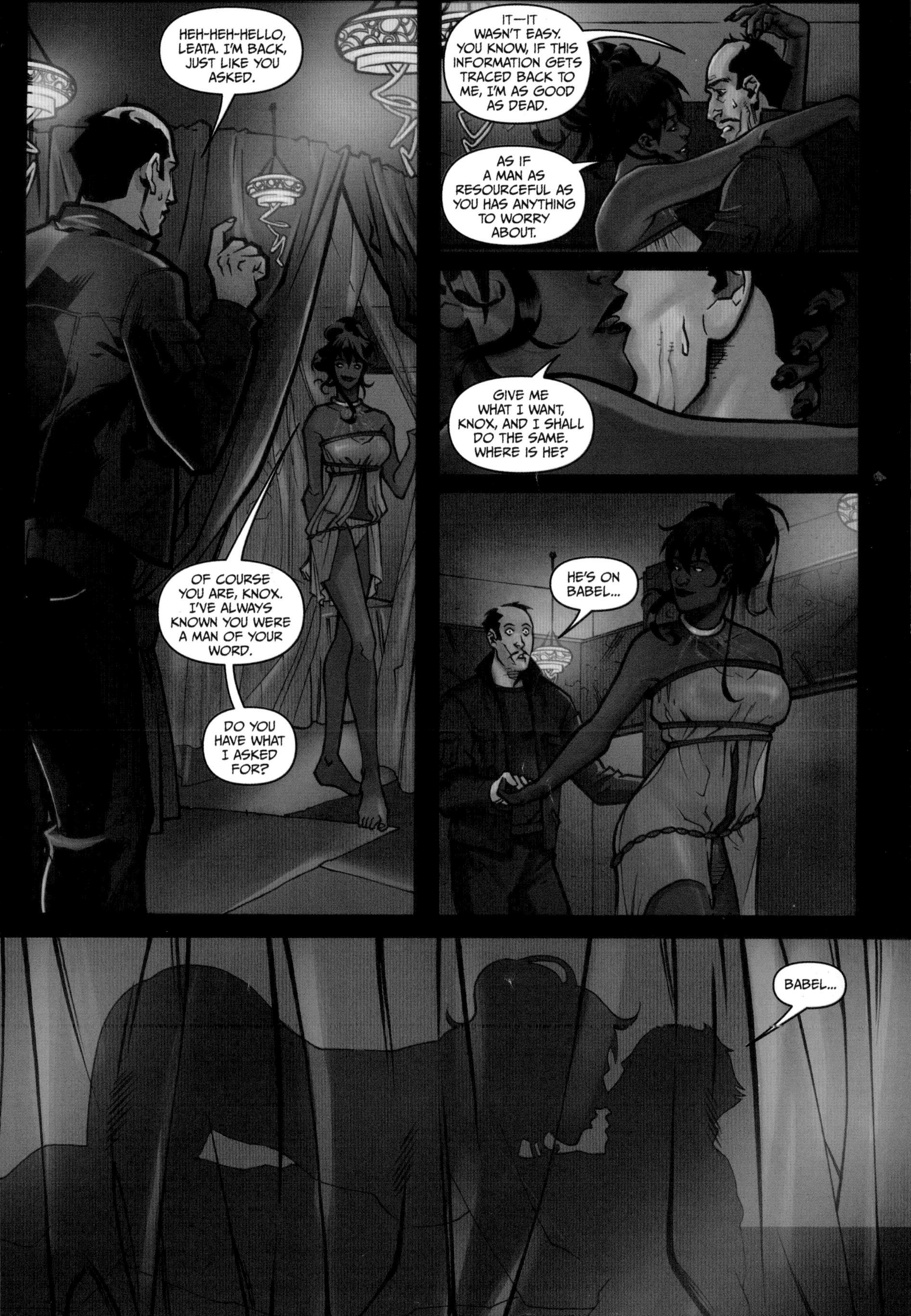
HEH-HEH-HELLO, LEATA. I'M BACK, JUST LIKE YOU ASKED.
OF COURSE YOU ARE, KNOX. I'VE ALWAYS KNOWN YOU WERE A MAN OF YOUR WORD.
DO YOU HAVE WHAT I ASKED FOR?
IT—IT WASN'T EASY. YOU KNOW, IF THIS INFORMATION GETS TRACED BACK TO ME, I'M AS GOOD AS DEAD.
AS IF A MAN AS RESOURCEFUL AS YOU HAS ANYTHING TO WORRY ABOUT.
GIVE ME WHAT I WANT, KNOX, AND I SHALL DO THE SAME. WHERE IS HE?
HE'S ON BABEL...
BABEL...

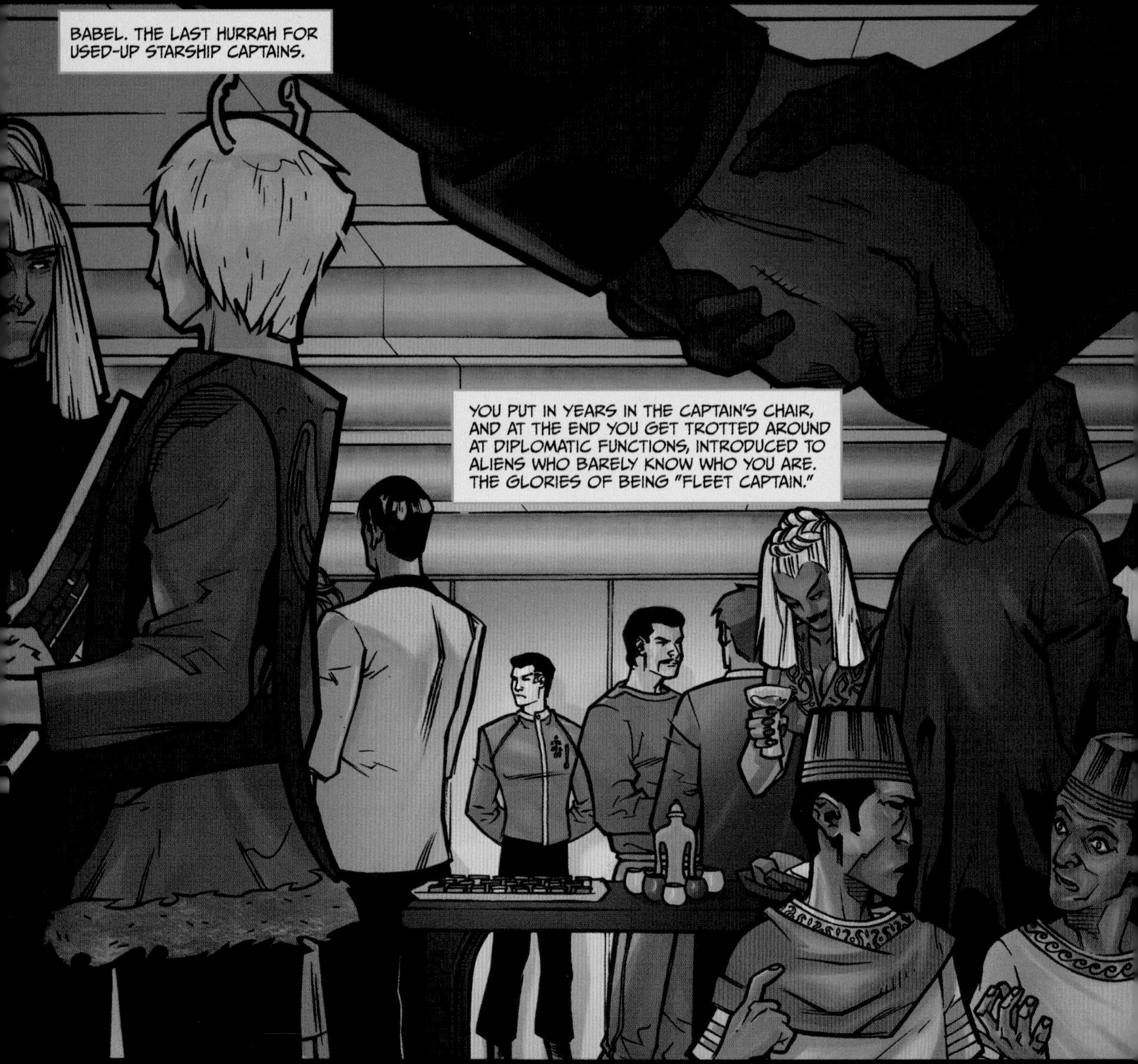
BABEL. THE LAST HURRAH FOR USED-UP STARSHIP CAPTAINS.
YOU PUT IN YEARS IN THE CAPTAIN'S CHAIR, AND AT THE END YOU GET TROTTED AROUND AT DIPLOMATIC FUNCTIONS, INTRODUCED TO ALIENS WHO BARELY KNOW WHO YOU ARE. THE GLORIES OF BEING "FLEET CAPTAIN."

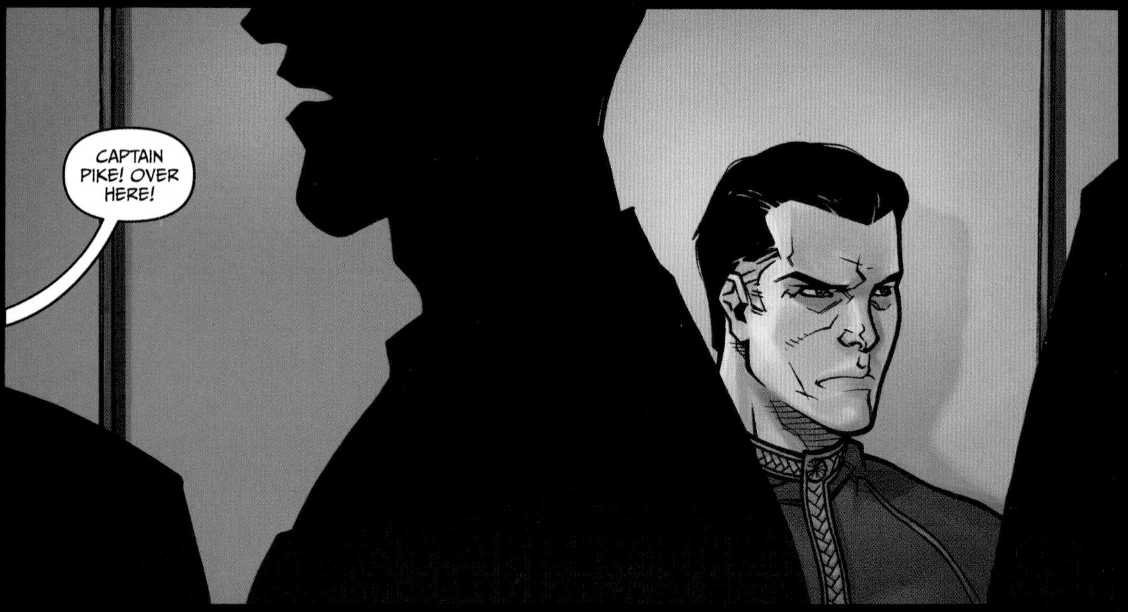
CAPTAIN PIKE! OVER HERE!

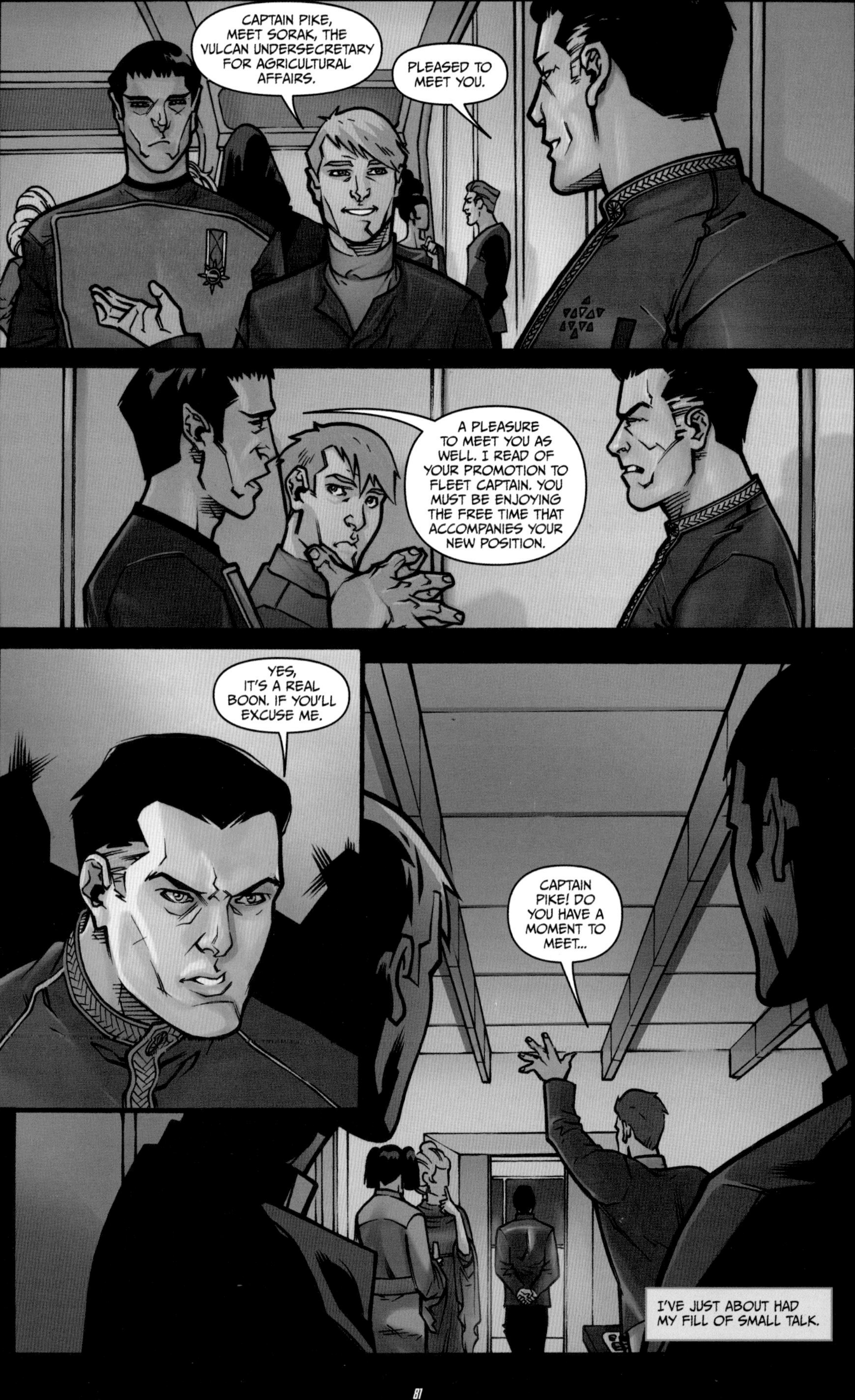
CAPTAIN PIKE, MEET SORAK, THE VULCAN UNDERSECRETARY FOR AGRICULTURAL AFFAIRS.
PLEASED TO MEET YOU.
A PLEASURE TO MEET YOU AS WELL. I READ OF YOUR PROMOTION TO FLEET CAPTAIN. YOU MUST BE ENJOYING THE FREE TIME THAT ACCOMPANIES YOUR NEW POSITION.
YES, IT'S A REAL BOON. IF YOU'LL EXCUSE ME.
CAPTAIN PIKE! DO YOU HAVE A MOMENT TO MEET...
I'VE JUST ABOUT HAD MY FILL OF SMALL TALK.

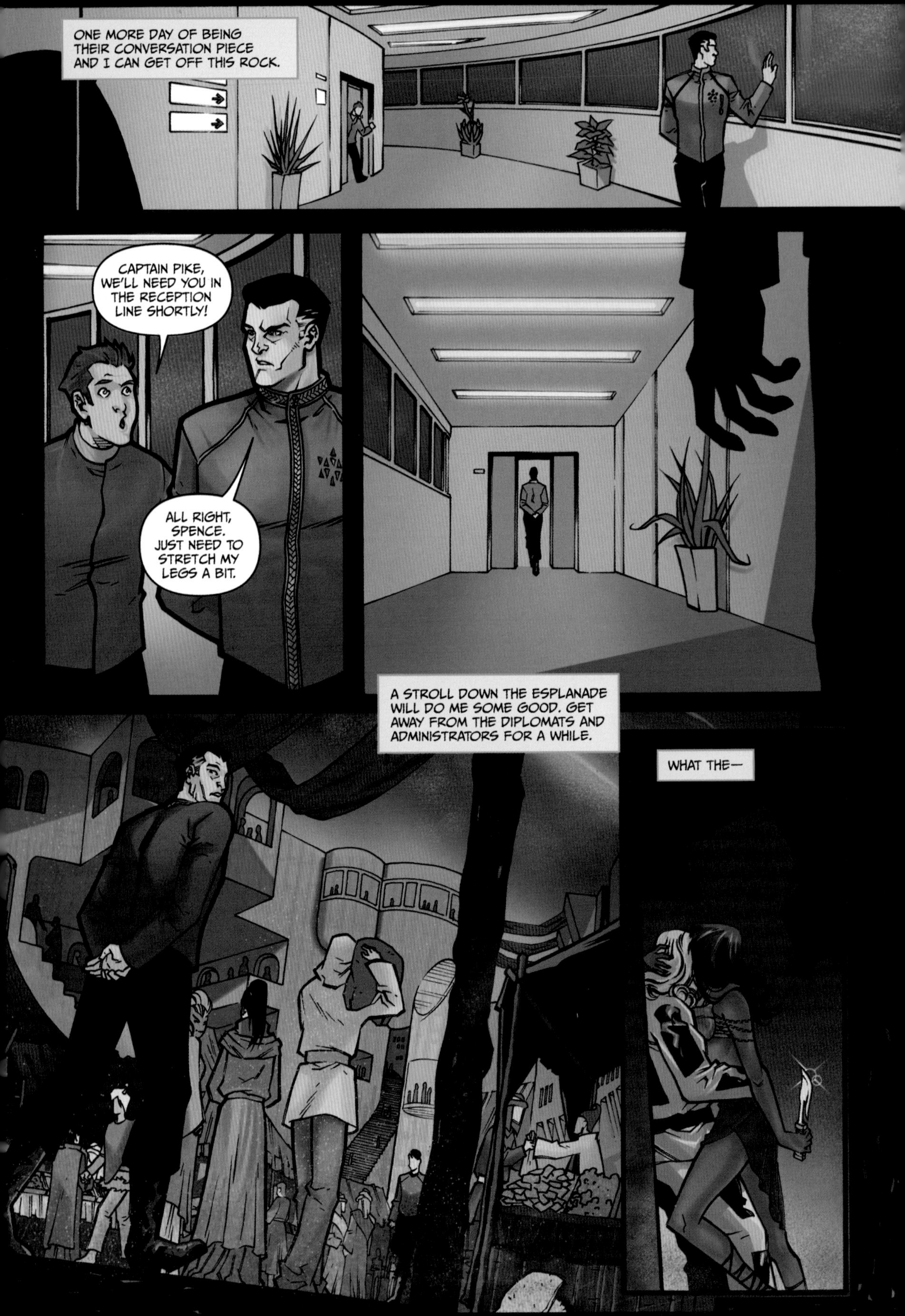
ONE MORE DAY OF BEING THEIR CONVERSATION PIECE AND I CAN GET OFF THIS ROCK.
CAPTAIN PIKE, WE'LL NEED YOU IN THE RECEPTION LINE SHORTLY!
ALL RIGHT, SPENCE. JUST NEED TO STRETCH MY LEGS A BIT.
A STROLL DOWN THE ESPLANADE WILL DO ME SOME GOOD. GET AWAY FROM THE DIPLOMATS AND ADMINISTRATORS FOR A WHILE.
WHAT THE—

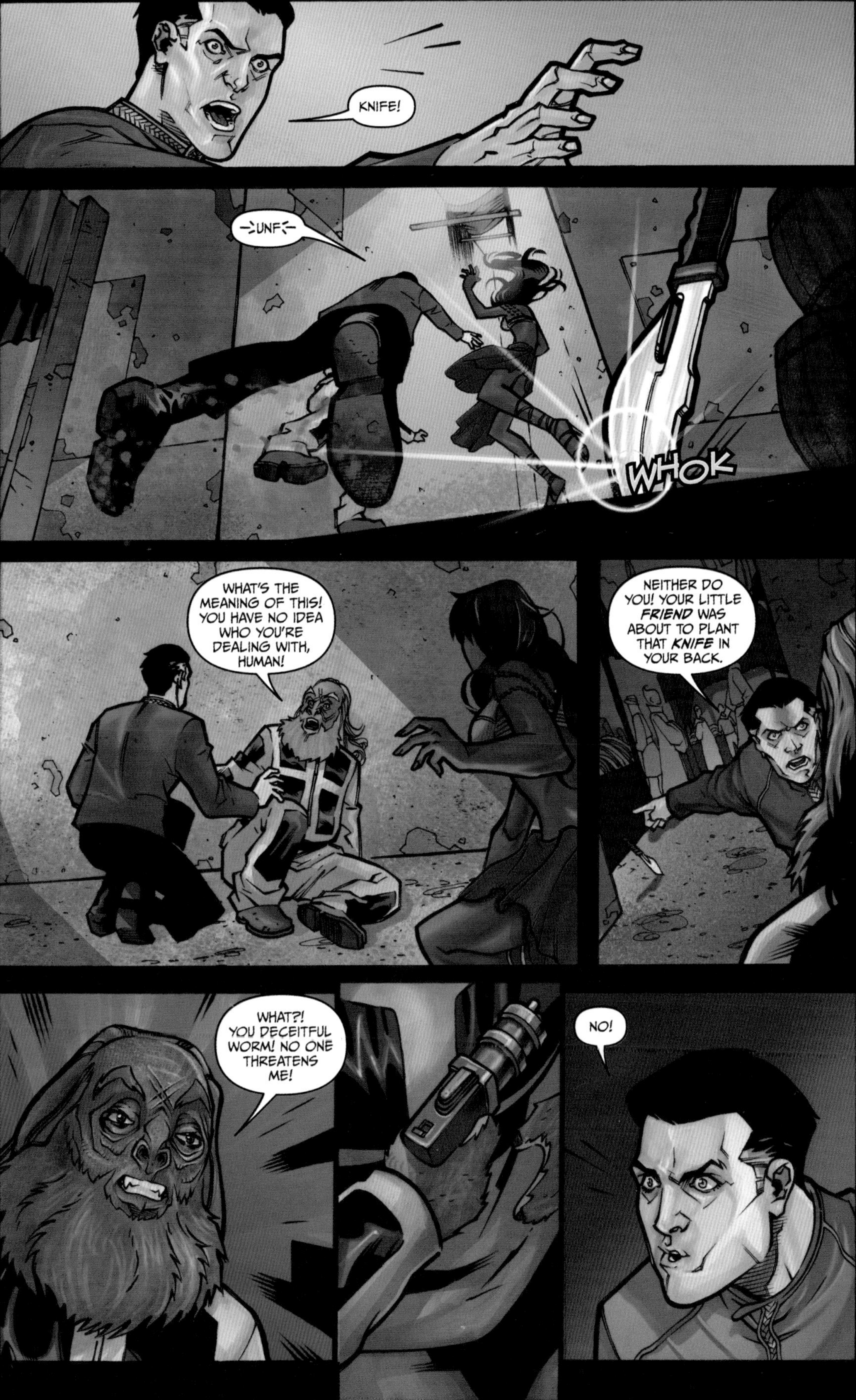
KNIFE!
UNF
WHOK
WHAT'S THE MEANING OF THIS! YOU HAVE NO IDEA WHO YOU'RE DEALING WITH, HUMAN!
NEITHER DO YOU! YOUR LITTLE FRIEND WAS ABOUT TO PLANT THAT KNIFE IN YOUR BACK.
WHAT?! YOU DECEITFUL WORM! NO ONE THREATENS ME!
NO!

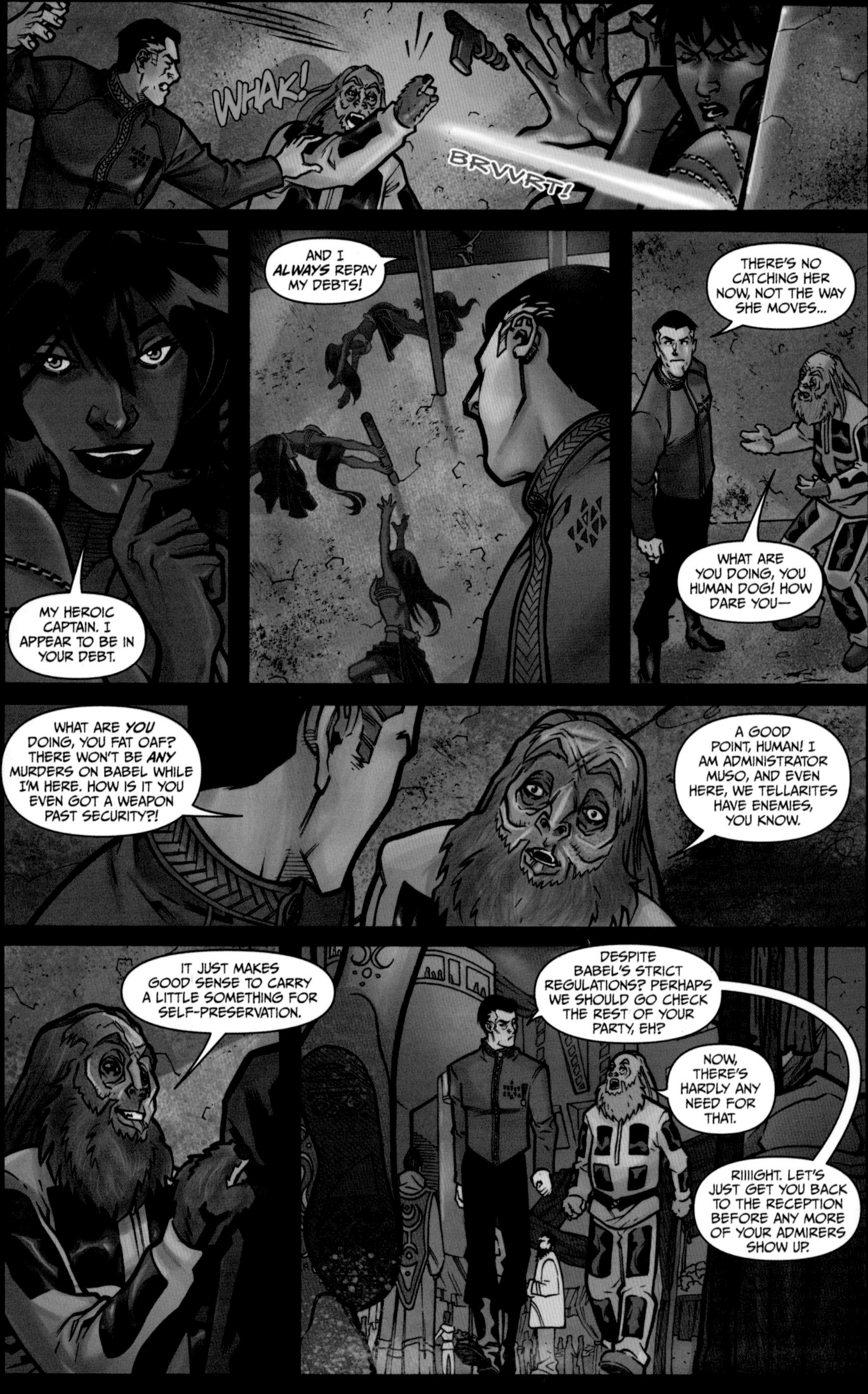
WHAK!
BRVVRT!
MY HEROIC CAPTAIN. I APPEAR TO BE IN YOUR DEBT.
AND I *ALWAYS* REPAY MY DEBTS!
THERE'S NO CATCHING HER NOW, NOT THE WAY SHE MOVES...
WHAT ARE YOU DOING, YOU HUMAN DOG! HOW DARE YOU—
WHAT ARE *YOU* DOING, YOU FAT OAF? THERE WON'T BE *ANY* MURDERS ON BABEL WHILE I'M HERE. HOW IS IT YOU EVEN GOT A WEAPON PAST SECURITY?!
A GOOD POINT, HUMAN! I AM ADMINISTRATOR MUSO, AND EVEN HERE, WE TELLARITES HAVE ENEMIES, YOU KNOW.
IT JUST MAKES GOOD SENSE TO CARRY A LITTLE SOMETHING FOR SELF-PRESERVATION.
DESPITE BABEL'S STRICT REGULATIONS? PERHAPS WE SHOULD GO CHECK THE REST OF YOUR PARTY, EH?
NOW, THERE'S HARDLY ANY NEED FOR THAT.
RIIIIGHT. LET'S JUST GET YOU BACK TO THE RECEPTION BEFORE ANY MORE OF YOUR ADMIRERS SHOW UP.

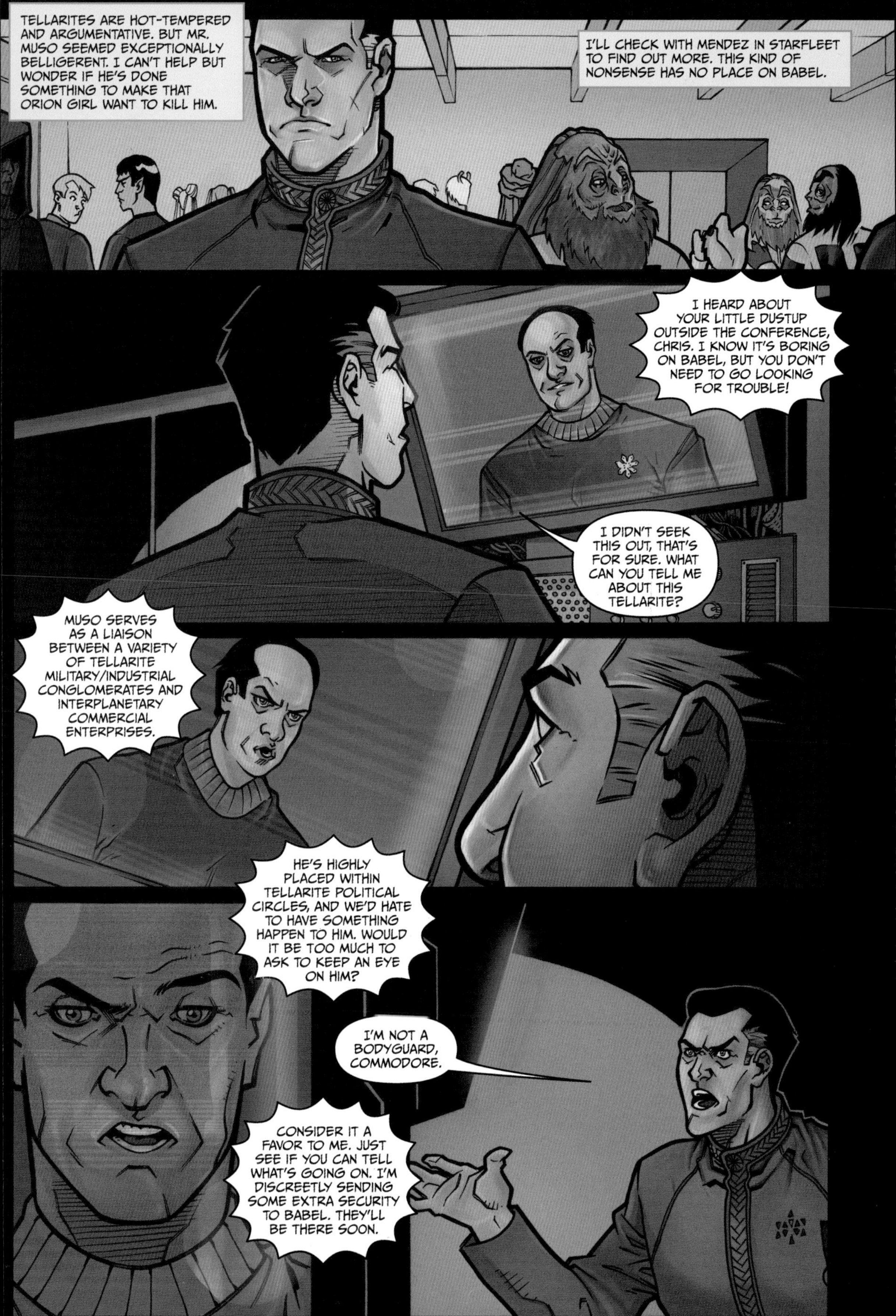
TELLARITES ARE HOT-TEMPERED AND ARGUMENTATIVE. BUT MR. MUSO SEEMED EXCEPTIONALLY BELLIGERENT. I CAN'T HELP BUT WONDER IF HE'S DONE SOMETHING TO MAKE THAT ORION GIRL WANT TO KILL HIM.
I'LL CHECK WITH MENDEZ IN STARFLEET TO FIND OUT MORE. THIS KIND OF NONSENSE HAS NO PLACE ON BABEL.
I HEARD ABOUT YOUR LITTLE DUSTUP OUTSIDE THE CONFERENCE, CHRIS. I KNOW IT'S BORING ON BABEL, BUT YOU DON'T NEED TO GO LOOKING FOR TROUBLE!
I DIDN'T SEEK THIS OUT, THAT'S FOR SURE. WHAT CAN YOU TELL ME ABOUT THIS TELLARITE?
MUSO SERVES AS A LIAISON BETWEEN A VARIETY OF TELLARITE MILITARY/INDUSTRIAL CONGLOMERATES AND INTERPLANETARY COMMERCIAL ENTERPRISES.
HE'S HIGHLY PLACED WITHIN TELLARITE POLITICAL CIRCLES, AND WE'D HATE TO HAVE SOMETHING HAPPEN TO HIM. WOULD IT BE TOO MUCH TO ASK TO KEEP AN EYE ON HIM?
I'M NOT A BODYGUARD, COMMODORE.
CONSIDER IT A FAVOR TO ME. JUST SEE IF YOU CAN TELL WHAT'S GOING ON. I'M DISCREETLY SENDING SOME EXTRA SECURITY TO BABEL. THEY'LL BE THERE SOON.

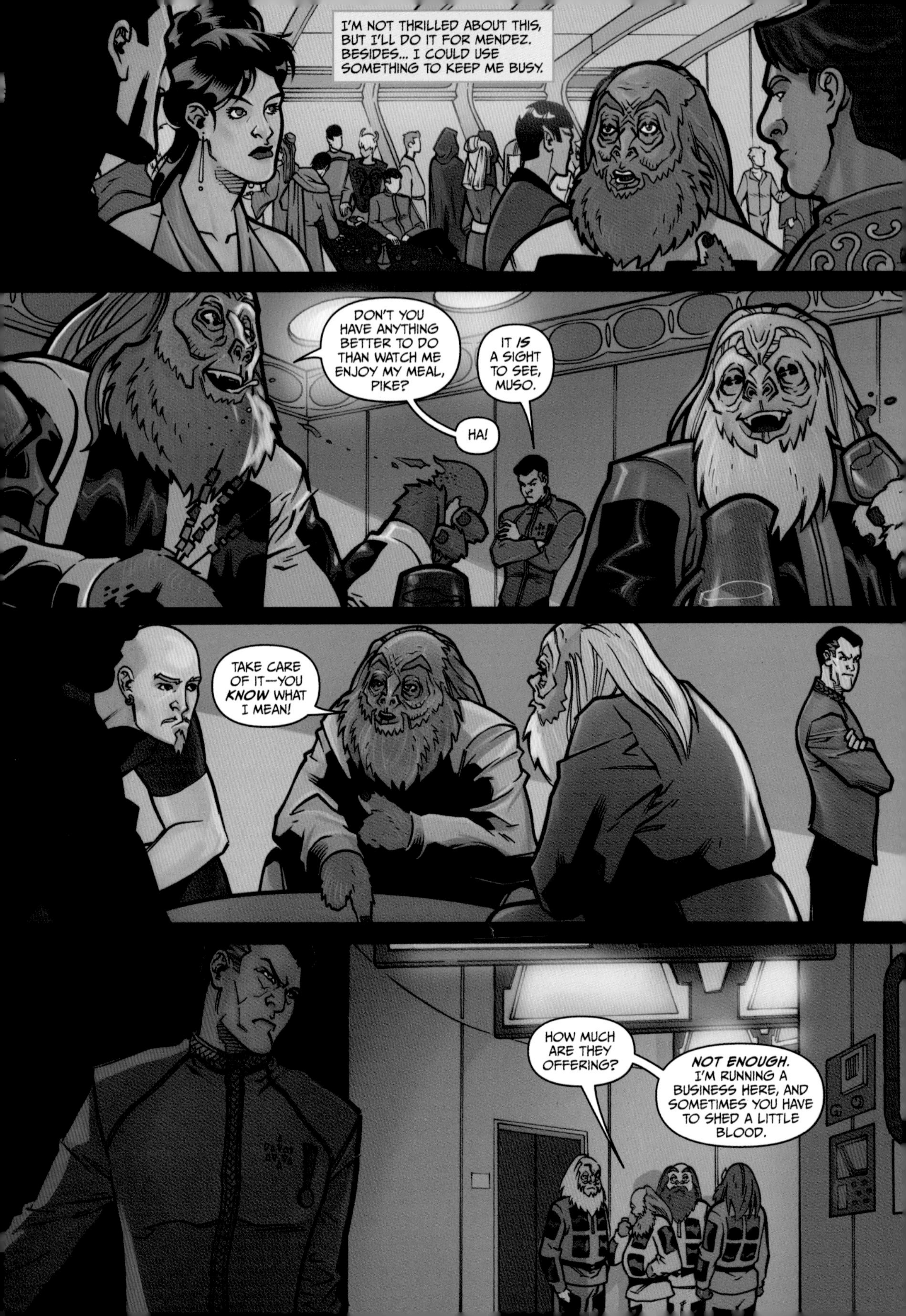
I'M NOT THRILLED ABOUT THIS, BUT I'LL DO IT FOR MENDEZ. BESIDES... I COULD USE SOMETHING TO KEEP ME BUSY.
DON'T YOU HAVE ANYTHING BETTER TO DO THAN WATCH ME ENJOY MY MEAL, PIKE?
HA!
IT *IS* A SIGHT TO SEE, MUSO.
TAKE CARE OF IT—YOU ***KNOW*** WHAT I MEAN!
HOW MUCH ARE THEY OFFERING?
NOT ENOUGH. I'M RUNNING A BUSINESS HERE, AND SOMETIMES YOU HAVE TO SHED A LITTLE BLOOD.

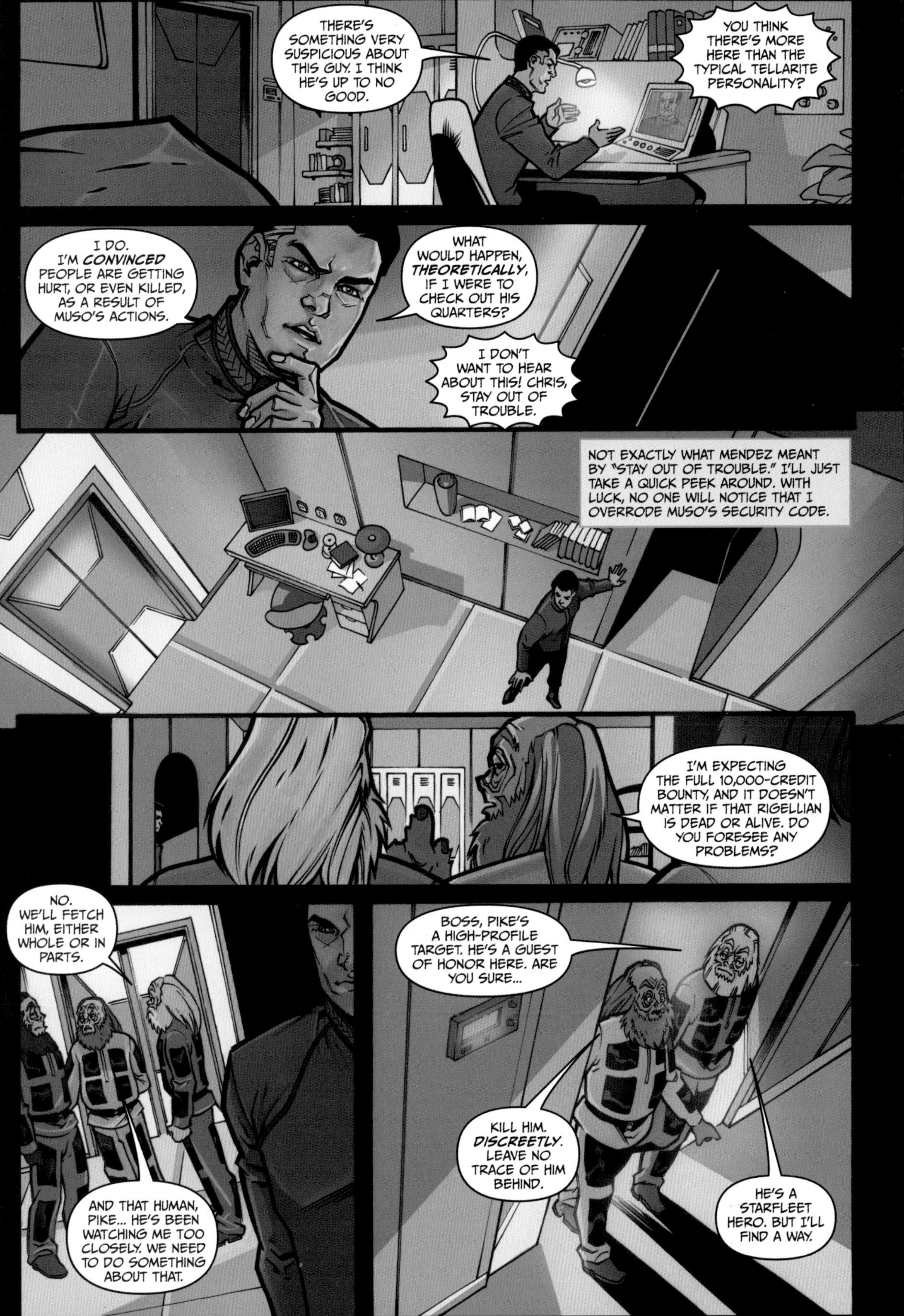
THERE'S SOMETHING VERY SUSPICIOUS ABOUT THIS GUY. I THINK HE'S UP TO NO GOOD.
YOU THINK THERE'S MORE HERE THAN THE TYPICAL TELLARITE PERSONALITY?
I DO. I'M *CONVINCED* PEOPLE ARE GETTING HURT, OR EVEN KILLED, AS A RESULT OF MUSO'S ACTIONS.
WHAT WOULD HAPPEN, *THEORETICALLY*, IF I WERE TO CHECK OUT HIS QUARTERS?
I DON'T WANT TO HEAR ABOUT THIS! CHRIS, STAY OUT OF TROUBLE.
NOT EXACTLY WHAT MENDEZ MEANT BY "STAY OUT OF TROUBLE." I'LL JUST TAKE A QUICK PEEK AROUND. WITH LUCK, NO ONE WILL NOTICE THAT I OVERRODE MUSO'S SECURITY CODE.
I'M EXPECTING THE FULL 10,000-CREDIT BOUNTY, AND IT DOESN'T MATTER IF THAT RIGELLIAN IS DEAD OR ALIVE. DO YOU FORESEE ANY PROBLEMS?
NO. WE'LL FETCH HIM, EITHER WHOLE OR IN PARTS.
AND THAT HUMAN, PIKE... HE'S BEEN WATCHING ME TOO CLOSELY. WE NEED TO DO SOMETHING ABOUT THAT.
BOSS, PIKE'S A HIGH-PROFILE TARGET. HE'S A GUEST OF HONOR HERE. ARE YOU SURE...
KILL HIM. *DISCREETLY*. LEAVE NO TRACE OF HIM BEHIND.
HE'S A STARFLEET HERO. BUT I'LL FIND A WAY.

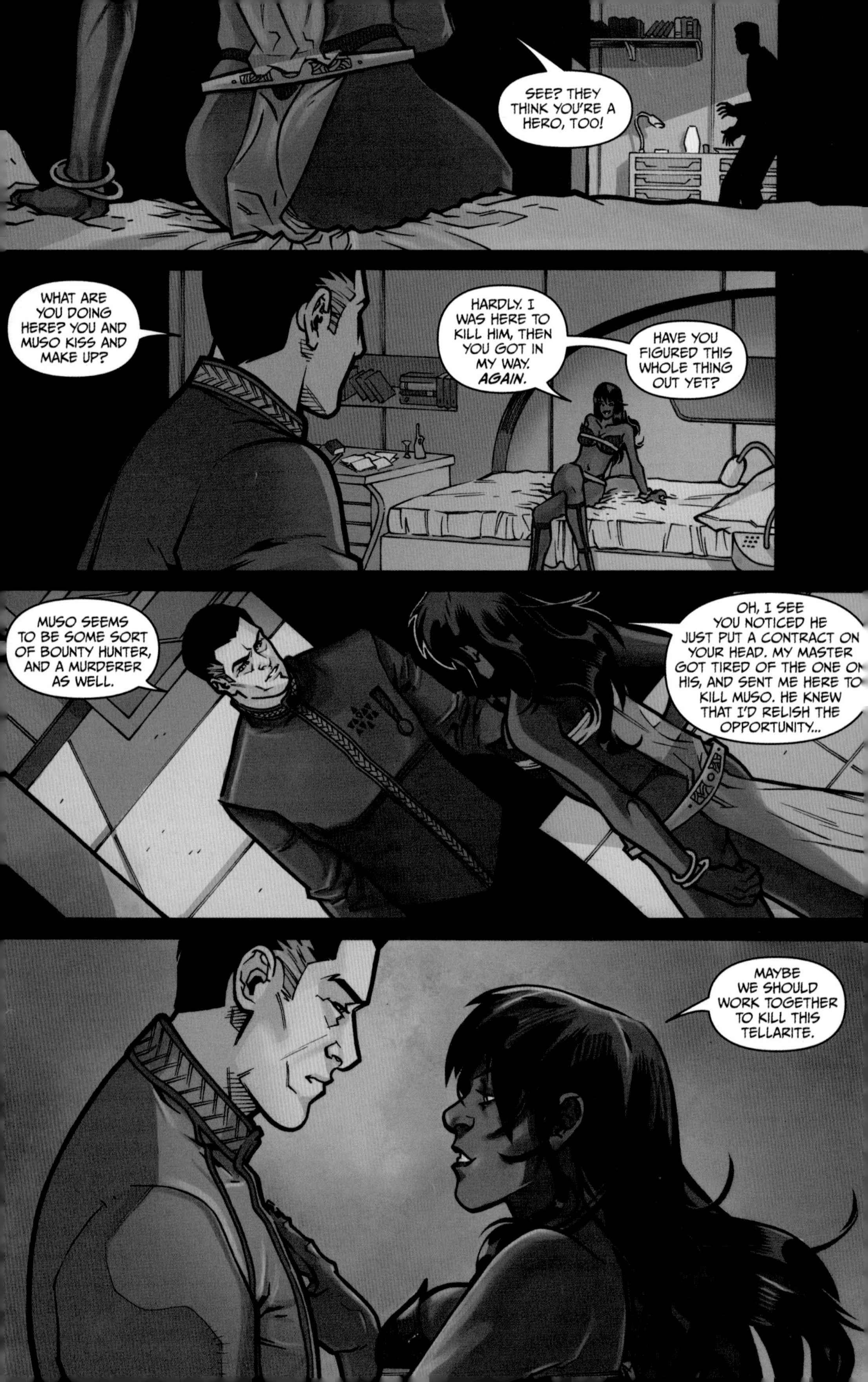
SEE? THEY THINK YOU'RE A HERO, TOO!
WHAT ARE YOU DOING HERE? YOU AND MUSO KISS AND MAKE UP?
HARDLY. I WAS HERE TO KILL HIM, THEN YOU GOT IN MY WAY. *AGAIN.*
HAVE YOU FIGURED THIS WHOLE THING OUT YET?
MUSO SEEMS TO BE SOME SORT OF BOUNTY HUNTER, AND A MURDERER AS WELL.
OH, I SEE YOU NOTICED HE JUST PUT A CONTRACT ON YOUR HEAD. MY MASTER GOT TIRED OF THE ONE ON HIS, AND SENT ME HERE TO KILL MUSO. HE KNEW THAT I'D RELISH THE OPPORTUNITY...
MAYBE WE SHOULD WORK TOGETHER TO KILL THIS TELLARITE.

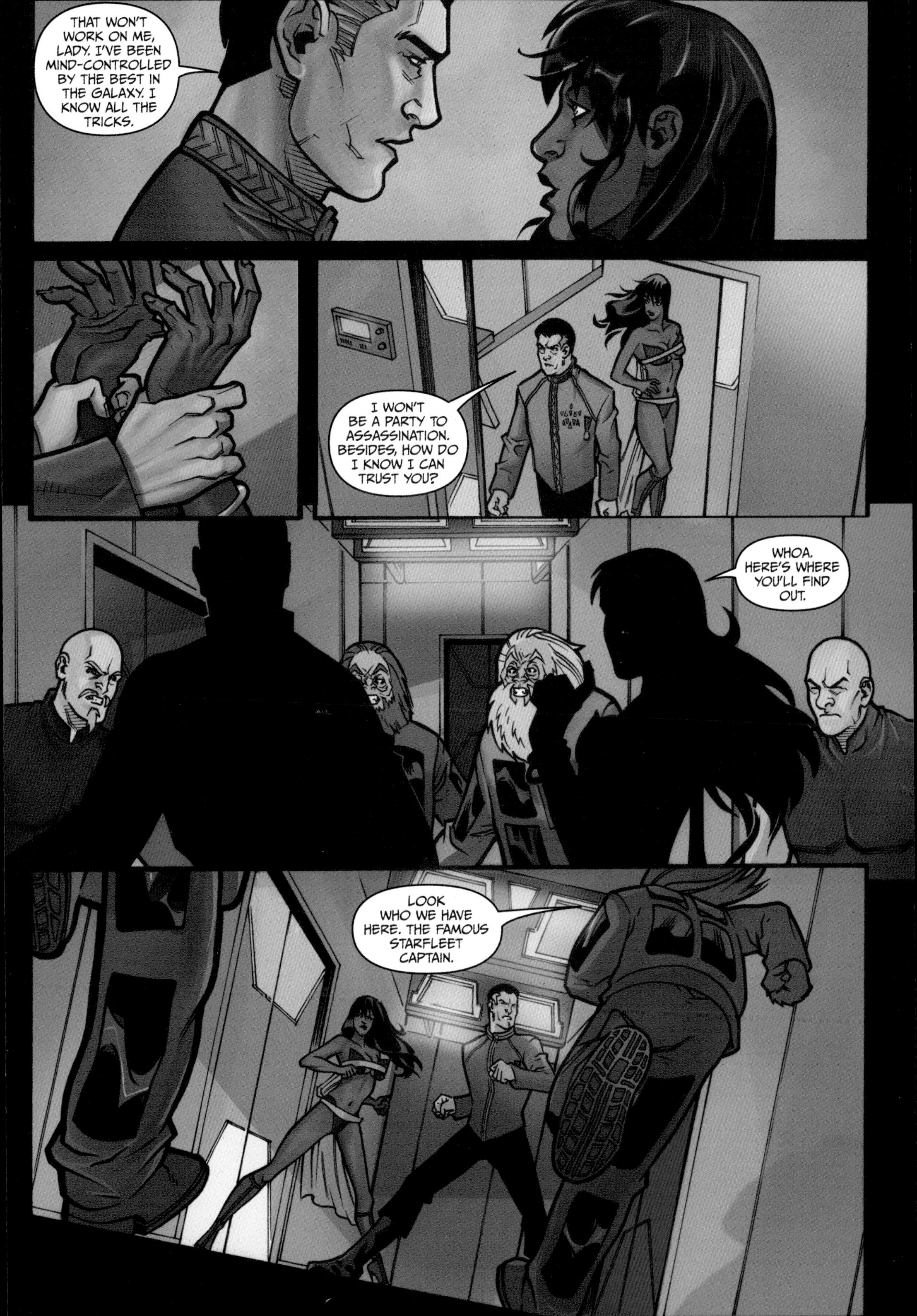
THAT WON'T WORK ON ME, LADY. I'VE BEEN MIND-CONTROLLED BY THE BEST IN THE GALAXY. I KNOW ALL THE TRICKS.
I WON'T BE A PARTY TO ASSASSINATION. BESIDES, HOW DO I KNOW I CAN TRUST YOU?
WHOA. HERE'S WHERE YOU'LL FIND OUT.
LOOK WHO WE HAVE HERE. THE FAMOUS STARFLEET CAPTAIN.

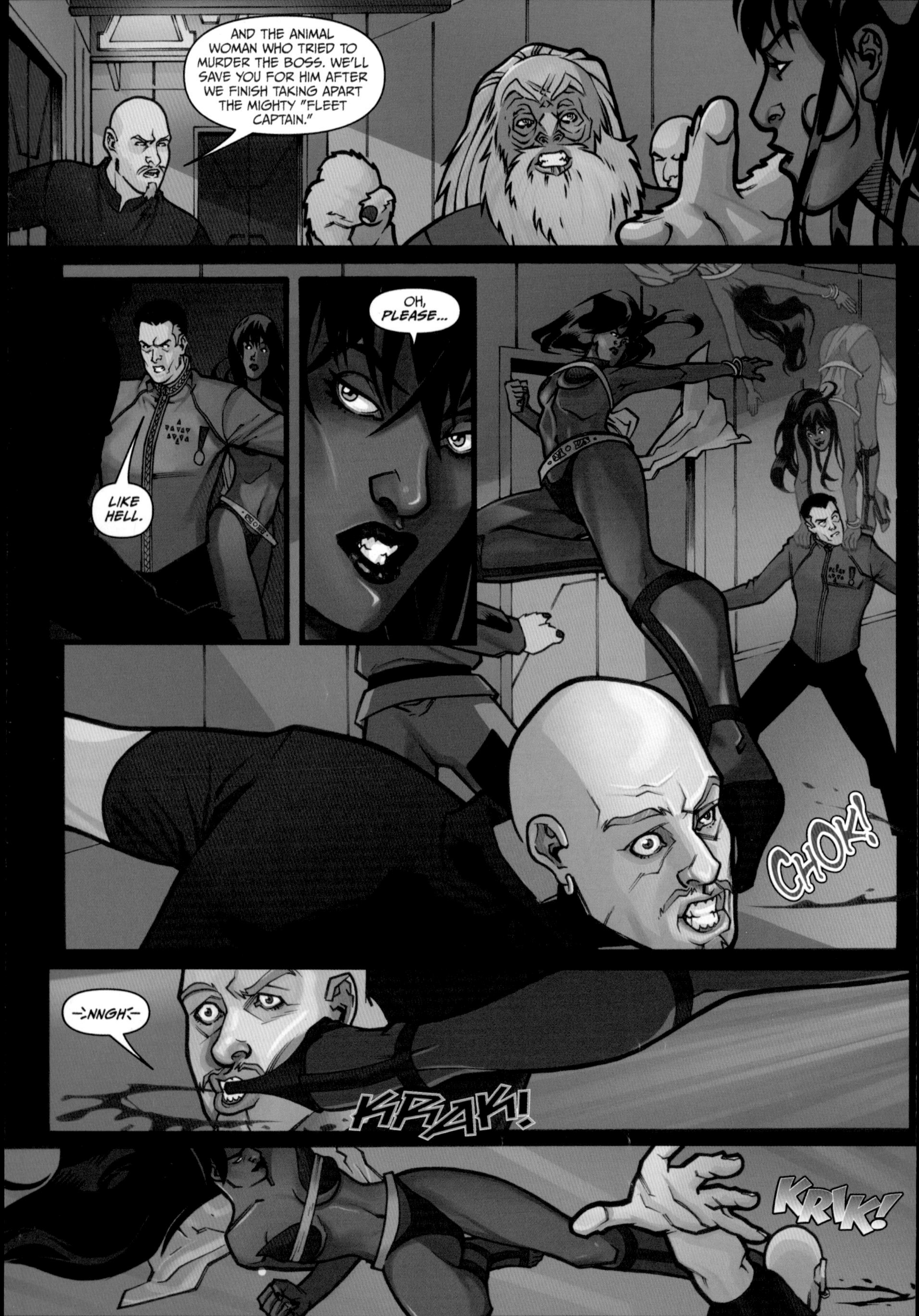
AND THE ANIMAL WOMAN WHO TRIED TO MURDER THE BOSS. WE'LL SAVE YOU FOR HIM AFTER WE FINISH TAKING APART THE MIGHTY "FLEET CAPTAIN."
LIKE HELL.
OH, PLEASE...
CHOK!
-NNGH-
KRAK!
KRIK!

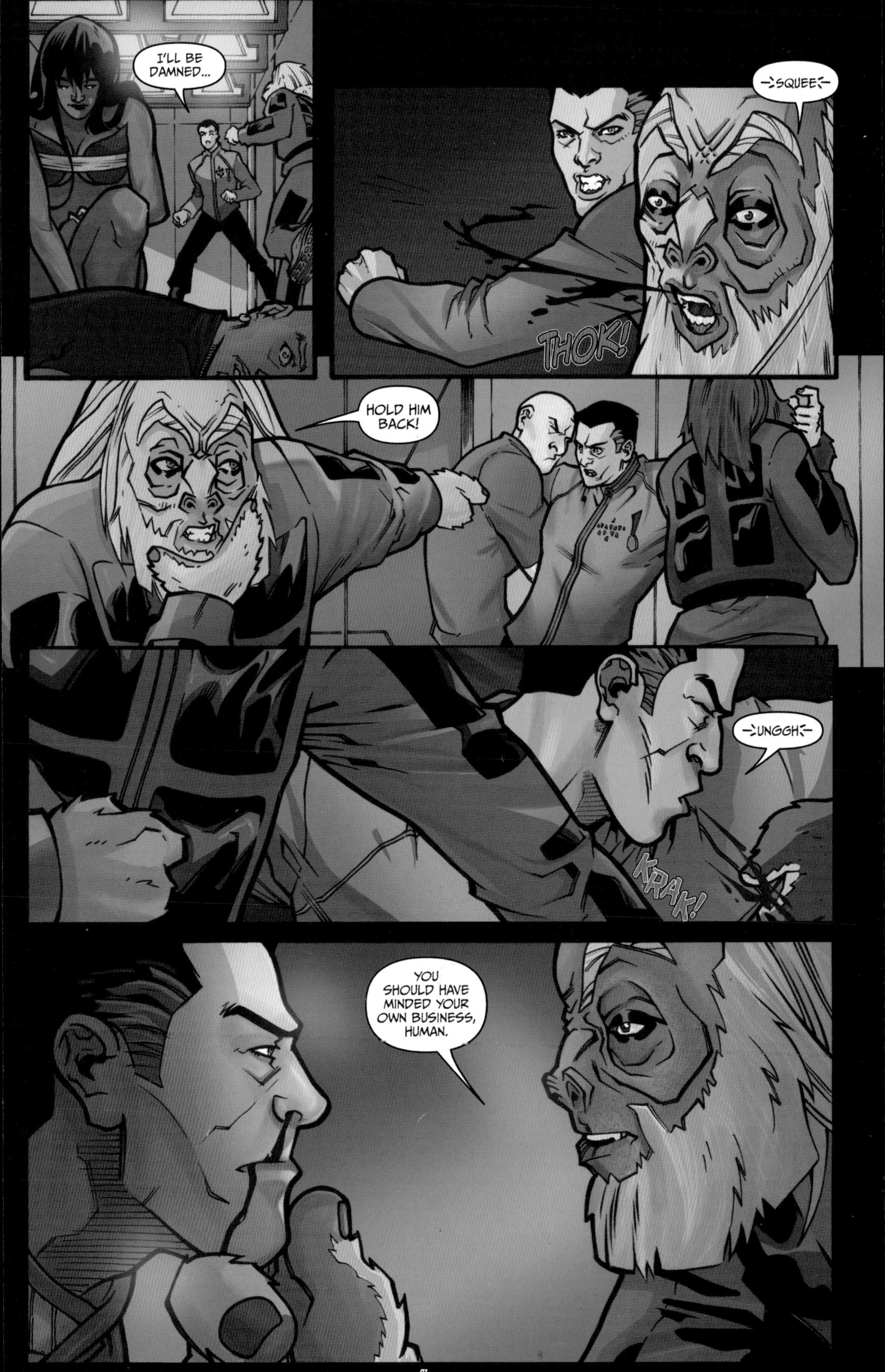
I'LL BE DAMNED...
-SQUEE-
THOK!
HOLD HIM BACK!
-UNGGH-
KRAK!
YOU SHOULD HAVE MINDED YOUR OWN BUSINESS, HUMAN.

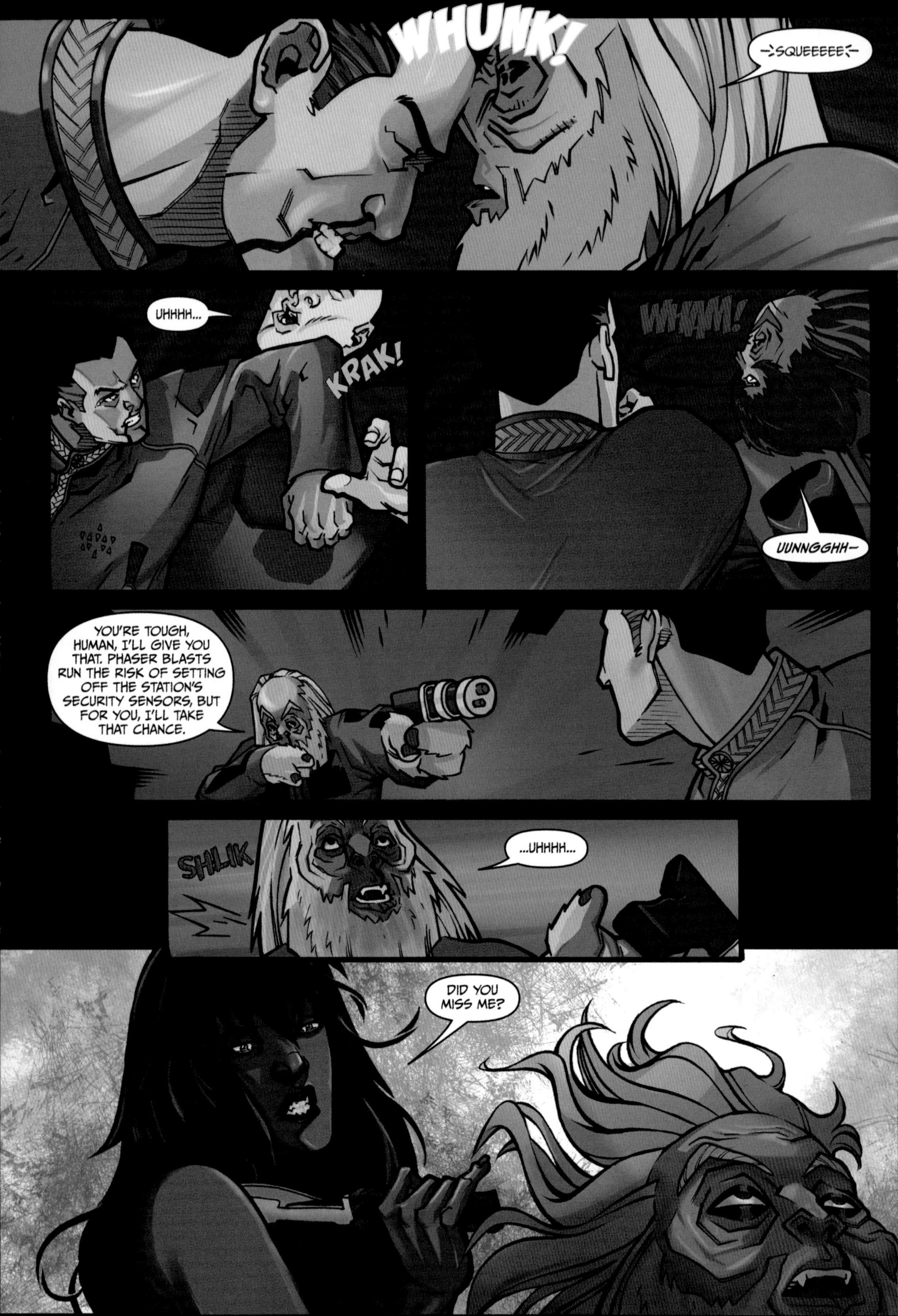
WHUNK!
-SQUEEEEEE-
UHHHH...
KRAK!
WHAM!
UUNNGGHH—
YOU'RE TOUGH, HUMAN, I'LL GIVE YOU THAT. PHASER BLASTS RUN THE RISK OF SETTING OFF THE STATION'S SECURITY SENSORS, BUT FOR YOU, I'LL TAKE THAT CHANCE.
SHLIK
...UHHHH...
DID YOU MISS ME?

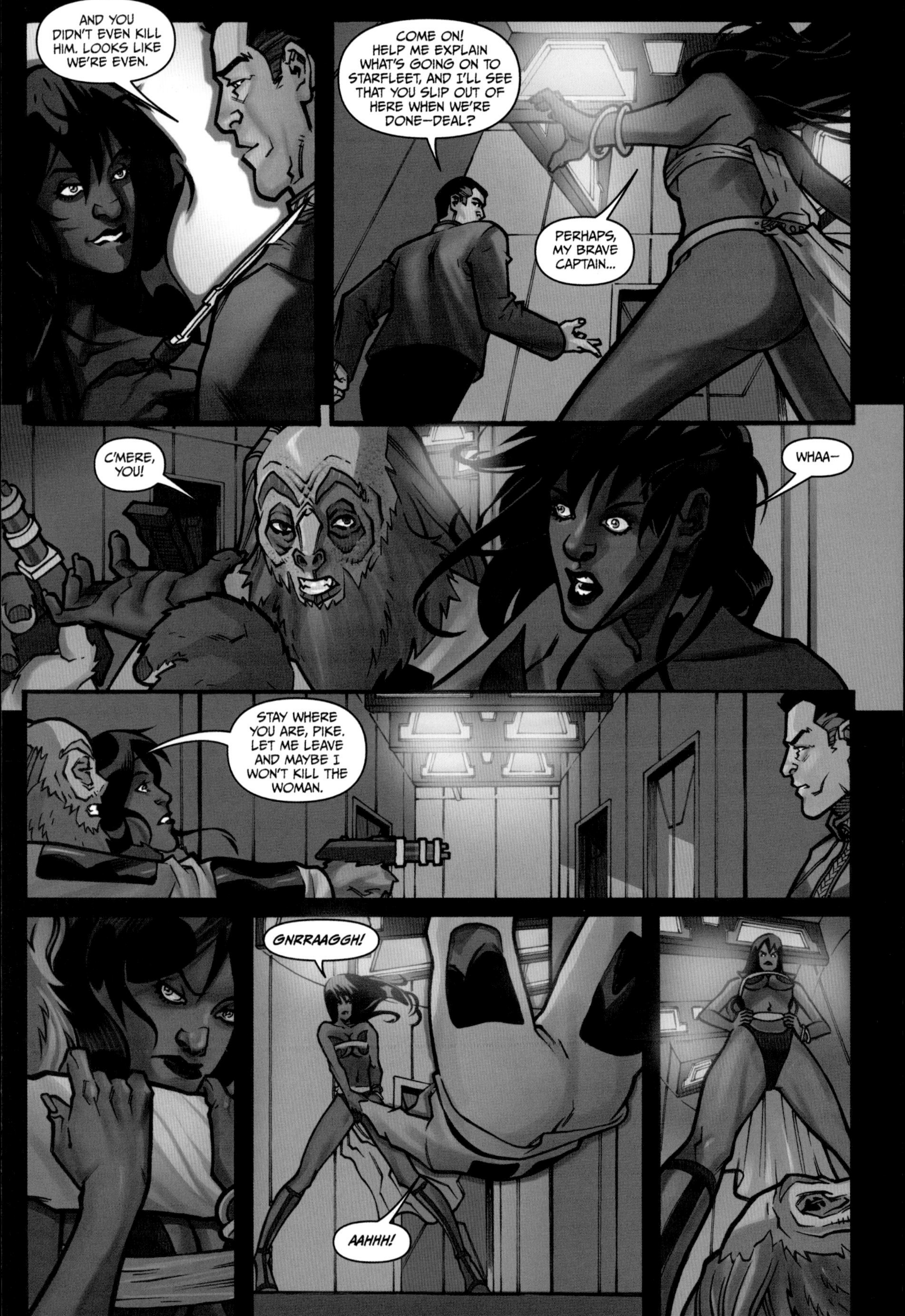
AND YOU DIDN'T EVEN KILL HIM. LOOKS LIKE WE'RE EVEN.
COME ON! HELP ME EXPLAIN WHAT'S GOING ON TO STARFLEET, AND I'LL SEE THAT YOU SLIP OUT OF HERE WHEN WE'RE DONE—DEAL?
PERHAPS, MY BRAVE CAPTAIN...
C'MERE, YOU!
WHAA—
STAY WHERE YOU ARE, PIKE. LET ME LEAVE AND MAYBE I WON'T KILL THE WOMAN.
GNRRAAGGH!
AAHHH!

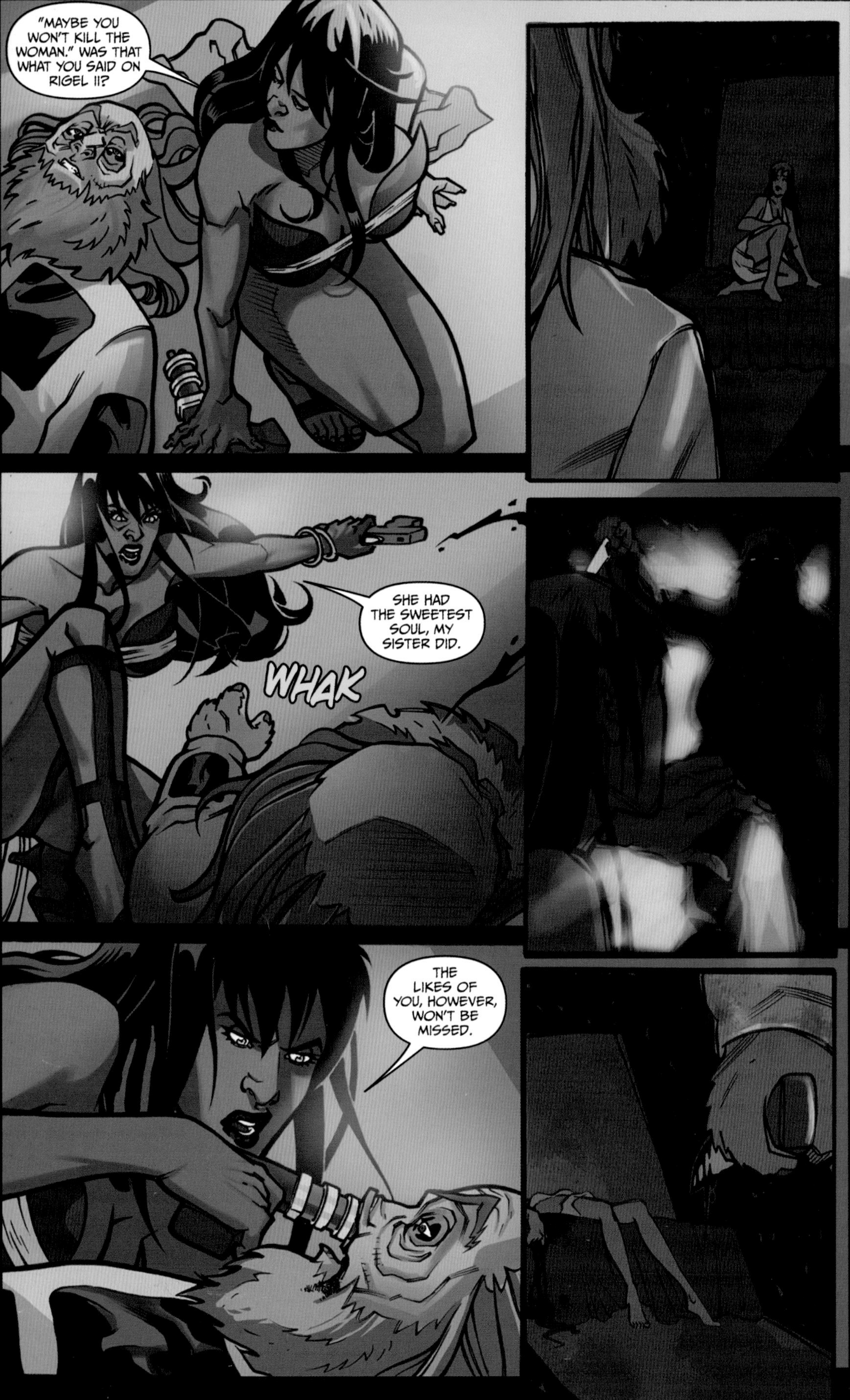
"MAYBE YOU WON'T KILL THE WOMAN." WAS THAT WHAT YOU SAID ON RIGEL II?
SHE HAD THE SWEETEST SOUL, MY SISTER DID.
WHAK
THE LIKES OF YOU, HOWEVER, WON'T BE MISSED.

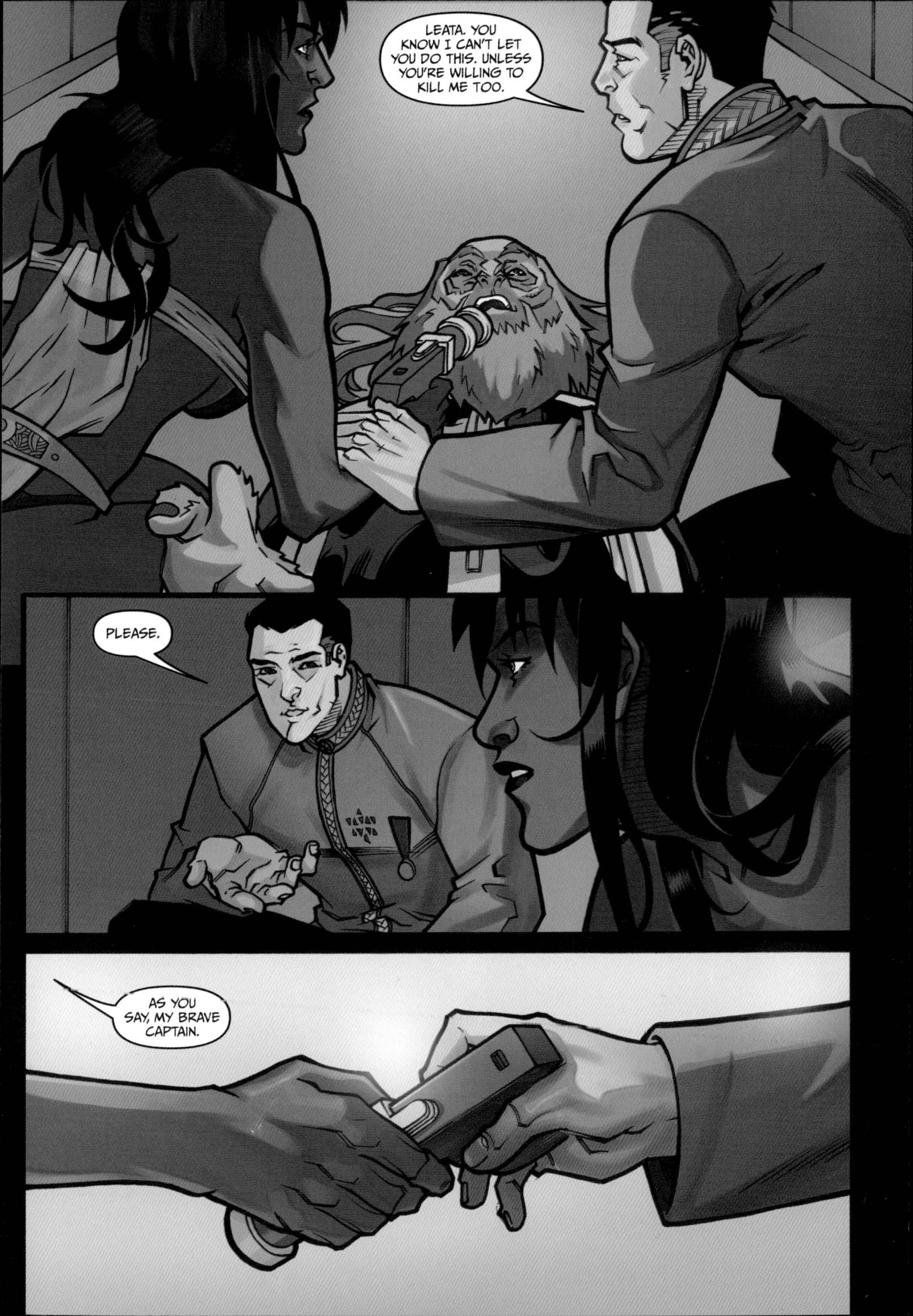
LEATA. YOU KNOW I CAN'T LET YOU DO THIS. UNLESS YOU'RE WILLING TO KILL ME TOO.
PLEASE.
AS YOU SAY, MY BRAVE CAPTAIN.

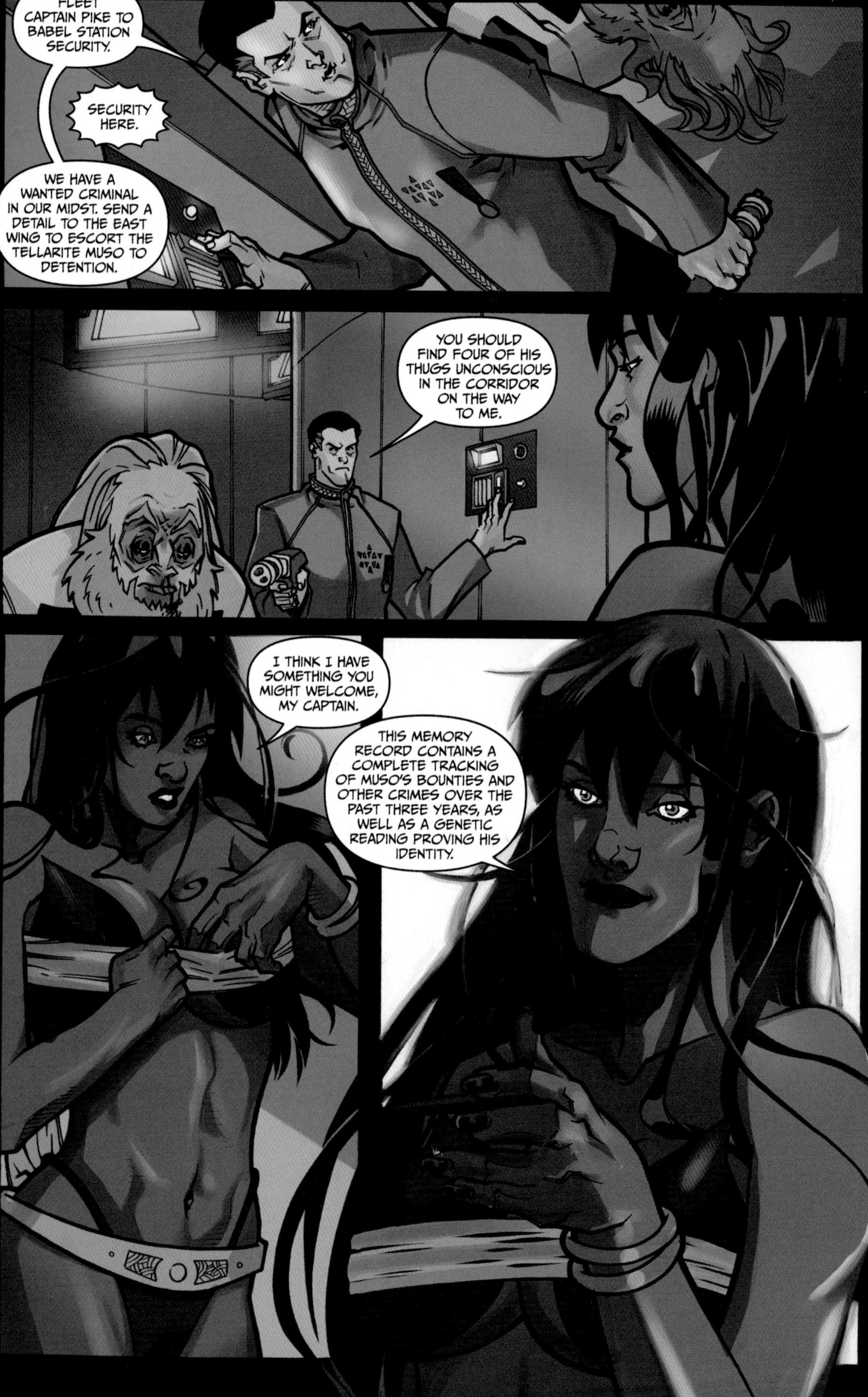
FLEET CAPTAIN PIKE TO BABEL STATION SECURITY.
SECURITY HERE.
WE HAVE A WANTED CRIMINAL IN OUR MIDST. SEND A DETAIL TO THE EAST WING TO ESCORT THE TELLARITE MUSO TO DETENTION.
YOU SHOULD FIND FOUR OF HIS THUGS UNCONSCIOUS IN THE CORRIDOR ON THE WAY TO ME.
I THINK I HAVE SOMETHING YOU MIGHT WELCOME, MY CAPTAIN.
THIS MEMORY RECORD CONTAINS A COMPLETE TRACKING OF MUSO'S BOUNTIES AND OTHER CRIMES OVER THE PAST THREE YEARS, AS WELL AS A GENETIC READING PROVING HIS IDENTITY.

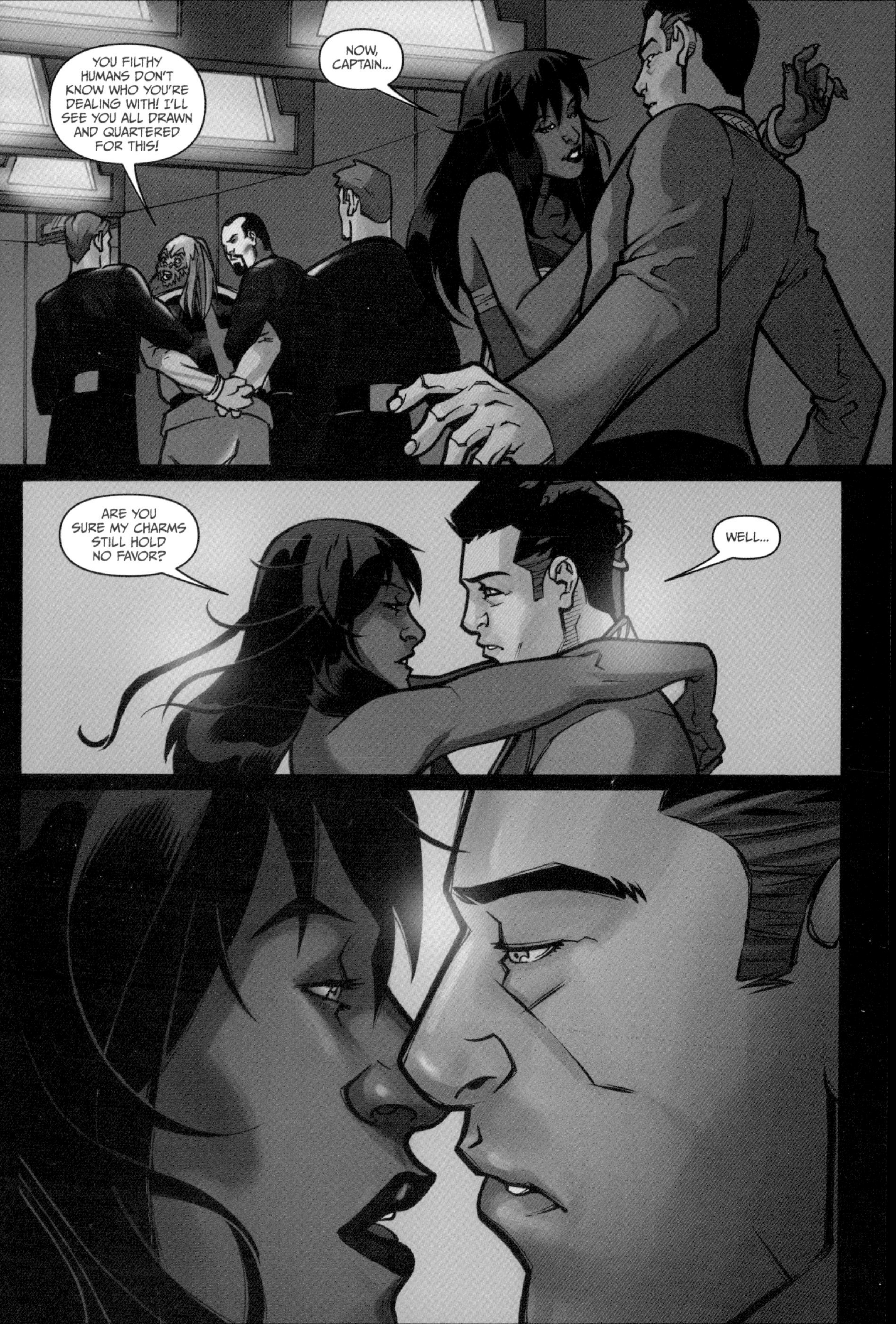
YOU FILTHY HUMANS DON'T KNOW WHO YOU'RE DEALING WITH! I'LL SEE YOU ALL DRAWN AND QUARTERED FOR THIS!
NOW, CAPTAIN...
ARE YOU SURE MY CHARMS STILL HOLD NO FAVOR?
WELL...

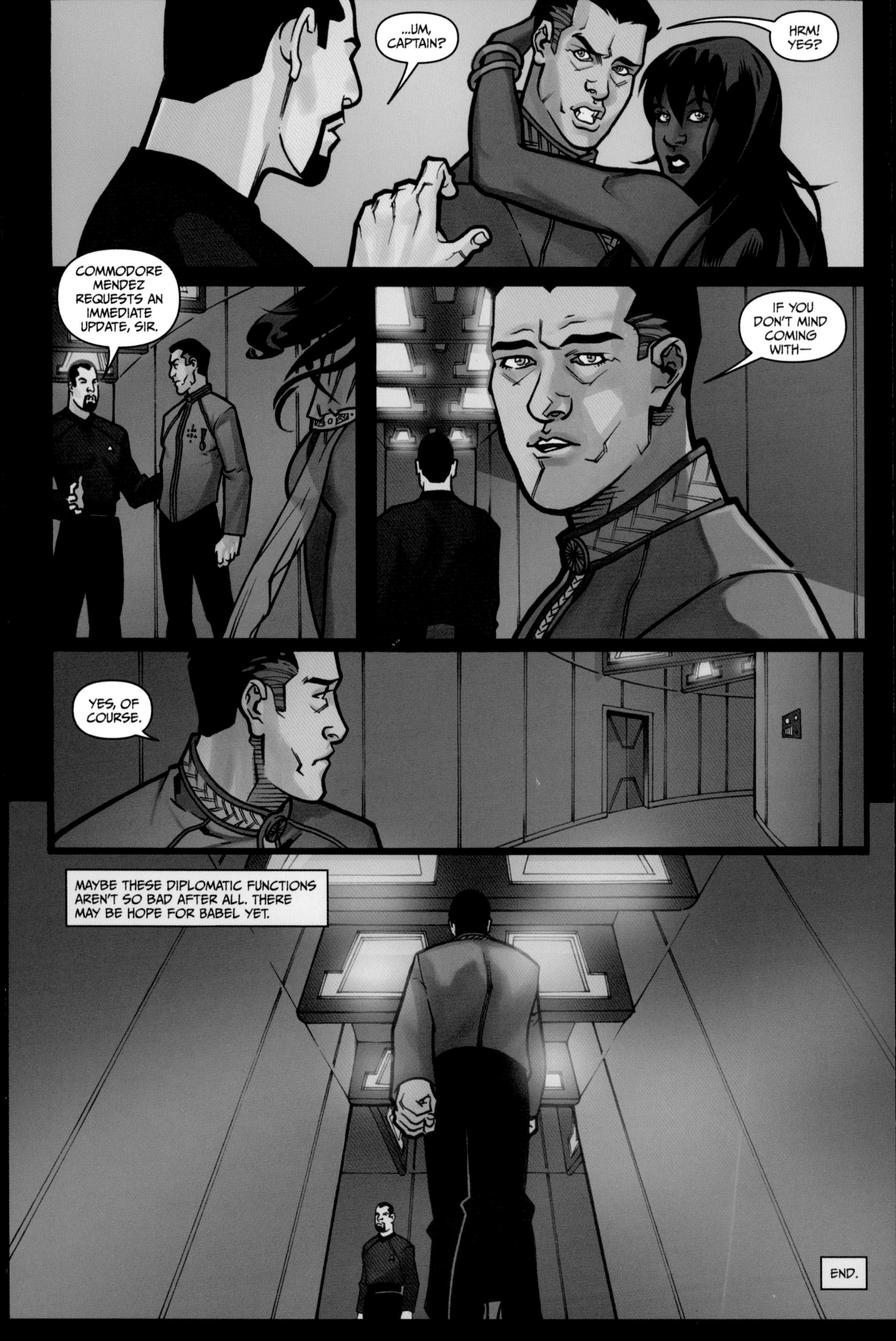
...UM, CAPTAIN?
HRM! YES?
COMMODORE MENDEZ REQUESTS AN IMMEDIATE UPDATE, SIR.
IF YOU DON'T MIND COMING WITH—
YES, OF COURSE.
MAYBE THESE DIPLOMATIC FUNCTIONS AREN'T SO BAD AFTER ALL. THERE MAY BE HOPE FOR BABEL YET.
END.

art and color by Elena Casagrande

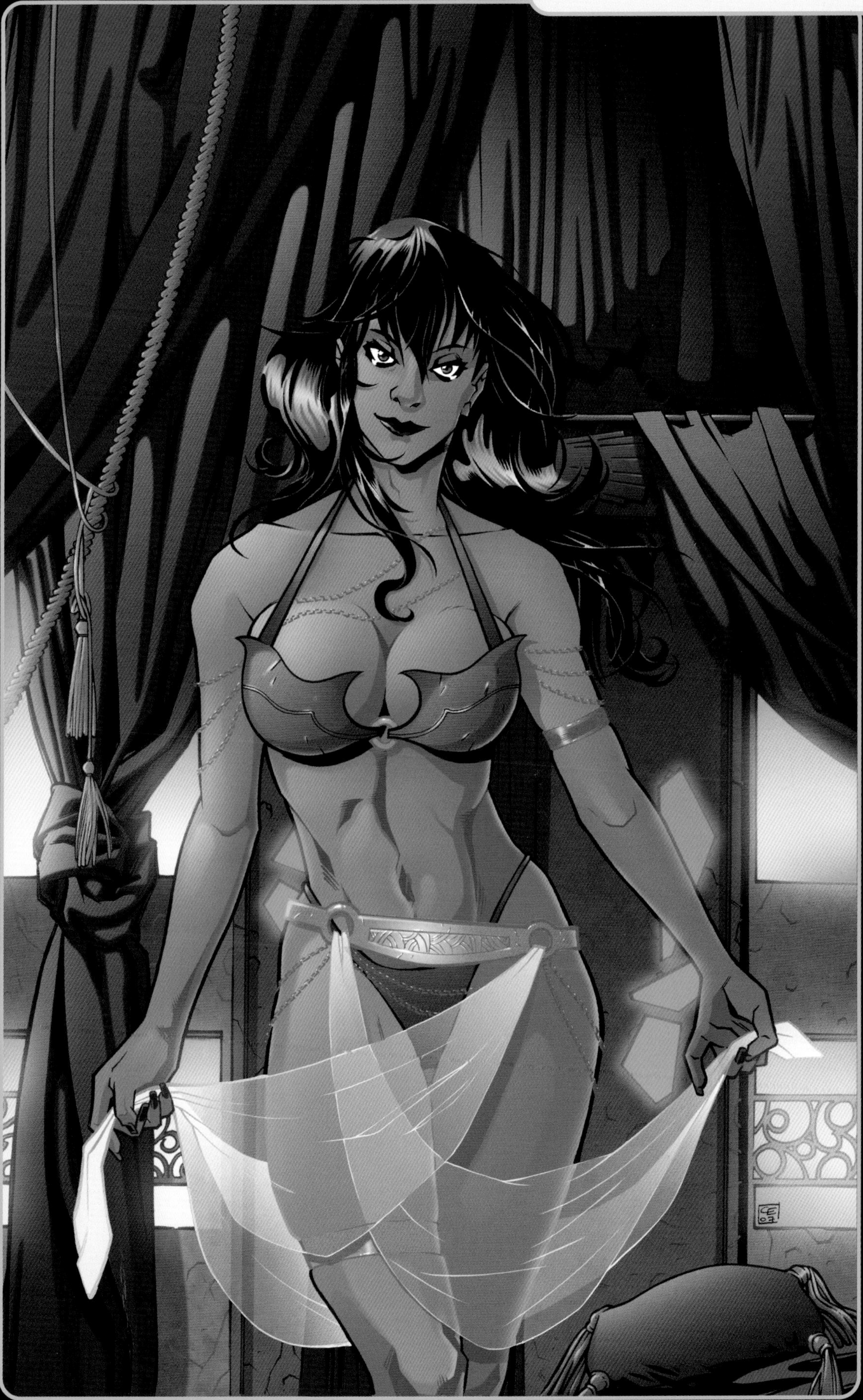

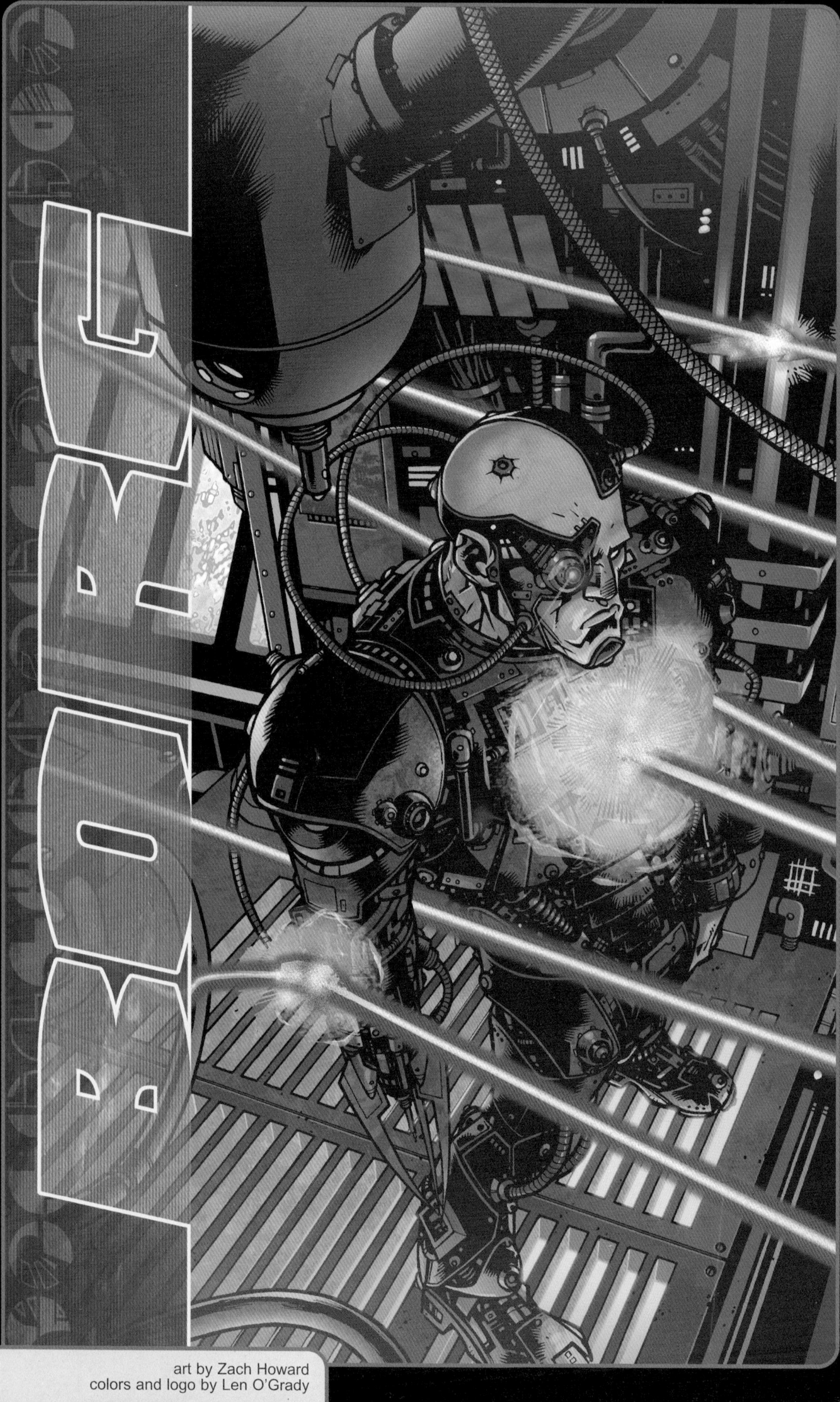
BORG

art by Zach Howard
colors and logo by Len O'Grady

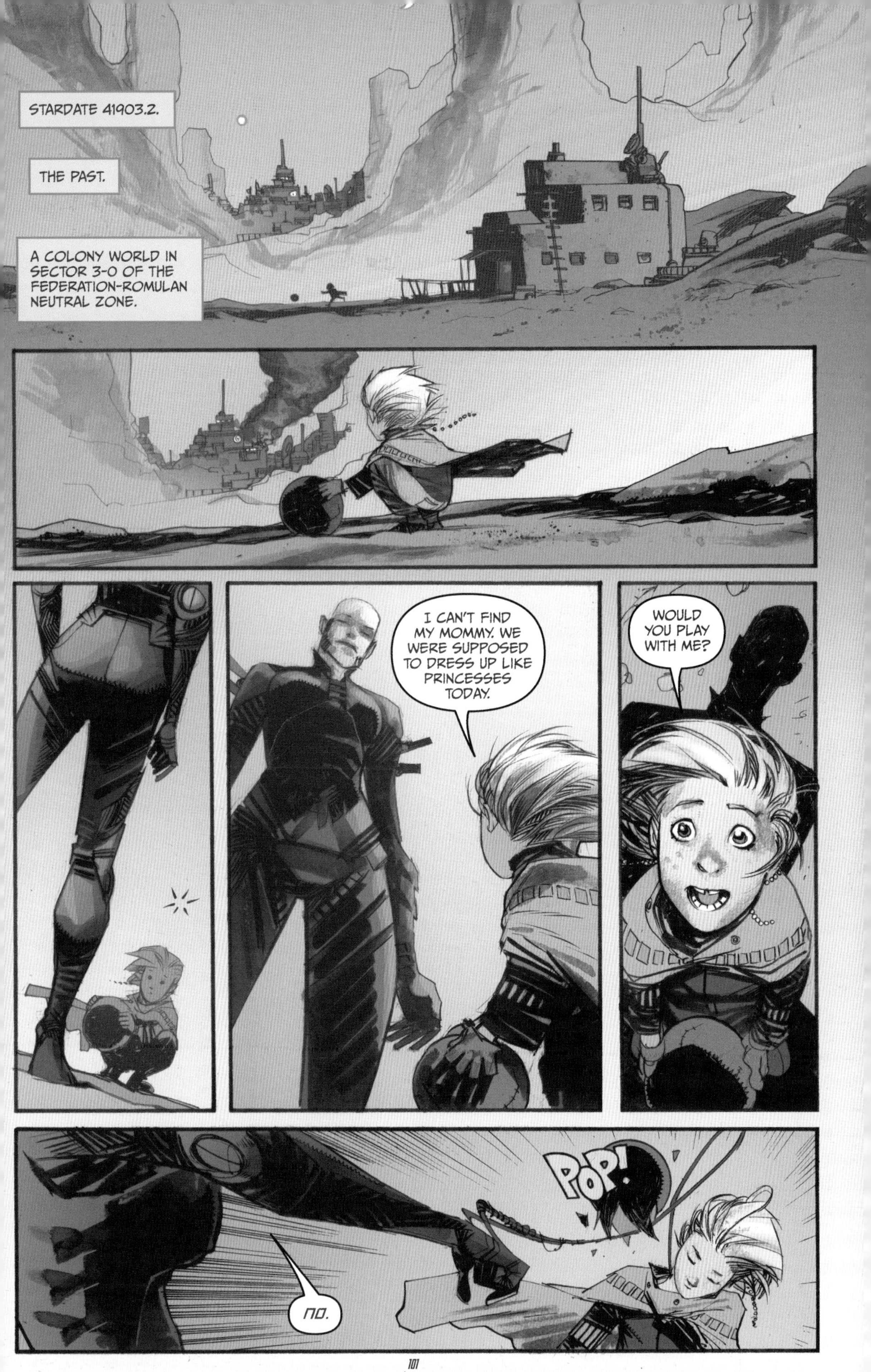
STARDATE 41903.2.
THE PAST.
A COLONY WORLD IN SECTOR 3-0 OF THE FEDERATION-ROMULAN NEUTRAL ZONE.
I CAN'T FIND MY MOMMY. WE WERE SUPPOSED TO DRESS UP LIKE PRINCESSES TODAY.
WOULD YOU PLAY WITH ME?
POP!
NO.

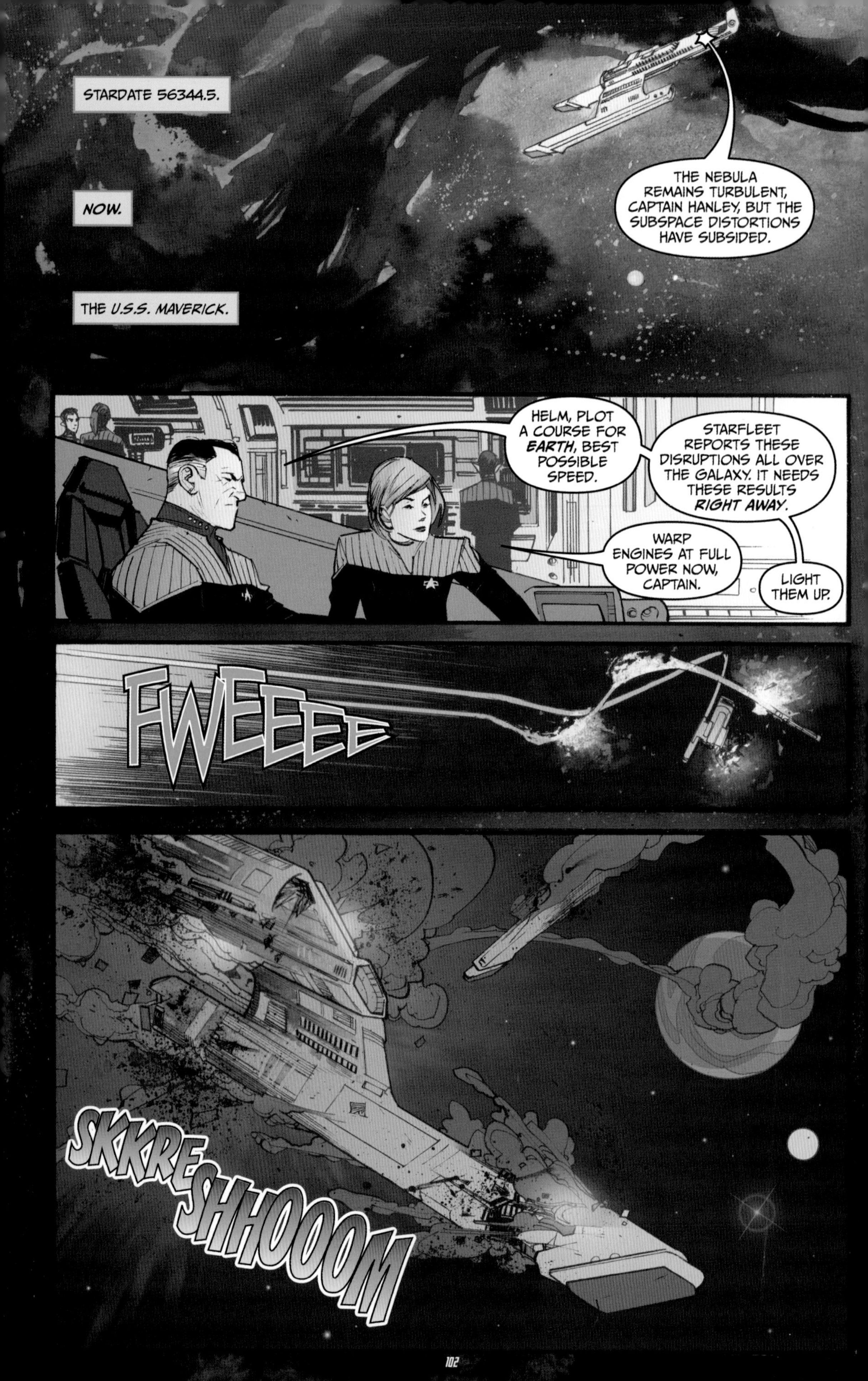

STARDATE 56344.5.
NOW.
THE U.S.S. MAVERICK.
THE NEBULA REMAINS TURBULENT, CAPTAIN HANLEY, BUT THE SUBSPACE DISTORTIONS HAVE SUBSIDED.
HELM, PLOT A COURSE FOR EARTH, BEST POSSIBLE SPEED.
STARFLEET REPORTS THESE DISRUPTIONS ALL OVER THE GALAXY. IT NEEDS THESE RESULTS RIGHT AWAY.
WARP ENGINES AT FULL POWER NOW, CAPTAIN.
LIGHT THEM UP.
FWEEEEE
SKKRESHHOOOM

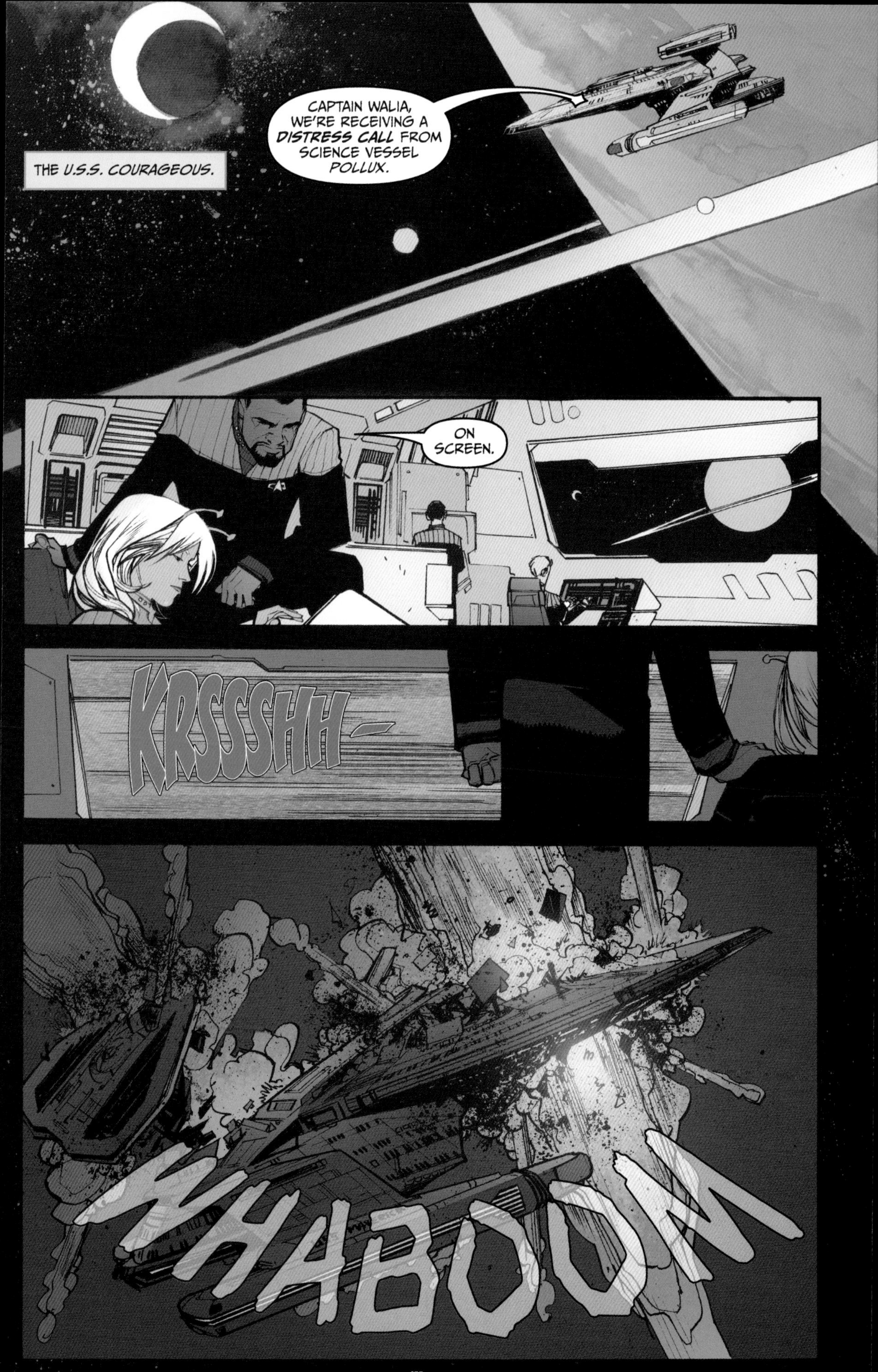
THE U.S.S. COURAGEOUS.
CAPTAIN WALIA, WE'RE RECEIVING A DISTRESS CALL FROM SCIENCE VESSEL POLLUX.
ON SCREEN.
KRSSSHH-
WHABOOM

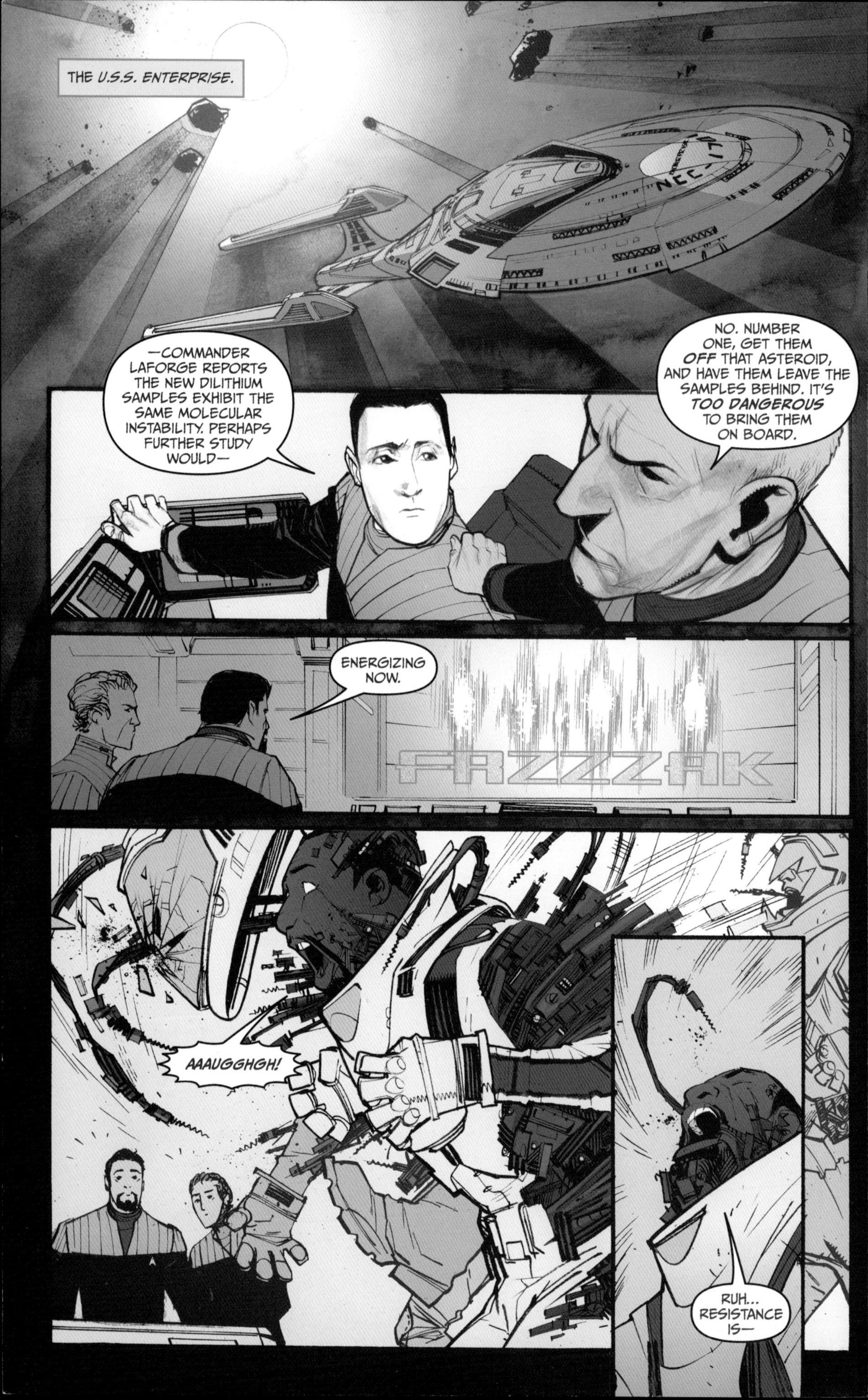
THE U.S.S. ENTERPRISE.
—COMMANDER LAFORGE REPORTS THE NEW DILITHIUM SAMPLES EXHIBIT THE SAME MOLECULAR INSTABILITY. PERHAPS FURTHER STUDY WOULD—
NO. NUMBER ONE, GET THEM OFF THAT ASTEROID, AND HAVE THEM LEAVE THE SAMPLES BEHIND. IT'S TOO DANGEROUS TO BRING THEM ON BOARD.
ENERGIZING NOW.
FRZZZAK
AAAUGGHGH!
RUH... RESISTANCE IS—

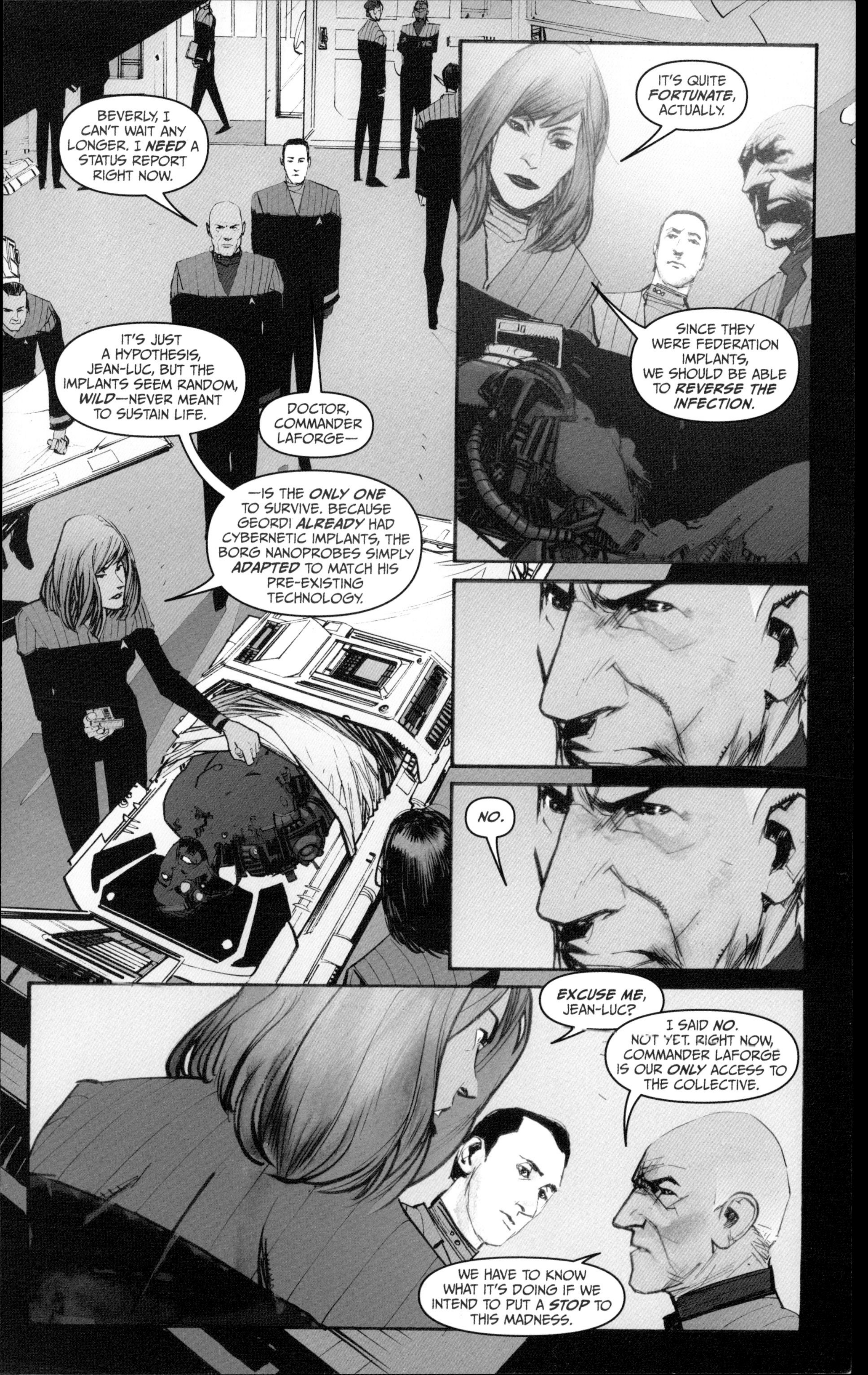
BEVERLY, I CAN'T WAIT ANY LONGER. I NEED A STATUS REPORT RIGHT NOW.
IT'S JUST A HYPOTHESIS, JEAN-LUC, BUT THE IMPLANTS SEEM RANDOM, WILD—NEVER MEANT TO SUSTAIN LIFE.
DOCTOR, COMMANDER LAFORGE—
—IS THE ONLY ONE TO SURVIVE. BECAUSE GEORDI ALREADY HAD CYBERNETIC IMPLANTS, THE BORG NANOPROBES SIMPLY ADAPTED TO MATCH HIS PRE-EXISTING TECHNOLOGY.
IT'S QUITE FORTUNATE, ACTUALLY.
SINCE THEY WERE FEDERATION IMPLANTS, WE SHOULD BE ABLE TO REVERSE THE INFECTION.
NO.
EXCUSE ME, JEAN-LUC?
I SAID NO. NOT YET. RIGHT NOW, COMMANDER LAFORGE IS OUR ONLY ACCESS TO THE COLLECTIVE.
WE HAVE TO KNOW WHAT IT'S DOING IF WE INTEND TO PUT A STOP TO THIS MADNESS.

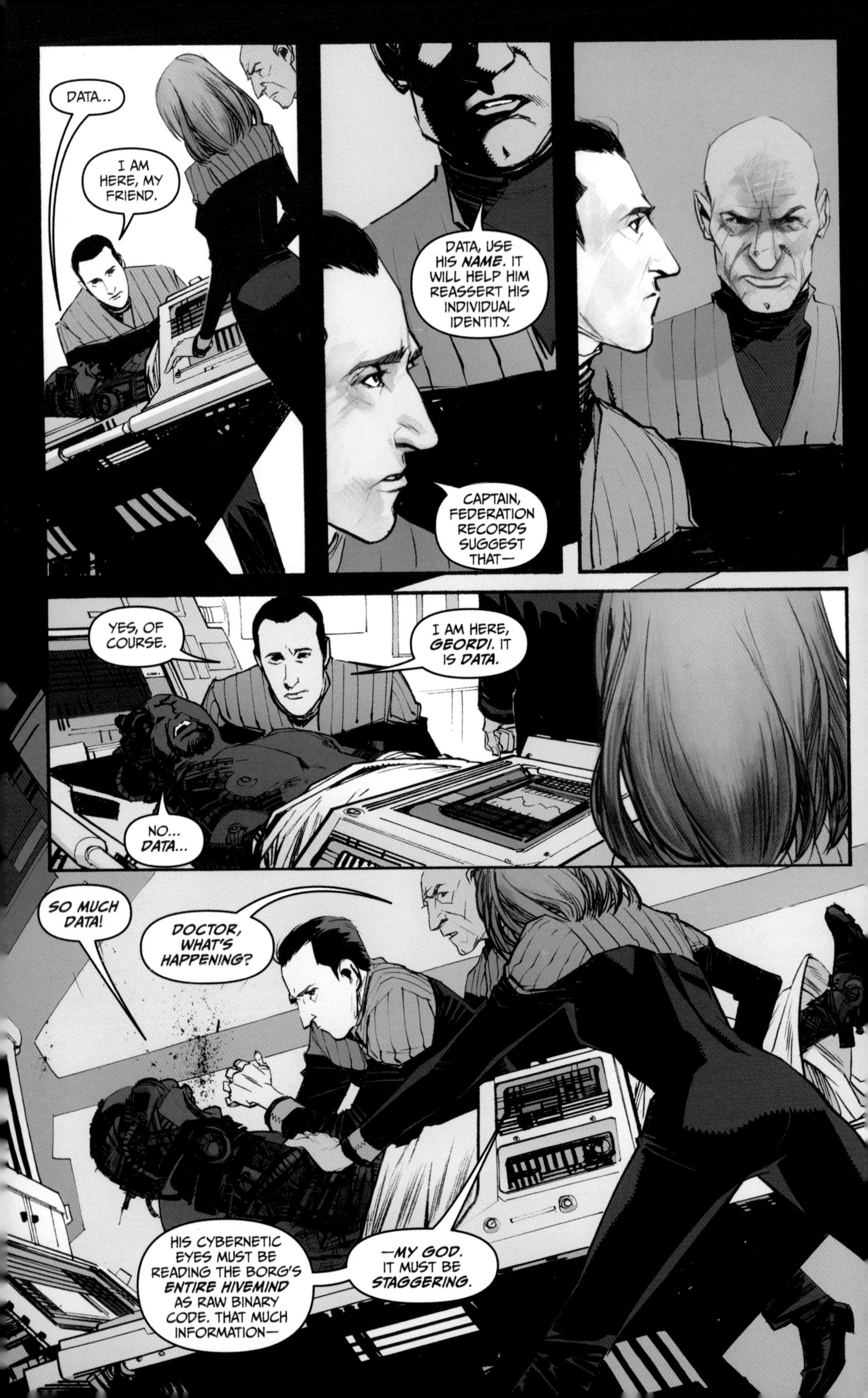
DATA...
I AM HERE, MY FRIEND.
DATA, USE HIS NAME. IT WILL HELP HIM REASSERT HIS INDIVIDUAL IDENTITY.
CAPTAIN, FEDERATION RECORDS SUGGEST THAT—
YES, OF COURSE.
I AM HERE, GEORDI. IT IS DATA.
NO... DATA...
SO MUCH DATA!
DOCTOR, WHAT'S HAPPENING?
HIS CYBERNETIC EYES MUST BE READING THE BORG'S ENTIRE HIVEMIND AS RAW BINARY CODE. THAT MUCH INFORMATION—
—MY GOD. IT MUST BE STAGGERING.

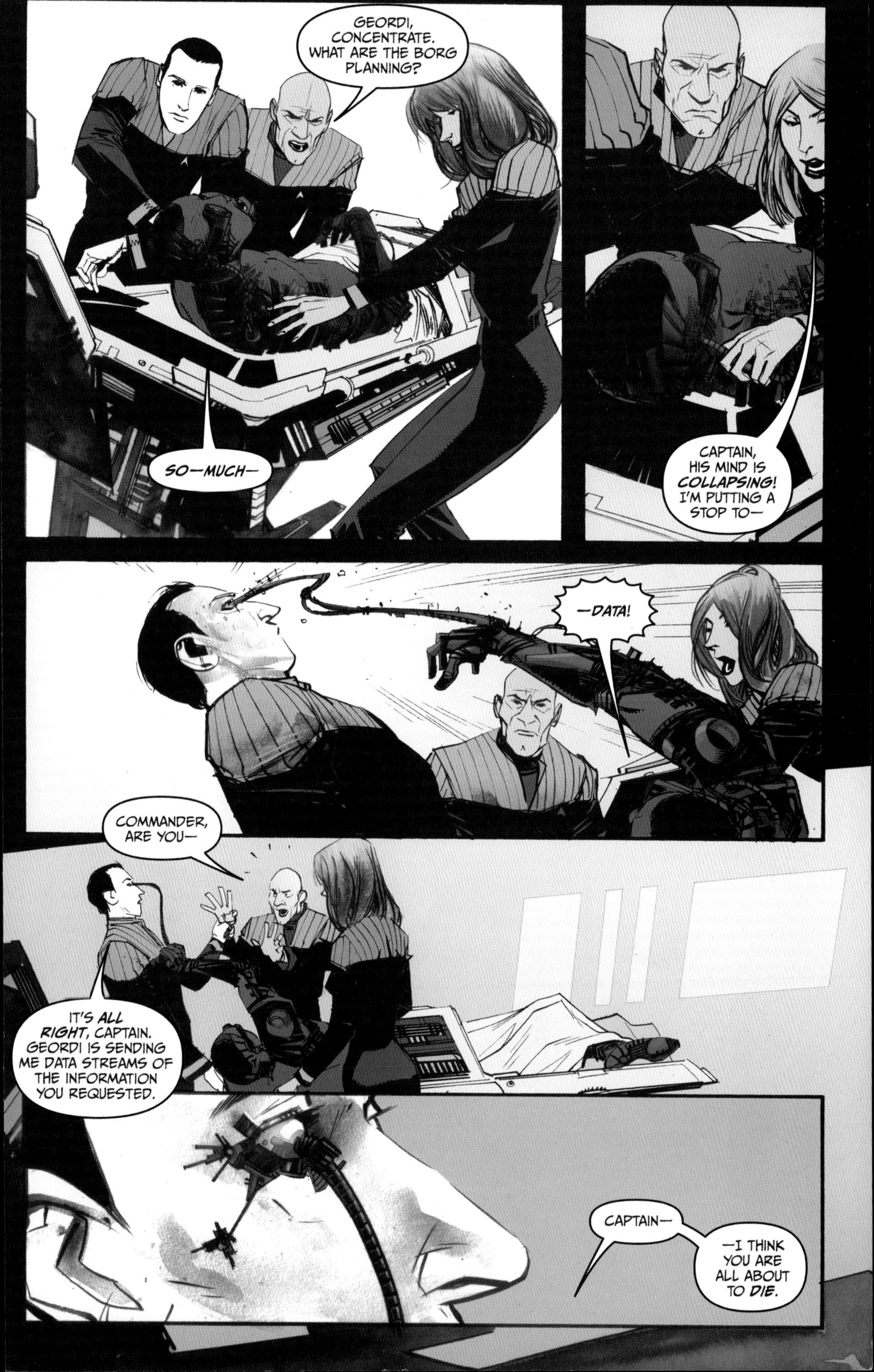
GEORDI, CONCENTRATE. WHAT ARE THE BORG PLANNING?
SO—MUCH—
CAPTAIN, HIS MIND IS COLLAPSING! I'M PUTTING A STOP TO—
—DATA!
COMMANDER, ARE YOU—
IT'S ALL RIGHT, CAPTAIN. GEORDI IS SENDING ME DATA STREAMS OF THE INFORMATION YOU REQUESTED.
CAPTAIN—
—I THINK YOU ARE ALL ABOUT TO DIE.

A *TIME WAVE.*

TRAVELING FROM THE FUTURE TOWARD THE PRESENT.

AN INTERSTELLAR CASCADE OF TACHYONS *RETHREADING* BORG HISTORY AS IT GOES.

THE FEDERATION'S EXPERT ON THE BORG...

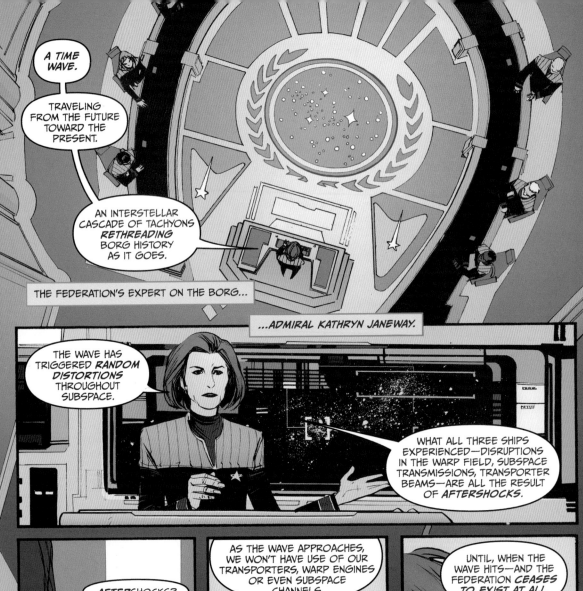

...ADMIRAL KATHRYN JANEWAY.

THE WAVE HAS TRIGGERED *RANDOM DISTORTIONS* THROUGHOUT SUBSPACE.

WHAT ALL THREE SHIPS EXPERIENCED—DISRUPTIONS IN THE WARP FIELD, SUBSPACE TRANSMISSIONS, TRANSPORTER BEAMS—ARE ALL THE RESULT OF *AFTERSHOCKS.*

AFTERSHOCKS?

YES, CAPTAIN AMASOV.

THE WAVE IS TRAVELING *BACKWARD* THROUGH TIME. ITS AFTERSHOCKS OCCUR *AHEAD* OF IT.

AS THE WAVE APPROACHES, WE WON'T HAVE USE OF OUR TRANSPORTERS, WARP ENGINES OR EVEN SUBSPACE CHANNELS.

THE ENTIRE FLEET WILL BE STRANDED AND UNABLE TO COMMUNICATE.

UNTIL, WHEN THE WAVE HITS—AND THE FEDERATION *CEASES TO EXIST AT ALL.*

THE BORG HAVE ATTEMPTED TO CHANGE PAST EVENTS BEFORE. TO ATTEMPT SO AGAIN, AFTER SUCH FAILURE, WOULD BE *INEFFICIENT*, AND THEREFORE *ILLOGICAL*.

ADMIRAL, IF I MAY?

THIS TACHYON WAVE DOES NOT CHANGE A *SINGLE* EVENT. IT CHANGES *ALL* EVENTS.

IT IS A *MASSIVE BURST* OF TEMPORAL ENERGY, REWRITING HISTORY SO THAT *ALL SPECIES* ARE *BORN BORG* AT THE MOMENT OF THEIR GENETIC INCEPTION.

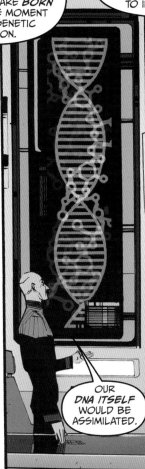

OUR *DNA ITSELF* WOULD BE ASSIMILATED.

AGAIN, ILLOGICAL. IF ALL SPECIES ARE BORN BORG, THERE WOULD BE NO DISTINCTIVENESS TO INCORPORATE.

THEY HAVE ASSIMILATED *VULCANS*, AND WOULD *CALCULATE* THIS.

INDEED. IT IS PRECISELY THAT VULCAN LOGIC THAT HAS REVEALED TO THE COLLECTIVE A PHILOSOPHICAL *PARADOX*.

THE BORG HAVE A *RACIAL IMPERATIVE* TO ACHIEVE PERFECTION. BUT THEY CAN NEVER BE AS PERFECT AS A SPECIES THAT WAS PERFECT FROM THE *BEGINNING*.

CONSEQUENTLY, THEY CONCEIVED THE *TACHYON WAVE*, TO BE USED ONCE THEY HAD ACHIEVED PERFECTION IN ALL BUT THEIR HISTORY.

IT IS, IN SHORT, AN ATTEMPT TO ASSIMILATE *THEIR PAST*.

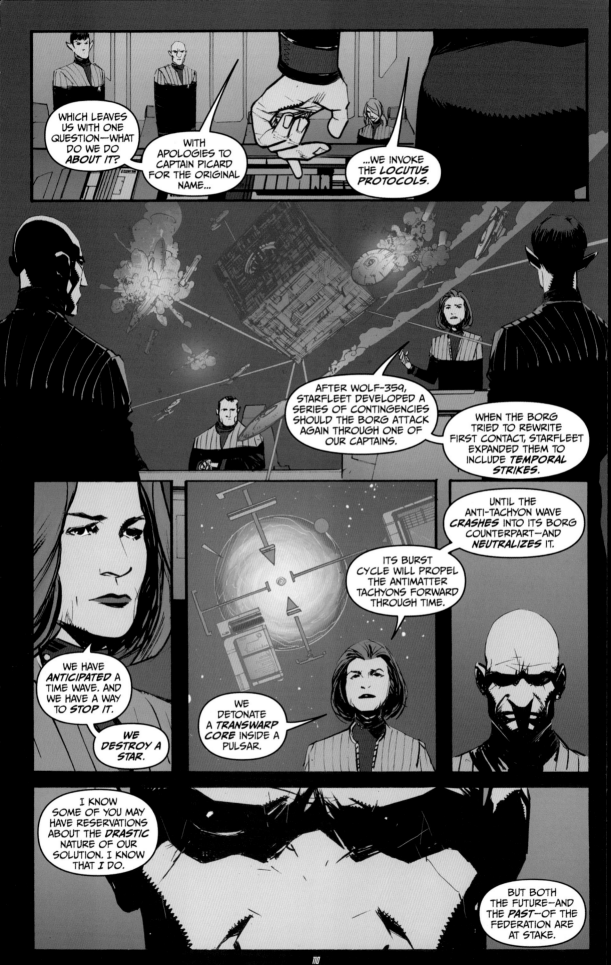

WHICH LEAVES US WITH ONE QUESTION—WHAT DO WE DO *ABOUT* IT?

WITH APOLOGIES TO CAPTAIN PICARD FOR THE ORIGINAL NAME...

...WE INVOKE THE *LOCUTUS PROTOCOLS.*

AFTER WOLF-359, STARFLEET DEVELOPED A SERIES OF CONTINGENCIES SHOULD THE BORG ATTACK AGAIN THROUGH ONE OF OUR CAPTAINS.

WHEN THE BORG TRIED TO REWRITE FIRST CONTACT, STARFLEET EXPANDED THEM TO INCLUDE *TEMPORAL STRIKES.*

UNTIL THE ANTI-TACHYON WAVE *CRASHES* INTO ITS BORG COUNTERPART—AND *NEUTRALIZES* IT.

ITS BURST CYCLE WILL PROPEL THE ANTIMATTER TACHYONS FORWARD THROUGH TIME.

WE HAVE *ANTICIPATED* A TIME WAVE. AND WE HAVE A WAY TO *STOP* IT.

WE *DESTROY* A STAR.

WE DETONATE A *TRANSWARP CORE* INSIDE A PULSAR.

I KNOW SOME OF YOU MAY HAVE RESERVATIONS ABOUT THE *DRASTIC* NATURE OF OUR SOLUTION. I KNOW THAT *I* DO.

BUT BOTH THE FUTURE—AND THE *PAST*—OF THE FEDERATION ARE AT STAKE.

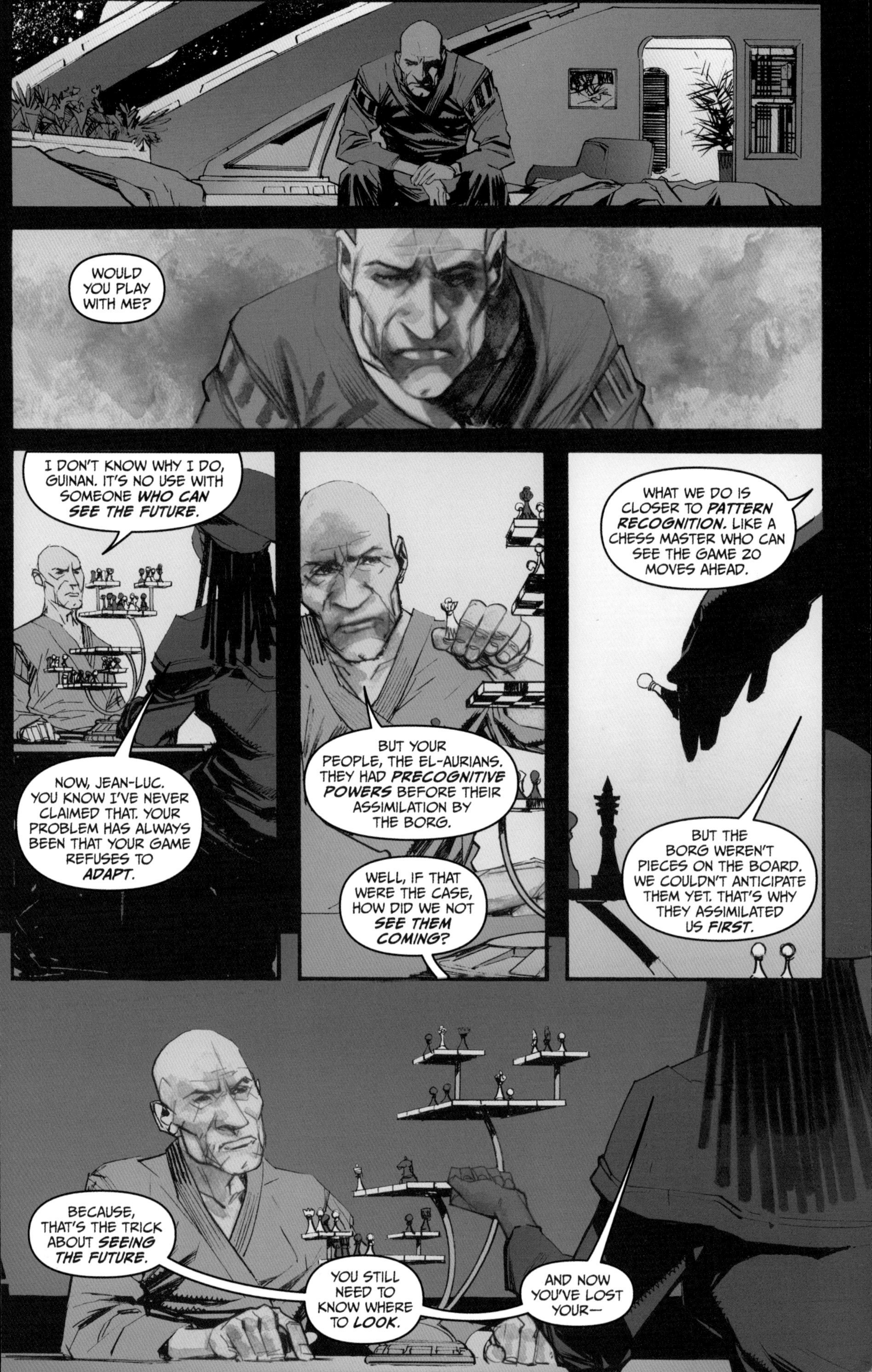
WOULD YOU PLAY WITH ME?
I DON'T KNOW WHY I DO, GUINAN. IT'S NO USE WITH SOMEONE *WHO CAN SEE THE FUTURE*.
NOW, JEAN-LUC. YOU KNOW I'VE NEVER CLAIMED THAT. YOUR PROBLEM HAS ALWAYS BEEN THAT YOUR GAME REFUSES TO *ADAPT*.
BUT YOUR PEOPLE, THE EL-AURIANS. THEY HAD *PRECOGNITIVE POWERS* BEFORE THEIR ASSIMILATION BY THE BORG.
WELL, IF THAT WERE THE CASE, HOW DID WE NOT *SEE THEM COMING?*
WHAT WE DO IS CLOSER TO *PATTERN RECOGNITION.* LIKE A CHESS MASTER WHO CAN SEE THE GAME 20 MOVES AHEAD.
BUT THE BORG WEREN'T PIECES ON THE BOARD. WE COULDN'T ANTICIPATE THEM YET. THAT'S WHY THEY ASSIMILATED US *FIRST*.
BECAUSE, THAT'S THE TRICK ABOUT *SEEING THE FUTURE*.
YOU STILL NEED TO KNOW WHERE TO *LOOK*.
AND NOW YOU'VE LOST YOUR—

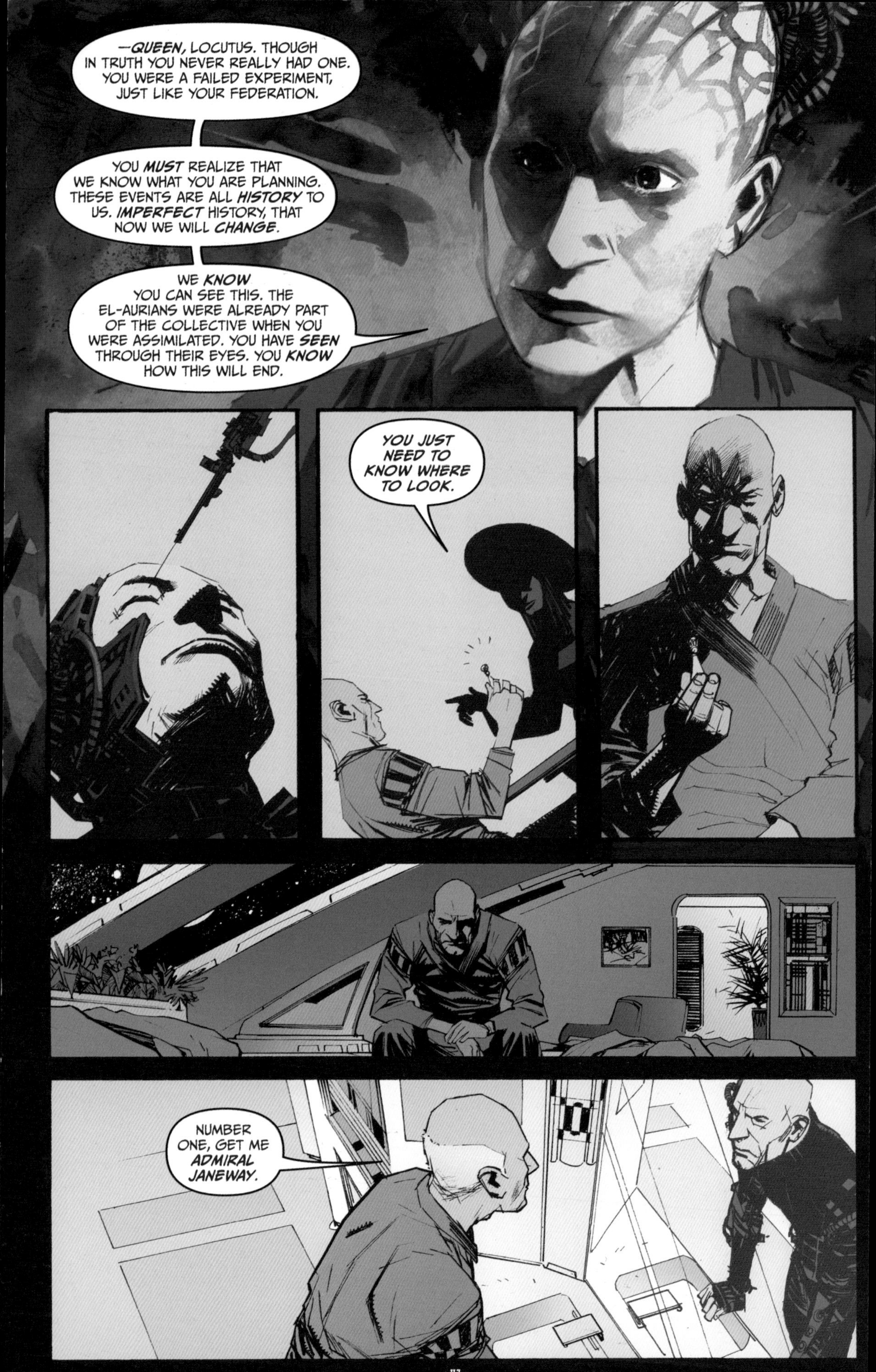

—QUEEN, LOCUTUS. THOUGH IN TRUTH YOU NEVER REALLY HAD ONE. YOU WERE A FAILED EXPERIMENT, JUST LIKE YOUR FEDERATION.
YOU MUST REALIZE THAT WE KNOW WHAT YOU ARE PLANNING. THESE EVENTS ARE ALL HISTORY TO US. IMPERFECT HISTORY, THAT NOW WE WILL CHANGE.
WE KNOW YOU CAN SEE THIS. THE EL-AURIANS WERE ALREADY PART OF THE COLLECTIVE WHEN YOU WERE ASSIMILATED. YOU HAVE SEEN THROUGH THEIR EYES. YOU KNOW HOW THIS WILL END.
YOU JUST NEED TO KNOW WHERE TO LOOK.
NUMBER ONE, GET ME ADMIRAL JANEWAY.

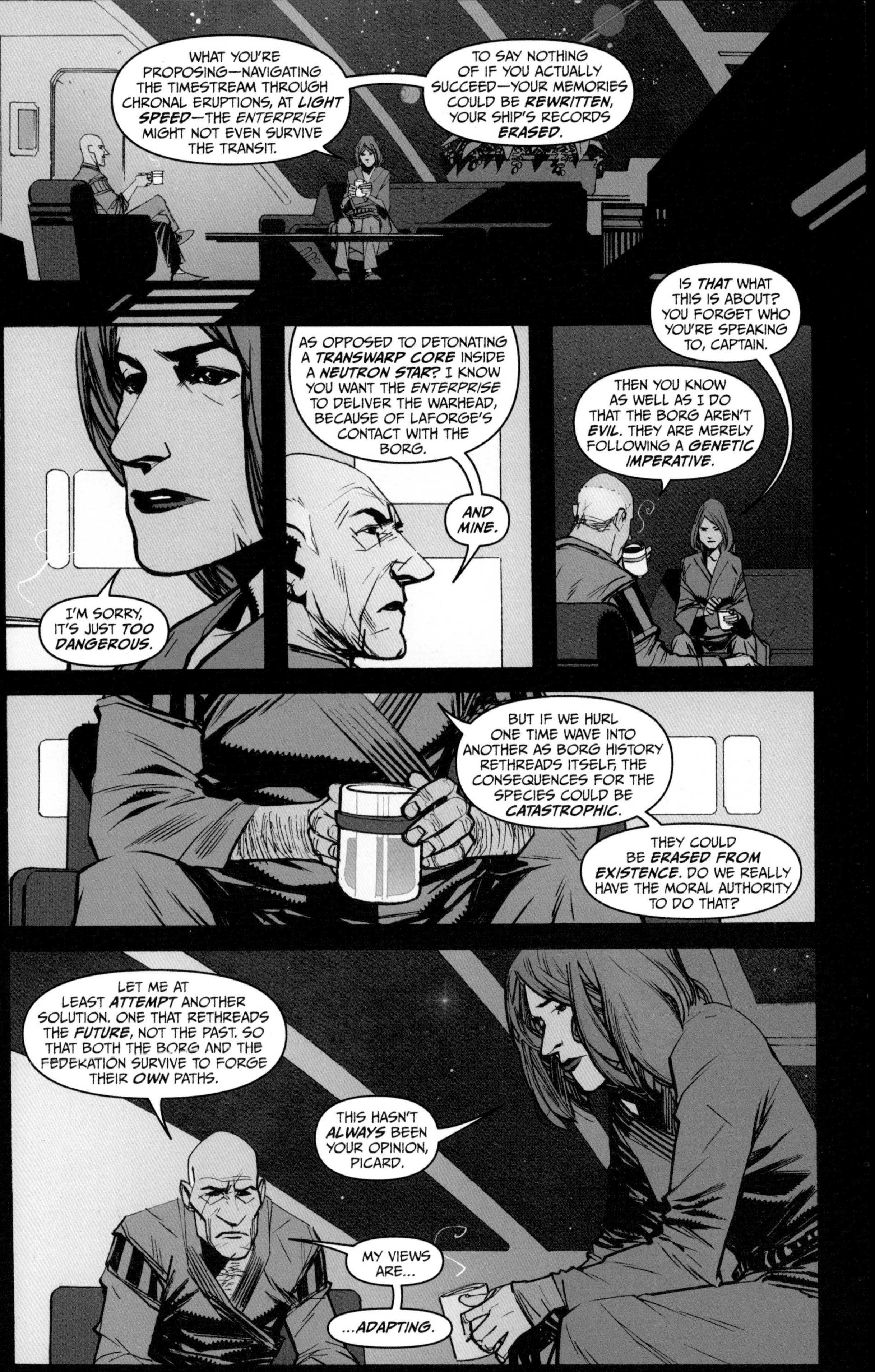
WHAT YOU'RE PROPOSING—NAVIGATING THE TIMESTREAM THROUGH CHRONAL ERUPTIONS, AT LIGHT SPEED—THE ENTERPRISE MIGHT NOT EVEN SURVIVE THE TRANSIT.
TO SAY NOTHING OF IF YOU ACTUALLY SUCCEED—YOUR MEMORIES COULD BE REWRITTEN, YOUR SHIP'S RECORDS ERASED.
I'M SORRY, IT'S JUST TOO DANGEROUS.
AS OPPOSED TO DETONATING A TRANSWARP CORE INSIDE A NEUTRON STAR? I KNOW YOU WANT THE ENTERPRISE TO DELIVER THE WARHEAD, BECAUSE OF LAFORGE'S CONTACT WITH THE BORG.
AND MINE.
IS THAT WHAT THIS IS ABOUT? YOU FORGET WHO YOU'RE SPEAKING TO, CAPTAIN.
THEN YOU KNOW AS WELL AS I DO THAT THE BORG AREN'T EVIL. THEY ARE MERELY FOLLOWING A GENETIC IMPERATIVE.
BUT IF WE HURL ONE TIME WAVE INTO ANOTHER AS BORG HISTORY RETHREADS ITSELF, THE CONSEQUENCES FOR THE SPECIES COULD BE CATASTROPHIC.
THEY COULD BE ERASED FROM EXISTENCE. DO WE REALLY HAVE THE MORAL AUTHORITY TO DO THAT?
LET ME AT LEAST ATTEMPT ANOTHER SOLUTION. ONE THAT RETHREADS THE FUTURE, NOT THE PAST. SO THAT BOTH THE BORG AND THE FEDERATION SURVIVE TO FORGE THEIR OWN PATHS.
THIS HASN'T ALWAYS BEEN YOUR OPINION, PICARD.
MY VIEWS ARE...
...ADAPTING.

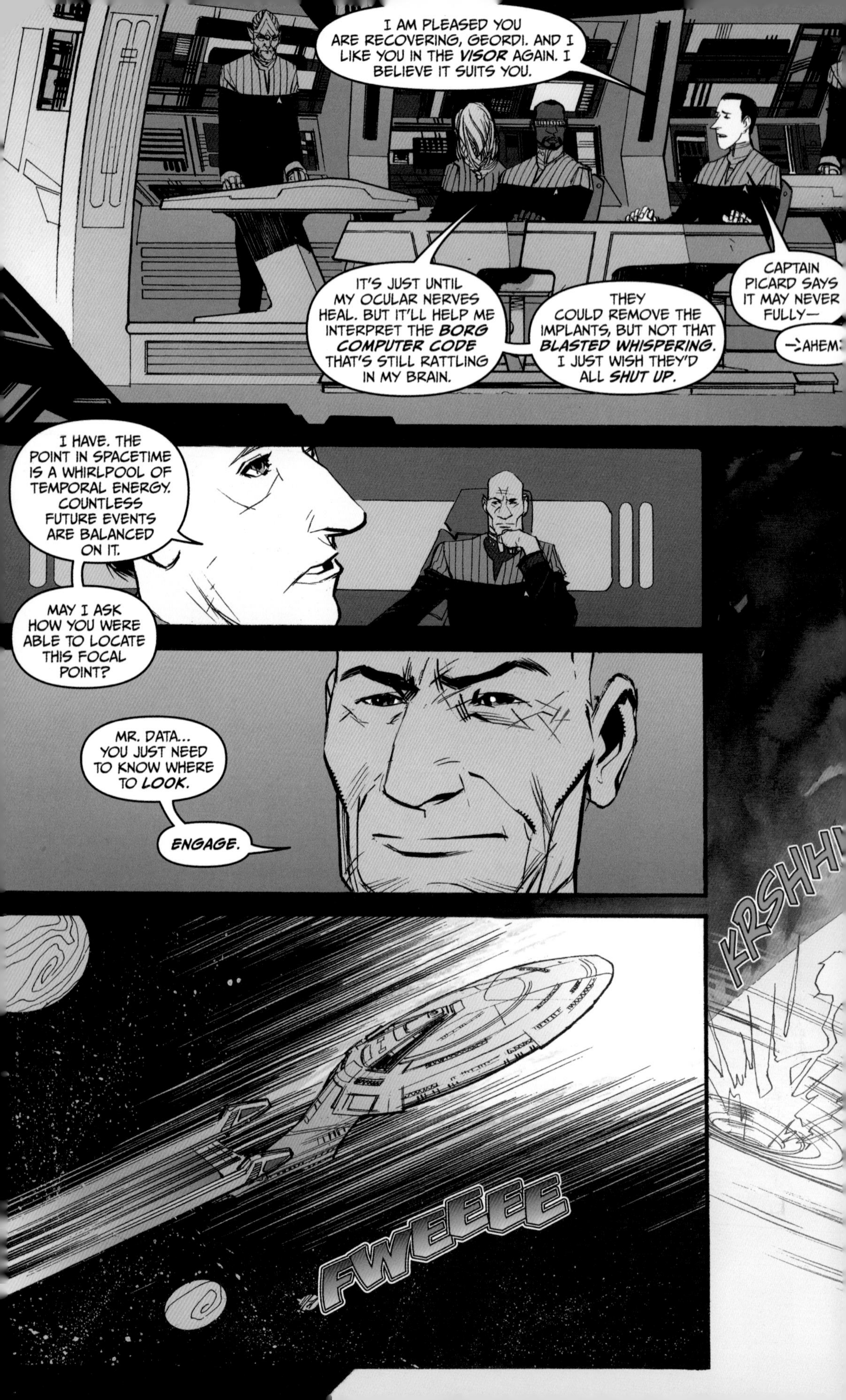
I AM PLEASED YOU ARE RECOVERING, GEORDI. AND I LIKE YOU IN THE VISOR AGAIN. I BELIEVE IT SUITS YOU.
IT'S JUST UNTIL MY OCULAR NERVES HEAL. BUT IT'LL HELP ME INTERPRET THE BORG COMPUTER CODE THAT'S STILL RATTLING IN MY BRAIN.
THEY COULD REMOVE THE IMPLANTS, BUT NOT THAT BLASTED WHISPERING. I JUST WISH THEY'D ALL SHUT UP.
CAPTAIN PICARD SAYS IT MAY NEVER FULLY—
—AHEM
I HAVE. THE POINT IN SPACETIME IS A WHIRLPOOL OF TEMPORAL ENERGY. COUNTLESS FUTURE EVENTS ARE BALANCED ON IT.
MAY I ASK HOW YOU WERE ABLE TO LOCATE THIS FOCAL POINT?
MR. DATA... YOU JUST NEED TO KNOW WHERE TO LOOK.
ENGAGE.
FWEEEE
KRSHHH

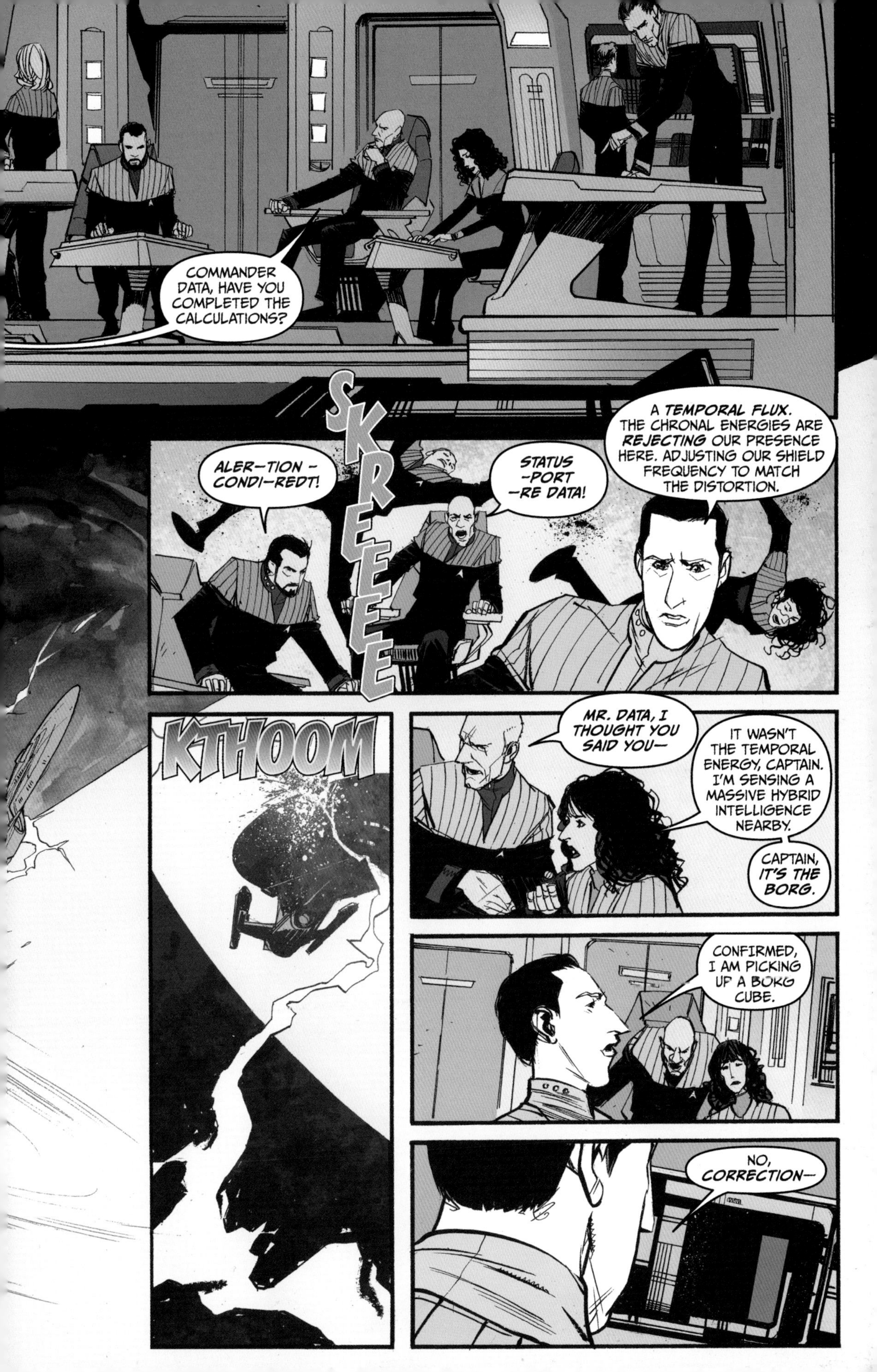
COMMANDER DATA, HAVE YOU COMPLETED THE CALCULATIONS?
SKREEEE
ALER–TION – CONDI–REDT!
STATUS –PORT –RE DATA!
A TEMPORAL FLUX. THE CHRONAL ENERGIES ARE REJECTING OUR PRESENCE HERE. ADJUSTING OUR SHIELD FREQUENCY TO MATCH THE DISTORTION.
KTHOOM
MR. DATA, I THOUGHT YOU SAID YOU—
IT WASN'T THE TEMPORAL ENERGY, CAPTAIN. I'M SENSING A MASSIVE HYBRID INTELLIGENCE NEARBY.
CAPTAIN, IT'S THE BORG.
CONFIRMED, I AM PICKING UP A BORG CUBE.
NO, CORRECTION—

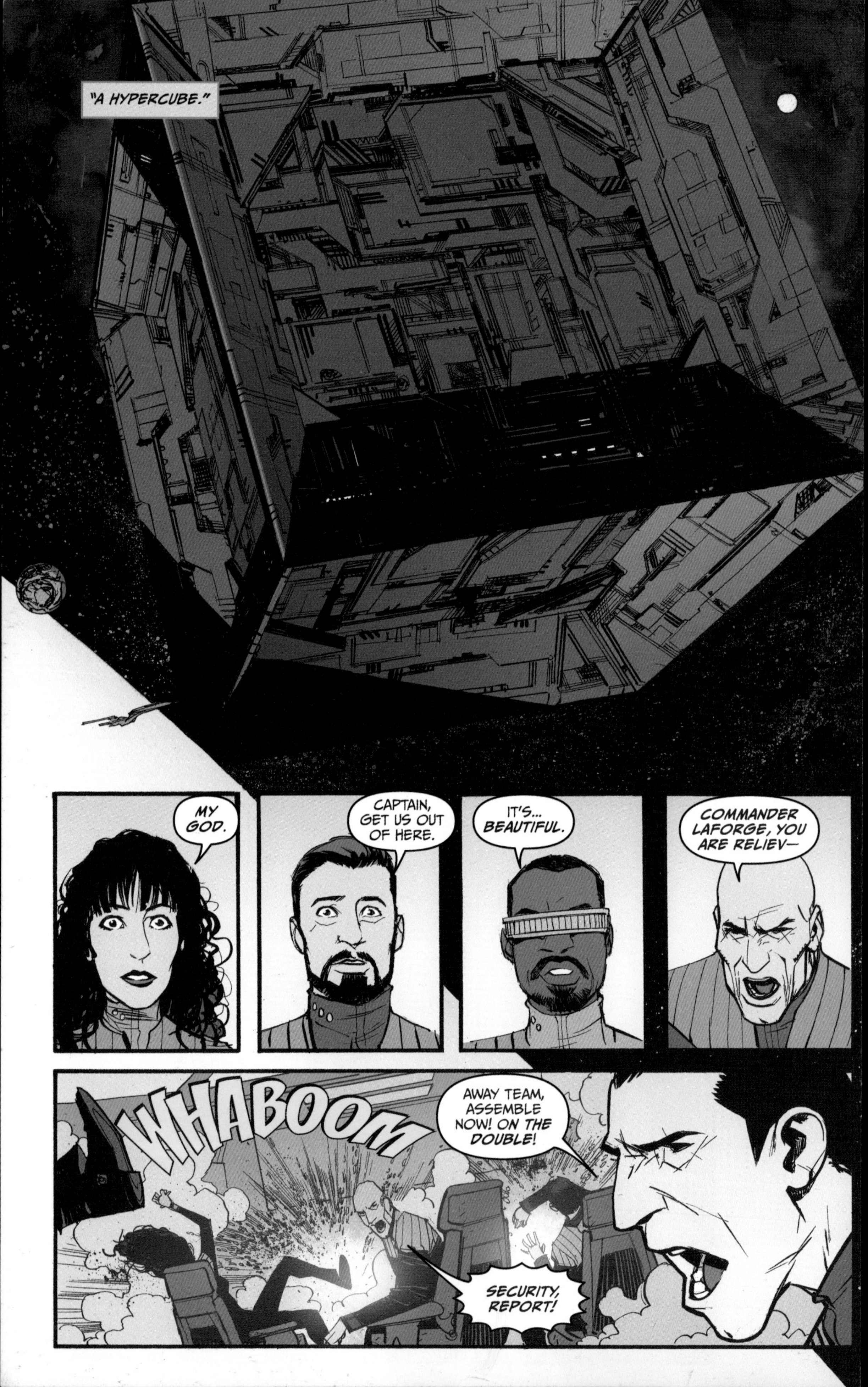
"A HYPERCUBE."
MY GOD.
CAPTAIN, GET US OUT OF HERE.
IT'S... BEAUTIFUL.
COMMANDER LAFORGE, YOU ARE RELIEV—
WHABOOM
AWAY TEAM, ASSEMBLE NOW! ON THE DOUBLE!
SECURITY, REPORT!

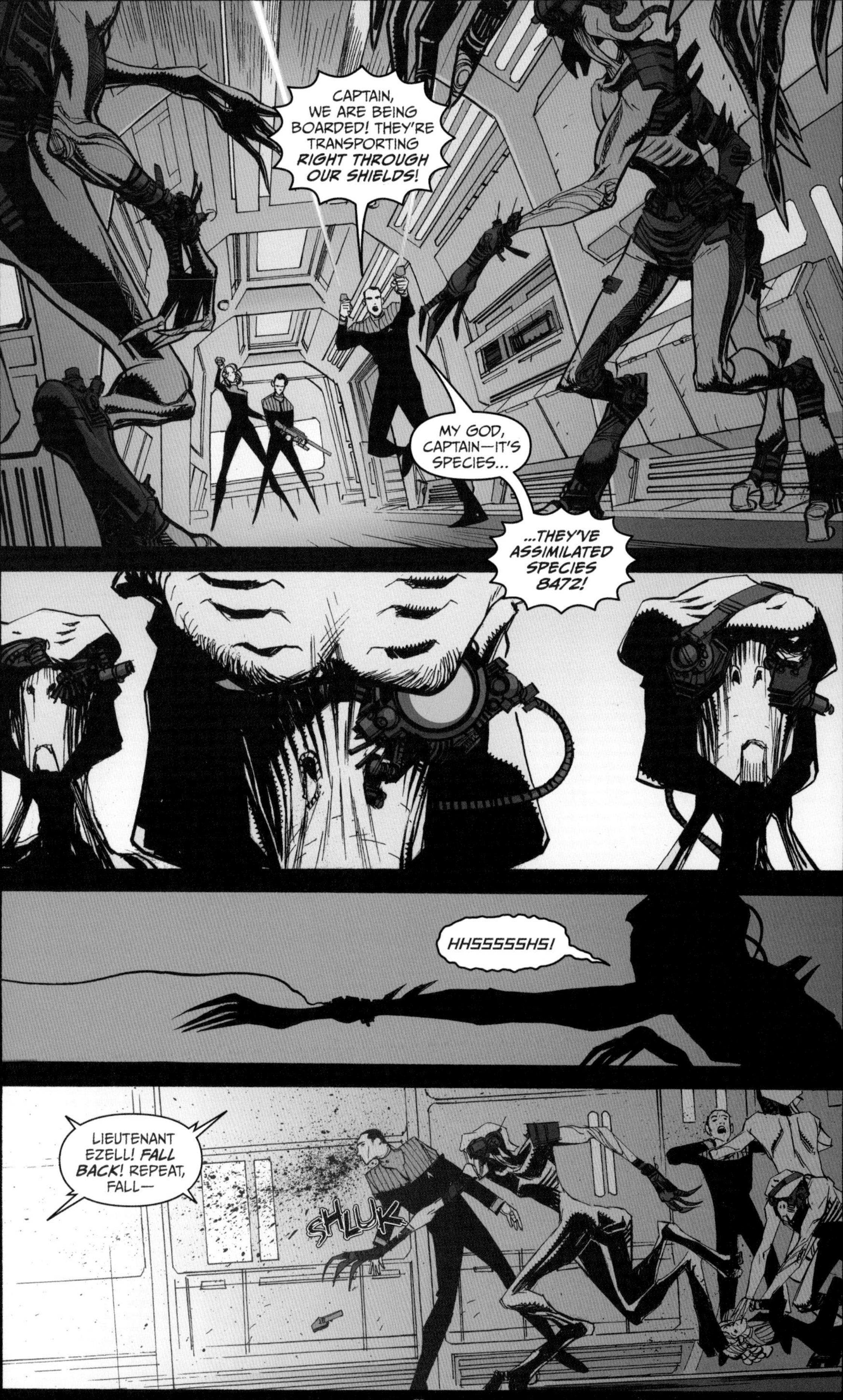
CAPTAIN, WE ARE BEING BOARDED! THEY'RE TRANSPORTING RIGHT THROUGH OUR SHIELDS!
MY GOD, CAPTAIN—IT'S SPECIES...
...THEY'VE ASSIMILATED SPECIES 8472!
HHSSSSSHS!
LIEUTENANT EZELL! FALL BACK! REPEAT, FALL—
SHLUK

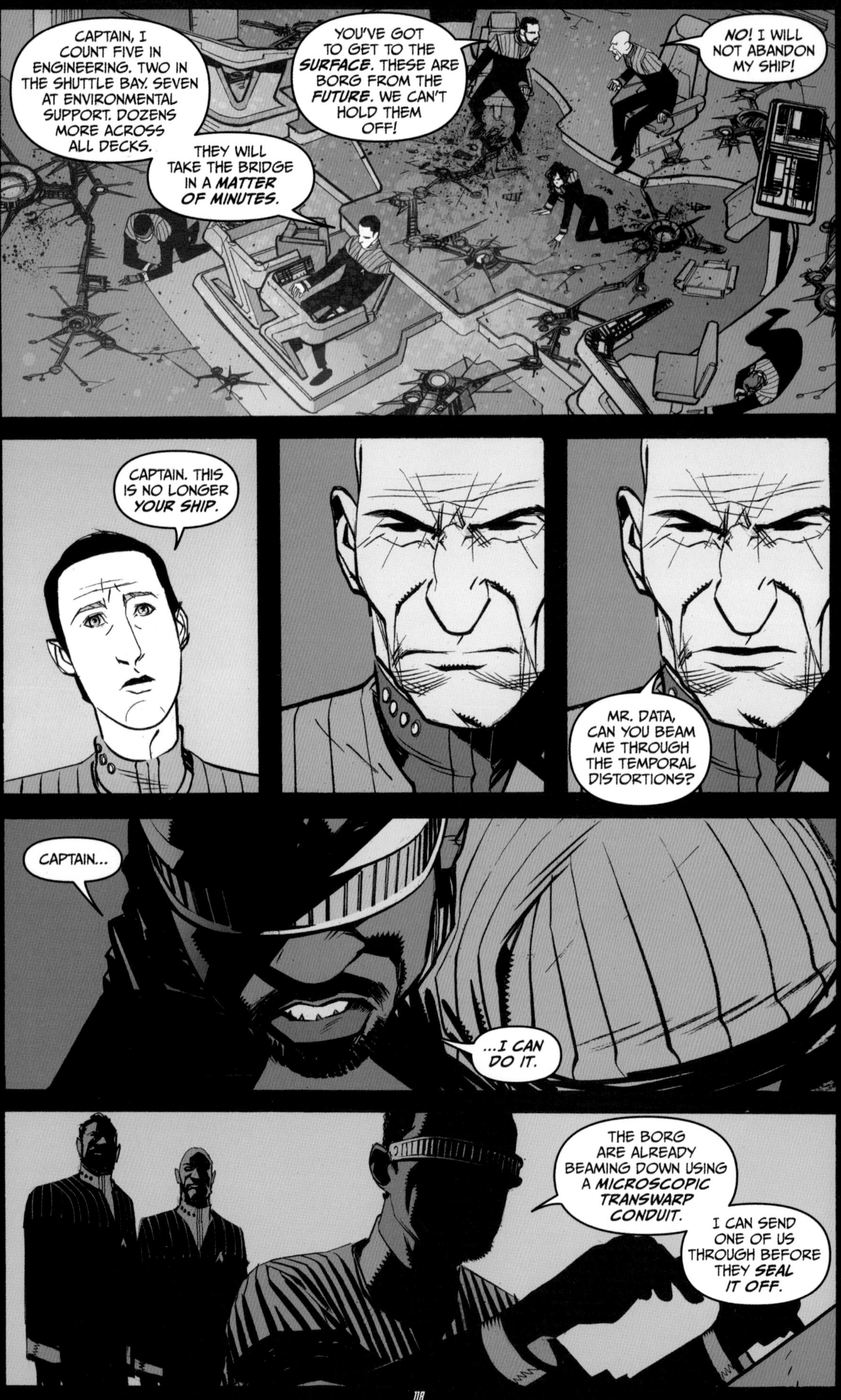
CAPTAIN, I COUNT FIVE IN ENGINEERING. TWO IN THE SHUTTLE BAY. SEVEN AT ENVIRONMENTAL SUPPORT. DOZENS MORE ACROSS ALL DECKS.
THEY WILL TAKE THE BRIDGE IN A MATTER OF MINUTES.
YOU'VE GOT TO GET TO THE SURFACE. THESE ARE BORG FROM THE FUTURE. WE CAN'T HOLD THEM OFF!
NO! I WILL NOT ABANDON MY SHIP!
CAPTAIN. THIS IS NO LONGER YOUR SHIP.
MR. DATA, CAN YOU BEAM ME THROUGH THE TEMPORAL DISTORTIONS?
CAPTAIN...
...I CAN DO IT.
THE BORG ARE ALREADY BEAMING DOWN USING A MICROSCOPIC TRANSWARP CONDUIT.
I CAN SEND ONE OF US THROUGH BEFORE THEY SEAL IT OFF.

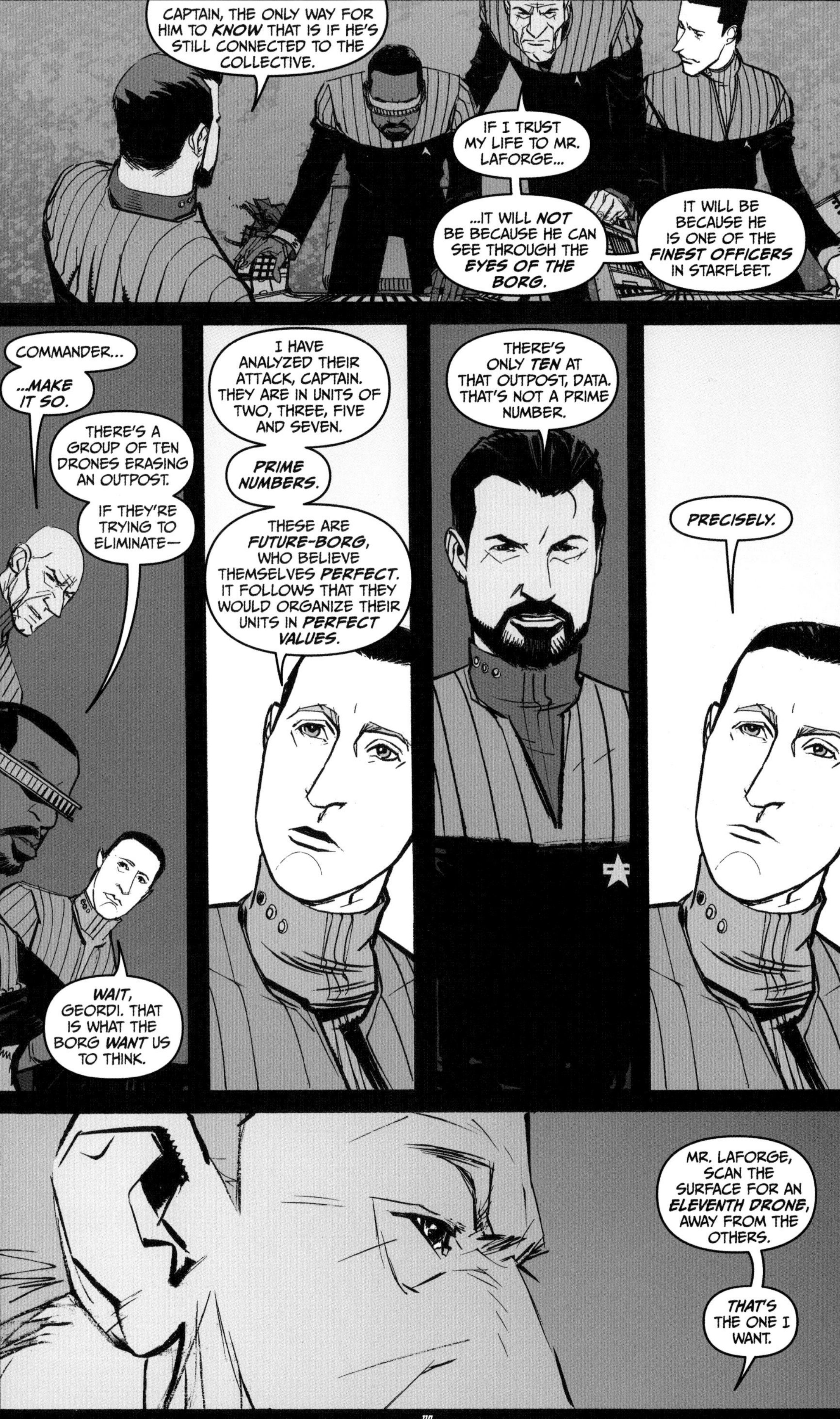
CAPTAIN, THE ONLY WAY FOR HIM TO KNOW THAT IS IF HE'S STILL CONNECTED TO THE COLLECTIVE.
IF I TRUST MY LIFE TO MR. LAFORGE...
...IT WILL NOT BE BECAUSE HE CAN SEE THROUGH THE EYES OF THE BORG.
IT WILL BE BECAUSE HE IS ONE OF THE FINEST OFFICERS IN STARFLEET.
COMMANDER...
...MAKE IT SO.
THERE'S A GROUP OF TEN DRONES ERASING AN OUTPOST.
IF THEY'RE TRYING TO ELIMINATE—
WAIT, GEORDI. THAT IS WHAT THE BORG WANT US TO THINK.
I HAVE ANALYZED THEIR ATTACK, CAPTAIN. THEY ARE IN UNITS OF TWO, THREE, FIVE AND SEVEN.
PRIME NUMBERS.
THESE ARE FUTURE-BORG, WHO BELIEVE THEMSELVES PERFECT. IT FOLLOWS THAT THEY WOULD ORGANIZE THEIR UNITS IN PERFECT VALUES.
THERE'S ONLY TEN AT THAT OUTPOST, DATA. THAT'S NOT A PRIME NUMBER.
PRECISELY.
MR. LAFORGE, SCAN THE SURFACE FOR AN ELEVENTH DRONE, AWAY FROM THE OTHERS.
THAT'S THE ONE I WANT.

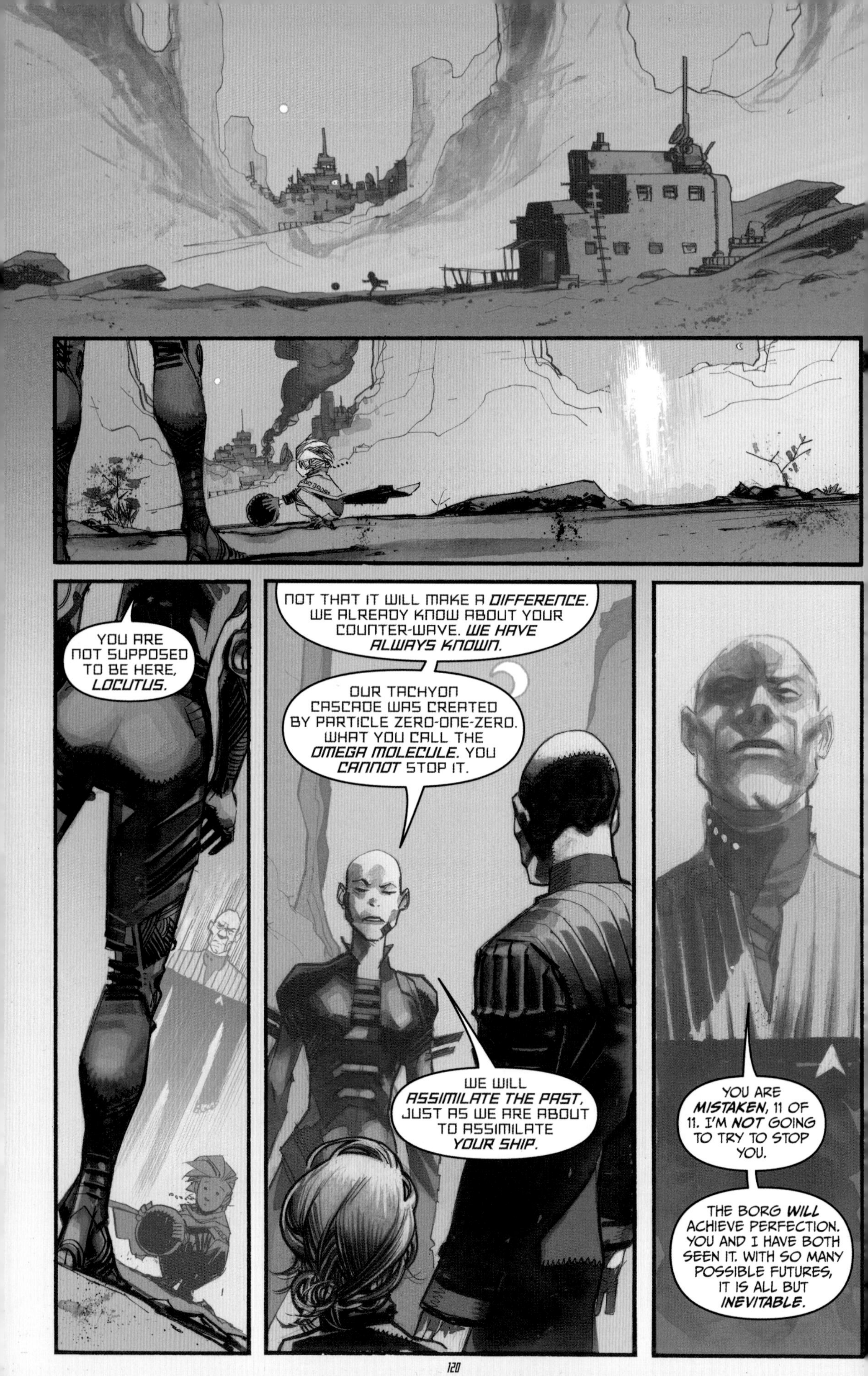
YOU ARE NOT SUPPOSED TO BE HERE, *LOCUTUS*.
NOT THAT IT WILL MAKE A *DIFFERENCE*. WE ALREADY KNOW ABOUT YOUR COUNTER-WAVE. *WE HAVE ALWAYS KNOWN*.
OUR TACHYON CASCADE WAS CREATED BY PARTICLE ZERO-ONE-ZERO. WHAT YOU CALL THE *OMEGA MOLECULE*. YOU *CANNOT* STOP IT.
WE WILL *ASSIMILATE THE PAST*, JUST AS WE ARE ABOUT TO ASSIMILATE *YOUR SHIP*.
YOU ARE **MISTAKEN**, 11 OF 11. I'M **NOT** GOING TO TRY TO STOP YOU.
THE BORG **WILL** ACHIEVE PERFECTION. YOU AND I HAVE BOTH SEEN IT. WITH SO MANY POSSIBLE FUTURES, IT IS ALL BUT **INEVITABLE**.

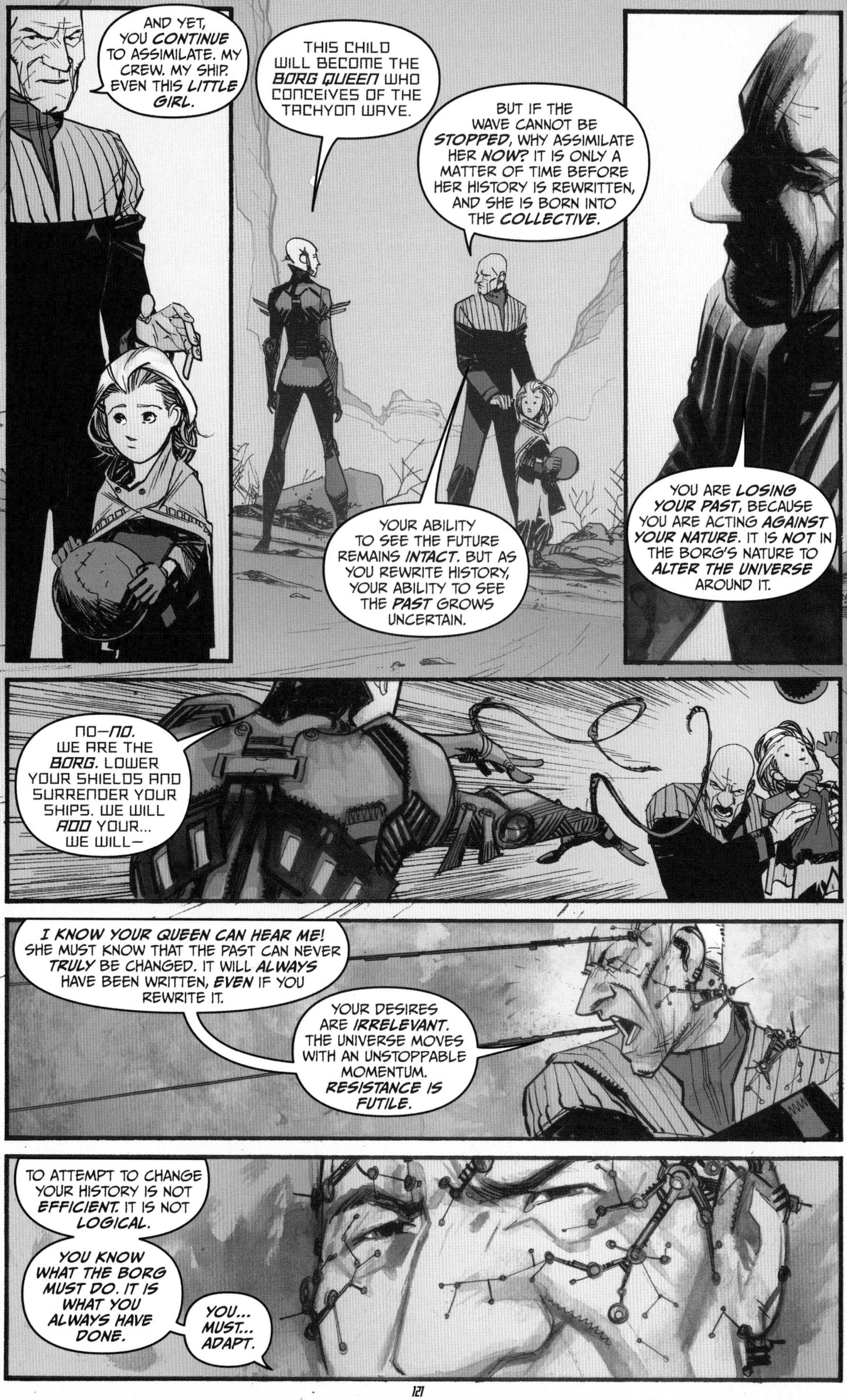
AND YET, YOU CONTINUE TO ASSIMILATE. MY CREW. MY SHIP. EVEN THIS LITTLE GIRL.
THIS CHILD WILL BECOME THE BORG QUEEN WHO CONCEIVES OF THE TACHYON WAVE.
BUT IF THE WAVE CANNOT BE STOPPED, WHY ASSIMILATE HER NOW? IT IS ONLY A MATTER OF TIME BEFORE HER HISTORY IS REWRITTEN, AND SHE IS BORN INTO THE COLLECTIVE.
YOUR ABILITY TO SEE THE FUTURE REMAINS INTACT. BUT AS YOU REWRITE HISTORY, YOUR ABILITY TO SEE THE PAST GROWS UNCERTAIN.
YOU ARE LOSING YOUR PAST, BECAUSE YOU ARE ACTING AGAINST YOUR NATURE. IT IS NOT IN THE BORG'S NATURE TO ALTER THE UNIVERSE AROUND IT.
NO—NO. WE ARE THE BORG. LOWER YOUR SHIELDS AND SURRENDER YOUR SHIPS. WE WILL ADD YOUR... WE WILL—
I KNOW YOUR QUEEN CAN HEAR ME! SHE MUST KNOW THAT THE PAST CAN NEVER TRULY BE CHANGED. IT WILL ALWAYS HAVE BEEN WRITTEN, EVEN IF YOU REWRITE IT.
YOUR DESIRES ARE IRRELEVANT. THE UNIVERSE MOVES WITH AN UNSTOPPABLE MOMENTUM. RESISTANCE IS FUTILE.
TO ATTEMPT TO CHANGE YOUR HISTORY IS NOT EFFICIENT. IT IS NOT LOGICAL.
YOU KNOW WHAT THE BORG MUST DO. IT IS WHAT YOU ALWAYS HAVE DONE.
YOU... MUST... ADAPT.

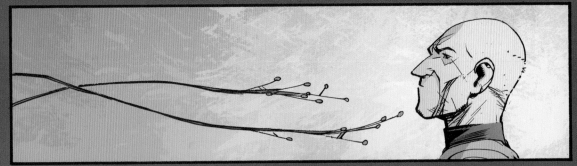

WE WILL— WE—

...

YOU MAY KEEP THE GIRL. HER PLAN IS *FLAWED.*

AND MY SHIP?

WE WILL RETURN IT TO YOU. AS CAPTAIN, YOU HAVE *UNIQUE QUALITIES* THAT WE WILL ADD TO OUR DISTINCTIVENESS WHEN THEY HAVE *TRANSCENDED THEIR IMPERFECTION.*

YOU ARE *NOT* YET LOCUTUS.

BUT YOU *WILL BE.*

THAT LADY WAS *MEAN.*

I KNOW. SHE'S VERY SORRY ABOUT IT.

I CAN'T FIND MY MOMMY. WE WERE SUPPOSED TO DRESS UP LIKE PRINCESSES TODAY.

WOULD YOU PLAY WITH ME?

YES.

THE END.

art by Sean Murphy
color by Len O'Grady

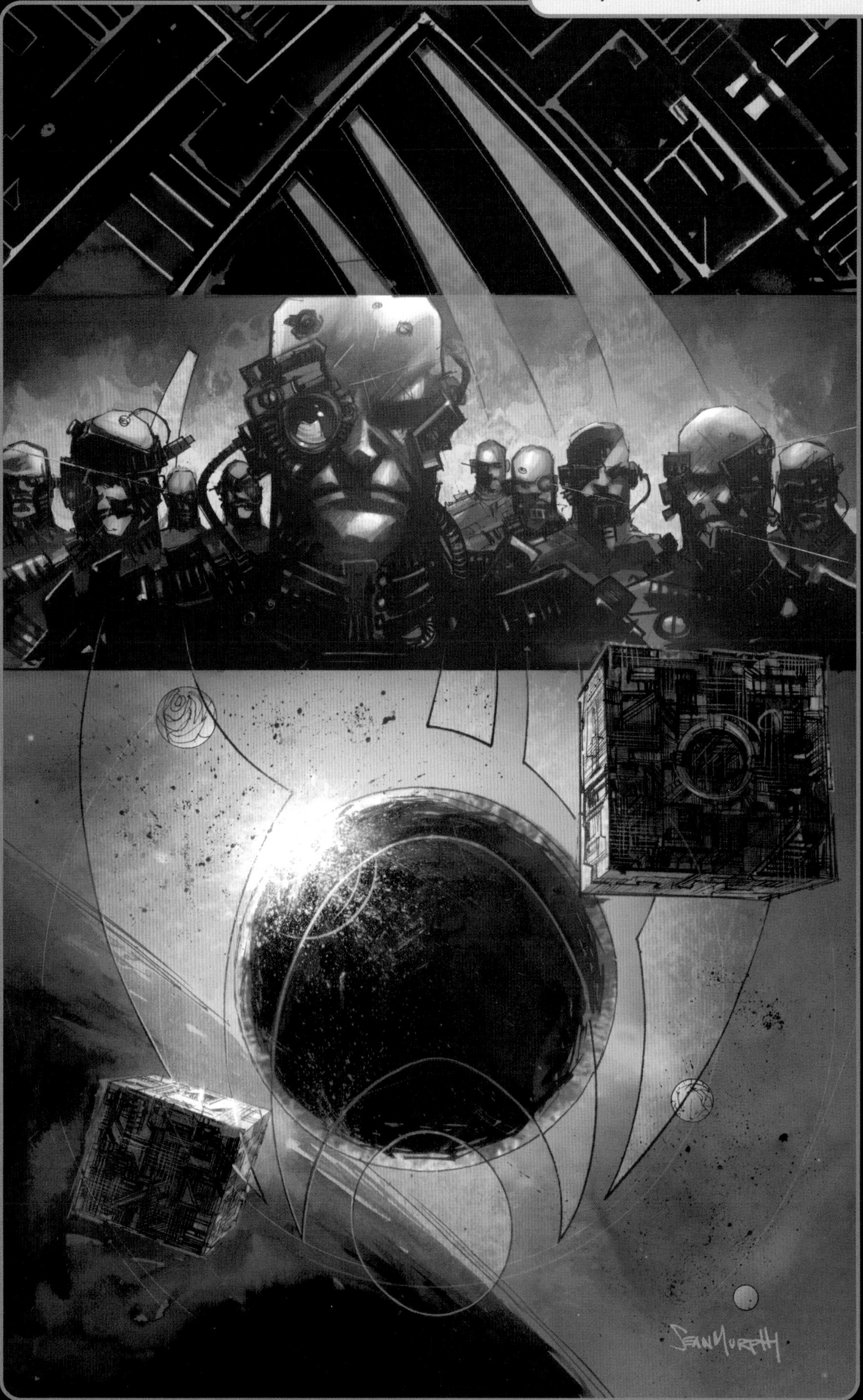

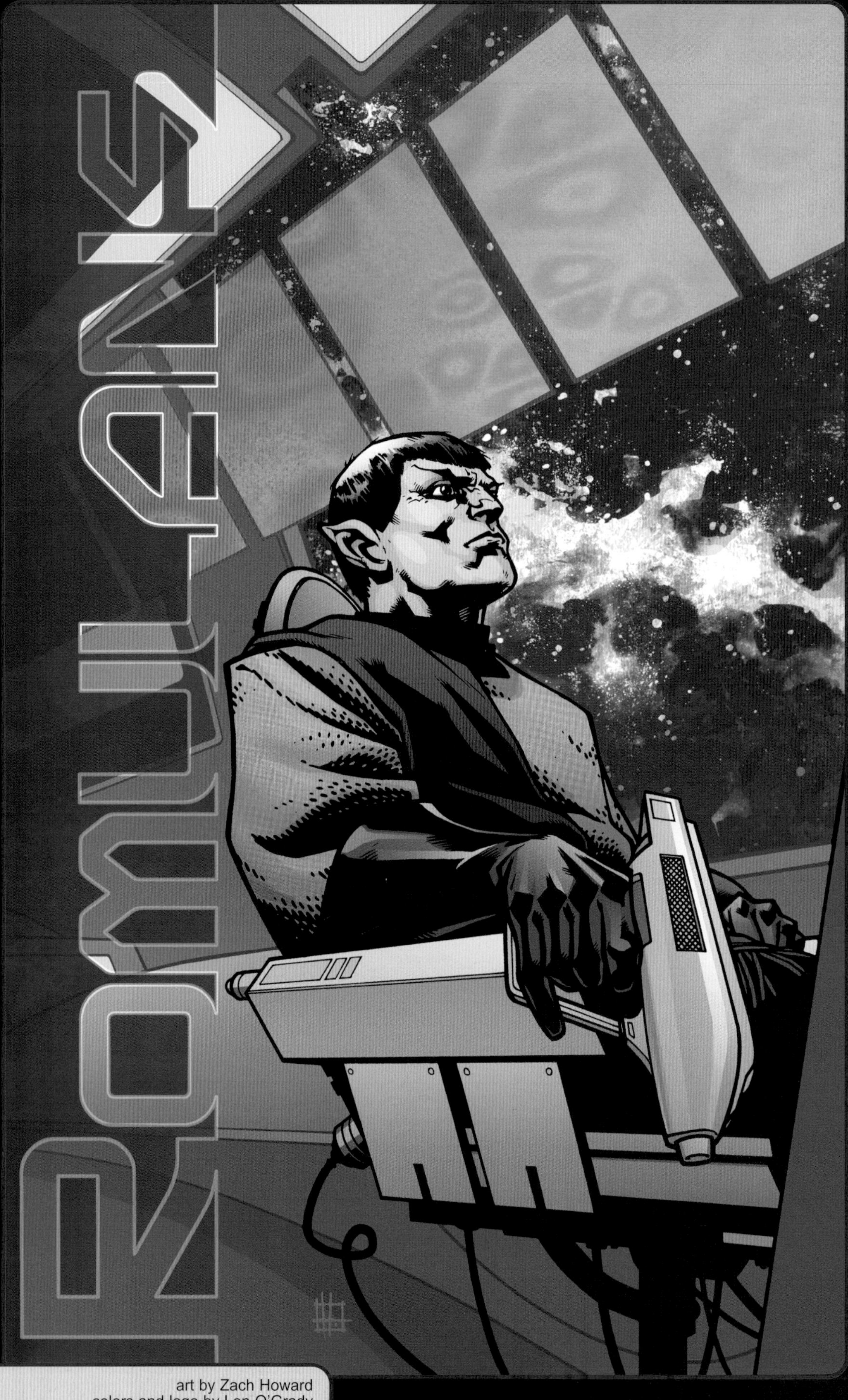
ROMULANS

art by Zach Howard
colors and logo by Len O'Grady

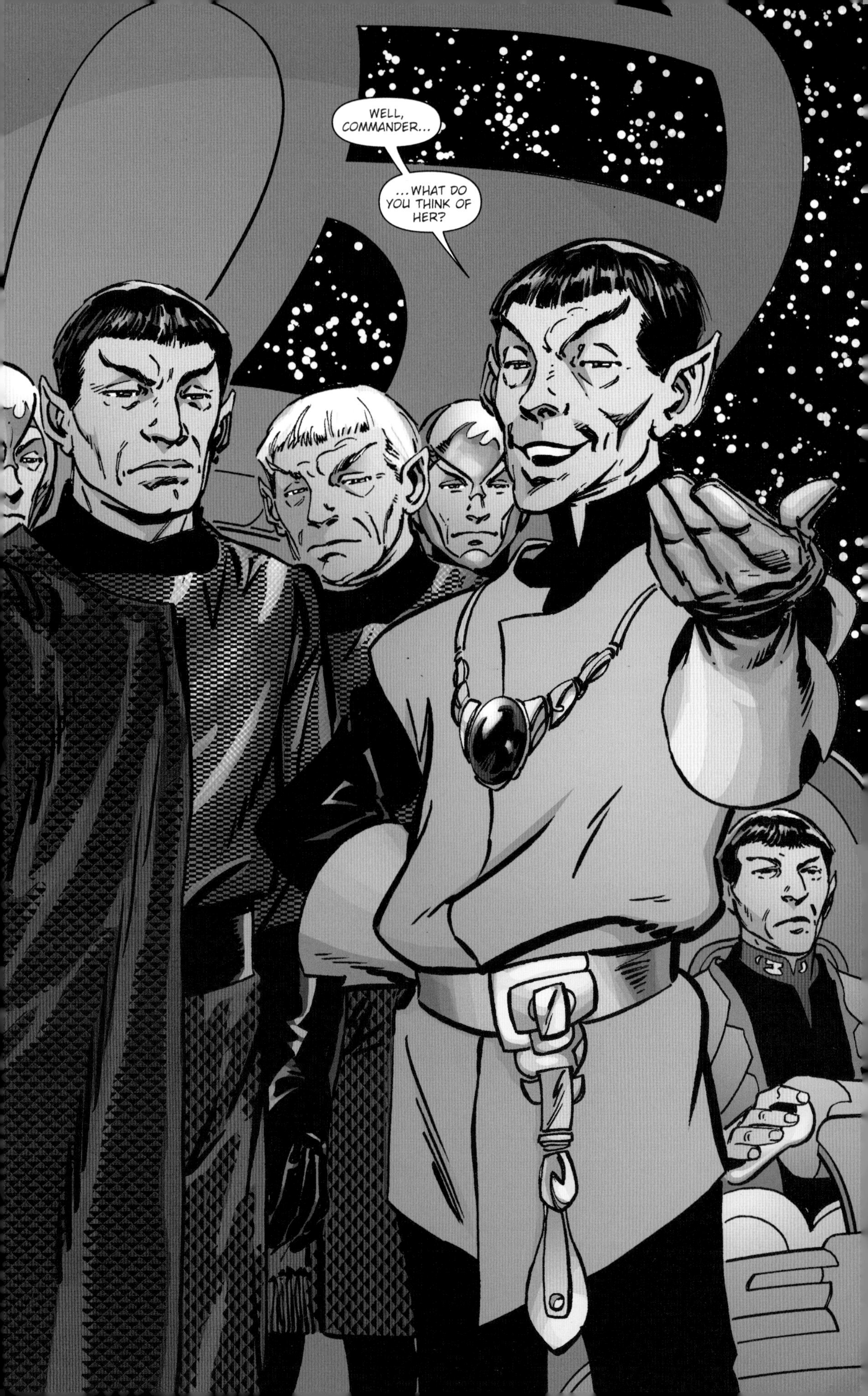
WELL, COMMANDER...
...WHAT DO YOU THINK OF HER?

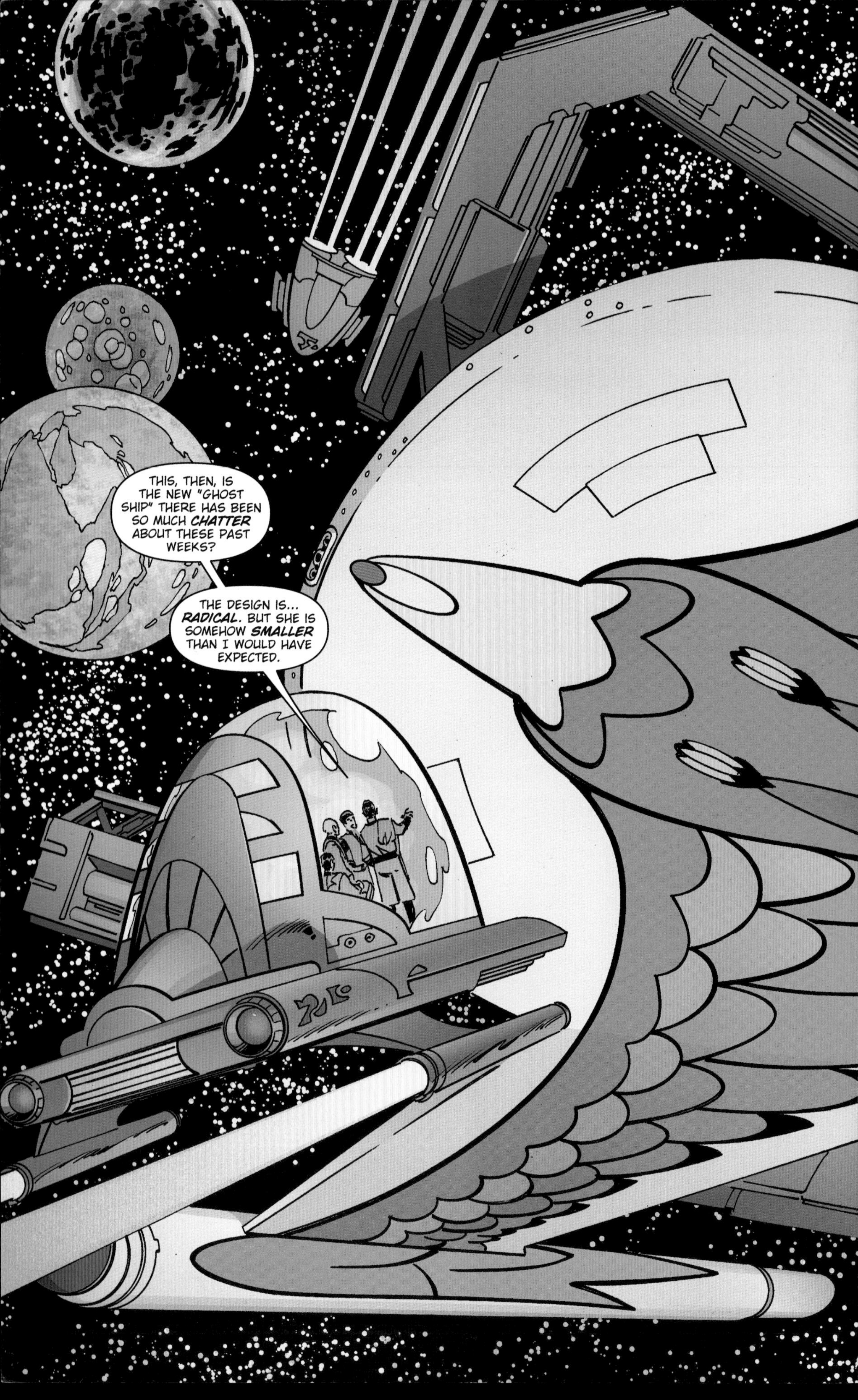
THIS, THEN, IS THE NEW "GHOST SHIP" THERE HAS BEEN SO MUCH CHATTER ABOUT THESE PAST WEEKS?
THE DESIGN IS... RADICAL. BUT SHE IS SOMEHOW SMALLER THAN I WOULD HAVE EXPECTED.

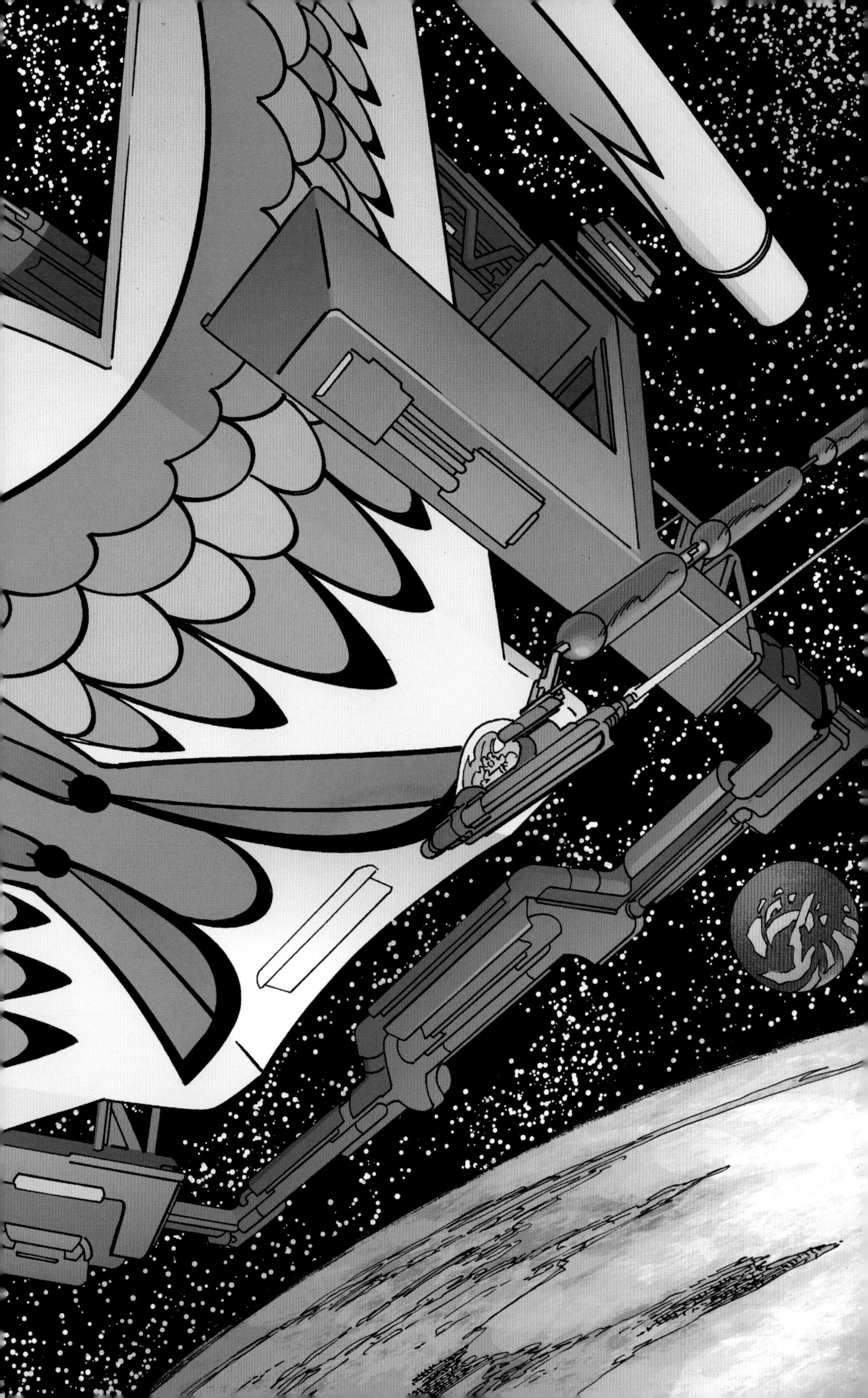

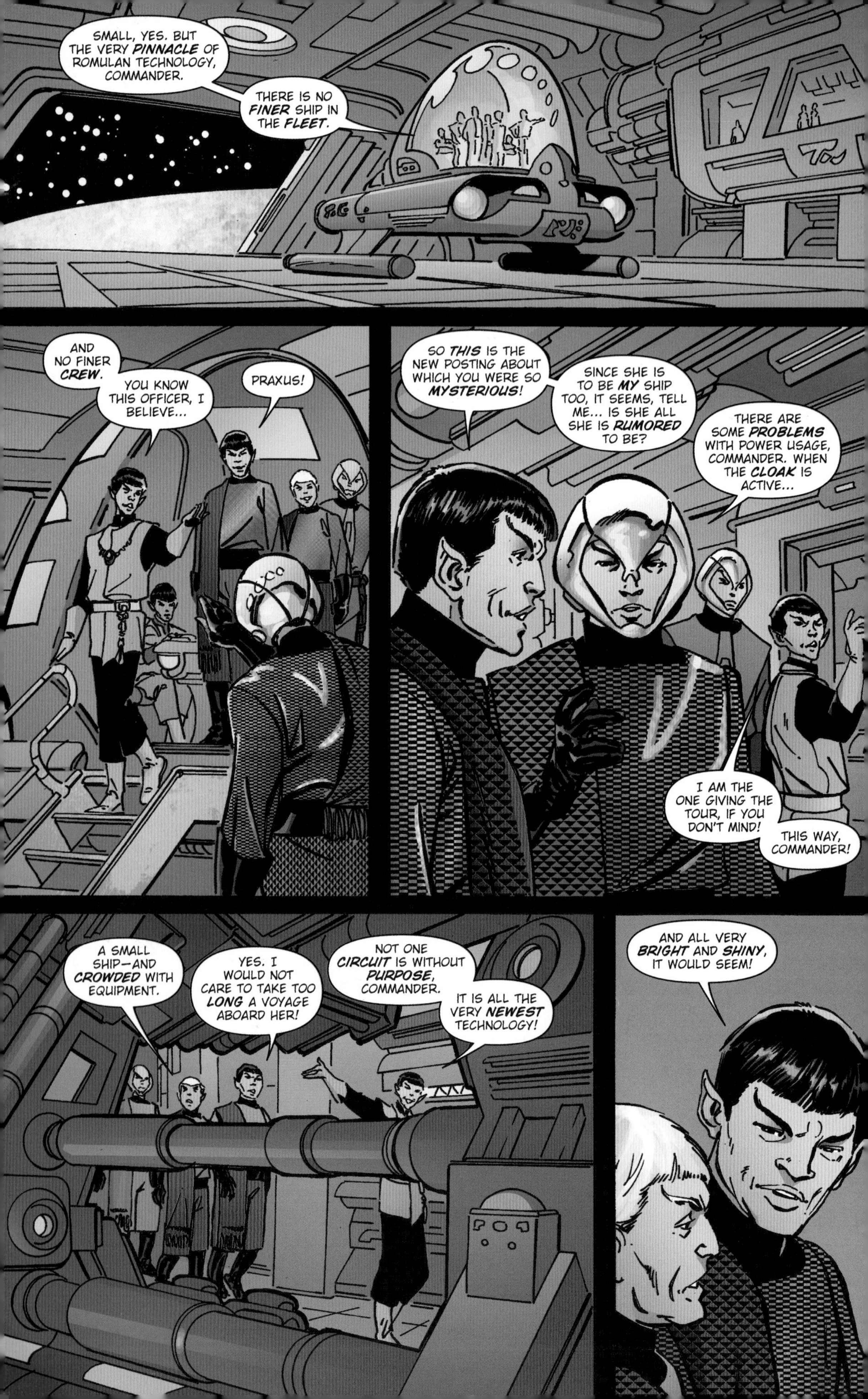
SMALL, YES. BUT THE VERY PINNACLE OF ROMULAN TECHNOLOGY, COMMANDER.
THERE IS NO FINER SHIP IN THE FLEET.
AND NO FINER CREW.
YOU KNOW THIS OFFICER, I BELIEVE...
PRAXUS!
SO THIS IS THE NEW POSTING ABOUT WHICH YOU WERE SO MYSTERIOUS!
SINCE SHE IS TO BE MY SHIP TOO, IT SEEMS, TELL ME... IS SHE ALL SHE IS RUMORED TO BE?
THERE ARE SOME PROBLEMS WITH POWER USAGE, COMMANDER. WHEN THE CLOAK IS ACTIVE...
I AM THE ONE GIVING THE TOUR, IF YOU DON'T MIND!
THIS WAY, COMMANDER!
A SMALL SHIP—AND CROWDED WITH EQUIPMENT.
YES. I WOULD NOT CARE TO TAKE TOO LONG A VOYAGE ABOARD HER!
NOT ONE CIRCUIT IS WITHOUT PURPOSE, COMMANDER.
IT IS ALL THE VERY NEWEST TECHNOLOGY!
AND ALL VERY BRIGHT AND SHINY, IT WOULD SEEM!

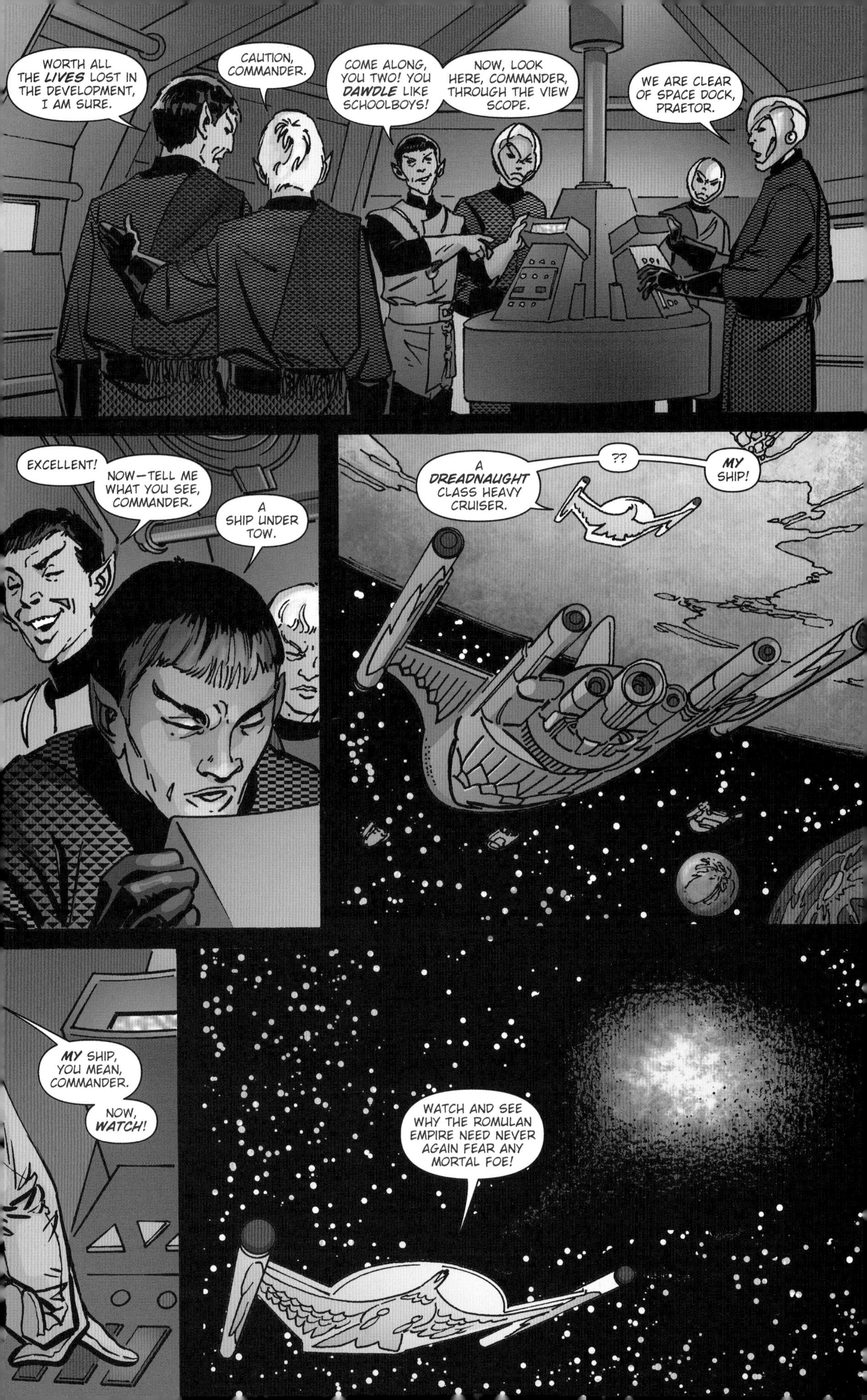
WORTH ALL THE LIVES LOST IN THE DEVELOPMENT, I AM SURE.
CAUTION, COMMANDER.
COME ALONG, YOU TWO! YOU DAWDLE LIKE SCHOOLBOYS!
NOW, LOOK HERE, COMMANDER, THROUGH THE VIEW SCOPE.
WE ARE CLEAR OF SPACE DOCK, PRAETOR.
EXCELLENT!
NOW—TELL ME WHAT YOU SEE, COMMANDER.
A SHIP UNDER TOW.
A DREADNAUGHT CLASS HEAVY CRUISER.
??
MY SHIP!
MY SHIP, YOU MEAN, COMMANDER.
NOW, WATCH!
WATCH AND SEE WHY THE ROMULAN EMPIRE NEED NEVER AGAIN FEAR ANY MORTAL FOE!

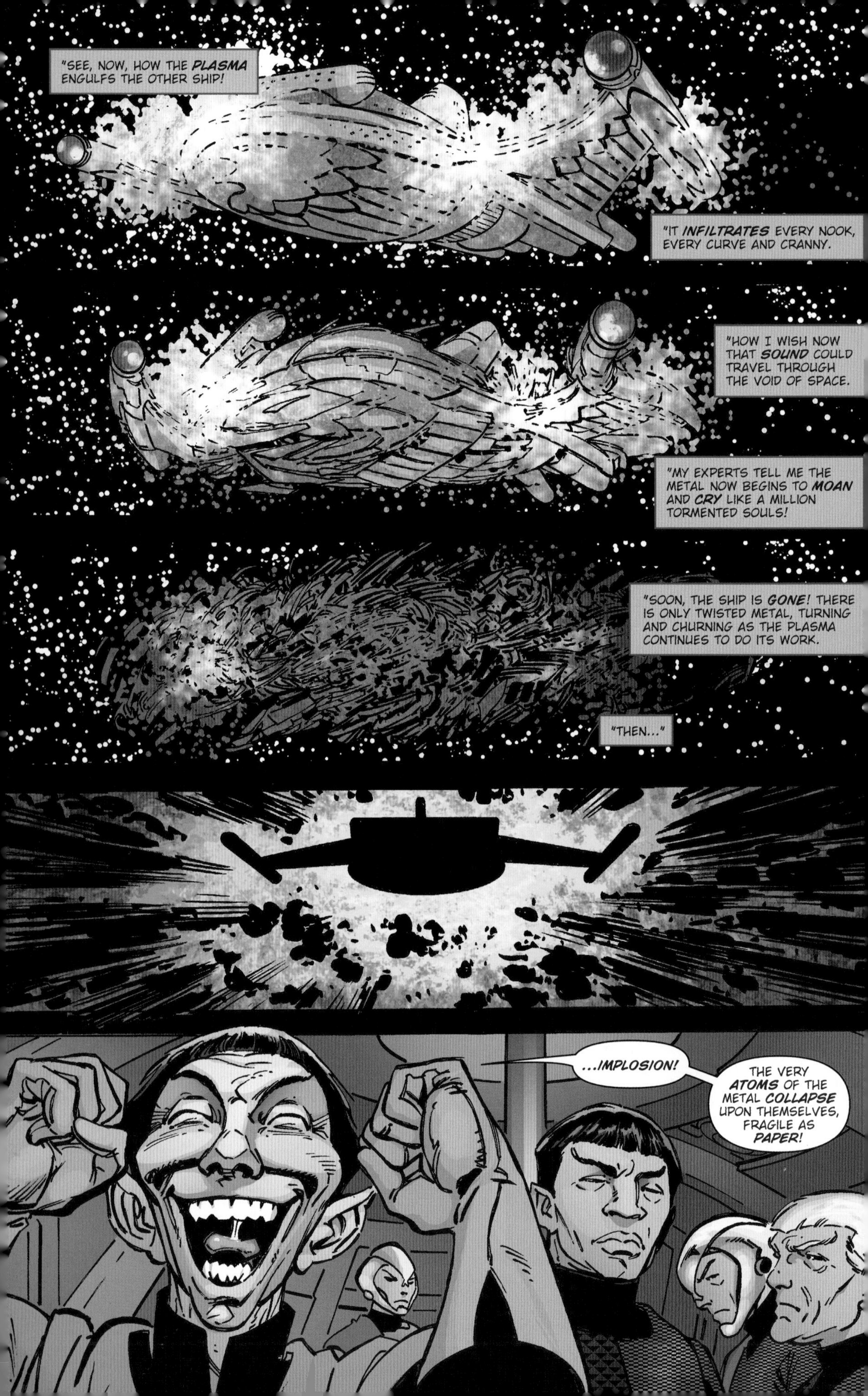
"SEE, NOW, HOW THE PLASMA ENGULFS THE OTHER SHIP!
"IT INFILTRATES EVERY NOOK, EVERY CURVE AND CRANNY.
"HOW I WISH NOW THAT SOUND COULD TRAVEL THROUGH THE VOID OF SPACE.
"MY EXPERTS TELL ME THE METAL NOW BEGINS TO MOAN AND CRY LIKE A MILLION TORMENTED SOULS!
"SOON, THE SHIP IS GONE! THERE IS ONLY TWISTED METAL, TURNING AND CHURNING AS THE PLASMA CONTINUES TO DO ITS WORK.
"THEN..."
...IMPLOSION!
THE VERY ATOMS OF THE METAL COLLAPSE UPON THEMSELVES, FRAGILE AS PAPER!

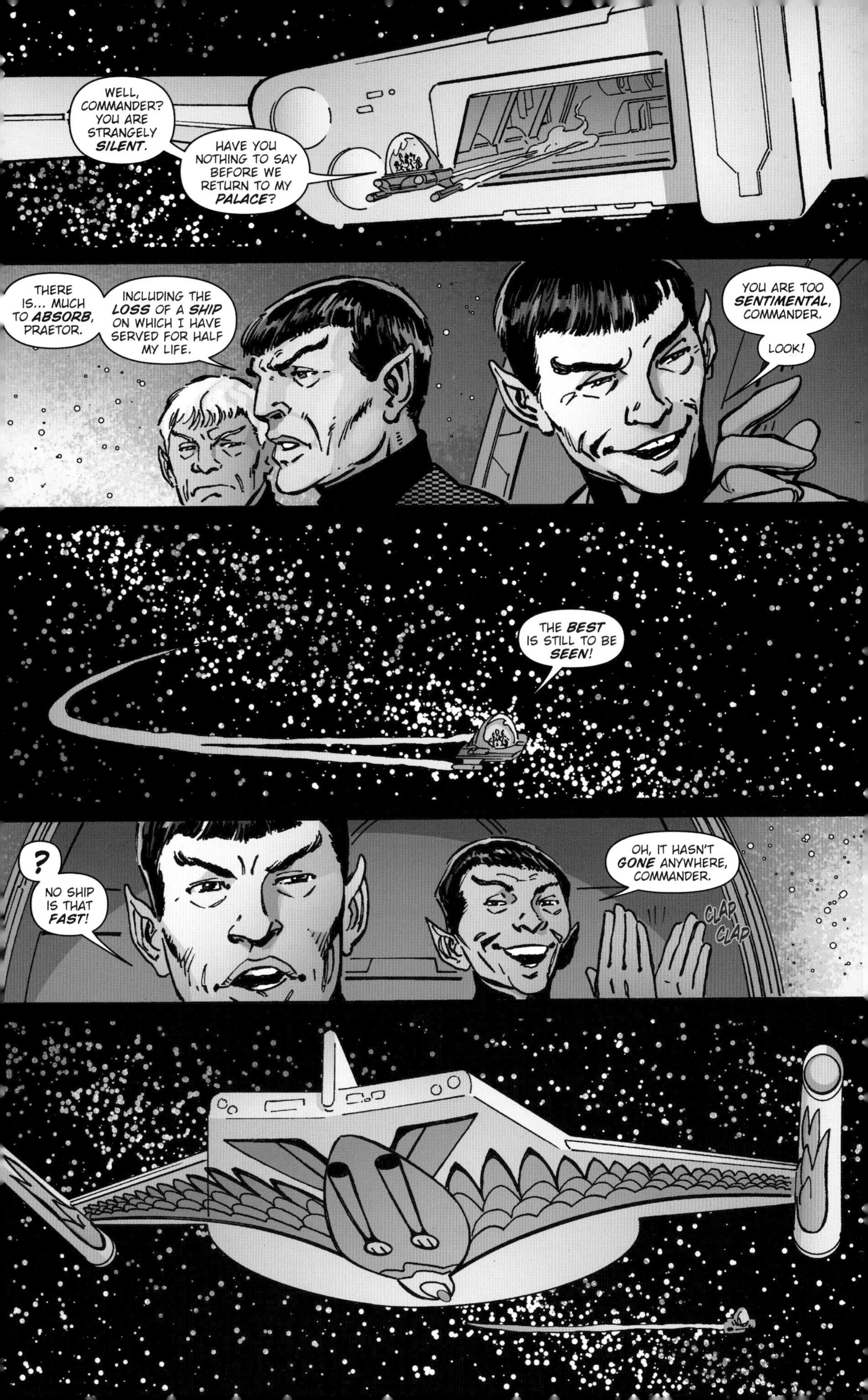
WELL, COMMANDER? YOU ARE STRANGELY SILENT.
HAVE YOU NOTHING TO SAY BEFORE WE RETURN TO MY PALACE?
THERE IS... MUCH TO ABSORB, PRAETOR.
INCLUDING THE LOSS OF A SHIP ON WHICH I HAVE SERVED FOR HALF MY LIFE.
YOU ARE TOO SENTIMENTAL, COMMANDER.
LOOK!
THE BEST IS STILL TO BE SEEN!
?
NO SHIP IS THAT FAST!
OH, IT HASN'T GONE ANYWHERE, COMMANDER.
CLAP CLAP

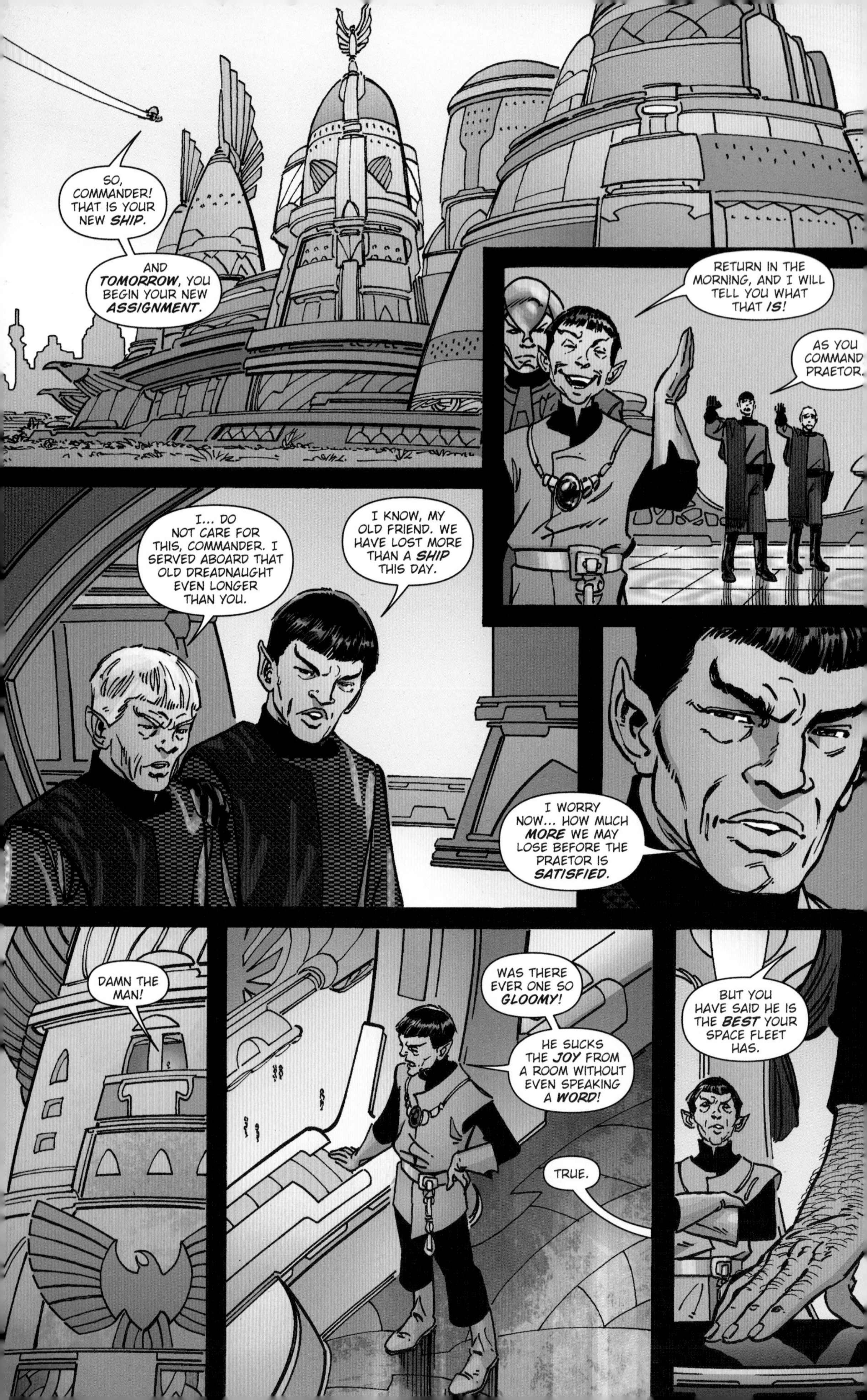
SO, COMMANDER! THAT IS YOUR NEW SHIP.
AND TOMORROW, YOU BEGIN YOUR NEW ASSIGNMENT.
RETURN IN THE MORNING, AND I WILL TELL YOU WHAT THAT IS!
AS YOU COMMAND PRAETOR.
I... DO NOT CARE FOR THIS, COMMANDER. I SERVED ABOARD THAT OLD DREADNAUGHT EVEN LONGER THAN YOU.
I KNOW, MY OLD FRIEND. WE HAVE LOST MORE THAN A SHIP THIS DAY.
I WORRY NOW... HOW MUCH MORE WE MAY LOSE BEFORE THE PRAETOR IS SATISFIED.
DAMN THE MAN!
WAS THERE EVER ONE SO GLOOMY!
HE SUCKS THE JOY FROM A ROOM WITHOUT EVEN SPEAKING A WORD!
BUT YOU HAVE SAID HE IS THE BEST YOUR SPACE FLEET HAS.
TRUE.

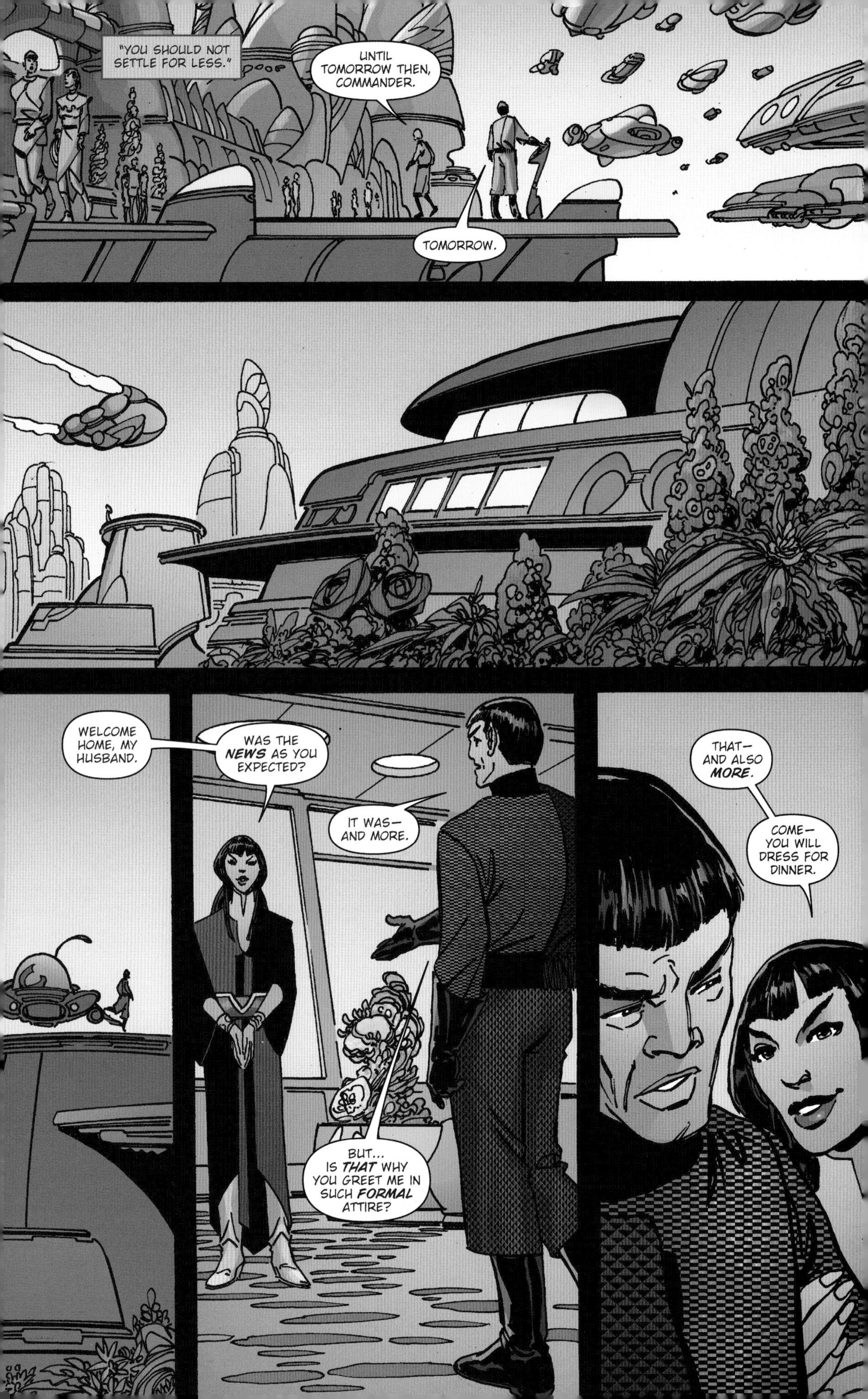
"YOU SHOULD NOT SETTLE FOR LESS."
UNTIL TOMORROW THEN, COMMANDER.
TOMORROW.
WELCOME HOME, MY HUSBAND.
WAS THE NEWS AS YOU EXPECTED?
IT WAS— AND MORE.
BUT... IS THAT WHY YOU GREET ME IN SUCH FORMAL ATTIRE?
THAT— AND ALSO MORE.
COME— YOU WILL DRESS FOR DINNER.

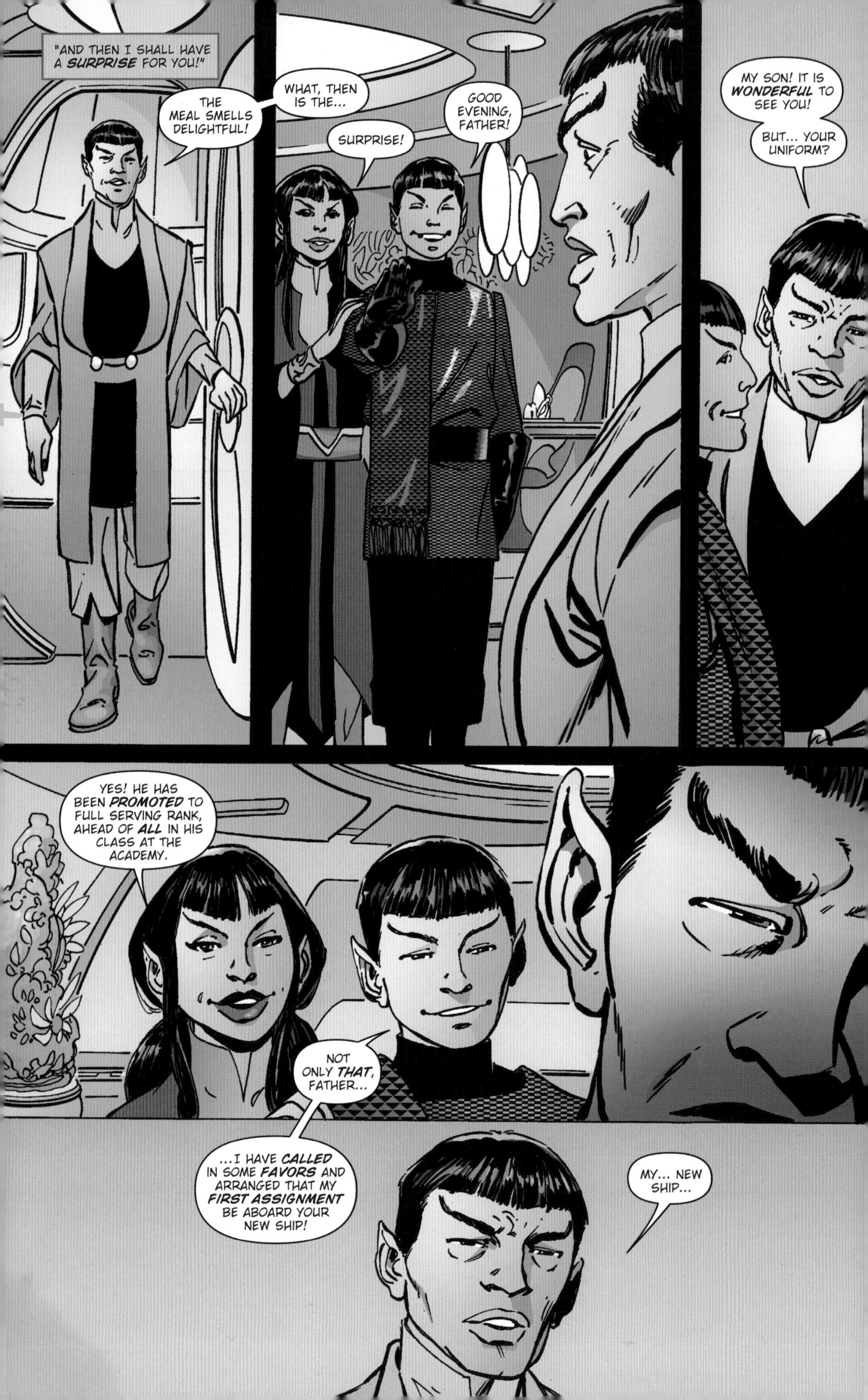
"AND THEN I SHALL HAVE A SURPRISE FOR YOU!"
THE MEAL SMELLS DELIGHTFUL!
WHAT, THEN IS THE...
SURPRISE!
GOOD EVENING, FATHER!
MY SON! IT IS WONDERFUL TO SEE YOU!
BUT... YOUR UNIFORM?
YES! HE HAS BEEN PROMOTED TO FULL SERVING RANK, AHEAD OF ALL IN HIS CLASS AT THE ACADEMY.
NOT ONLY THAT, FATHER...
...I HAVE CALLED IN SOME FAVORS AND ARRANGED THAT MY FIRST ASSIGNMENT BE ABOARD YOUR NEW SHIP!
MY... NEW SHIP...

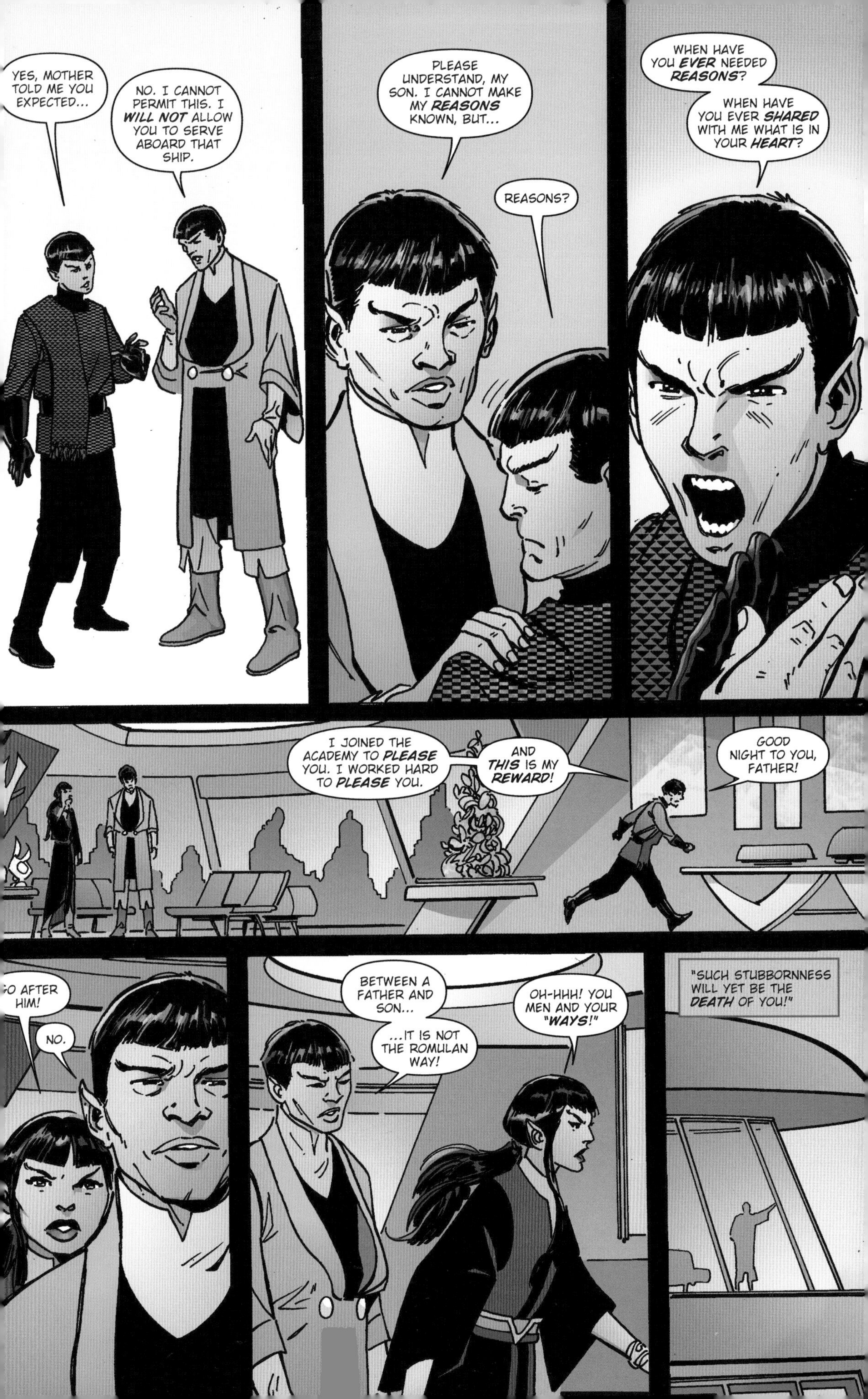

YES, MOTHER TOLD ME YOU EXPECTED...
NO. I CANNOT PERMIT THIS. I **WILL NOT** ALLOW YOU TO SERVE ABOARD THAT SHIP.
PLEASE UNDERSTAND, MY SON. I CANNOT MAKE MY **REASONS** KNOWN, BUT...
REASONS?
WHEN HAVE YOU **EVER** NEEDED **REASONS**?
WHEN HAVE YOU EVER **SHARED** WITH ME WHAT IS IN YOUR **HEART**?
I JOINED THE ACADEMY TO **PLEASE** YOU. I WORKED HARD TO **PLEASE** YOU.
AND **THIS** IS MY **REWARD**!
GOOD NIGHT TO YOU, FATHER!
HIM!
NO.
BETWEEN A FATHER AND SON...
...IT IS NOT THE ROMULAN WAY!
OH-HHH! YOU MEN AND YOUR "**WAYS**!"
"SUCH STUBBORNNESS WILL YET BE THE **DEATH** OF YOU!"

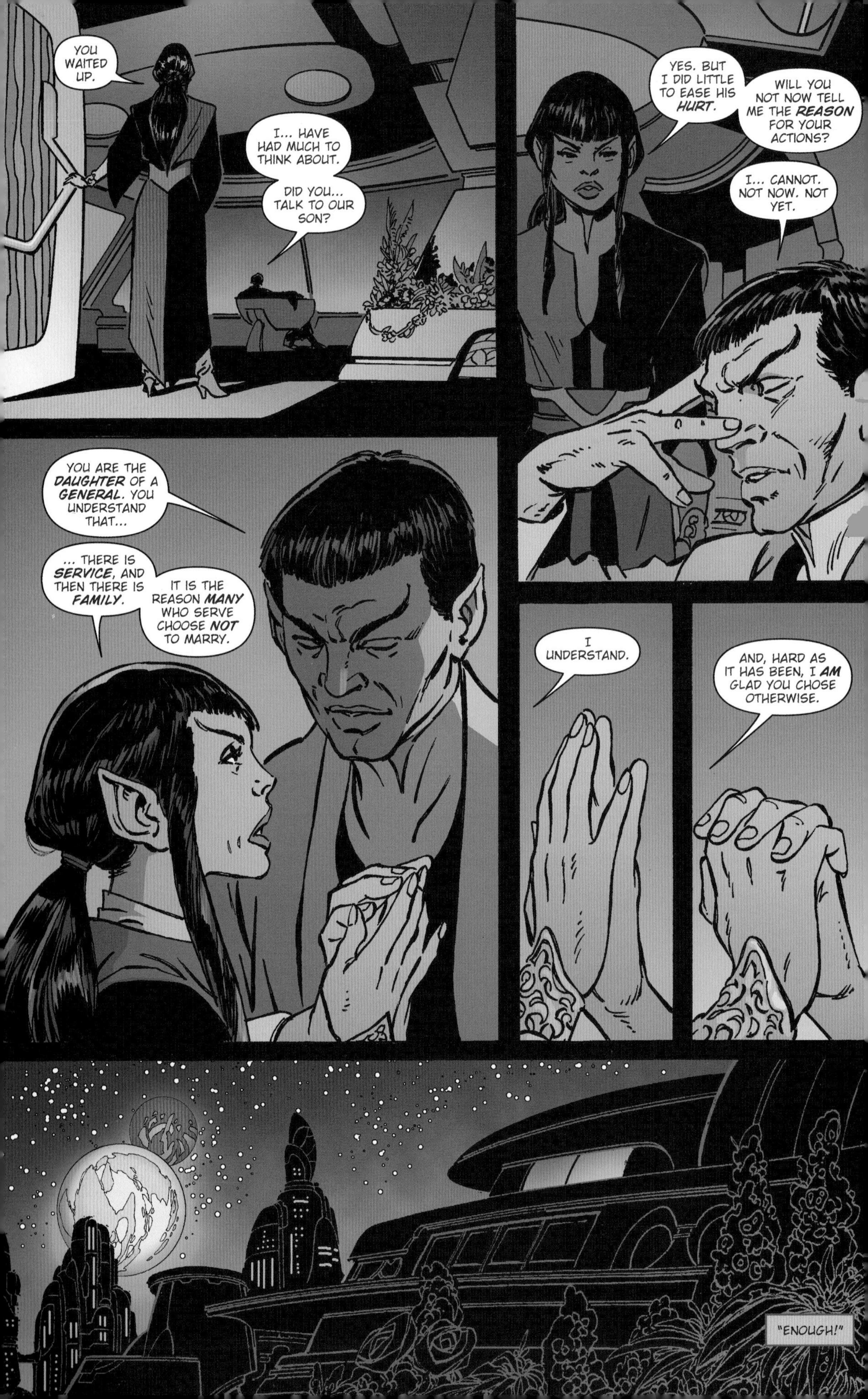
YOU WAITED UP.
I... HAVE HAD MUCH TO THINK ABOUT.
DID YOU... TALK TO OUR SON?
YES. BUT I DID LITTLE TO EASE HIS HURT.
WILL YOU NOT NOW TELL ME THE REASON FOR YOUR ACTIONS?
I... CANNOT. NOT NOW. NOT YET.
YOU ARE THE DAUGHTER OF A GENERAL. YOU UNDERSTAND THAT...
... THERE IS SERVICE, AND THEN THERE IS FAMILY.
IT IS THE REASON MANY WHO SERVE CHOOSE NOT TO MARRY.
I UNDERSTAND.
AND, HARD AS IT HAS BEEN, I AM GLAD YOU CHOSE OTHERWISE.
"ENOUGH!"

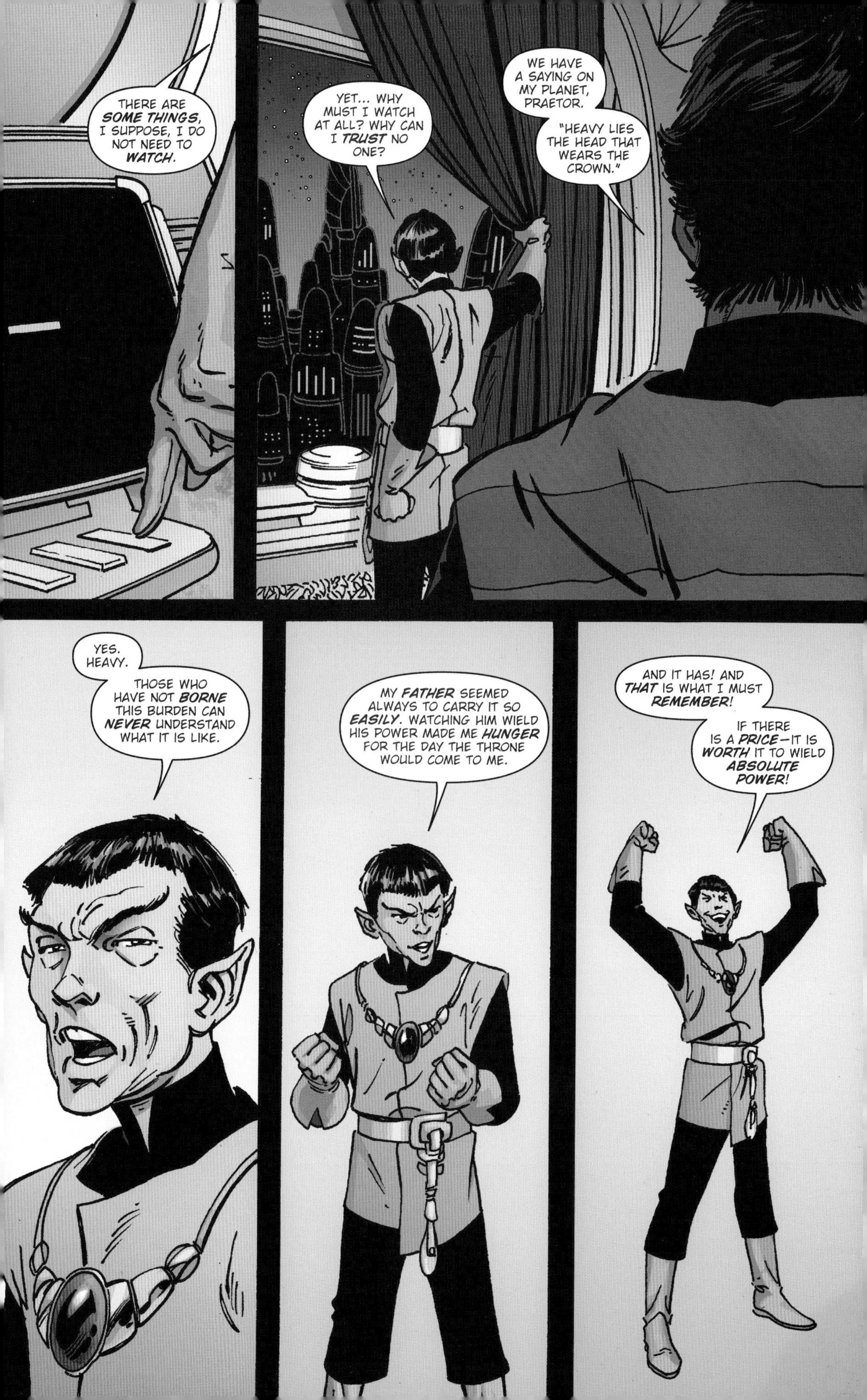
THERE ARE SOME THINGS, I SUPPOSE, I DO NOT NEED TO WATCH.
YET... WHY MUST I WATCH AT ALL? WHY CAN I TRUST NO ONE?
WE HAVE A SAYING ON MY PLANET, PRAETOR.
"HEAVY LIES THE HEAD THAT WEARS THE CROWN."
YES. HEAVY.
THOSE WHO HAVE NOT BORNE THIS BURDEN CAN NEVER UNDERSTAND WHAT IT IS LIKE.
MY FATHER SEEMED ALWAYS TO CARRY IT SO EASILY. WATCHING HIM WIELD HIS POWER MADE ME HUNGER FOR THE DAY THE THRONE WOULD COME TO ME.
AND IT HAS! AND THAT IS WHAT I MUST REMEMBER!
IF THERE IS A PRICE—IT IS WORTH IT TO WIELD ABSOLUTE POWER!

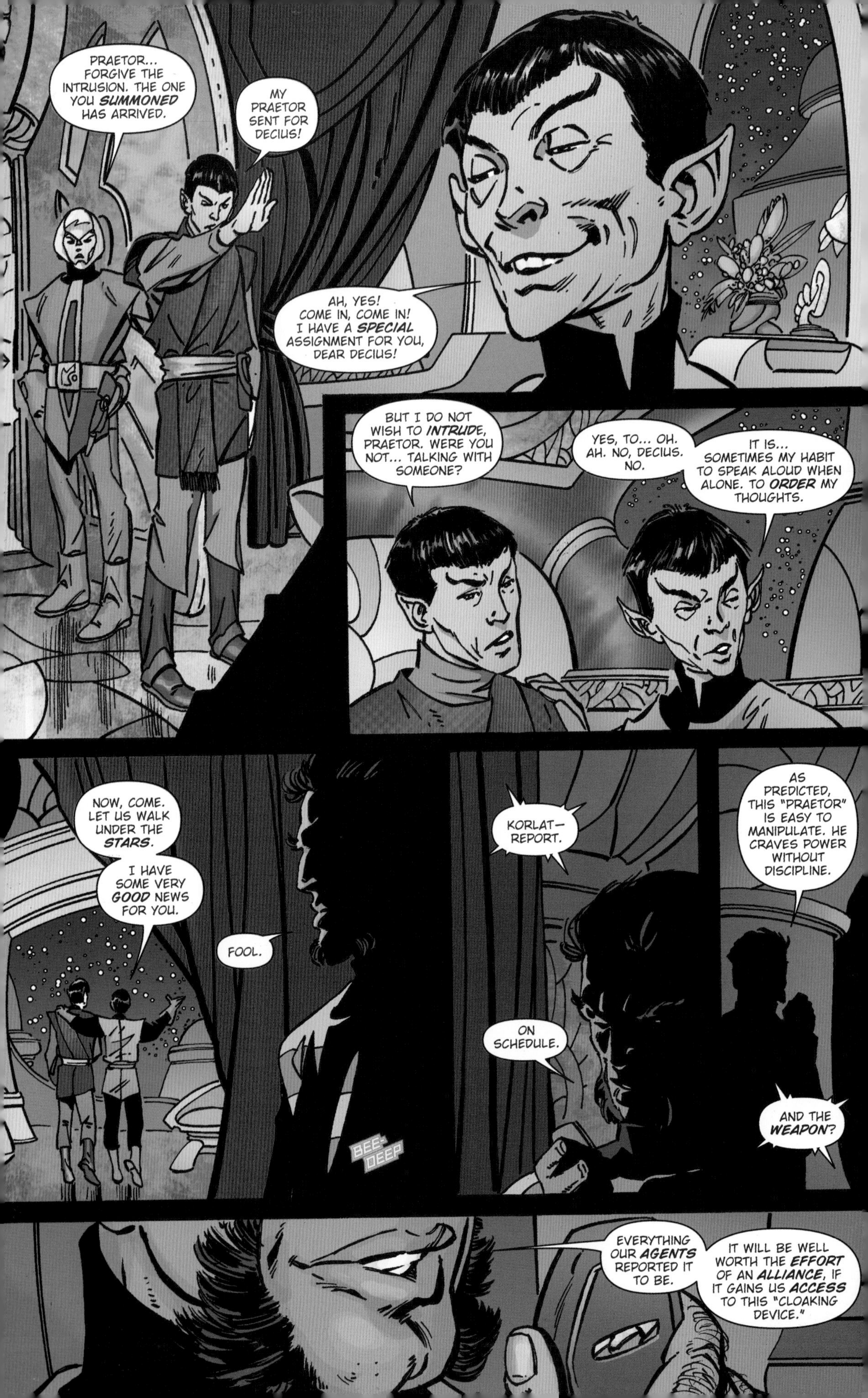
PRAETOR... FORGIVE THE INTRUSION. THE ONE YOU SUMMONED HAS ARRIVED.
MY PRAETOR SENT FOR DECIUS!
AH, YES! COME IN, COME IN! I HAVE A SPECIAL ASSIGNMENT FOR YOU, DEAR DECIUS!
BUT I DO NOT WISH TO INTRUDE, PRAETOR. WERE YOU NOT... TALKING WITH SOMEONE?
YES, TO... OH. AH. NO, DECIUS. NO.
IT IS... SOMETIMES MY HABIT TO SPEAK ALOUD WHEN ALONE. TO ORDER MY THOUGHTS.
NOW, COME. LET US WALK UNDER THE STARS.
I HAVE SOME VERY GOOD NEWS FOR YOU.
FOOL.
BEE-DEEP
KORLAT— REPORT.
AS PREDICTED, THIS "PRAETOR" IS EASY TO MANIPULATE. HE CRAVES POWER WITHOUT DISCIPLINE.
ON SCHEDULE.
AND THE WEAPON?
EVERYTHING OUR AGENTS REPORTED IT TO BE.
IT WILL BE WELL WORTH THE EFFORT OF AN ALLIANCE, IF IT GAINS US ACCESS TO THIS "CLOAKING DEVICE."

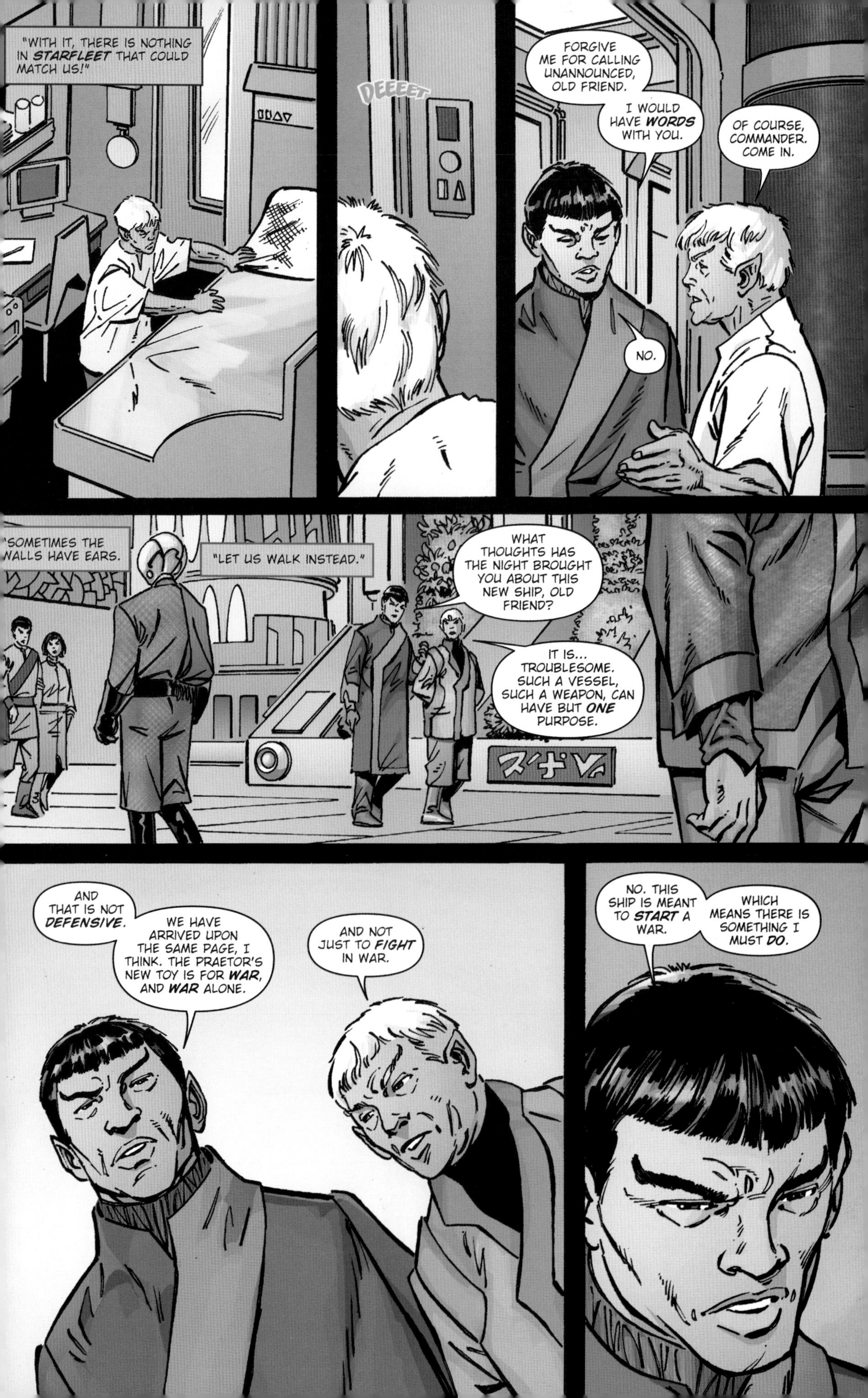

"WITH IT, THERE IS NOTHING IN STARFLEET THAT COULD MATCH US!"
DEEEET
FORGIVE ME FOR CALLING UNANNOUNCED, OLD FRIEND.
I WOULD HAVE WORDS WITH YOU.
OF COURSE, COMMANDER. COME IN.
NO.
"SOMETIMES THE WALLS HAVE EARS.
"LET US WALK INSTEAD."
WHAT THOUGHTS HAS THE NIGHT BROUGHT YOU ABOUT THIS NEW SHIP, OLD FRIEND?
IT IS... TROUBLESOME. SUCH A VESSEL, SUCH A WEAPON, CAN HAVE BUT ONE PURPOSE.
AND THAT IS NOT DEFENSIVE.
WE HAVE ARRIVED UPON THE SAME PAGE, I THINK. THE PRAETOR'S NEW TOY IS FOR WAR, AND WAR ALONE.
AND NOT JUST TO FIGHT IN WAR.
NO. THIS SHIP IS MEANT TO START A WAR.
WHICH MEANS THERE IS SOMETHING I MUST DO.

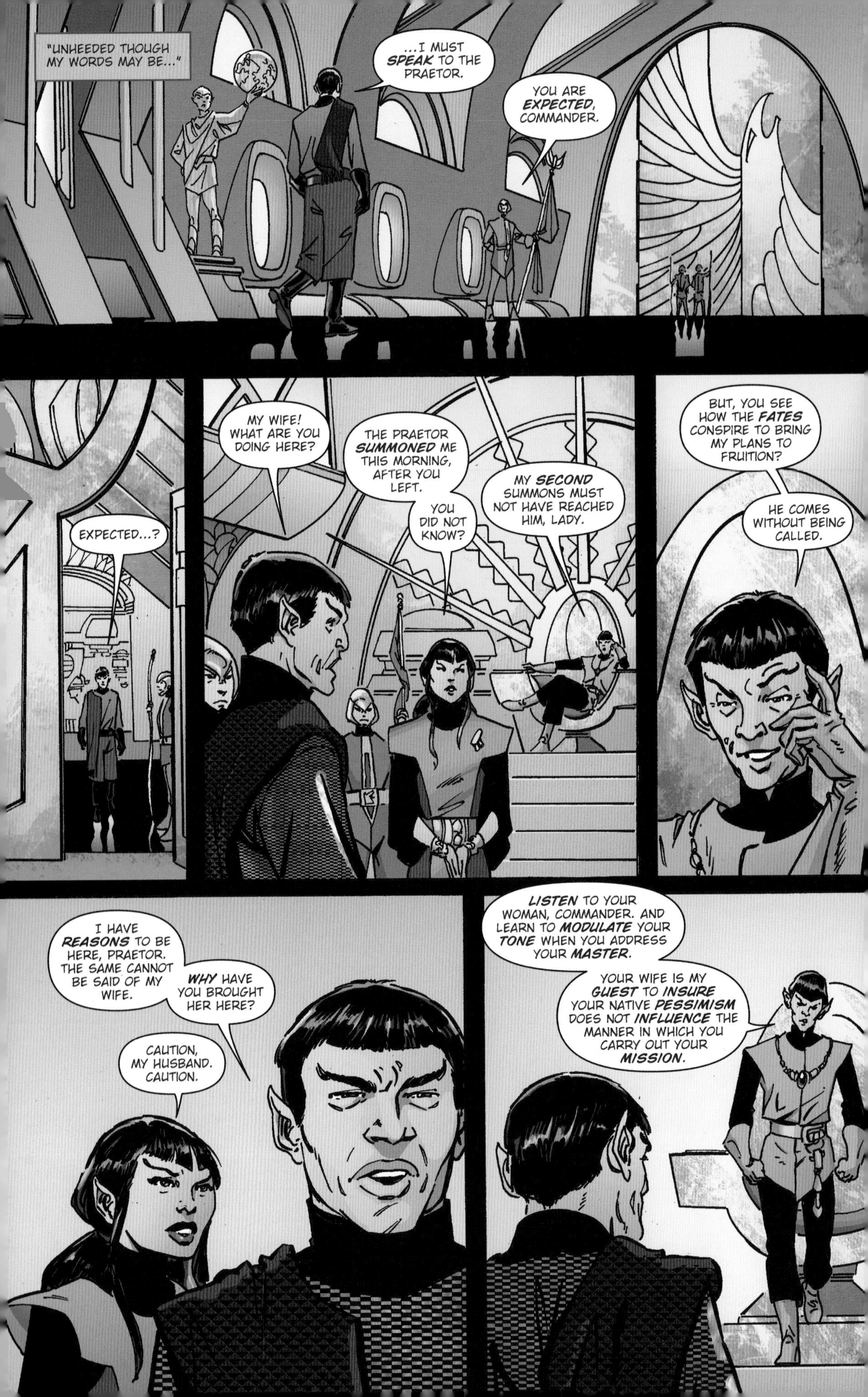
"UNHEEDED THOUGH MY WORDS MAY BE..."
...I MUST SPEAK TO THE PRAETOR.
YOU ARE EXPECTED, COMMANDER.
EXPECTED...?
MY WIFE! WHAT ARE YOU DOING HERE?
THE PRAETOR SUMMONED ME THIS MORNING, AFTER YOU LEFT.
YOU DID NOT KNOW?
MY SECOND SUMMONS MUST NOT HAVE REACHED HIM, LADY.
BUT, YOU SEE HOW THE FATES CONSPIRE TO BRING MY PLANS TO FRUITION?
HE COMES WITHOUT BEING CALLED.
I HAVE REASONS TO BE HERE, PRAETOR. THE SAME CANNOT BE SAID OF MY WIFE.
WHY HAVE YOU BROUGHT HER HERE?
CAUTION, MY HUSBAND. CAUTION.
LISTEN TO YOUR WOMAN, COMMANDER. AND LEARN TO MODULATE YOUR TONE WHEN YOU ADDRESS YOUR MASTER.
YOUR WIFE IS MY GUEST TO INSURE YOUR NATIVE PESSIMISM DOES NOT INFLUENCE THE MANNER IN WHICH YOU CARRY OUT YOUR MISSION.

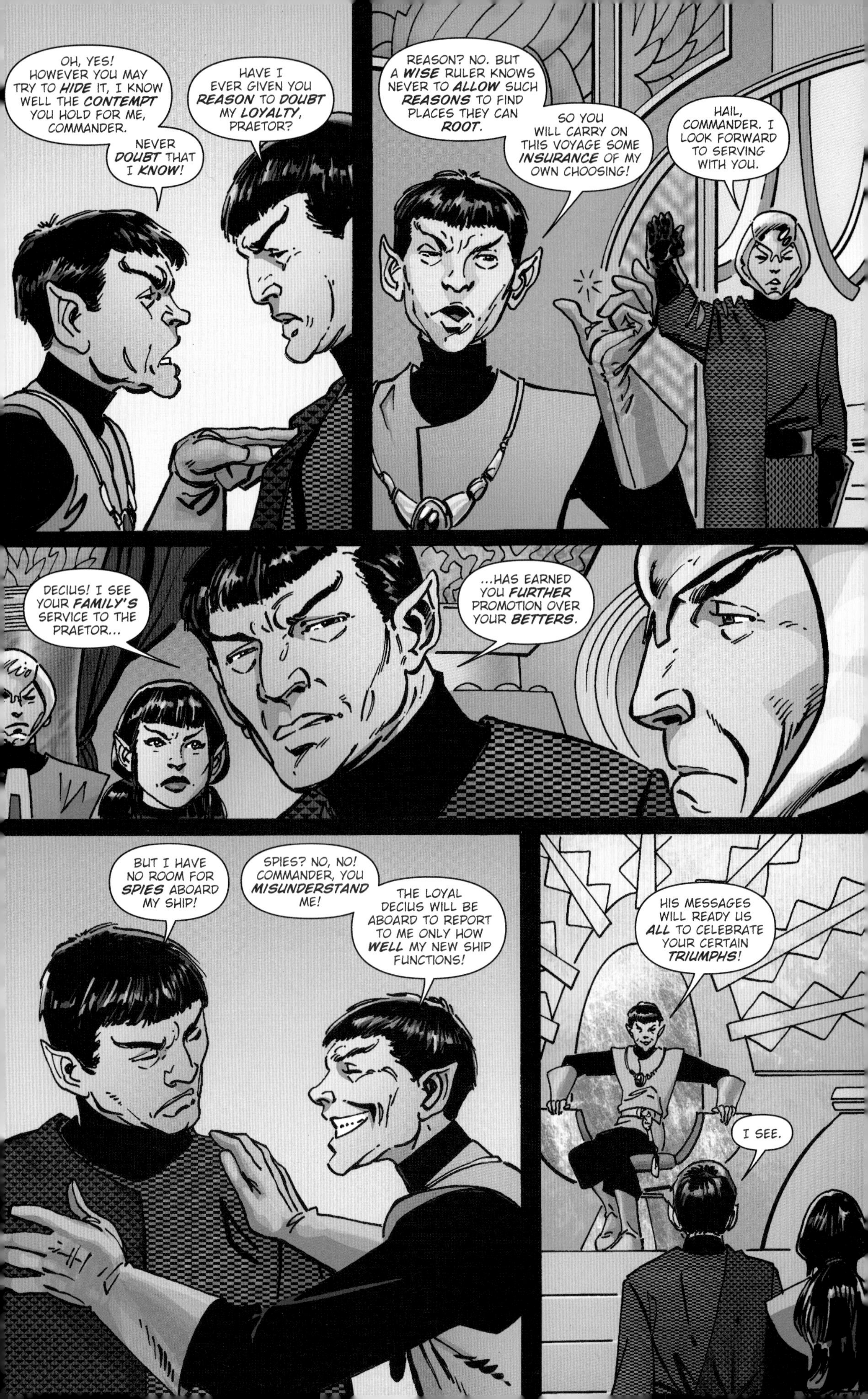

OH, YES! HOWEVER YOU MAY TRY TO HIDE IT, I KNOW WELL THE CONTEMPT YOU HOLD FOR ME, COMMANDER.
NEVER DOUBT THAT I KNOW!
HAVE I EVER GIVEN YOU REASON TO DOUBT MY LOYALTY, PRAETOR?
REASON? NO. BUT A WISE RULER KNOWS NEVER TO ALLOW SUCH REASONS TO FIND PLACES THEY CAN ROOT.
SO YOU WILL CARRY ON THIS VOYAGE SOME INSURANCE OF MY OWN CHOOSING!
HAIL, COMMANDER. I LOOK FORWARD TO SERVING WITH YOU.
DECIUS! I SEE YOUR FAMILY'S SERVICE TO THE PRAETOR...
...HAS EARNED YOU FURTHER PROMOTION OVER YOUR BETTERS.
BUT I HAVE NO ROOM FOR SPIES ABOARD MY SHIP!
SPIES? NO, NO! COMMANDER, YOU MISUNDERSTAND ME!
THE LOYAL DECIUS WILL BE ABOARD TO REPORT TO ME ONLY HOW WELL MY NEW SHIP FUNCTIONS!
HIS MESSAGES WILL READY US ALL TO CELEBRATE YOUR CERTAIN TRIUMPHS!
I SEE.

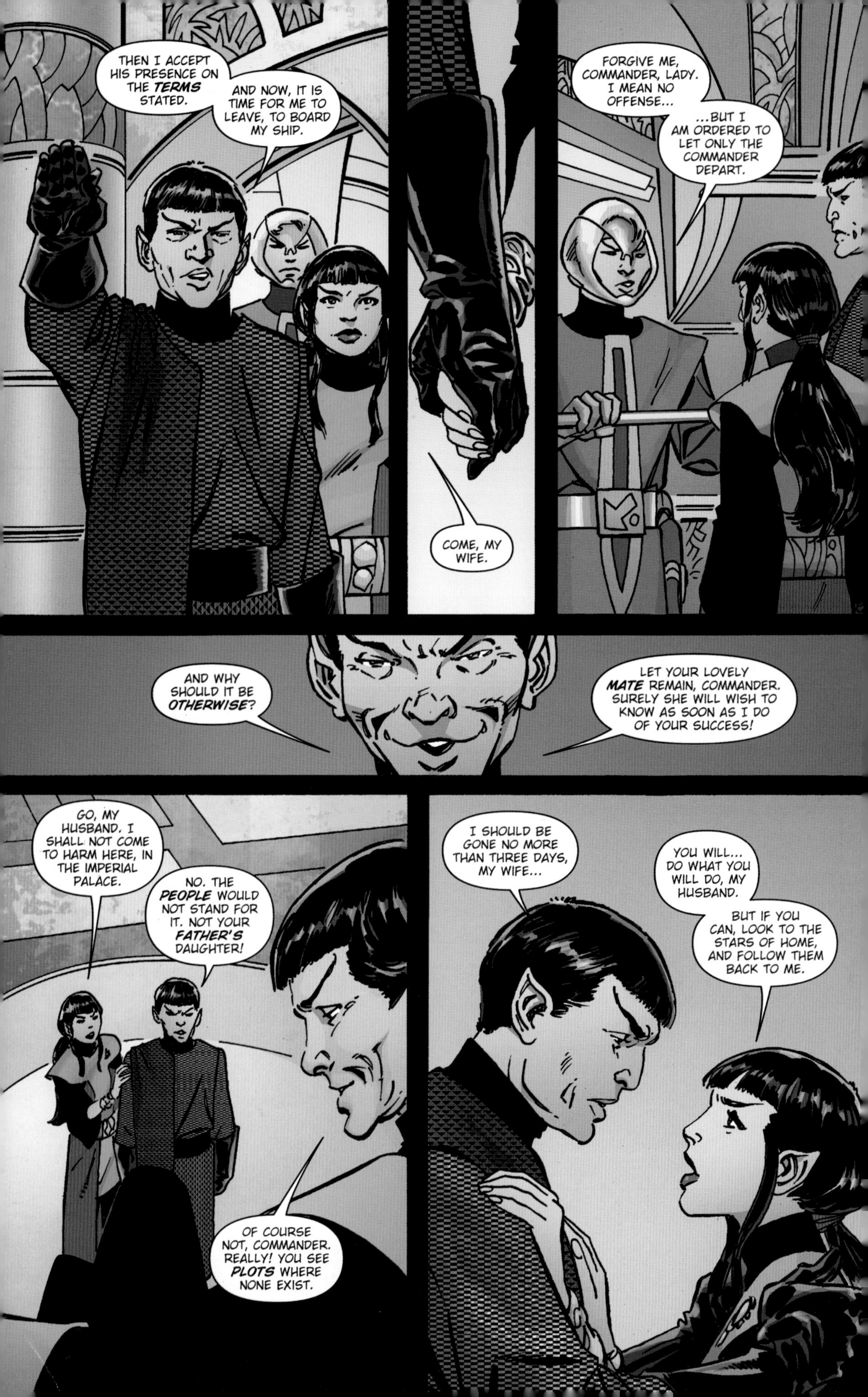
THEN I ACCEPT HIS PRESENCE ON THE **TERMS** STATED.
AND NOW, IT IS TIME FOR ME TO LEAVE, TO BOARD MY SHIP.
COME, MY WIFE.
FORGIVE ME, COMMANDER, LADY. I MEAN NO OFFENSE...
...BUT I AM ORDERED TO LET ONLY THE COMMANDER DEPART.
AND WHY SHOULD IT BE **OTHERWISE**?
LET YOUR LOVELY **MATE** REMAIN, COMMANDER. SURELY SHE WILL WISH TO KNOW AS SOON AS I DO OF YOUR SUCCESS!
GO, MY HUSBAND. I SHALL NOT COME TO HARM HERE, IN THE IMPERIAL PALACE.
NO. THE **PEOPLE** WOULD NOT STAND FOR IT. NOT YOUR **FATHER'S** DAUGHTER!
OF COURSE NOT, COMMANDER. REALLY! YOU SEE **PLOTS** WHERE NONE EXIST.
I SHOULD BE GONE NO MORE THAN THREE DAYS, MY WIFE...
YOU WILL... DO WHAT YOU WILL DO, MY HUSBAND.
BUT IF YOU CAN, LOOK TO THE STARS OF HOME, AND FOLLOW THEM BACK TO ME.

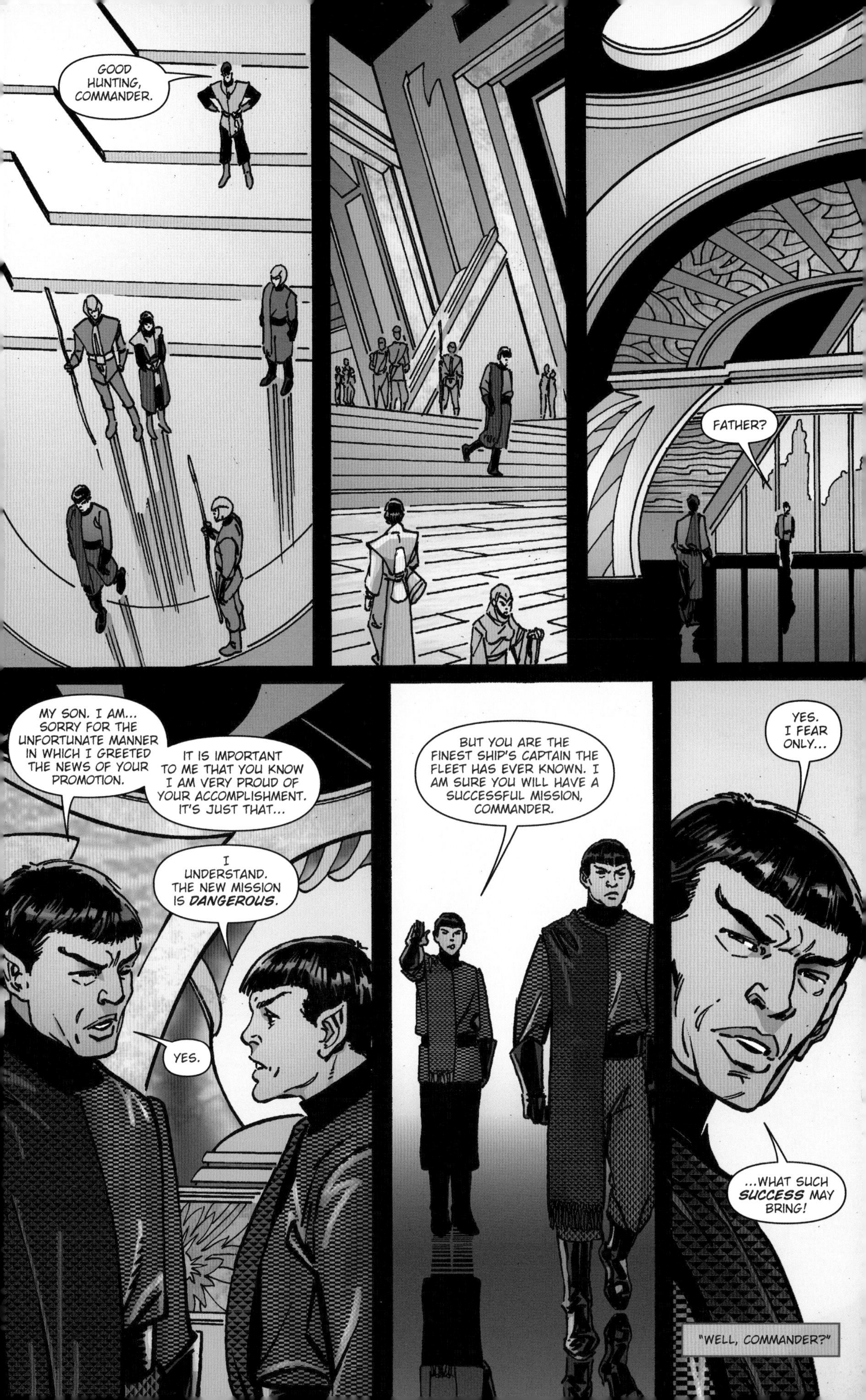
GOOD HUNTING, COMMANDER.
FATHER?
MY SON. I AM... SORRY FOR THE UNFORTUNATE MANNER IN WHICH I GREETED THE NEWS OF YOUR PROMOTION.
IT IS IMPORTANT TO ME THAT YOU KNOW I AM VERY PROUD OF YOUR ACCOMPLISHMENT. IT'S JUST THAT...
I UNDERSTAND. THE NEW MISSION IS ***DANGEROUS***.
YES.
BUT YOU ARE THE FINEST SHIP'S CAPTAIN THE FLEET HAS EVER KNOWN. I AM SURE YOU WILL HAVE A SUCCESSFUL MISSION, COMMANDER.
YES. I FEAR ONLY...
...WHAT SUCH ***SUCCESS*** MAY BRING!
"WELL, COMMANDER?"

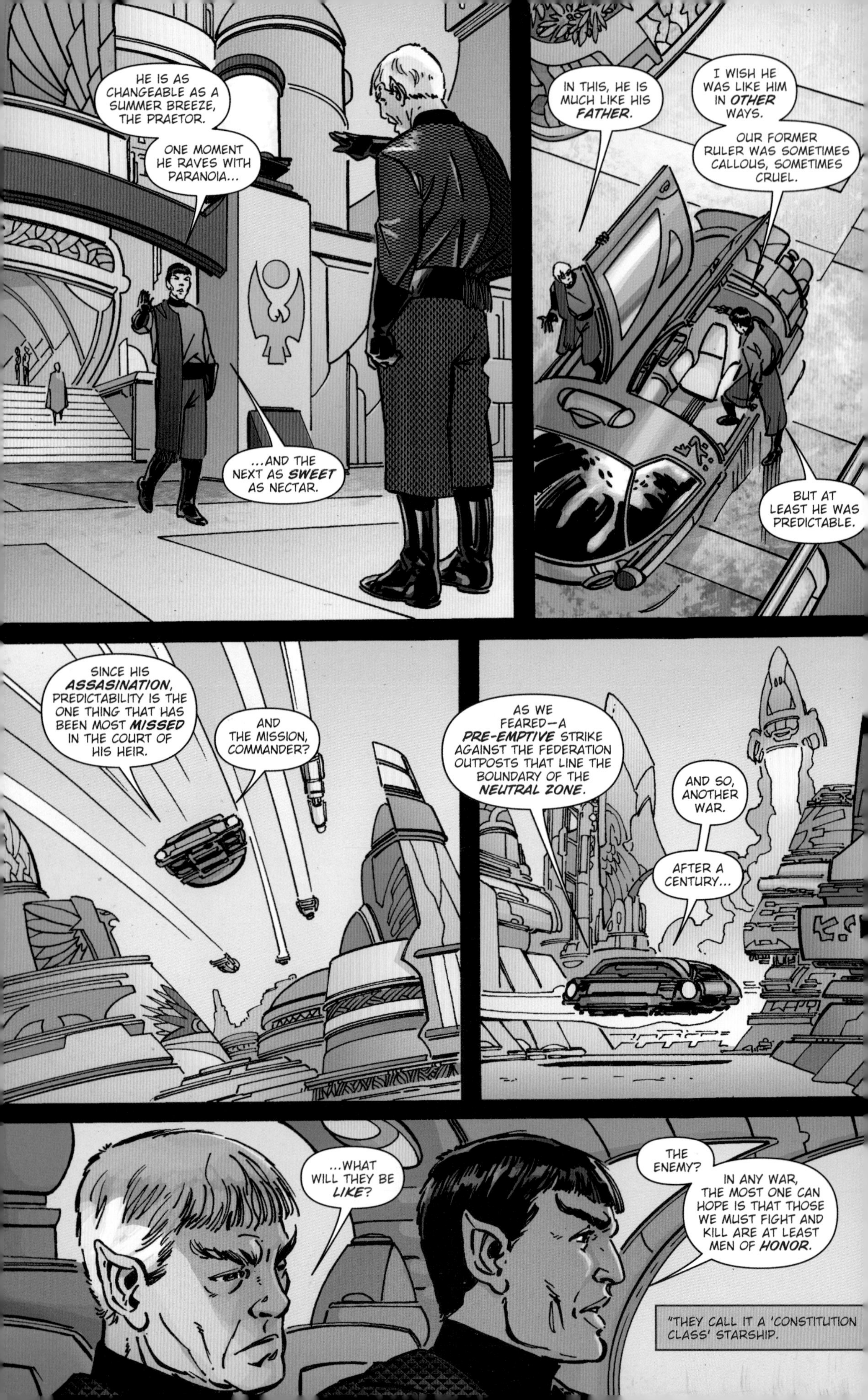
HE IS AS CHANGEABLE AS A SUMMER BREEZE, THE PRAETOR.
ONE MOMENT HE RAVES WITH PARANOIA...
...AND THE NEXT AS SWEET AS NECTAR.
IN THIS, HE IS MUCH LIKE HIS FATHER.
I WISH HE WAS LIKE HIM IN OTHER WAYS.
OUR FORMER RULER WAS SOMETIMES CALLOUS, SOMETIMES CRUEL.
BUT AT LEAST HE WAS PREDICTABLE.
SINCE HIS ASSASINATION, PREDICTABILITY IS THE ONE THING THAT HAS BEEN MOST MISSED IN THE COURT OF HIS HEIR.
AND THE MISSION, COMMANDER?
AS WE FEARED—A PRE-EMPTIVE STRIKE AGAINST THE FEDERATION OUTPOSTS THAT LINE THE BOUNDARY OF THE NEUTRAL ZONE.
AND SO, ANOTHER WAR.
AFTER A CENTURY...
...WHAT WILL THEY BE LIKE?
THE ENEMY?
IN ANY WAR, THE MOST ONE CAN HOPE IS THAT THOSE WE MUST FIGHT AND KILL ARE AT LEAST MEN OF HONOR.
"THEY CALL IT A 'CONSTITUTION CLASS' STARSHIP.

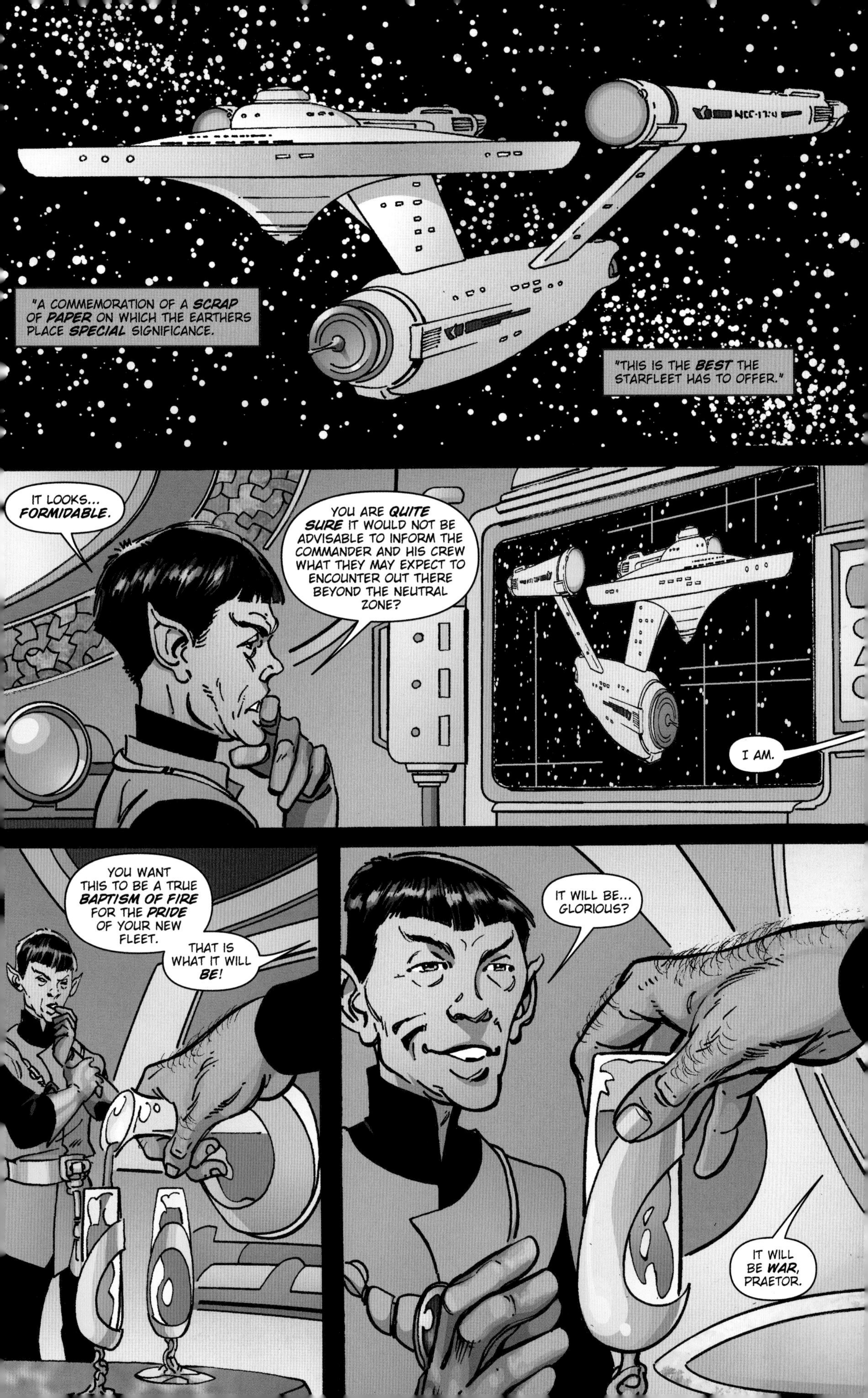
"A COMMEMORATION OF A SCRAP OF PAPER ON WHICH THE EARTHERS PLACE SPECIAL SIGNIFICANCE.
"THIS IS THE BEST THE STARFLEET HAS TO OFFER."
IT LOOKS... FORMIDABLE.
YOU ARE QUITE SURE IT WOULD NOT BE ADVISABLE TO INFORM THE COMMANDER AND HIS CREW WHAT THEY MAY EXPECT TO ENCOUNTER OUT THERE BEYOND THE NEUTRAL ZONE?
I AM.
YOU WANT THIS TO BE A TRUE BAPTISM OF FIRE FOR THE PRIDE OF YOUR NEW FLEET.
THAT IS WHAT IT WILL BE!
IT WILL BE... GLORIOUS?
IT WILL BE WAR, PRAETOR.

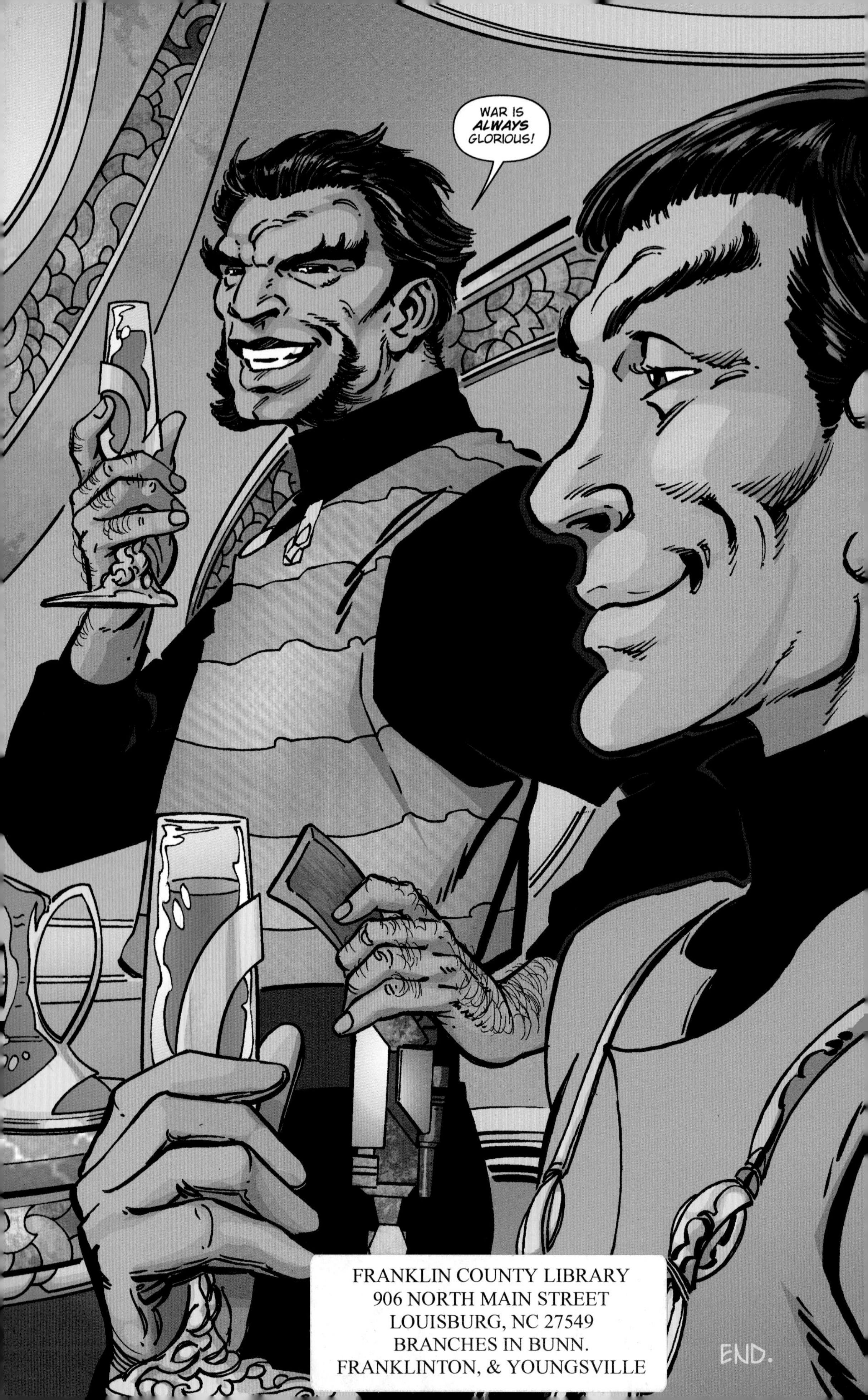
WAR IS ALWAYS GLORIOUS!
END.

CHARACTER SKETCHES BY JOHN BYRNE

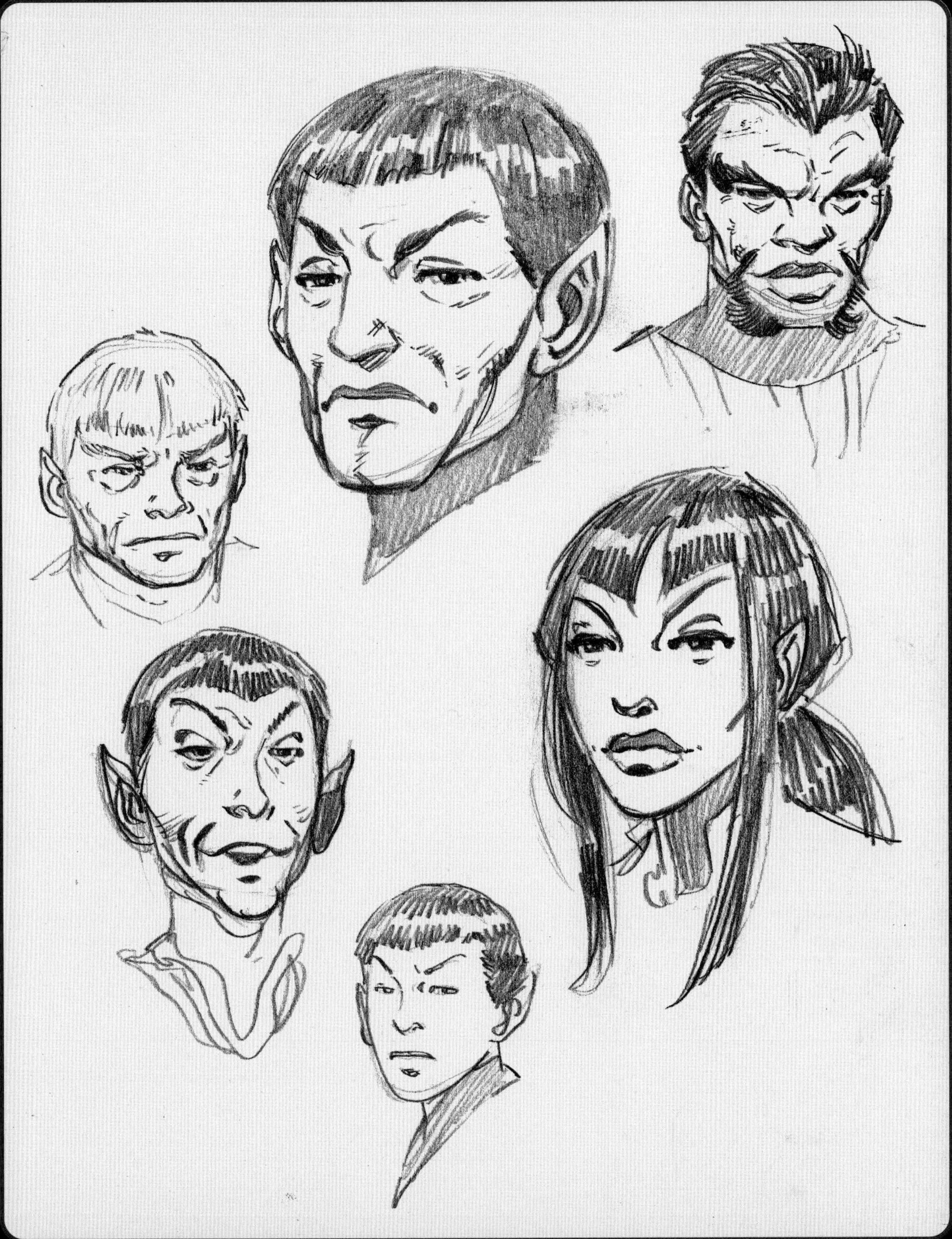

EVOLUTION OF A COVER

BY JOHN BYRNE

›››
It all starts with the cover sketch.

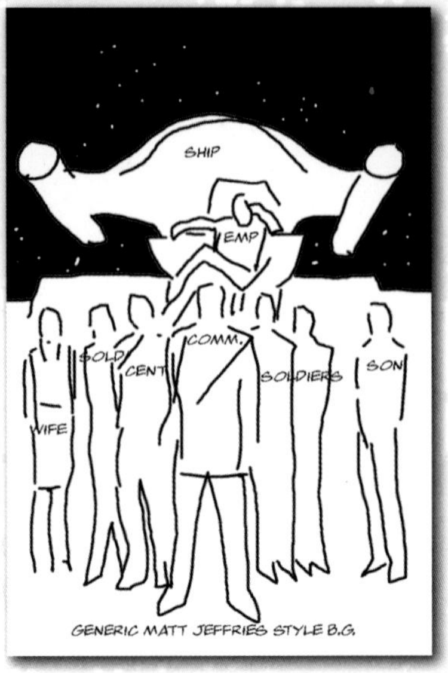
SHIP
EMP
SOLD
CENT
COMM.
SOLDIERS
SON
WIFE
GENERIC MATT JEFFRIES STYLE B.G.

‹‹‹
From there, John pencils the cover.

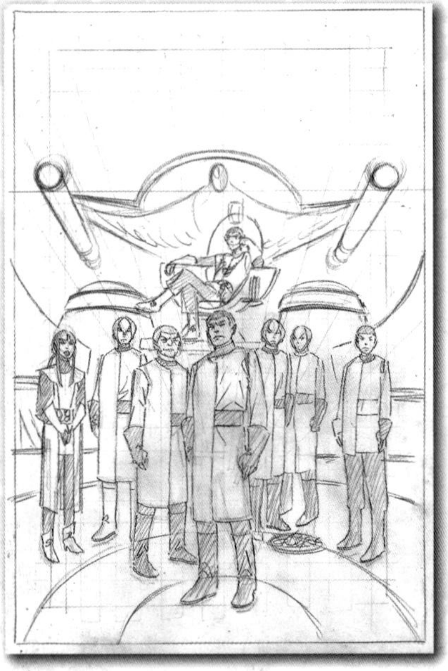

›››
Then, the cover base is laid down with inks.

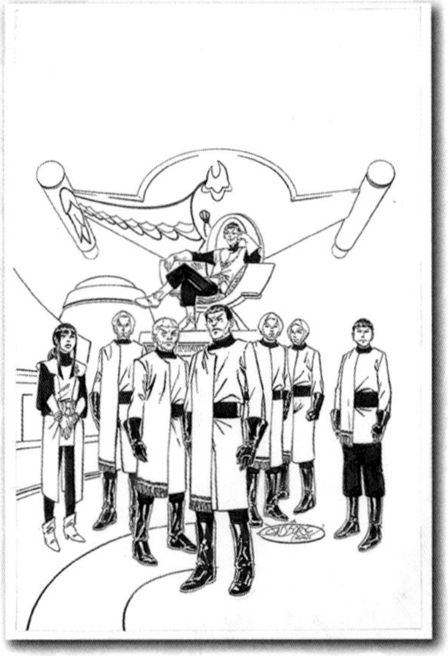

‹‹‹
Effects and finishes are added, completing the final b&w art.

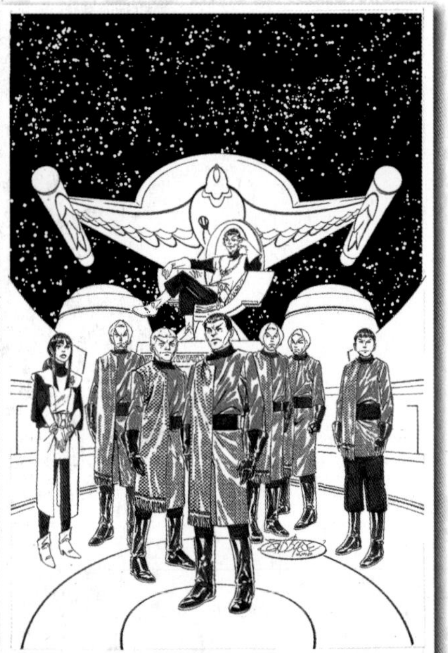

›››
Finally, Leonard O'Grady colors the art, giving us the finished cover.

colors by Leonard O'Grady

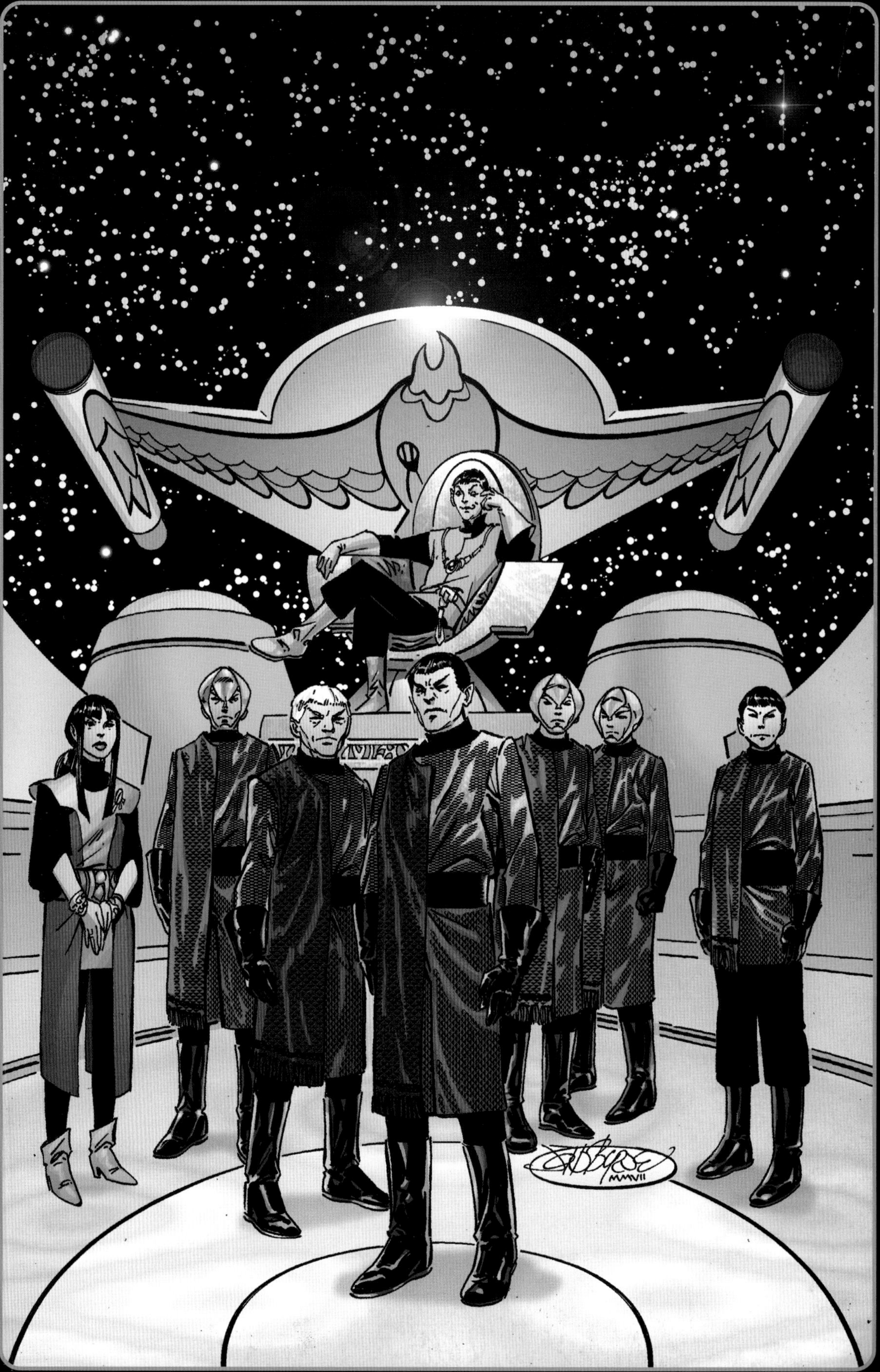
MMVII

Gorn Tech Designs

BY PAOLO MADDALENI

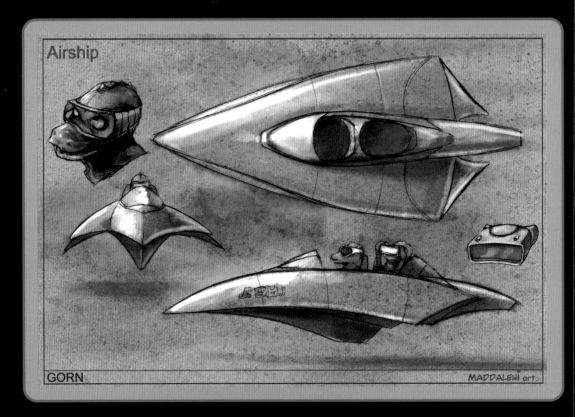

Airship

GORN

MADDALENI art.

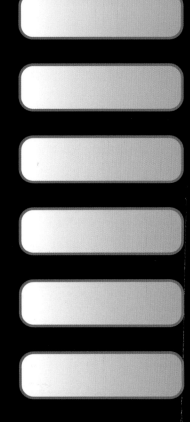

GORN

MADDALENI art.

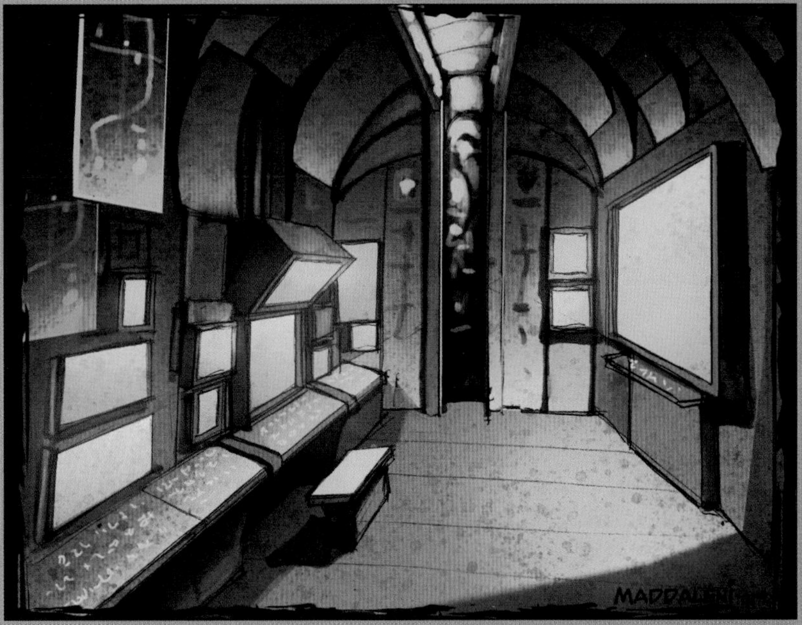
MADDALENI

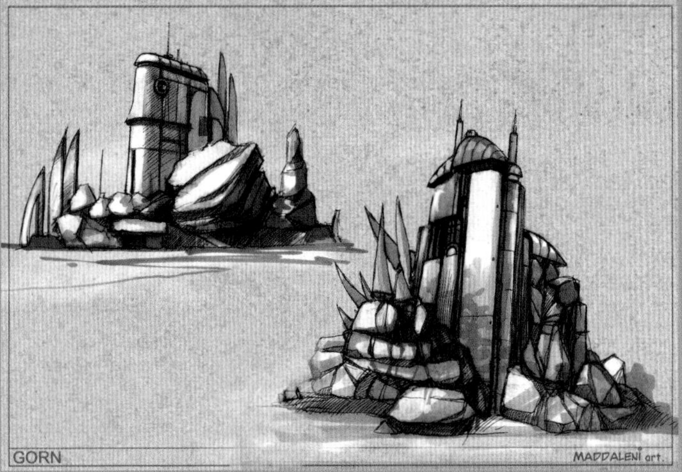
GORN
MADDALENI art.

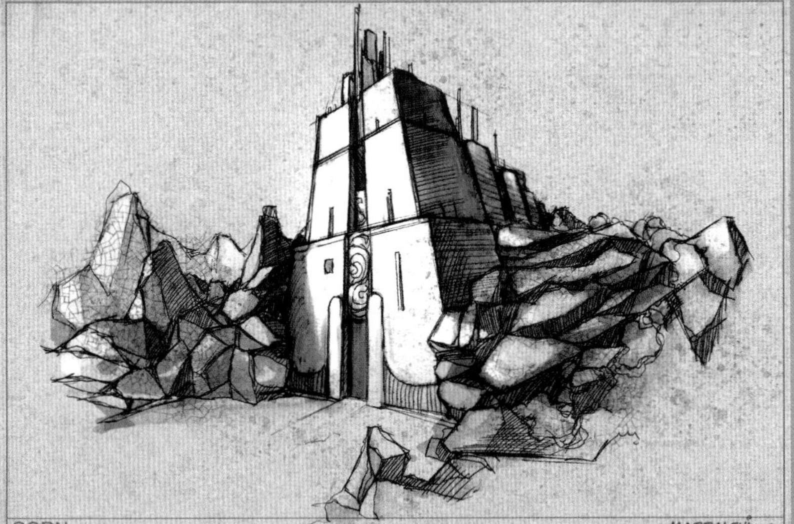
GORN
MADDALENI art.

STAR TREK
ALIEN SPOTLIGHT

ALIENS,

FRIEND

AND FOE,

INVADE

SUMMER

2008

NEW SERIES
FEATURES:

KLINGONS

BETAZOIDS

FERENGI

THOLIANS

THE Q

ART BY DAVID MESSINA